THE ONCE AND FUTURE UNION

Ohio History and Culture

THE ONCE AND FUTURE UNION

THE RISE AND FALL OF THE UNITED RUBBER WORKERS, 1935—1995

BRUCE M. MEYER

THE UNIVERSITY OF AKRON PRESS

AKRON, OHIO

All inquiries and permissions requests should be addressed to the publisher,
The University of Akron Press, Akron, OH 44325–1703

Manufactured in the United States of America

First edition 2002

05   04   03   02   5   4   3   2   1

LIBRARY OF CONGRESS CATALOGING-IN-PUBLICATION DATA

Meyer, Bruce, 1962

    The once and future union : the rise and fall of the united rubber
workers / Bruce Meyer.

        p.   cm. — (Ohio history and culture)

    Includes bibliographical references and index.

    ISBN 1-884836-84-4 (hc : acid-free) — ISBN 1-884836-85-2
(pb : acid-free)

    1. United Rubber, Cork, Linoleum, and Plastic Workers of America.
2. Labor unions—United States. 3. Rubber industry workers—United
States. I. Title. II. Series.

    HD6515.R92 U556 2002

    331.88'1782'0973—dc21

                          2001007067

To my wife, Megan,
whose constant support helped me
turn my vision of this project
into a reality.

C O N T E N T S

ILLUSTRATIONS

TABLES

ACKNOWLEDGMENTS

A work such as this could never be published without the help of many people. I cannot name everyone by name who pitched in, but I will name as many as I can in this brief space. First and foremost, I would like to thank the more than sixty people who consented to personal interviews for this work. This history of the United Rubber Workers union is in a large sense the story of all those who over the years called themselves URW members, their personal stories and recollections helped give this narrative life, depth, and perspective. I would have liked to include all their stories, but unfortunately space limitations made that impossible. I especially will remember my week in Gadsden, Alabama, visiting with current and former members of Local 12. The hospitality of Larry Thrasher, Local 12 vice president, was particularly appreciated, along with the opportunity to meet and interview in person E. K. Bowers, who served as the local's president in three different decades. I also cherished the time I spent in Kitchener, Ontario—the "Akron of Canada"—to hear the stories of many of the Canadian contingent, including those of George Goebel, Leonard Bruder, John Fuhrman, and a number of others. Special thanks also goes to former URW Presidents Mike Stone and Kenneth Coss, who gave of their time and memories, as did former International Officers J. Michael Stanley and Glenn Ellison; John Sellers, who took over for Coss as an executive vice president with the United Steelworkers of America; Dan Borelli, who served as an assistant to both Coss and Sellers; Louis Beliczky, who gave invaluable insight on the union's fight for health and safety; and Steve Clem, former URW research director, who shared his recollections and also provided an invaluable index to his department's archives.

Other commendations go to Edward Noga, my editor at *Rubber & Plastics News,* and Mike McNulty, a senior reporter at *Rubber & Plastics News,* who volunteered to read and edit the manuscript as it was being written. David Giffels, from the *Akron Beacon Journal* and a co-author of *Wheels of Fortune,* and Brad Dawson, from *Rubber & Plastics News,* also chipped in with some reading and observations. John Miller and his staff at the University of Akron archives also were helpful in aiding my research of the URW Archives, which are housed at the university. My wife, Megan, helped expedite my research of the 1976 strike and some of the early years of the union, and helped with reading and observations on the final manuscript. Also receiving my gratitude are the staff of the University of Akron Press (Director Michael Carley and Production Coordinator Amy Petersen) for their patience and guidance as the project proceeded; Elton Glaser, former University of Akron Press director, who first expressed interest in the project and helped me form my outline for the book into a workable guideline; the staff of the former United Steelworkers of America (USWA) office in Akron, who provided me access to their photo files as well as a place to conduct a number of my interviews; former URW Public Relations Director J. Curtis Brown, who parted temporarily with some of his cherished *United Rubber Worker* magazines, which represent much of his life work; University of Akron Professor David Meyer, who gave invaluable insight into labor issues throughout the century; Katie Byard of the *Akron Beacon Journal,* who gave me use of the paper's coverage of the 1976 strike; the USWA public relations staff, who provided me with the unpublished manuscript of John House; my brother, Harold, who has been a constant presence in my life; and my employers, Crain Communications Inc., for access to *Rubber & Plastics News* photo files and for providing a work environment that led to the idea for this book.

I also want to express my appreciation to two people I have never met. First to Stu Feldstein, who covered the 1976 strike for the *Akron Beacon Journal.* It was his compilation of clips that Katie Byard passed on to me, and his excellent coverage of not only the day-to-day activities of the strike but also the issues behind the walkout proved invaluable. Feldstein's coverage definitely was first-rate. Secondly, I'd like to pass on my thanks to the late John House, the first president of URW Local 2 at Goodyear and later a longtime staff member of the URW. House shared his views of the early years of the URW through his unpublished manuscript titled *Birth of a Union,* provided to me by the USWA. His recollections helped provide color and insight into some events that otherwise would have been just rote historical listings. In the introduction to *Birth of a Union,* House said he hoped all his hours of typing would not be in vain. Should any of his descendants read *The Once and Future Union,* they will know that House's work was not in vain.

CAST OF CHARACTERS

William Green: American Federation of Labor (AFL) president who presented the charter to delegates at the United Rubber Workers of America founding convention in September 1935.

Coleman Claherty: AFL organizer who recruited union members in the rubber industry in the mid-1930s and whom Green unsuccessfully tried to appoint as the first URW president.

John House: First president of Local 2 at Goodyear in Akron and longtime URW staff member; in 1922 came from the South to Akron to work in the rubber factories, as tens of thousands of others had.

Frances Perkins: Secretary of Labor under Franklin Delano Roosevelt who in 1935 brokered the "Tea Cup Agreement."

Paul W. Litchfield: Anti-union Goodyear executive who developed the Goodyear Industrial Assembly, the firm's longtime company union that operated from before 1920 until it was ruled unconstitutional in 1937; refused to sign the company's first contract with the URW in 1941.

Sherman H. Dalrymple: Elected the first URW International president after he was seen as a voice of reason at the founding convention in 1935; served in the office until 1945.

John L. Lewis: United Mine Workers president who formed the CIO, of which the URW was an original member, and in 1937 urged the rubber workers to "Organize, organize, organize."

Thomas F. Burns: Challenged William Green at the founding convention in 1935 to let the rubber workers choose their own officers; served as the URW's first vice president.

Rex Murray: President of the URW local at General Tire in Akron who led the nation's first-known "sit-down strike" in 1934.

Leland Buckmaster: Second URW president, serving from 1945 to 1960, save for a short period when he was removed from office in 1949.

George Bass: URW staff member who unsuccessfully tried to wrest the union's presidency from Buckmaster at the 1948 and 1949 conventions.

H. R. "Whitey" Lloyd: Served as URW vice president in 1948 and was named interim URW president in 1949 when Buckmaster was temporarily removed from office.

Joe Childs: URW vice president under Buckmaster who died in 1960 before getting his chance at the union's presidency.

E. K. Bowers: Goodyear worker in Gadsden, Alabama, who first promised never to join the union when going to work at the plant in 1936, then served as president of Local 12 for most the 1940s, '50s, and '60s.

John Nardella: Local 2 president for twenty-three years, both during the good times and when Goodyear started closing plants in Akron; ran on the ticket opposing Peter Bommarito in 1978.

George Burdon: Third URW International president, serving from 1960 to 1966; preferred what he called "responsible militancy."

Peter Bommarito: Fourth URW International president, who towered over the union as its leader from 1966 to 1981.

Ike Gold: URW vice president under Burdon and Bommarito from 1960 to 1978; teamed with Bommarito to oust Burdon in 1966.

Louis Beliczky: Hired by the URW in 1971 as the first full-time industrial hygienist employed by an industrial union in the United States; served in the post until 1993.

Leonard Bruder: Onetime URW district director in Canada who, as president of the URW's staff union in the 1970s, filed National Labor Relations Board charges against Bommarito.

Gilbert Laws: President of the URW local at the Goodyear plant in Lincoln, Nebraska, who ran against Bommarito in 1975.

Bob Long: A longtime Bommarito supporter who headed up the "Reform Group" that tried to unseat Bommarito in 1978.

Steve Clem: URW research director who worked for the URW and United Steelworkers of America (USWA) for nearly thirty years, from late 1969 until 1998.

J. Curtis Brown: Longtime URW public relations director and editor of the union's monthly newspaper, the *United Rubber Worker;* joined the union's staff in 1974.

Reginald Duguay: URW district director in Canada who was certain the union had won organizational votes in 1979 at two Michelin plants in Nova Scotia—but the votes were never counted.

Don Weber: URW organizer who led the union's successful campaign at the Oklahoma City tire plant in 1981.

Mike Stone: First served as URW vice president under Bommarito before being elected fifth URW International president in 1981, serving until 1990; presided over union during the era of plant closings.

Frank Tully: Goodyear chief negotiator from 1980–93.

James Warren: Goodyear negotiator who succeeded Tully in his position and headed the firm's negotiating team in 1994.

Kenneth Coss: Defeated Stone in 1990 to become sixth—and final—URW International president; led the crusade to merge with the United Steelworkers of America.

Glenn Ellison: Final secretary/treasurer of the URW and an earlier candidate in 1981 for president against Mike Stone.

J. Michael Stanley: Final URW vice president, elected with Kenneth Coss and Glenn Ellison in 1981, who also chaired the URW Merger Committee that put together the merger agreement with the USWA.

Annalee Benedict: Longtime treasurer of Local 626 who was one of the few women ever to serve on the URW's International Executive Board, sitting on the board in the early 1990s.

Dan Borelli: Kenneth Coss's right-hand man who served as his assistant from 1991–96 and then held the same post under John Sellers.

John Sellers: Took over in 1996 for Kenneth Coss as leader of the USWA's Rubber/Plastics Industry Conference after Coss retired; also was the URW coordinator for contract talks with Bridgestone/Firestone in the War of '94.

Yoichiro Kaizaki: Brought in from Japan parent Bridgestone Corp. to be chairman of Bridgestone/Firestone; was responsible for drastic change in firm's labor management philosophy in 1993–94.

INTRODUCTION

"YEARNING FOR A UNION"

The tale of the United Rubber Workers (URW) union was one that just begged to be told. While never one of the biggest unions in the United States, the Akron, Ohio-based labor organization wielded power for decades that seemed far disproportionate to the union's size. To tell the story of the URW is to tell a saga of conflict—internal and external. If the Rubber Workers were not battling a tire or rubber company at the bargaining table or on the picket line, they were fighting with each other. Throughout the URW's history, its members operated a democratic union where the rank and file always made sure their leaders knew who really was in charge. They expected a lot from their officers, and if they were less than satisfied, the leader would hear about it (and sometimes lose his job because of it). When the URW merged with the larger United Steelworkers of America (USWA) union in 1995, it was clear the URW's history needed to be chronicled soon. It needed to be told while those who had lived through the battles and the conventions, the strikes and the organizational campaigns, were still around to tell the story. It is these memories that give the URW's history the life and dimension it so deserved. Just as the union was theirs for nearly six decades, so too this story belongs to them.

EARLY EFFORTS

The United Rubber Workers union officially began September 12, 1935, in the Portage Hotel in Akron, Ohio, but the fight to unionize rubber industry employees started decades earlier. One of the first efforts of the twentieth century involved a strike in Trenton, New Jersey, by the Amalgamated Rubber Union of North America, formed in November 1902 under an American Federation of Labor (AFL) charter. The union claimed it represented "all persons working at the trade of making rubber goods." At the time the rubber industry was centered in New England, near where Charles Goodyear in 1839 had discovered vulcanization, the process of heating rubber and sulfur to make rubber usable. The Amalgamated Rubber Union did have fourteen locals, with the largest outside of Trenton in Massachusetts, Chicago, and Akron. The union staged nineteen strikes from 1901 to 1905, mainly related to organizational activities. In Trenton, the union wanted the rubber companies to begin using the union label. The firms balked because they knew it would mean recognizing the union. In early 1904 the union put in writing its request for recognition, adoption of the union label, and a 10 percent wage hike. When the companies again refused, about 850 workers went on strike against nine rubber firms in Trenton. AFL President Samuel Gompers addressed a meeting of the strikers on January 25. The companies said they would deal with the workers as individuals rather than through a union—a mantra rubber executives would repeat continuously for decades as they fought ruthlessly to keep labor organizations out of their plants. The rubber companies brought in strikebreakers, and police squads were used as guards. The strike ended April 13 when the remaining strikers voted 83 to 58 to return to work. The Amalgamated, which probably never had membership much above two thousand, folded by 1906.

As some rubber companies had started locating in Akron by this time, moguls from the Ohio city followed the Trenton situation closely and organized the Akron Employers Association to stop any labor moves. The association was said to pay labor spies eighty-five dollars a month to watch out for possible union men in the plant, later increasing that to one or two hundred dollars. Companies weeded out rebellious workers, created a blacklist, established worker welfare programs, and did everything in their power to keep labor organizations at bay.

The next major push to unionize rubber workers came in 1913, this time in Akron. The city was in the early stages of an unprecedented growth spurt that would land it the title of "Rubber Capital of the World." Benjamin Franklin Goodrich set up the first rubber shop in Akron in 1870; Goodyear Tire & Rubber Co. was established in 1898 and Firestone Tire & Rubber Co. in 1900. From 1910 to 1920, Akron's population exploded from 69,067 to 208,435, with employment in the city's rubber factories more than tripling from 22,000 to 70,000.

As tire manufacturers began to introduce machines to replace hand processes in tire building, the workers' most hated person in the factory became "the man with the stopwatch," who determined at which pace the workers should be performing specific tasks on the job. In the world of the rubber shop, the workers often worked on a "piece rate," meaning they

A street scene during the 1913 rubber industry strike in Akron. *(USWA/URW photo files)*

were paid based on the number of tires or other rubber products they made during a given shift. The employee "made out" when he reached the top rate of pay for the shift, meaning he did not have to work any more that day even if two or more hours remained on his shift. At Goodyear, for example, Frank A. Seiberling had introduced a bonus system and then began a speedup system. As workers "made out" on the bonus rates, the rates were cut. Because the companies did not take kindly to paying these high rates, they countered by hiring pacesetters to set the rate at which other workers would have to perform their jobs to make the top rate of pay. The role of the pacesetters was simple: to go full out and set a cadence that no normal worker could match. That way the employers would have to pay less than the top rate to nearly all their workers.

Firestone, which had just introduced new tire-building equipment, also implemented what the workers viewed as a speedup, leading to the start of the 1913 strike. The spontaneous walkout spread to workers from other Akron plants. Protesters paraded down Main Street with red ribbons pinned to their coats. The walkout was encouraged and supported by the most radical labor organization of the time—the Industrial Workers of the World (IWW), commonly known as the Wobblies. IWW leader "Big Bill" Haywood, fresh off a famous Wobblies strike in Lawrence, Massachusetts, addressed strikers in Akron several times. The IWW had been founded in Chicago in 1905 with pure socialist aims. The Wobblies wanted to combine the American working class into one industrial-based trade union, then lead a revolution through a series of strikes where the capitalists would give in and the IWW would step in to control the workers' commonwealth. The Wobblies, which lasted as a viable organization roughly until 1924, seemed to make strides early on in the Akron strike. More than five thousand strikers joined the IWW, and the walkout at one point included about fifteen thousand of the twenty-two thousand hourly rubber workers in Akron. But the strike was not well led, as the strikers put no demands to the company until nearly two weeks into the work stoppage.

The American Federation of Labor also tried to get in on the action. The AFL, founded in 1881, was organized on the basis of crafts, rather than on a broad industrial basis, and as a conservative labor organization it had nothing in common with the IWW. So, with the AFL and the Wobblies working against each other, the friction between the two unions further diluted the effectiveness of the strike.

Firestone executives viewed the strike from a much different perspective than that of the workers. The company had developed its first tire-building machine in the second half of 1912. Other firms had been paying Goodyear a royalty on each tire made on Goodyear-designed machinery. On September 1, 1912, the first machine-built Firestone tires were produced, meaning that tire builders no longer would need to stretch plies over the iron-forming core and smooth them down after each layer. By the end of the year Firestone had twenty of its new machines in operation with ten more near completion. Like any other advance in which technology replaced human labor, the company felt a wage adjustment was in order. On the old machinery, the tire builder performed all the stages of constructing a tire by himself. With Firestone's advancement, the tire was built by machine and finished by hand, bringing about the new classification of tire finisher. Firestone tentatively set the piecework scale at about one-third the rate previously paid for making a whole tire by hand. The company claimed that a finisher doing a good job would be able to maintain his prior rate of $3.50 a day. The workers disagreed. Most of the workers found that $2.50 a day was the most they could make under the new rates. When the night-shift workers arrived on February 11, 1913, the entrance was blocked as 150 men in the tire-finishing area walked out when the company refused to restore the old scale. The next morning six hundred workers failed to report for work, and the strike was on.

By February 20 about half the Firestone plant's workers were out. On February 24, the factory turned out just two hundred tires and two hundred tubes. Despite the meager output, the manufacturers were determined to beat the strike. Employees who crossed the line were paid their regular wages—even when there was no work—and given free meals. On March 1, an Ohio senate committee chaired by William Green—who later would make his mark as AFL president—opened hearings on the strike in Akron. Firestone Chairman Harvey S. Firestone testified that the rate was not intended to speed up work because that could lead to poor quality. In contrast, Firestone striker O. S. Miller outlined grievances that included a general wage reduction of 35 percent, a docking system where a worker lost a whole hour if late even by a minute, fumes and dust in the factory, and even the lack of clean washbowls.

Goodyear's Seiberling returned to town during the strike's second week and said he would not deal with any collective bargaining group—that his company would continue to deal with the employees as individuals. "Under no circumstances will we enter into a wage discussion now, and under no circumstances will we deal with anyone, now or hereafter, except our own employees," he said. "That is our position now; it will be our position next year; and 10 years from now."

Both Seiberling and Harvey Firestone testified before the senate committee that they did not oppose unionization and always were willing to meet with employees to discuss grievances. But when the strikers sent committees to meet with each company, both executives hid behind their rhetoric. Since all committee members remained on strike, Seiberling considered them former employees and claimed no obligation to meet with them. At Firestone, the committee was given a statement that said the strikers had misconstrued Harvey Firestone's testimony as an invitation for a conference. Instead, it was meant as a statement that the company would meet with employees whether they belonged to a labor union or not, but that the company would not deal with a committee representing a labor union.

Anti-union forces joined in a Citizens Welfare League, which took the form of a Citizens' Police Association. About one thousand men were sworn in and given police badges and clubs to intimidate the strikers. They wore yellow ribbons in distinction to the red ribbons of the Wobblies and the red, white, and blue ribbons worn by AFL members. The sheriff placed the city under martial law. Parading and general picketing were prohibited, and such action effectively was stopped after several skirmishes between strikers and the city police and citizens' police groups. The most serious altercation occurred March 11, 1913, when several shots were fired, police clubbed strikers, and twenty were arrested.

While both Harvey Firestone and Seiberling came across well in testifying before the senate committee, the first witness for the striking workers hurt their cause considerably. H. E. Polka was chair of the strikers' executive committee but had been working both sides of the dispute. He had helped the strikers' case by revising its early demand of a complicated wage scale to one that called for an across-the-board increase and later tried to ease public perception by saying the strike organization was "not entirely" tied to the IWW. Polka, though, had designs on gaining wealth and power, a taste the strike organization was not likely to satisfy. Each night after the strikers' executive board met, he would give a copy of the meeting's minutes to his sister to type. But his sister was a stenographer in Seiberling's office, and she made a copy of the minutes for Seiberling. In addition, Polka had been seen with company agents at times. When he opened the senate committee hearings as the first witness, Polka proclaimed he had no grievances and no real complaints. Three days later the IWW forced him to resign from the executive committee on charges of spying. Later labor witnesses helped little, talking of unsanitary conditions rather than speedups, blacklists, and discrimination.

The senate committee's final report indicated that while the committee opposed the speedup system, its members found tire industry wages high. The committee criticized the militancy of the IWW, but observers felt the main problem for the strikers was the lack of a clear-cut strategy. The strike began as a spontaneous walkout without specific issues around which the strikers could rally. That meant there was no clear definition of victory. Spokesmen eventually called for reinstatement of all workers, an eight-hour day and six-day week, a minimum starting rate of at least 22½ cents an hour, and time and a half for overtime. But the workers were not unified on these issues, and the companies had far superior resources with which to fight. During March, Firestone eventually got more than one thousand people working in the plant, which then operated twenty-four hours a day.

The six-week strike collapsed on March 15 and officially ended March 30 with only two hundred strikers participating in the vote to return to work. The strike also lost momentum when a tremendous flood hit the area on March 24, the largest natural disaster in the state. The flood shut down the rubber factories, including Goodyear, more effectively than the strike had, and it took the IWW's work stoppage off the front page of the newspaper.

Following the strike, there was no substantial labor action in the Rubber Capital of the World for the next two decades. Akron had become, without a doubt, a strong "open shop town."

AN ERA OF PATERNALISM

Goodyear President Paul W. Litchfield felt the 1913 strike was started by outsiders who did not represent the sentiments of the majority of the workforce. Of course, that was a common excuse among employers of the era. It could never be "his workers" who were unhappy, Litchfield thought, so there had to be somebody else to blame for the unrest—an "outside agitator" of some unknown origin. But Litchfield did realize that as the companies had grown large, the resulting depersonalization created a labor-management relations problem. So he made changes to show that labor and the employers both benefited when they worked together. By 1916, Goodyear had put in the eight-hour day (one of the demands in the 1913 strike), provided vacations for workers with five years' experience, and established a pension plan.

Firestone, too, went to eight-hour shifts as Akron became known as "Ohio's eight-hour town." Harvey Firestone said there was nothing sentimental or paternalistic in adopting the eight-hour system. "But you can't make men do their best unless you get them fully interested, proud of what they are doing, happier in mind, better in body and spirit, and producing something for themselves while they produce something for the business organization of which they are a part," he said.

Despite Firestone's statement, it was during this twenty-year period from 1913 to 1933 that many rubber industry employers tried to take a paternalistic approach toward managing workers. This effort included many initiatives that became known as "worker welfare" programs. Goodyear especially was active in this area, although most other companies participated to varying degrees. Workers were provided sport teams and leagues, music and theater groups, company picnic and recreation areas, and countless other activities. Goodyear and Firestone even bought huge tracts of land and built affordable houses for resale to employees to try to ease the housing shortage created by the sudden rise of the rubber industry in Akron. The city, in fact, still has residential areas known as Firestone Park and Goodyear Heights.

Much of the worker welfare efforts were aimed at reducing the high employee turnover that plagued all Akron operations. Rubber industry employment nationwide doubled to 159,000 workers between 1914 and 1919, with the workforce in the Akron plants leaping from nearly 20,000 in 1914 to a peak of about 73,500 in April 1920. Before World War I the companies did not care much about retaining workers as thousands of young people migrated from the South to come to the Rubber Capital of the World. Turnover figures surged during this period—both in and outside of Akron. For example, Firestone said company turnover sometimes exceeded 20 percent per month. At U.S. Rubber Co., which had no Akron facilities, annual turnover ranged from 50 percent a year to more than 200 percent.

Another outgrowth of this era was the company union, not a free labor organization in any sense. The representatives were elected from within the workforce, but any decisions made were always subject to management veto—so the ultimate effectiveness of such organizations still was tied to the whim of management. Again, Goodyear had the most elaborate structure of all the company unions with its Goodyear Industrial Assembly—the brainchild of company President Litchfield. The Industrial Assembly was set up to mimic the U.S. Congress. There was the upper body, known as the Senate—for which a worker had to have more seniority to be eligible for election—and a second, lower body, known as the House, for which the length of service requirement was much less. Litchfield viewed the Industrial Assembly as the perfect way to give workers a say in the operation of the company. It was an honor to sit on the assembly, whose members were given some special privileges and paid for time spent on assembly business. Yet Litchfield also knew that the management, with its veto power, still carried the ultimate authority.

U.S. Rubber also introduced factory councils into most of its footwear plants in 1919 under the direction of Cyrus S. Ching, a Canadian who had managed unionized workers at the Boston Elevated Railway Co. His approach was much like other postwar efforts, with elected employee representatives joining with management officials in a council. That council then would appoint standing committees to resolve grievances and coordinate plant activities. Labor unions said the council initiative fragmented the workforce and did not focus on wage issues. Ching countered that he did not want to duplicate a conventional union, but wanted "the fullest possible use of the ideas and energies of the workers in the conduct of industry."

During World War I, labor unions made some gains, with total U.S. membership doubling from 2.5 million in 1915 to more than 5 million in 1920. Rubber workers formed unions and conducted many strikes, but most gains were short-lived. The majority of the larger-scale rubber plant labor campaigns during the period occurred in the eastern plants. One of the biggest walkouts involved more than forty-five hundred workers at the Bristol, Rhode Island, plant of National India Rubber Co., a U.S. Rubber subsidiary. The dispute included a riot at the plant toward the end of May, where private guards fired into the crowd and wounded three people.

The AFL did make another attempt in late 1917 and early 1918 to organize Akron's tire plants. Cal Wyatt came to the city, proclaiming that prior campaigns had failed because of the industry's seasonal nature and the long lines of job seekers—both obstacles taken away by the war. In January, Wyatt formed a federal labor union, and rubber workers jammed the Central Labor Union hall to hear the AFL organizer extol the virtues of "patriotic duty, loyalty to government and peaceful methods." But the effort petered out.

NOT SO WELL OFF

Despite the declarations of Litchfield and Firestone about how they cared for their workers, there was much evidence that the rubber workers did not have it so good. Working conditions in the rubber factories could be abhorrent. Howard and Ralph Wolf wrote in their book *Rubber: A Story of Glory and Greed* what plant workers faced during this era. "It was still the era of dust and flying soapstone loading the lungs; of workers nodding drunkenly in the benzene vapors above cement tanks; of unventilated calender rooms below the street level where men withered in the heat and the skin peeled from their bodies; of hell-hot pits where the toilers yet slipped about in the wet underfoot," the Wolfs wrote. "Mills had no hoods to carry poisonous fumes away and the result was lassitude and loss of appetite on the job, a splitting headache to carry home every day. 'Blue men' baffled physicians who didn't know the companies were using aniline. Lead poisoning was common." Not only were the workers facing deadly chemicals, but also the companies were making the employees work at an inhuman pace, speeding up the work to a level that no one could possibly meet. "[The problem] is with the system that sucks out his life and leaves him broken at forty, the average age at which the caouthchouc (rubber) toiler is through despite the squadron of twenty-year employees which each factory trots out for publicity purposes," they wrote. "It is with the system that, to quote Frank Seiberling, 'employs these men for one season in the year to full capacity and then throws them out on the streets for a period of three to six months hunting a job.' It is with the system that recruits or takes back the young men when the plants swing into peak production and leaves the older ones on the scrap heap."

It was a system with which workers like John House became much too familiar. Like many other men who came to Akron on the promise of high wages in the rubber and tire plants—not so lovingly called the gum mines—the first thing House saw when he arrived at the Akron Union Station was a vast billboard across the tracks from the stations saying: "Welcome to Akron, City of Opportunity." The year was 1922 and House was seventeen, having just graduated from high school in Cleveland, Georgia, a small rural community of some four hundred residents. House's older brother had found a job as a rubber worker in Akron during a period of peak production at the end of World War I and was getting ready to return to the city. House was hoping to earn enough money to pay his tuition for the first year of college, so his father gave permission for him to accompany his brother and wife on their return to Akron. By 1922, Akron was overflowing with more than two hundred thousand citizens, so by comparison House was coming to a "vast metropolis."

House's brother got a job immediately at B. F. Goodrich Co. (BFG), where he had worked previously and compiled an excellent work record. For House, the going was a bit tougher at the start. "I would join the long line of men, stretching for at least a city block, long before the employment office would be opened for interview—men who, like me, had been

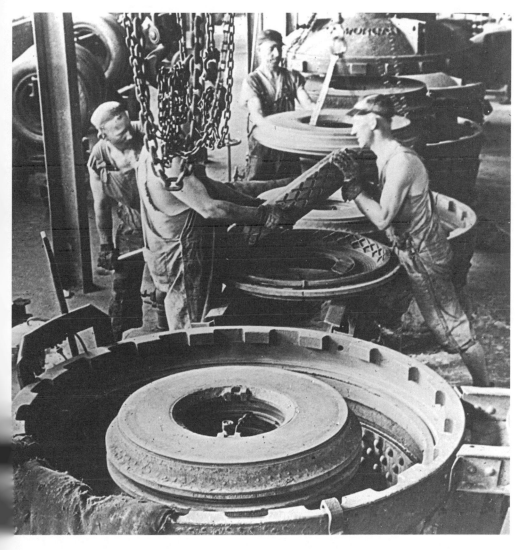

Workers take automotive tires from the curing pits in an early-century tire shop.
(USWA/URW photo files)

lured to Akron by the widely advertised promise of good jobs at high wages," House said. "It is said that it was a deliberate policy of the Akron rubber companies to keep a big surplus of manpower seeking employment in their plants as one means of keeping their employed workforce docile." After several days of waiting in line for as long as four or five hours before reaching the man who did the hiring and being told there was no work, he finally got a job at Goodrich paying a minimum of thirty-five cents an hour—and up to as much as forty to forty-five cents an hour by "rawhiding," or going all out to surpass standard production rates. He then got another job in the same department paying fifty-five cents an hour and later moved into another division of the factory which paid more, but he got laid off two weeks later along with a group of fifty. After being off work two months he was rehired, worked two weeks, and was laid off again.

House then moved to the inner tube department as part of a two-man tire-building team producing cross-woven fabric tires. After just a few days' training, he was "making out," or earning the top rate of about eighty-five to eighty-eight cents an hour. "On this job the several men working as tire builders had rather informally agreed among themselves that no two-man team would produce more than 114 tires in an eight-hour shift," House said. "This would pay them each a few cents over seven dollars (a day). The reason for this limitation of production was that it had been common practice for the company to reduce the piecework price whenever the earnings of workers on the same job exceeded a certain level." In February 1924 he and his tire-building partner were given a raw material that was dry and difficult to use. The next day the foreman brought up a cured tire that could be identified as one they had made the previous day out of the dry stock. Though the tire was worth no more than three or four dollars at most, the two were given a thirty-day penalty layoff. "Without a union, there wasn't a damned thing we could do but take it," he said.

House decided he did not want to work for such an unfair employer, so he got a job at Firestone. As was common among the "gum workers," House got laid off from that job after a time. He then got another job at the Firestone plant in the curing department. He had the job of cleaning the green—uncured—tires of any foreign substance and placing the green tire into the empty mold from which the cured tire had been removed. It was important that he place the proper size tire into the mold in the proper position. Once he put the tire into the wrong size mold. When the cured tire was removed from the mold, his supervisor brought it over to where he was working and said, "John, I guess you know what that means." The tire was identified as one he had laid by the number on the little piece of tin each tire layer was required to place in the mold with the tire. "Realizing that I was about to lose my job because of the mistake, as soon as the supervisor turned his back, I quickly destroyed the evidence," House said. "When he returned with the foreman to show him the ruined tire and could not prove what I had done he just about blew his top. From then on he was extremely critical of everything I did and I knew that he was looking for some excuse to be rid of me." House soon became fed up with the constant surveillance and decided to quit and take the job his father-in-law had offered on his peach and apple orchard crew in Georgia. He did not want to wait around, however, for the next regular payday to get his final week's wages, so he deliberately picked a fight with the foreman and got fired. That way he got his money the next day.

House, though disturbed by the working conditions in the rubber factories, did not stay in the peach groves long and later returned to Akron to be an integral part of the union-organizing efforts at the Goodyear plant in the city.

UNIONS MAKE LITTLE HEADWAY

During the 1920s, massive labor turnover continued to plague rubber product manufacturers. A severe recession in 1920–21 first reduced the industry's total workforce. Employment in Akron's rubber plants had grown from 40,000 at the end of World War I to a peak of 73,000 in 1920. By December, however, the city's rubber industry workforce plummeted to 19,600, effectively erasing all job gains in the Akron facilities since 1915. Rubber workers elsewhere lost jobs as well, with 10,000 U.S. Rubber employees laid off just in Rhode Island. But even as the industry started to recover through the rest of the decade, workers were not shy about changing jobs as long as economic times were good and jobs plentiful. Between 1921 and the end of 1929, Goodyear hired about 87,500 workers to maintain a workforce that averaged just 13,000 and never reached 19,000. Goodyear had added about 10,000 jobs from the low point of the recession in 1921, so the rest of the hired workers replaced those who had quit or had been laid off. Likewise, the annual turnover percentage for Detroit industries averaged 150 to 200 percent. Annual wages did climb slowly during the decade, from $1,222 in 1919 to $1,390 in 1929. That dropped to $1,134 in 1931 and even further to $1,076 in 1933.

During the decade there were three efforts to organize tire workers. The first, in 1922–23, was predominantly by conventional trade unions that tried to continue earlier efforts to bring the Akron rubber workers into the AFL fold. This attempt led to a return of worker militancy and more strikes. Following a strike at B. F. Goodrich, the Central Labor Union (CLU) held a mass meeting January 14, 1923, to organize an AFL union. The initial session drew a crowd of 500, with 200 of those enlisting in the union afterward. AFL organizer J. J. Conboy said he would stay in Akron until the union was established. The weekly rally attracted 800 rubber workers on January 21, somewhat fewer on January 28, and only 240 on February 24. Conboy stayed just through January, with the Akron CLU leaders in charge after that. The campaign, like earlier efforts, was dormant by March.

The second effort to organize rubber workers was political and started in south Akron. The group that looked to organize the rubber workers was the Ku Klux Klan, which was prominent on the Akron political scene from 1921 to 1926. The Klan's message crossed many lines. It appealed to the pro-union and the anti-union, Republicans and Democrats, several religions, and the rich and poor. The Klan was anti-immigrant, anti-black, and anti-Catholic. But the group did not resort to violence in Akron, instead wanting to bring a larger political role to south Akron and more representation and power on the city's school board. The city's school population had grown fivefold from 1910 to 1930 as young rubber workers married and started families. The Protestant working class in south Akron, where schools were most overcrowded, saw how Akron's westside economic elite dominated the school board. Rubber workers themselves did not lead the rebellion from south Akron. The Klan elected or got appointed to the school board a wide range of representatives—all of whom had some association with rubber workers. By 1923–24, the mayor, sheriff, county prosecutor, clerk of courts, two of three county commissioners and several city council members reportedly were Klansmen. At a July 4, 1925, rally in Akron, a national Klan official declared that the Akron organization, with fifty-two thousand members, was the largest local Klan body in the United States. But the Klan began attracting a larger legion of opponents, primarily because of its association with violence elsewhere. In October 1925, just before that year's school board elections, a prominent attorney and local minister attacked the Klan. The south Akron Klan members soon found themselves on the defensive, and the group's heavy-handed tactics frightened or offended many who initially had been sympathetic. Klan candidates lost big in the 1925 elections. Scandals involving the Klan in other states and a power struggle in the Ohio Klan disillusioned others. The Akron Klan ceased to function in 1928, leaving the rubber workers without a public advocate.

The third organizational effort among rubber workers in the 1920s involved the role of the company unions set up at many plants, especially Goodyear and U.S. Rubber. Some U.S. Rubber factories still did not have company unions by the end of the decade as some lower executives disliked Cyrus Ching, resented the demands that company unionism imposed, and thought it could lead to the entrance of outside unions. Even in U.S. Rubber's Footwear Division, the factory councils did not seem to have any type of influence over a massive consolidation that led to the loss of thousands of jobs. But Goodyear's Industrial Assembly was different because Litchfield had carefully chosen subordinates, meaning there would be no sabotage of the assembly by managers. So any uprising would come from below—and it did to a certain extent. During the recession of 1920–21, Litchfield—trying to pass on the painful job of making layoffs to the workers—encouraged assembly leaders to discuss retrenchment policies. They first proposed a layoff plan emphasizing the retention of workers with houses and families, but Litchfield vetoed the bill because it did not consider merit or service. They then asked that foremen and assembly members jointly determine who would go, and Litchfield approved. As the recovery began in March 1921, the assembly won company approval for shift assignments by seniority. In early 1922 the assembly demanded and won a small wage increase. So the five thousand to six thousand Goodyear workers in Akron not laid off—from a high of more than thirty thousand workers—came out of the recession with relatively high wages, fringe benefits, shop floor preferences, and access to most executives. The assembly in effect became a "union" of the oldest and most experienced Goodyear employees.

While tensions at other plants led to strikes, at Goodyear they caused conflicts within the Industrial Assembly. But that was not to say Litchfield got off without problems. For example, in the October 1922 assembly elections, all six incumbent senators and nine of seventeen representatives were defeated, meaning Litchfield had a whole new set of people to deal with. The new assembly demanded a 15 percent wage increase, but Litchfield refused to approve the proposal. The Goodyear executive ordered a study of wages and living costs in Akron to show that the increase was not justified. After listening to the report, the representatives voted to raise the minimum wage from $4 to $5 a day for men and from $2.80 to $3.50 for women. Litchfield ordered a 10 percent increase in the form of a temporary bonus that helped torpedo the AFL organizational campaign going on at the time. Litchfield was troubled by the uprising of the Industrial Assembly. As the assembly became more active it also cost the company more. In 1919, worker representatives averaged a total of 900 hours a month on assembly work, but by 1925 they averaged 2,860 hours a month, or about 25 percent of each representative's workday. In December 1925 Litchfield showed how the Goodyear assembly was not a real union in the truest sense when he declared he would not pay for more than 1,500 hours a month toward assembly work. Assembly members countered by passing a bill calling for a 12.5 percent wage increase, a measure that Litchfield promptly vetoed. The House then voted to adjourn until management would agree to a more flexible time budget, thus waging what is called the only recorded company union strike of the decade. It was becoming clear that the assembly was what it was: an organization that could provide input but not the final decision, which still rested with Goodyear management.

Some workers met privately to form the Ameliorate Club, a group modeled after the assembly but free from management control. While the Ameliorate Club gained membership of from three thousand to six thousand members, the group collapsed in January 1927 when a fight between two rival factions led to a riot at the group's office. After 1926, the Industrial Assembly operated smoothly, with the decline of the AFL and Ameliorate Club contributing to a more placid atmosphere, as Litchfield desired.

In the years leading up to what would be the heyday of labor organizing in the United States there was little activity to speak of. Then came the Great Depression and President Franklin Delano Roosevelt.

LABOR BACK IN THE GAME

Organized labor, after having little or no influence for two decades, was about to grab the spotlight, with a lot of help from FDR and his New Deal legislation. The Great Depression that followed the Black Friday stock market crash led to great layoffs in the rubber industry as well as all parts of domestic industry. Total employment in the Akron plants declined from a pre-Depression high of more than 58,000 in June 1929 to a low of about 27,400 in March 1933. In a move to try to preserve a skilled labor force—and to follow suggestions by President Hoover's Emergency Committee on Employment—rubber companies adopted "share-the-work" policies. At Goodyear, Litchfield in July 1930 first put into effect a plan whereby each worker would be laid off every eighth week. But when the economy continued to weaken, the workers had to be laid off more often—first every seventh week and so on, until the layoff came every fifth week. By November, Goodyear had adopted the four-day week and then the six-hour workday. Rubber companies changed to the six-hour day so that as many people as possible could be kept on the payroll—and also on hand when the Depression ended. Wage rates that had been considered high at times during the 1920s now were cut to the bone. Rubber workers on average earned $1,046 from March 1932 to March 1933, 37 percent less than they had made in 1928. The Depression also made those lucky enough to keep their jobs more likely to stay put. In 1929, 37.5 percent of Goodyear employees quit. But that percentage dropped to 10.2 percent in 1930, 0.5 percent in 1931, and 5.9 percent in 1932.

It was, in fact, an act of government that changed everything as far as union organizing was concerned. An integral part of FDR's May 1933 New Deal initiatives was the National Industrial Recovery Act (NIRA) and its Section 7(a), which basically called on workers to form into labor unions. The section stated that "employees shall have the right to organize and bargain collectively through representatives of their own choosing and shall be free from interference, restraint or coercion of employers in the designation of such representatives." The government was telling workers that they could organize into labor unions and the law would protect them.

From the 1920s to the 1930s, the United States saw a 180-degree turn of events. During the 1920s there were good times and everybody was working—and there was little union activity to speak of in the decade. But by the 1930s nobody was working and the country was suffering from political division, with a large number of the nation's adults registered to vote as either socialists or communists. Roosevelt tried to construct a large, planned economy to keep people working—with the government calling the shots and labor unions playing an integral role. Corporate America, however, did not agree with FDR's philosophy and challenged the constitutionality of the NIRA.

In the meantime, with this call to arms from the NIRA, the AFL became active in trying to recruit members for its union. The AFL would set up what it called Federal Labor Unions, or FLUs for short, at individual plants. The AFL unions mostly were set up along craft lines, with the FLUs serving as a sort of holding group where new members from a factory would stay until one of two things happened: Either enough similar FLUs were formed so they could be joined into an international union, or the individual members would be divided among the various craft unions in the AFL. In union terms, an "international union" did not normally operate on an international basis. It was just the term to name the umbrella organization that oversaw all of the union locals under its direction. Most of the international unions, in fact, had members only in the United States, with some expanding into Canada.

In a rubber factory, the AFL had identified as many as sixteen distinguishable crafts. That meant workers who initially had joined one FLU could end up in as many as sixteen different unions—all from one plant. But in mass production industries—such as rubber, auto, and steel—workers normally felt more affinity for their fellow workers in the plant than for others practicing the same craft in other factories with whom they likely would have no contact.

On June 26, 1933, just ten days after FDR signed the NIRA, fifty thousand leaflets were distributed at plant gates in Akron and nearby Barberton telling of a mass meeting to be held in the Akron Armory on June 30. More than five thousand showed up to hear the AFL's Paul Smith tell rubber workers the benefits of union membership. Within a few weeks FLU charters were issued to rubber workers in at least nine plants in and around Akron, and at other factories across the United States. By the end of the year as many as seventy-five FLU charters had been issued to rubber worker groups in all parts of the country, with total membership of the locals as high as fifty thousand late in 1933. In Akron alone, it was estimated that 60 percent of Akron's rubber workers signed up.

What helped more than the New Deal, though, was an upturn in business. Between March and July 1933, the workforce in the tire industry jumped from 39,000 to 59,100, and the average workweek climbed from 24.2 to 42 hours per week. The gains erased the employment losses of the prior three years.

Coleman Claherty was the man the AFL charged with organizing the rubber workers. Claherty, a former sheet-metal worker and member of the Boilermakers' Union, originally was supposed to concentrate on workers in Cleveland, but saw such an opportunity in Akron that he convinced AFL President William Green that Akron was where he should be spending his time. Claherty had good early success as laborers in the city's rubber plants were eager to join up.

But the issue of craft unions helped slow down the progress of these FLUs. Claherty's job—besides trying to recruit members—was to protect the jurisdictional claims of the sixteen AFL craft unions that claimed jurisdiction over these workers. It was not unusual for scores of workers to initially join up, then drop their union membership once they were transferred into the separate craft unions. Many of the rubber workers favored an industrial form of unionism, with an "international union" set up to oversee the needs of all workers involved in the production of rubber products. As the rubber workers began to lose faith in Claherty as a viable leader, they called a clandestine meeting to be held in Indianapolis, Indiana, in December 1933 to set up an independent international union. Claherty used his dwindling power to convince the main Akron FLUs that they should send only an observer to the session and not participate in an official capacity. Without the presence of the Akron locals, the forty delegates at the Indianapolis convention failed to accomplish their main goal of establishing an international—but that did not mean the rubber workers' zest for industrial unionism had waned. The AFL disciplined three of the leading delegates at the Indianapolis session because the delegates had said that if a charter for a rubber workers' international could not be obtained, then the group would form an independent union. The statement opened the meeting to a charge of dual unionism.

The AFL tried to ease the concerns of those workers by setting up a loosely organized Rubber Council in June 1934 within the federation, with

Claherty as president of the council. Delegates were named by crafts, so while production workers made up 90 percent of the membership, they made up a minority of the delegates. The FLUs within the Rubber Council were ordered to surrender their skilled tradesmen and maintenance men to the various AFL craft unions and to surrender funds collected from the craftsmen for initiations and dues. Claherty also bought time by coming up with the idea of gaining a blanket agreement between the Rubber Council and the rubber industry. He devised the proposal and presented it for consideration to the Rubber Manufacturers Association (RMA), to which all of the major tire and rubber companies belonged. The RMA, of course, immediately rejected the blanket pact, saying that as an industry association it had no bargaining power for any of its member firms.

The tens of thousands of rubber workers who had signed up with FLUs became disenchanted with the lack of any bargaining success, and membership fell. In the fall of 1933, BFG, Firestone, and General Tire & Rubber Co. all created company unions, while Goodyear put Industrial Assemblies in all of its plants. BFG was one company that was not openly hostile to the AFL, but privately felt the unions did not have good enough leadership to take care of all the increased activities in the area of worker representation. Though BFG Vice President T. G. Graham did not have much faith in company unionism, he felt the company was better prepared than the AFL to train men for employee representation work. Workers, meanwhile, believed that the representatives only won what the company wanted to give up. The General Tire representation plan was more outwardly anti-union. The company granted such concessions as an improved group insurance plan and generous vacation allowances. General Tire Vice President Charles Jahan also argued that the council satisfied the Section 7(a) provisions of the NIRA. At Goodyear in Akron, the Industrial Assembly and the AFL FLU initially coexisted, but Goodyear continued to favor the company union by raising the pay of assembly members. In August 1934 the AFL union officially banned participation of its members in the Goodyear Industrial Assembly. Outside of Akron, relations between unionized rubber workers and management were more hostile and confrontational. Goodyear laid off eighty-four veteran employees, including many union activists, at Gadsden, Alabama, in August 1933, and Kelly-Springfield Tire Co. in Maryland laid off most of the local union's officers in June 1934.

Workers who tried to organize at various non-tire plants also encountered problems. Eagle Rubber Co. in Ashland, Ohio, laid off the local's officers. Employees at Ohio Rubber Co. in Willoughby, Ohio, formed an FLU in July 1933 and struck for recognition. The management agreed to recognize the union but soon after Ohio Rubber formed a company union and laid off many of the FLU members. At Aetna Rubber Co. in Ashtabula, Ohio, company President S. T. Campbell discharged fifty union members in early 1934, prompting a strike by the remaining 450 FLU members. On April 5 Campbell personally led an attack on the picket line and was injured in the battle that followed. Troubles at Barr Rubber Co. in Sandusky, Ohio, led to a bitter 190-day strike in 1934 after the company fired several union activists.

"TEA CUP AGREEMENT"

By 1935, the rubber workers' patience with their employers, Claherty, and the AFL had grown thin, prompting talk of a strike. The AFL, in an attempt to try to get the union movement going again, presented Goodyear, Goodrich, and Firestone with new demands for signed agreements recognizing the AFL as collective bargaining agents. When Goodyear was given the proposed agreement in late 1934, Factory Manager Clifton C. Slusser—keeping with the company's well-known anti-union stance—wrote John House a letter claiming the workers already had better conditions than those proposed.

The other rubber firms refused to bargain as well, so some of the more militant leaders of the Akron FLUs wanted a general strike to be called. Claherty and the AFL leaders were concerned that the time was not right for a walkout, that public sentiment likely would not be in the strikers' favor. The locals did take strike votes, but the results—though appearing to favor a walkout—were ambiguous and far from overwhelming. Even the AFL refused to call the workers out on strike. As a countermeasure, each of the rubber companies had its company unions take referendum votes on the simple question: "Do you wish to go on strike?" In each case the result was overwhelming: the employees wanted to stay on the job. Had the companies failed with these loaded votes, they were prepared to take the cowardly approach of crushing the labor organization with force. Each company had Sheriff Jim Flower deputize five hundred of its men. National Guard drillmasters had been hired to instruct foremen, assistant foremen, and other trusted factory hands in the art of billy-club swinging. Barbed wire fences and sandbag entrenchments were constructed, submachine guns and searchlights mounted, and strikebreakers arranged for. The firms also had stockpiled their warehouses with tires.

But the unions—being baited in many ways by the companies—still used the threat of a strike to try to make some gains with the employers. Under this threat, the union and companies enlisted the aid of Secretary of Labor Frances Perkins. She brought the two sides to Washington and devised during a most unusual set of negotiations what would become known as the "Tea Cup Agreement." During these talks, culminated on April 13, 1935, she kept the sides in separate rooms, presumably drinking tea, hence the nickname for the negotiations. First she would talk with one group, then switch rooms and talk to the other. Perkins had warned that the president would intervene if the two sides failed to avert a strike. She first suggested that the manufacturers withdraw their legal challenges to organizational elections or agree to organizational elections before the courts had acted on the constitutionality of the NIRA. When the companies rejected those ideas, Perkins devised a temporary arrangement that would delay talk of a strike.

At no time would company executives meet face-to-face with labor representatives, who included Claherty, House, Walter R. Kriebel from Firestone, and Sherman H. Dalrymple of Goodrich. Each side signed a separate document with Perkins. That way the executives could deny that they had granted recognition in any manner to the union. They could claim the agreement they entered into was with Secretary Perkins, not the unions. Under the understanding, labor agreed not to strike until the U.S. Supreme Court had decided on the constitutional questions regarding the NIRA. The manufacturers agreed to meet with representatives of any group of employees and act promptly on their requests and complaints. There also was a provision for a three-person fact-finding board to address unsettled grievances.

Although the union leaders were not happy with the Tea Cup Agreement, they were convinced it was the best they could get without a strike. And since Green had told them the AFL would not support a strike under the existing circumstances, they reluctantly agreed to recommend ratification. They knew that the militant workers would view the gains as a sellout—clearly not a victory of any kind. All three of the big Akron locals did ratify the Perkins agreement, but not without heated discussion. At the Goodyear local meeting—the most bitter of the local sessions—someone questioned House's integrity and accused him of selling out. "Deeply hurt and angered by such an unfair accusation I took off my coat, rolled up my shirt sleeves and suggested that if that person or anyone else wished to pursue the point he should come forward and meet me man to man," House said. "No one accepted my challenge and the meeting moved smoothly and quickly to a standing vote in which only a handful of members voted against ratification." While the leaders may have been able to push through ratification, they could not stop the workers from effectively dropping out of the FLUs by failing to pay the monthly one dollar dues. By September all of the rubber worker locals in Akron could claim just thirty-one hundred paid members.

All through this process, large corporations—both inside and outside the rubber industry—fought the constitutionality of the NIRA, along with other parts of FDR's New Deal. They felt the government had no business giving such rights to workers. Yet even if the courts let the NIRA stand, the firms still maintained the company unions satisfied the infamous Section 7(a) that covered workers' rights to join labor organizations. In the end, the Supreme Court on May 27, 1935, did strike down the NIRA, along with Section 7(a), and the circuit court two weeks later voided organization election orders issued earlier by the government.

But following soon after the NIRA's demise came the National Labor Relations Act—known as the Wagner Act and signed into law July 5, 1935—that had in some ways even stronger provisions than its predecessor in terms of workers' rights to join together in unions. Though also challenged by the companies, which said that this bill too would not hold up to a constitutional test, the basis of the law was simple. It encouraged "the practice and procedure of collective bargaining and by protecting the exercise by workers of full freedom of association, self-organization, and designation of representatives of their own choosing, for the purpose of negotiating the terms and conditions of their employment or other mutual aid or protection." The law, sponsored by Senator Robert F. Wagner of New York, also said, "Employees shall have the right to self-organization, to form, join, or assist labor organizations, to bargain collectively through representatives of their own choosing, and to engage in concerted activities, for the purpose of collective bargaining or other mutual aid protection." Employers under the statute were forbidden from discriminating against union members, interfering with self-organization of employees, supporting company unions, or refusing to bargain collectively with employees' representatives. Finally, the law, which had little initial impact, created a National Labor Relations Board (NLRB) to investigate, try cases, and give redress to workers.

While most employers blamed FDR for the rapid rise of unionism, House said the administration's new labor laws just gave rise to something that was already within the workers. "The desire, the yearning, for real opportunity to have a bona fide union through which they might bargain collectively without restraint or coercion and without the threat of reprisal by employers," House said, "had always existed as a result of unfair treatment by employers and the failure of employers and the public generally to give them their rightful recognition as first-class citizens."

Although the battle was just beginning, it was becoming clear that the rank-and-file workers disagreed with Litchfield and the other rubber executives: they did indeed need a union of their own to make sure their voice was heard loudly and clearly.

PART I

THE BEGINNING

CHAPTER 1

THE BIRTH OF A UNION

The United Rubber Workers liked to refer to itself as "A Mighty Fine Union" throughout its history. It very easily could have been "A Mighty Democratic Union." For during the union's six decades of existence, one thing was always clear—the final decision was always in the hands of the rank and file. Be it a question of raising dues, going on strike, or removing one of the top officers, the delegates to the URW conventions held the supreme power of approval or disapproval.

And so it was at a special convention in July 1995 that delegates were asked to merge the URW with the much larger United Steelworkers of America union. The Rubber Workers had fallen on hard times. Membership had fallen, and the union's coffers were nearly bare after an ill-fated strike against Bridgestone/Firestone and three other foreign tire makers in the "War of '94." Following a hectic couple of months during which the URW first had called off its strike against Bridgestone/Firestone and then hastily put together the merger agreement with the USWA, the nearly sixty years of URW history culminated in mass confusion at this special convention. Had the union's merger with the much larger USWA passed or failed? Delegates to the gathering in Pittsburgh had cast ballots several hours earlier and yet the outcome was still in doubt. URW and USWA officials scrambled about yelling at each other, mostly in terms not suitable for family television. Word filtered down that the merger had not surpassed the 614 votes—two-thirds of the 921 votes cast by 624 delegates—required to bring a halt to the independence of the always proud URW. Or had it?

As people from both unions scurried around, those from the URW sought out Dan Borelli, assistant and right-hand man to URW President Kenneth Coss, the main force behind the merger and the person who first proposed this union of unions. URW members frantically told Borelli the vote had come up short. "Bullshit, there's no way," Borelli told them. URW

Secretary/Treasurer Glenn Ellison ran upstairs to see what he could find out. An assistant to USWA President George Becker, who had focused much of his union's manpower and financial resources on making this merger happen, got wind of the situation and was visibly upset. When Borelli found Coss and brought him up to speed on the vote count, the URW president said, "It can't be." Borelli tried to comfort him, saying: "I don't know what to say. They called for us. Glenn's up there now. I'll see what the situation is and come back and tell you." J. Curtis Brown, then URW public relations director, was sitting in a room waiting to write a news release—whether the merger passed or failed—as the now-tense situation simmered to a near boil. "I saw Coss's face drop. He looked crushed," Brown said.

But had the merger actually failed? Had all the effort and money the USWA and merger supporters from within the URW put forth been wasted? The Steelworkers had spared no expense. Officers of the larger, Pittsburgh-based USWA had treated this potential merger as its largest organizational campaign in decades. They saw the benefits of adding more than ninety thousand members to the union's dues-paying rolls, more members than nearly a decade of successful plant organizing would deliver at a time when the U.S. public was becoming less and less enamored with the benefits of union membership. USWA officials were frantic that their crusade might have come up short.

When Borelli arrived where the convention's Tellers Committee had gathered to count up the secretly cast paper ballots, the scene had calmed a bit. Because the tally was so close, the committee—chosen by a random draw of delegates—already had set about recounting the ballots before an official recount was mandated by the convention. During a vote count, it was normal procedure to put ballots for or against the merger into separate stacks of tens. During the course of the recount, the Tellers Committee members apparently found a few instances where the wrong number of ballots had been placed in a particular pile. The new final tally: 617 votes in favor of the merger, 304 opposed. The URW's merger with the Steelworkers union had passed with three votes to spare. "By the time I got up there they'd recounted what they had, and they had the right number to get three votes over what we needed," Borelli said. He then went to Coss to give him the good news. The URW president's reaction, rather than elation, was one of relief that all the hard work of the harried past few months had not been squandered.

The chaotic manner in which the United Rubber Workers union ended its reign as perhaps the nation's most democratic trade union also was a fitting end to the frantic months that led up to the historic merger convention. As for remembering the URW's history and tradition, the Rubber Workers took it upon themselves to pass on the unending tales of victories and losses, of strikes and negotiations, of leaders and unsung heroes. Or as Local 677's John Cunningham told delegates at the merger convention: "I'm proud to be URW. History doesn't go away. It's how you tell the story." And what a story it was.

THE FOUNDING CONVENTION

As 1935 moved forward, the rubber workers never swayed in their belief that an industrial union was in their best interests, even though it was clearly against the main tenets of the American Federation of Labor. The AFL long had been set up along craft lines, so workers who shared a trade belonged in the same union regardless of their place of employment. Thus, machinists would be in one union, plumbers in another, and electricians in yet another. So when scores of workers from the rubber shops joined up with the AFL, they first were put in the Federal Labor Union assigned to the plant, then doled out to the AFL international union umbrella organization that covered the specific trades. But those who toiled in the rubber factories felt kinship toward each other—not for an electrician who worked in some unrelated plant across town.

Finally, the AFL acquiesced and announced the intention to issue separate industrial union charters for auto and rubber—the 106th and 107th international unions to be affiliated with the AFL. But it was clear that the rubber workers were not going to be pushovers and accept whatever the AFL offered. What the AFL had in mind was clear when AFL President William Green presented the charter to the Auto Workers for the formation of the United Auto Workers (UAW). Green wanted the power to appoint the officers of the newly formed internationals, and he wanted the jurisdiction of the unions to be restricted to pure production workers. The AFL president was not above holding the specter of losing AFL financial aid over the heads of the unionists in order to keep that power. That way, Green figured, the leader would be working in the interest of the AFL rather than trying to push an agenda of his own. When the Auto Workers union was formed—just a matter of weeks before Green traveled to Akron to present the charter for a United Rubber Workers union—Green was able to appoint his organizer, Francis J. Dillon, as UAW president over the protests of many of the delegates by using this hammer of financial support.

The founding convention to form what would become the United Rubber Workers of America bore clear evidence of the independent-mindedness of those who would form the union's early leadership. And the paltry number of eligible members for the new organization showed how the AFL's method of signing up workers and then transferring the members into various craft unions had been an utter failure in the rubber industry. Coleman Claherty and others had signed up tens of thousands of members while chartering sixty-nine FLUs in the rubber industry since the organizing drive began in June 1933. But a convention call that went to fifty-plus eligible FLUs brought replies from just twenty-six, representing fewer than four thousand paid-up members in good standing—hardly a sizable group from which to start an international union. It was evident that the rubber workers were not taken with the AFL's vision of union organization; they wanted to be together in one union and not separated along craft lines.

So when Claherty and Green gathered with the convention delegates on September 12, 1935, they did not find a group of conciliatory workers glad to have the mighty AFL at their service. Delegates had hard questions for Green and clearly were not afraid to air their views. Foremost on their minds: Did this charter give Green the power to appoint officers of his choosing, or would the delegates get to name their own leaders? Under the sponsorship of Fisk Rubber worker Thomas F. Burns, forty of forty-nine delegates in attendance presented a resolution asking for "democratic procedure" and the right to elect all officers. Green was angered over having the petition handed to him when he arrived at the lobby of the Portage Hotel, but seemed in much better spirits when speaking at the convention. "Now the American Federation of Labor will stand by you," Green told delegates. "We will never, never desert you. I am glad that I can serve you as the mere instrumentality through which this international union can be launched, and because I am launching it, it will ever be close to my heart, and as long as I live and breathe, I will give my life and service to protect it from its enemies from within and without."

Still, debate on the topic of how officers would be selected was heated. Delegate Salvatore Camelio from Boston Woven Hose in Cambridge, Massachusetts, said to Green, "I would like to ask if we, the delegates

The delegates to the URW's founding convention gather at the Portage Hotel in Akron. *(USWA/URW photo files)*

assembled, accept this charter, does this give the president the right to appoint the officers?" To which Green snapped back: "It is not for you to decide as to whether or not you will accept the charter. That has been decided by the convention of the American Federation of Labor and by the Executive Council. . . . It cannot be amended and it cannot be accepted and it cannot be rejected."

One group, however, was afraid that without the financial backing of the AFL, the newly formed Rubber Workers would die as quickly as it was born. Among this group was John House, by then president of the FLU at Goodyear in Akron, and Charles Lanning, both members of the convention's Resolutions Committee. They and delegate E. L. Gray of Gadsden, Alabama, met privately with Green and Claherty and came up with a compromise—dubbed Resolution No. 21—in which Green could appoint Claherty as the union's president for one year with the salary paid by the

AFL, and the delegates could elect the other officers and pay those salaries. At future conventions, the delegates would elect all convention officers. In turn, the AFL would continue its financial backing as the new URW tried to gain stature and membership.

But this compromise measure clearly was not the will of the delegates. House and Lanning were the only members of the Resolution Committee to support the resolution. Undaunted, Claherty and Green had Resolution No. 21 considered first—clearly out of order—with the recommendation to accept the minority report. Delegates were not pleased. They made impassioned pleas for democracy and self-government. Then Green turned on Burns, the leader of the opposition at that point, and accused him of being associated with a "dual union" movement stemming from Burns's involvement in the earlier ill-fated convention in Indianapolis that attempted to start an independent union. Burns countered by reminding Green that the AFL president himself had appointed a leader of the "dual union" movement to a high post, and that Green merely was trying to deflect attention from the real issue: the right of the rubber workers to elect their own officers and conduct the union as they saw fit.

Sherman Dalrymple, from the BFG local in Akron, arose as a voice of reason during the debate. He said the charges were false, that no one had questioned the integrity of the AFL. Dalrymple also brushed aside Green's threats, saying the union would be happy to have the assistance of the AFL but the rubber workers would finance their own organization if they had to. "When we get the membership, the finances will be there," Dalrymple said. He told the convention that the AFL constitution guaranteed the democratic autonomous rights of affiliates, so these rights should not be denied to the rubber workers. "Financial help is less important to me than democracy," Dalrymple said to the delegates. "Do not vote the democratic principles of this union away." The roll call was a mere formality, with delegates overwhelmingly voting not to allow Green to appoint officers.

Green gave one more response before leaving the convention. "You have decided to refuse to request me and the Executive Council of the American Federation of Labor to appoint Brother Claherty during a probationary period," he told delegates. "You have said in a most decisive way that you will not make that request. . . . Secondly, you have decided to refuse to request me and the Executive Council to establish and finance your International headquarters. You have said you don't want that from the American Federation. I accept your words as final. . . . Now the con-

Sherman Dalrymple, the
first president of the
United Rubber Workers
of America. *(USWA/URW
photo files)*

vention is turned over to you. You may elect your officers from top to bottom and you may arrange to finance your convention and your organization work and carry on."

The next three days at the convention were spent writing the constitution, acting on the remaining resolutions, and getting ready for the
upcoming elections of the first officers of the United Rubber Workers of
America. Burns and House—the leaders of the main two factions of the
convention—were two of the candidates for president. Burns had led
those who wanted an independent union, while House had been more
conciliatory toward allowing the AFL some power over the fledgling
union in return for the financial backing. But the field also included Dalrymple as a wild card third choice. Though Burns likely would easily have
defeated House in a head-to-head contest, Dalrymple gave a different
complexion to the race.

Dalrymple was not the type of person who normally would be expected to head a growing international union during a time of change and

turmoil. He was not the bombastic, fiery type of orator who could work the crowd into a frenzy. Although not highly educated—he did not go past the fourth grade—he was seen as an intelligent man. More importantly, he was an honest man whose integrity was beyond reproach. That meant the rank and file could take his word as gold. Born in Walton, West Virginia, on April 4, 1889, he came to Akron in 1903 to help pay off debts on the family farm and began working in the rubber industry in 1909. "We worked ten hours a day, six days a week," Dalrymple said. "Sometimes the foreman would come around on Saturday without any previous notice and tell us to work Sunday—and of course no overtime pay. If you refused you would get reprimanded or laid off or maybe even fired. The foreman always had his way and the worker didn't have a chance."

He turned to oilfield work from 1911 to 1914 before returning to the rubber industry for three years beginning in 1914. He served in World War I in the U.S. Marine Corps as a private, corporal, sergeant, and second lieutenant, returning a decorated war hero. Some of the early members of the Rubber Workers told Glenn Ellison, the union's final secretary/treasurer, that Dalrymple was a natural leader who was very strong in his ways. "They said when he made a decision, that was it," Ellison said. "He was a strong leader, but I've never heard any one of those old-timers who didn't have the utmost respect for him. So it always seemed to me like he set the URW on a certain pathway that lasted for many, many years." George Freiberger, one of the founding members of Local 87 in Dayton, had the opportunity to sit in on skilled trade meetings that Dalrymple chaired at later URW conventions. "You couldn't believe that he knew so much about organization, as young as he was at the time," Freiberger said. "He told us what we can do and can't do. He said, 'If you live by the rules, you'll never have any problems.'"

And at the URW's founding convention, it was this integrity that drew the delegates to him. Dalrymple was a Green critic and an influential local president, but foremost he was an honest man the delegates trusted. He also was the one candidate who could unite the Akron delegates, who accounted for twenty-four of the convention's fifty-five votes. Delegate Rex Murray recalled that Burns desperately wanted to be president but the Akron delegates opposed him vehemently. Dalrymple did not really want the office or feel he was qualified to handle it, but Murray said the Akron leaders "knew the honesty and integrity of the individual, and there was

Table 1.1 First URW Leaders

PRESIDENT
Sherman H. Dalrymple

VICE PRESIDENT
Thomas F. Burns

SECRETARY/TREASURER
Frank Grillo

EXECUTIVE BOARD
George B. Roberts
Salvatore Camello
W. W. Thompson
N. H. Eagle
Walter J. Welsh
John Marchiando
John House

Source: House, *Birth of a Union.*

no one else that we could feel the same way about." In the end, Dalrymple took twenty-nine votes to nineteen for Burns and seven for House. The vote indicated that Dalrymple likely took the votes of nearly all the Akron and Ohio delegates except the Goodyear group, with Burns getting the backing of his core non-Akron delegate followers. Dalrymple promised to "upbuild" the union and to maintain his sense of perspective. He pledged that his head would "never get larger than the position."

Burns easily defeated Lanning 41–14 for vice president and helped steer the victory of Frank Grillo, from the Goodrich local in Los Angeles, as secretary/treasurer from a pool of three candidates, meaning that two of the top three officers hailed from outside of Akron. Burns's supporters also won a majority of the General Executive Board seats. The three top officers—while opposed occasionally at later URW conventions—continued as the URW's top three officers until the 1941 convention, when Burns did not seek re-election (table 1.1).

Convention delegates in 1935 also adopted a constitution that listed as the first objective of the union "to unite in one organization all men and women eligible for membership, employed in and around factories engaged in the manufacture of rubber products." The AFL Executive

Council balked at the extent of industrial unionism embraced by the new constitution that clearly defied the setup of the AFL as a craft union stronghold. They demanded the language be changed to read "to unite in one organization of men and women eligible for membership employed and engaged in the manufacturing of rubber products." The URW also had to add a new section under the title "Jurisdiction" that read: "All those in the rubber industry who are engaged in the mass production of rubber products, same not to cover or include such workers who construct buildings, manufacturing of machinery, or engage in maintenance work or in work outside the plants or factories." To avoid an open break with the AFL, the URW Executive Board approved the changes demanded by the AFL, and by December 1, thirty-nine locals officially were transferred from the AFL into the URW.

Though shunned by delegates as a potential president for the new union, Claherty did remain as the presiding officer throughout the Constitutional Convention and presented the AFL charter which he had received from Green to the newly elected officers. He chastised delegates one last time for their treatment of Green—a statement answered strongly by Dalrymple—but he also assured the new officers of his continued support, made the office available to the new organization, and agreed to give the new union his guidance and advice when called upon.

Immediately after the convention, the three officers—looking basically to start up an international union from scratch—traveled to Washington, D.C., where Green agreed to give some help to the fledgling organization. During the URW's first year, the AFL granted $1,000.00 in cash; a balance of $1,846.78 that remained in the treasury of the Rubber Workers' Council; office furniture, fixtures, and equipment valued at $677.50; and the cash deposit of $25.00 with the telephone company. The union's financial position was so poor that Dalrymple remained on the payroll of his local union for a month after he was elected URW president, and Vice President Burns stayed in an extra room at Dalrymple's home. Immediate and needed cash was secured by voluntary advances of $350.00 from three local unions. "We opened our headquarters in two small rented rooms," Dalrymple said later. "We didn't have a dollar in the bank. We had exactly 3,080 dues-paying members. We had two worn-out typewriters. We did not have a single contract with a major rubber company. We had no staff. We had no money to print our constitution and the proceedings of our first Constitutional Convention. However, our printer, Alex Eigenmacht, never squawked about the bills. He told us: 'I am right with you boys. I know you have no money. If you do all right, that's fine. If you go broke, I go broke with you.'" In November and December the URW's deficit exceeded $300.00 a month, and by mid-January the URW's bank balance dipped below $1,000.00. The Executive Board investigated and decided to fire two clerks and return some of the furniture. The officers voluntarily took pay cuts of $25.00 a month.

JOINING UP WITH THE CIO

A few weeks after the founding convention of the URW, an incident at the AFL national convention in Atlantic City, New Jersey, cemented the future direction of the new Rubber Workers union. A URW delegate had presented a resolution objecting to a committee report rejecting rubber- and auto-worker petitions that craft unions be kept out of their industries. The resolution asked the AFL to extend the union's jurisdiction to cover "all employees in and around the respective factories without segregation of the employees in the industry." It was just another way of trying to impress upon the AFL that the Rubber Workers viewed those in their own plant as union brothers and sisters—not someone who shared a trade but worked elsewhere. A delegate from Akron pointed out that in his local, 432 organized members had been turned over in 1934 to the machinists union and only five of those 432 were paid-up members in the machinists union a year later.

During debate, William L. Hutcheson, president of the carpenters union, raised a point of order saying that the issue of industrial unionism had been settled, which Green sustained. John L. Lewis, president of the United Mine Workers, and another delegate rose to defend the right of the URW delegate to present his case. "This thing of raising points of order all the time on minor delegates is rather small potatoes," Lewis said. Hutcheson took offense, saying he had been raised on small potatoes, and a fist fight broke out between the two, with Hutcheson being knocked across a convention table. Though the AFL convention sustained the committee report—meaning the jurisdictional lines of the craft unions would remain—the URW cast its lot with Lewis as he formed the Committee for Industrial Organization (later renamed the Congress for Industrial Organization, CIO) in November 1935 as the basis to organize unions in mass production industries. Lewis said it was natural that the Rubber Workers, many of whom were former United Mine Workers, would be part of his new labor organization. "The labor movement is organized upon the principle that the strong shall help the weak," Lewis said. "[Rubber Workers] are not content to be further exploited in these feeble craft attempts to establish collective bargaining in the haunts of the rubber barons."

The URW's Executive Committee in July 1936 officially approved affiliation with the CIO, even though it meant suspension from the AFL. The URW joined the auto and steel workers as industrial unions that cast their lot with Lewis and the CIO rather than the longer-established AFL. The AFL and CIO continued this philosophical debate, often battling to organize the same group of workers, until reuniting as the AFL-CIO in 1955.

THE GOODYEAR STRIKE OF 1936: "COME ON, BOYS, LET'S GO"

With the United Rubber Workers of America fresh from its historic Constitutional Convention, it did not take long for tire companies to test the fledgling union. The economy by late 1935 was in the midst of a recovery. But the tire makers were hurt by vicious price competition among firms that left profits at low, pre-Depression levels. This drain on profits helped lead to a round of labor turmoil that began in October, just a month after the URW's founding. Between October and December 1935, disturbances broke out at all of the major plants in Akron. General Tire locals protested against layoffs; the Goodrich union was hit by continuous rumors that hours would be increased and wages cut; and tire builders at Firestone became involved in a dispute over rate cuts.

But the major dispute of the era would come at Goodyear. Despite the Tea Cup Agreement earlier in 1935, relations between Goodyear and its workforce remained tense at best. More so than the other firms, Goodyear felt that unions had no place in its factories. Goodyear's Litchfield steadfastly stuck to the notion that the company and workers were best off when Goodyear could deal with each employee individually, without the outside influence of a labor organization. At least it was better for Goodyear and Litchfield, who could more easily control individual workers not banded together with union solidarity. So workers seethed when in October 1935 Goodyear cut rates without first notifying union leaders, as had been agreed to in the Tea Cup accord. Litchfield wanted his huge operation to make money, and to this end he first planned to combine a longer workweek with lower rates. His first plan called for hourly earnings to drop from 96 cents to 86 cents, with monthly earnings increasing from $122 to $125 because of the longer workweek. He later raised the plan to 92 cents an hour and $133 a month. Litchfield's plan was not any more severe than cuts accepted by Firestone workers, but the Goodyear leader also wanted to end the six-hour day. Litchfield did not understand that workers equated longer hours with layoffs rather than higher earnings, despite his assurance that new business would create more jobs. This time the company had perturbed even members of the Goodyear Industrial Assembly. The members of this company union finally were seeing that the assembly had no power, that in the end Litchfield truly made all the decisions. Some assembly members even came to Local 2 headquarters to see if the union would join them in a strike. Local 2 officials responded that if the assembly joined the AFL organization, then the AFL would call the strike. The assembly tried to take action, voting to return to the six-hour day in the Plant 2 tire departments. On October 30, Litchfield, talking to an assembly committee, refused to order a return to the six-hour day in Plant 2. The assembly, though, decided against appealing to Secretary of Labor Perkins at that time. It was clear that the company union had reached its limitations when it could make no inroads on an issue of such importance to workers.

Local 2, however, continued to hold rallies and pressure Perkins to intervene. A group of tire builders staged a sit-down strike on November 5 when the superintendent of the Plant 2 truck tire department announced piece-rate reductions of 10 to 15 percent. The company agreed to revise the rates after the foreman met with a group of day- and night-shift workers. By mid-November Perkins decided to act because a confrontation looked more likely. She appointed a fact finding board of several Labor Department officials along with Fred C. Croxton of Ohio State University, who chaired the board. The board members came to Akron on November 22, interviewed union and company officers, and collected data on Goodyear's workforce. They also listened to assembly leaders and returned to Washington to present conclusions. Croxton's report was quite damning to Goodyear, saying there was no justification for the eight-hour day, reduced wages, or the firm's refusal to permit a referendum. Goodyear, he found, also had favored the Industrial Assembly over the URW and had indeed violated the Tea Cup Agreement from earlier in 1935. Croxton concluded that wage cuts and layoffs would reduce demand for Goodyear products; he proposed higher tire prices rather than lower wages to bring profits up. Perkins and her advisers were so shocked by the report that they delayed its issuance, fearing that it would cause more trouble in the industry. Although Croxton said on December 18 that the report was complete, Labor Department officials refused even to acknowledge its existence until three days later. When Perkins released the report January 6 and Goodyear officials refused to make any comment, the news value of the document diminished quickly. The company did, however, schedule work in Plant 2 in six-hour shifts, giving in to the main demand of the workers.

But the incident did little to calm the growing tempest building between the workers and the company. The report had the firm thinking that the government was biased while union leaders thought the Labor Department was no more helpful than the NLRB. Adding fuel to the flames was a January 19, 1936, rally at which CIO President Lewis clearly set the tone for what actions the workers must take. "Your destiny is in your own hands. I hope you'll do something for yourselves," he told a crowd of two thousand. "Organize, organize, organize" was his message. Three days after the Lewis rally, Firestone cut piece rates in the truck tire department, and the suspension of a union man who got in a fight with a non-union pacesetter prompted a fifty-five-hour sit-down action. URW President Dalrymple conferred with the plant's labor manager, and an agreement was reached whereby the men would receive their usual base rate for the time they had not worked and the suspended union member would get half-pay. It seemed to escape notice that the rate cuts that started the fiasco were not discussed and remained in effect. Other sit-downs occurred in following weeks at Goodyear and Goodrich.

It was clear that the tensions soon would come to a head in one manner or another. Fourth-shift tire builders at Goodyear were likely to be the most militant as they would face the brunt of layoffs if the plant went to a permanent three-shift, eight-hour-a-day schedule. The fourth-shift workers sat down on February 14 when the foreman began passing out layoff notices. When a meeting between a six-man, non-union group and management proved unsuccessful, they sat down for the rest of their shift and half of the next, leaving only after the Plant 2 superintendent promised another meeting. Local 2 President House met them at the gate to offer the help of the union and suggest a meeting of tire builders at the union hall.

Second-shift tire builders sat down to protest the fourth-shift layoffs until plant management agreed to meet them, and third-shift tire builders staged their own sit-down at 6:00 P.M. that evening. They were ordered back to work or face discharge, with only three members of the elite Flying Squadron—workers specially trained by the company whom Goodyear normally could count on to follow its policies under all circumstances— going back to their machines and the other 137 tire builders remaining idle. At 9:30 P.M. the foremen distributed "pass-out checks" that said, "Quit, no notice," but still the men refused to leave. After 11:00 P.M., the men gradually went back to their machines and built at least one tire each. Supervisors sent home hundreds of other workers and canceled the fourth shift. As no work was scheduled for Saturday or Monday, the plant was not scheduled to reopen until Tuesday, February 18.

The firing of the third-shift workers, who had not been involved in earlier protests, helped bring the tensions to the boil-over point. A committee from the Industrial Assembly met with plant management on Saturday evening, and the company promised to rehire the 137 men on Monday if they applied at the employment office. After another conference Monday, Goodyear said the layoff would be suspended and the production schedule re-examined. Union militants got angrier, as it appeared that Goodyear would cooperate with the company union but not Local 2. A Local 2 rally Sunday called for the union to shut down Plant 2 if the tire builders were not reinstated. On Monday it was reported that Personnel Director Fred Climer refused to meet with the local union committee. About one thousand rubber workers attended another rally at the Local 2 hall that evening; the tire builders voted not to work, and other workers pledged to join them. Local 2 President House—who had tried to help forge a compromise with Green during the URW's founding convention—did not personally favor a strike. He thought continued negotiations would be more prudent. But as wintery February temperatures continued to drop and the weather reached blizzard proportions, the temperature of the men inside the union hall reached fever level. "Needless to say, I was scared and wanted to suggest to the meeting that we postpone the establishment of a picket line and try again to set up a meeting with management but was dissuaded by one of my most trusted fellow officers, George Hull, who said he could see no possibility of holding the infuriated assemblage," House said. "At this point, Cibert M. 'Skip' O'Harrah, a member of the local union Executive Board and a former coal miner, grabbed the U.S. flag from the speakers' platform and, yelling, 'Come on boys, let's go,' marched out of the union hall down the stairway to East Market Street with the entire crowd following him up East Market to Martha Avenue and on to the Plant 2 gatehouse through a raging blizzard that had begun while the meeting was in progress and dropping the outside temperature to nine degrees below zero with the chill factor several degrees lower."

By 11 P.M., five hundred men and women marched outside the gate and turned away several hundred fourth-shift employees at midnight. The picketers surrounded the whole eleven-mile perimeter of the Goodyear complex—the longest picket line in U.S. strike history. A few hours later, five hundred Plant 1 tire builders and pit workers sat down in support of the strike, gradually putting that plant out of operation as well. By late Tuesday, all of Goodyear operations in Akron had come to a halt.

The historic Goodyear strike of 1936 differed markedly from the walkout of 1913. This time the workers were organized, though they did have to scramble at first to put a full-fledged strike organization in place; the leaders knew how to run a strike of this proportion; and the workers' demands were clear and understood from the outset. While the AFL offered some support, the CIO leaders took charge and placed the URW local strikers under their wing. It became clear that the Rubber Workers' ideal of industrial unionism much more closely matched the beliefs of the CIO rather than the AFL. In later years, the Goodyear work stoppage was widely looked on as the first CIO strike. Skip O'Harrah took responsibility for the picketers, adopting the title of "field marshal." He provided each picket outpost with a steel drum stove, and the men erected huts for further protection from the elements. Most of the outposts took names such as "Camp Roosevelt" or "John L. Lewis Post," and the local post office even authorized mail delivery to these named shacks.

Dalrymple insisted that the other URW plants in town continue to work, but many from the other factories helped picket when off duty or brought in help when it seemed like there would be trouble at the picket line. The CIO especially threw all its resources into the battle. Adolph Germer worked with the strike leaders behind the scenes, while Powers Hapgood and Rose Pesotta came to town February 26 to manage public relations for the strikers. Only Claherty from the AFL came to town, and no strike leader greeted him when he toured the picket line.

Local 2 pickets parade in front of the Goodyear office during the strike of 1936. (*USWA/URW photo files*)

Litchfield dug in his heels to try to stop the union's growing popularity and power. On February 19 he went to the Plant 1 gates and demanded that the police help first-shift workers cross the picket line. But that tactic failed, and the Goodyear leader spent the first twelve days of the strike inside the plant, sleeping on a couch in his office. When interviewed inside the plant on February 20, he said he was bitter toward the union malcontents he claimed caused the strike, and also against the Local 2 officers, with whom he said he would not deal, even if that meant closing the plants indefinitely. With a crew of about one thousand supervisors and nonstrikers who also took up residence inside the huge factory complex, Litchfield tried, but failed, to keep up some semblance of production.

Litchfield was trying to employ various steps in the so-called Mohawk Valley Formula, the step-by-step plan developed by the president of Remington Rand, to try to break labor strikes. But for the Goodyear leader, the formula did not work as planned. After ending his seclusion, Litchfield took up residence at the Mayflower Hotel and began giving interviews and making radio broadcasts. Despite these efforts, however, it was clear that the Rubber Workers—with huge assistance from the CIO leaders—were winning the public relations war as the public clearly sided with the working men.

The walkout was conspicuous for its virtual lack of violence. In the early weeks of the strike, in fact, there was more threat of violence from a group of nonstrikers who were long-service men and veterans of the Industrial Assembly and the Ku Klux Klan. On February 19 several hundred of them jammed city hall demanding police protection. Many volunteered to serve as special deputies, but the mayor and sheriff refused to deputize them. Mayor Lee D. Schroy even traded words with Litchfield, who criticized the mayor's evenhanded approach in asking for negotiations. On February 22 the county's common pleas judges issued an injunction permitting only ten pickets per gate and prohibiting intimidation against Goodyear employees. This was good news to the group of nonstrikers, and they were confident they would be back at work within a couple of days.

Sheriff Jim Flower—with just twenty-three regular and nine special deputies—did not attempt to enforce the injunction until February 24, when he planned to go to the Local 2 hall. As word of Flower's impending arrival spread, thousands of picketers crowded around the hall. House met Flower at the door and escorted him to the microphone, where the sheriff pledged not to deputize nonstrikers. Someone in the crowd yelled, "Are we going to let them in?" And the crowd screamed, "No!"

The sheriff went to city hall and, after talking to Goodyear executives, decided he would confront the strikers the next morning. He had 130 city police officers and 18 deputies assembled at the intersection of Exchange and East Market streets, one block from the plant. He ordered traffic blocked in the area and planned to have the police and deputies march to the main gate and arrest pickets who continued to violate the injunction. House was asleep in the Local 2 board room about 6:30 A.M. when someone alerted him that "all hell's about to pop." He dressed in a hurry and

Akron police try to force their way through the picket line during the 1936 strike.
(*USWA/URW photo files*)

took a position in the front line of men that stretched across all six lanes of East Market Street and extended to the top of the steps leading into the Goodyear gatehouse. "Behind this line as far as the eye could see eastward, a vast throng of [strikers] filled the street awaiting the threatened attack of the sheriff and his deputies, backed up by the entire Akron police force under the leadership of Police Chief Frank Boss," House said.

URW officials had alerted the pickets and other union members and by 9:00 A.M. thousands of sympathizers had assembled on East Market Street, many carrying guns and other weapons. By 9:30, five thousand people were blocking the street from the edge of Plant 1 to the main gate a hundred yards to the southeast. When the mayor and police chief learned of Flower's plan, they decided the tactics were not a good idea. The police chief revoked Flower's authority to command the police and rushed to the scene. Boss led the police officers single file up the hill to their usual posts. When people saw that the police would not attack, the mood of the crowd became much more pleasant. County Prosecutor Herman Werner then entered the Goodyear office and asked Litchfield to negotiate—a request the Goodyear executive refused. So Werner told strikers there would be no more attempts to enter the plant or to break the picket line until the strike was settled. The strikers hoisted Werner on their shoulders along with House, who said, "Fellows, I'm so full of feeling I can hardly talk. . . . There is nothing that can stop us. We are in this fight to win and we are going to win in spite of hell and high water."

Mayor Schroy then persuaded Secretary of Labor Perkins to send Undersecretary Edward F. McGrady to try to keep peace. McGrady arrived February 26 and called for an immediate end to the strike, reinstatement of the strikers, and arbitration of differences between the company and union. Union negotiators felt they should accept the plan, but at an impromptu meeting at the Local 2 hall, Dalrymple announced the decision and called for a membership vote. Much opposition broke out, as the leader of the union militants opposed the plan and asked the union officers to postpone the vote. When URW leaders tried to defend the actions of the union negotiators, they were shouted down, and Dalrymple called off the vote.

Litchfield decried McGrady, vowed to stand by the Industrial Assembly, and held fast that he would never enter into an agreement with the United Rubber Workers. Goodyear Vice President E. J. Thomas advocated a more conciliatory approach toward the union. Thomas, while agreeing with Litchfield on the basics, was prepared to live with the union but did not want the company to make additional concessions. While the company and union made offers and counteroffers to no avail, secret negotiations without a set agenda began March 5 and continued off and on through the remainder of the work stoppage.

The next nervous moment occurred the morning of March 7 when the group of nonstrikers insisted on the removal of the makeshift shacks that had been protecting the strikers to some degree from the harsh winter weather. Mayor Schroy conferred with House and O'Harrah several times, and the two apparently promised to remove the shelters but never acted. The mayor ordered sanitation workers, accompanied by seventy-five police officers, to remove the shelters. The fifty-six sanitation workers destroyed four of the shacks before the workers realized what was going on and sounded the alarm. Pickets poured out of the nearby Local 2 hall.

Workers at General Tire heard that trouble was brewing down Market Street at Goodyear and shut down their presses and rushed to help. URW members from the Firestone Local 7 headquarters came to the scene. Within minutes nearly three thousand people filled the street to protect the shanties. Schroy at first wanted to renew the attack, but police said they would have to shoot if that took place. The mayor then met with Local 2's House and O'Harrah, and postponed any action as long as the union removed the shelters from major roadways. Thereafter, strikers sat in cars near the plant gates.

By the end of March 7 the secret negotiations had produced understandings on a number of issues. The company would reinstate all employees, give Local 2 equal representation with the Industrial Assembly, notify union leaders of layoffs and rate changes, reconsider recent rate cuts, reduce the number of Flying Squadron members, and maintain the six-hour day. Local 2 leaders were to report the results to membership at a meeting the following day, Sunday, March 8, but a local reporter learned of the agreement and published the story in that morning's paper. When Goodyear officials objected, House merely summarized negotiations to that point, realizing he probably did not have the votes anyway. Litchfield also had second thoughts and broadcast a new, less generous proposal the next day. His offer did not mention hours in non-tire operations, the February wage cuts, Flying Squadron members, or the union's role in grievances. The Goodyear leader also insisted that the Industrial Assembly would continue to operate just as it had since its inception. Litchfield was willing to scrap all the work his more pragmatic executives had accomplished in negotiations.

Despite the public problems, the negotiators continued talking, and on March 11 Thomas assured the union they would abide by the original agreement despite Litchfield's broadcast. Thomas also insisted there would be no more movement by the company and demanded a ratification vote. The union negotiators scheduled a vote for that Saturday, March 14, and it looked as though the measure might pass. But the night prior to the vote found one of the local union militants speaking out vehemently against the pact. At the meeting, one of the activists proposed to amend the agreement and bring back earlier union demands.

After the strikers adopted the amended report, Litchfield retreated to prior stances. He vowed to reopen the plant and withdrew his offer to reinstate strikers. At this point, former Akron Mayor C. Nelson Sparks came on the scene with the formation of a so-called Law and Order League. Sparks wanted to unite various non-union groups into an anti-union strike majority. Litchfield pitched in fifteen thousand dollars in cash to support Sparks and paid for the group's headquarters at the Mayflower Hotel. In a Sunday evening speech, Sparks claimed to have fifty-two hundred vigilantes, and URW leaders pledged to resist any attack on the picket line. Hundreds of union members came to strike headquarters and thousands more planned to be there Monday morning at the factory gates if Goodyear and the Law and Order League tried to reopen the plant. Mayor Schroy, though, figured that any attempt to open the plant would lead to violence, and he refused to give assistance to the anti-strike forces. Sparks and the league were attacked by Akron newspapers in editorials, and the governor refused to intercede. The *Akron Beacon Journal* wrote in its March 17 editorial about the Law and Order League: "The name is a misnomer. Resort to organization of a citizens' vigilante to open the Goodyear plants is an open invitation to rioting and violence. It is deliberately provocative and inflammatory. It will produce the exact opposite of law and order."

Secretary Perkins called for House and Litchfield to renew renegotiations, and Litchfield, finding that the Law and Order League had failed, finally seemed open to the idea. By that Wednesday, Thomas and Climer agreed to a thirty- to forty-hour week in the non-tire departments and employee referendums before the workweek was increased in both tire and non-tire units. The company's attorney also signed an addendum spelling out more explicit verbal assurances. Goodyear did refuse to abolish the Industrial Assembly, and the union dropped demands for piece-rate adjustments, the end to the assembly, and a signed contract. The second ratification meeting, on Saturday, March 21, was anticlimactic, with only a small last-minute opposition arising. Local 2 members voted almost unanimously to accept the agreement and return to work.

In the end, Local 2 did not gain recognition or a written contract, but it did earn something that at this point was just as important: the respect of the workers. After the strike, the plant laborers unquestionably saw the ineffectiveness of the Goodyear Industrial Assembly as the company union it was, and viewed the URW as its best hope of making gains and having a true say in the business. Hourly employees began signing up for the URW in droves. "After the strike, instead of a weak 500- or 600-member union, we had more than 10,000 members," House said. "The chief thing we won from this strike was our union. We demonstrated that the courage of the people in the plant was complete; that we could do things through organization and working together that would be impossible without the union."

TROUBLE IN GADSDEN

While relations between Goodyear and the URW in Akron calmed a bit for the time being, it was only a matter of a few months before the two sides clashed violently in Gadsden, Alabama. Goodyear never made any secret in 1928 about why Gadsden was chosen to be the home of the company's coveted Dixie plant. "While we are building the plant in Gadsden, it is in a larger sense an addition to the industrial importance of the new South," Goodyear's Clifton Slusser said when the firm made the announcement on December 11, 1928. "We believe that we can make tires here cheaper than anywhere; that is the reason we came and the only reason. It was an economic proposition." Goodyear President Litchfield wanted a production site away from Akron, where the company had experienced much labor turmoil. Litchfield was said to be impressed by residents of the Sand Mountain area north of Gadsden, where hill farmers were not likely to be swayed by the lure of trade unions. Goodyear personnel workers followed the lead of the two other major Gadsden factories, screening all applicants and requiring each to have a sponsor who would "vouch that the individual would be a hard worker, give a full day's labor and not join a union," wrote Charles H. Martin in "Southern Labor Relations in Transition: Gadsden, Ala., 1930–1943."

Goodyear's Gadsden plant did not immediately live up to the great expectations the company had for the facility because of the Depression and a Federal Trade Commission decision that struck down an exclusive contract the tire maker had with Sears, Roebuck & Co. But in April 1936, Goodyear announced a major expansion of the Gadsden factory, likely because of the Rubber Workers strike earlier that year at the Akron tire plant. What made Gadsden attractive to the tire maker was its leaders' sense of insecurity. Gadsden citizens were more worried about plant closings because all three of the town's major employers—Dwight Manufacturing, Gulf States Steel, and Goodyear—were northern companies that had opened up satellite facilities in the South. The three manufacturers used this leverage to win financial and legal favors and to fight organized labor without interference.

Despite these tactics, unionism did come to the Gadsden Goodyear plant—but not without a fight. The AFL chartered FLU 18372 at the factory in August 1933 and nearly half the workforce joined the union within a few months. The FLU made little progress, with the sporadic meetings attended by just thirty to forty members. E. L. Gray, president of the FLU, and F. D. Love attended the founding convention of the URW in September 1935, and the group became URW Local 12. When the AFL officially transferred the local to the URW in October 1935, Local 12 had just sixty-one members.

With that few members, the URW knew it needed to better establish Local 12, and URW President Dalrymple came personally to Gadsden in June 1936 to help out. He had been president of the newly formed union for less than nine months when he was called to aid Local 12. Attendance at Local 12 meetings had dropped to just five or six members. At the beginning of June, Goodyear management fired Gray and fellow union officer B. E. Afferson, saying only that the company had no use for them anymore. Gray tried to talk to plant management, but the company adamantly refused to reinstate him. So Dalrymple and his wife, Grace, came to Gadsden, where the URW president was to address a special meeting of Local 12 the evening of June 6. When the Dalrymples arrived in Gadsden on June 4, he found that Gray had been arrested for passing out the *United Rubber Worker* newspaper. Dalrymple also met with Plant Manager A. C. Michaels and asked him to attend the June 6 meeting, but Michaels declined. He said that Dalrymple was okay personally, but the Goodyear executive wanted nothing to do with a union meeting. As the meeting approached, Goodyear managers told workers in the plant about the recent strike in Akron and how the employees lost money. The day of the rally, a Goodyear Flying Squadron member proposed that they go to the meeting, beat up the URW president, and run him out of town. He said it was arranged with police that nobody would be arrested.

The night of June 6, several hundred union men with their wives and children went to the courthouse auditorium for the meeting, joined by an extensive contingent of squadron members and their allies. When Gray introduced Dalrymple, those in attendance booed and began yelling, "Who the hell sent for you?" Dalrymple tried in vain to explain and quiet the crowd, but they started throwing rocks and eggs at him. At that point, Sheriff Bob Leath and his deputies came in and advised Dalrymple to break up the meeting. The sheriff asked Dalrymple to go out the back with him, supposedly to lead him back to his hotel. The crowd had gathered at the back of the building, where Leath was taking Dalrymple. "Sheriff, you are leading me out here into a mob," Dalrymple said. The sheriff answered, "Never mind, I'll take care of you." As they got outside, the group of Goodyear anti-union workers started beating the union leader. Grace Dalrymple witnessed the beating up close and later gave a detailed explanation of the attack for a one hundred thousand dollar lawsuit against Goodyear, which the URW president ended up not pursuing. "There was a man on each side of him who took his wrists and pulled his hands clear up in the back of his neck, and I could just hear his shoulders give," Grace Dalrymple said. "And then two men got him by the hair and pulled his head back. Then they just held him there and let the men beat him on the head, face and in the eyes. . . . He said he thought he was gone."

Somehow, Dalrymple made it to the front of the hotel and the beating began again. He grabbed the screen door but several men pulled him back so forcefully that he tore off the screen. The sheriff had been walking behind, saying, "Boys, don't do that," but not raising a hand to help Dalrymple, his wife said. The URW leader finally made it to the hotel, and Dalrymple asked the sheriff to get him some medical help. The sheriff told him, "Dalrymple, the whole city is up in arms against you, and I won't be responsible for a thing that happens to you." As Grace Dalrymple tried to get the sheriff to get medical attention, about four or five members from the crowd got in her face and told her: "Now, God damn you, if you want him now, you had better take him out of here." They also warned her "not to let the sun shine on him again in Gadsden." She drove about thirty miles to Collinsville, Alabama, and stopped at a tourist camp there. They got a doctor out of bed, and he looked at Dalrymple. "This man has lost enough blood to kill him, let alone the injuries he has," the doctor said. He begged Dalrymple to let him take him to see another doctor, but Dalrymple refused. "The doctor saw that he was going on, so he put some shots in his nose, eyes and mouth to clot the blood so that he wouldn't bleed so much, and he fixed me some ice bags to put on his head when we stopped," Mrs. Dalrymple said.

She drove about 130 miles before stopping at another tourist camp and putting ice on him. "We had only been in bed a couple of hours when he turned over and laid his arm on me and said, 'Oh mom, please let's go to Akron,'" she said. So she drove 480 miles to her sister's place at Blanchester, Ohio. There he let his wife call URW Secretary/Treasurer Grillo, but he warned Grillo not to tell anyone in Akron about what had happened. They stayed the night at his wife's sister's house, and left there at 5 A.M. to return to Akron. Dalrymple had Grillo bring out some URW members so he could tell them the story personally, and photographers took his picture in his beaten-up state. Then he started back into the house and went to lie on the davenport, but he could not make it and fell across the end of the sofa. He told his wife, "Now, mom, there is nothing to worry about. If I die now, it won't make any difference. I explained everything to the boys, and I know they won't leave a stone unturned." The URW president spent a week in the hospital recovering and had earned the honor of being the highest-ranking labor leader to be so violently attacked in the 1930s.

That was not the end of the violence in Gadsden. On June 8 the anti-union group in the factory attacked three union members and drove them from the plant. The Rubber Workers union turned to the federal government for help. A group of URW leaders went to Washington, where they obtained promises of investigation from Labor Secretary Perkins, Warren Madden, chairman of the National Labor Relations Board, and Senator Robert M. LaFollette Jr. The URW also decided to answer the attacks with a militant campaign to organize the local. They brought Gray and three other Local 12 men to Akron to relate their stories, and the union started a one hundred thousand dollar fund-raising effort to finance a southern organizing campaign. An advance team was sent first, consisting of field representative George Roberts, Chuck Lesley, and William Boyle. A second contingent, led by Local 2's House and W. W. Thompson, followed soon after.

House and Dalrymple were close. Dalrymple had met with House just before the URW president went to Gadsden. They had received reports from various sources concerning the strength of the Gadsden anti-union forces. "When he told me of his intention to go to Gadsden despite the recognized element of danger in having anyone identified with the Akron-Goodyear situation, I strongly urged him to let me go in his stead," House said. But Dalrymple insisted on going himself. Within hours after word of Dalrymple's beating had reached other URW officers in Akron, a group of

Sherman Dalrymple (center) talks with Local 2 President John House (left) and URW Secretary/Treasurer Frank Grillo after Dalrymple was beaten by a mob during an organizational rally in Gadsden, Ala. *(USWA/URW photo files)*

local union officers in the Akron area held a meeting at the Local 5 union hall and determined that they would participate in a planned June 20 open meeting. "When I was asked to be a member of this group, even though I seriously doubted the wisdom of the proposition, I could hardly refuse after having volunteered previously to substitute for Dalrymple," House said.

Roberts and Birmingham, Alabama, labor lawyer Yelveton Cowherd met with Gadsden city commissioners on June 19 to get permits for the meeting. They assured the commissioners of the peaceful intent of the gathering and asked that Gadsden city police be present because the unionists feared that anti-union employees from Goodyear, Gulf States

Steel, and Dwight Manufacturing would attempt to disrupt the meeting. With the presence of the police and highway patrol and numerous out-of-town newspaper reporters, the mass meeting was attended by a crowd of two thousand and took place without incident.

After the meeting, the Akron union contingent took rooms on the tenth floor of the Reich Hotel and the following day rented a suite of offices on the second floor of the Tolson Building on Fifth Street, about a block from the Gadsden police station. They learned that the anti-union workers at Goodyear had beaten up and run out of the plant all Local 12 officers and several other active local members. Word also filtered through that the group planned to run the out-of-town URW contingent out of Gadsden and Etowah County. The attack first was to take place at 3 P.M. on June 24, but the union office was closed that day, with the Akron men holed up in their hotel rooms all day.

They reopened the office the following morning, and Roberts received a phone call from Goodyear employee Grady Cleere, with whom Roberts had become acquainted some years earlier. Cleere, who was supposed to be part of the attacking group, told him the attack on the union group would take place about noon that day. Roberts called the police chief at 11:30 A.M. and told him what he heard. Goodyear supervisors recruited workers in the plant to take part, and about two hundred to three hundred men left the factory. By noon men had started gathering at a pool room directly across from the Tolson Building and on the adjacent sidewalk. As the size of the crowd grew, someone in the crowd began calling for the Akron men to come down to the street. "I attempted to dissuade the mob from proceeding with the attack, talking to them through an open window and explaining the peaceful purpose of our being in Gadsden and that I was a graduate of the Goodyear Flying Squadron," House said. "Instead of mollifying the crowd, my words seemed only to antagonize them further." Roberts kept trying to reach the police chief and, being unsuccessful at that, he called Sheriff Leath to ask for protection. He could not reach either law enforcement official so he phoned the governor, who promised to send in the highway patrol. The union men could see three Gadsden police officers standing on the outskirts of the mob, but they made no effort to interfere. "The union men had previously reached an understanding amongst themselves that, in the event they were attacked, they would not resist or retaliate for the reason that this would give members of the mob grounds to claim self-defense if any of the union men were killed," House said.

The door leading from the hallway to the union suite of offices had been locked, but the upper part of the door was made of colored glass. The union group, trying to delay the inevitable, put their heavy oak table on end against the door, with several of them trying to hold the table against it. When the mob could not open the door, one used the handle of his pistol to break out the glass from the top portion of the door. One union man then made a futile attempt to stop the onslaught by throwing pepper through the opening into the faces of the mob leaders. The attacking group then got a two-by-four scantling and used it as a battering ram to break down the door and enter the reception room. Roberts continued to try unsuccessfully to reach law enforcement agencies. Three of the URW men escaped through a back window, sliding down the sloping roof and jumping into the next-door church yard. Gray and House were left face-to-face with the mob. A person from the second line of the group hit House in the eye, and Gray instinctively drew out his claw hammer from a loop on the right leg of his overalls. Remembering their pledge not to actively fight back, House told Gray to get rid of the hammer, which he did. House soon realized that he would have to try to escape down the stairway. At the landing at the top of the stairs leading to the street, he received a kick in the pants which sent him bouncing down the stairs to the sidewalk.

As he walked through the mob down the street toward the hotel, the anti-union men kept striking House in the head and back. At the corner of the street where his hotel was, he noticed a police officer just standing there with his billy club hanging loose from his hand and with his gun it its holster. "I grabbed him by the arm and demanded that he protect me," House said. "He took me by the arm and said to the men nearest him, 'That's enough boys. I'll take care of him now.'" House and the other union men who had not escaped the mob were brought into the police station where the chief offered first aid, which the men refused. The chief also declined to let them retrieve their cars and belongings from the hotel. Instead he sent some of his police force, accompanied by several members of the mob, to the hotel to get their autos and belongings, and to meet them in Attalia, where the union men were taken in police cars. Except for the Local 12 officers, the union men from up North with no ties to Gadsden took the brunt of the beatings. The anti-union force viewed the "Yankees" as trying to stick their noses in where they were not wanted, and trying to assure that job growth came to the Akron plant rather than Gadsden. By the time the unionists reached Birmingham, Cowherd already had initiated another wave of protests and appeals. Labor Secretary Perkins promised a new investigation. At an Akron rally on June 28, Dalrymple made his first public appearance since his beating and called on the workers to not seek revenge, but instead to concentrate on organizing Gadsden. But rather than fire up the workers in support of Local 12, the violence had helped to destroy what little remained of the local. Even the Alabama governor told URW leaders not to send organizers to Gadsden in the near future. House and two other union men remained in Birmingham for a short while, trying to continue the effort, but they returned to Akron in early July. The URW's grand southern organizing strategy had failed.

ERA OF THE SIT-DOWN STRIKE

Although the URW had no success making management listen in Gadsden, the union found a way to make the companies pay attention elsewhere: by using the sit-down strike. The sit-down strike was popularized by the United Auto Workers as a means of stopping a company dead in its tracks, getting a point across, and—most importantly—wielding a powerful stick when they felt their employers failed to bargain in good faith. In fact, though, it was the United Rubber Workers that first used the leverage of the sit-down strike, where workers literally would stop their machines and sit down at their work stations. This prevented the company from bringing in replacement labor to keep production going and generally brought the assembly line to a screeching halt. The sit-down strike also was usually much quicker at bringing a dispute to resolution.

For the record, the first major sit-down occurred at the General Tire plant in Akron on June 19, 1934. General Tire had cut piece rates, and the tire builders protested. The local demanded a response from the company within twenty-four hours, but heard nothing, even after giving two extra hours. Rex Murray, president of the FLU there at the time, orchestrated the plan and put it into motion. This is how Murray described what happened: "The strike started when I walked through the plant and gave workers the signal to shut it down. . . . And as fast as I could walk from one department to another throughout the plant, that's when it went down. And one of the plant guards was following me from about the time I got to the second department, telling me I couldn't do it. 'You have to stay in your own department.' I said, 'I'll go back to my department in a little while,' and I just kept walking, one floor to the other. When I gave them the signal they pulled the switches and shut it down." The workers just sat by the machines until time to change shifts. Then the next shift of workers came in and sat down right beside their machines. After the two sides met and could come to no agreement, the General Tire local commenced a traditional strike on June 21. The strike was not settled until July 17 when General Tire President William O'Neil brought Murray and other members of the local's Executive Committee to his home for negotiations. O'Neil promised to reinstate the strikers, raise wages, end all support for the company union, meet union representatives on request, and consider seniority in layoffs and recalls. The document, however, made no mention of the union or the AFL and was signed only by O'Neil.

The peak of the sit-down strike movement came in July 1936, not long after the Goodyear strike was settled. URW membership soared, workers found they could get much accomplished because they had some leverage, and union militants found they were immune from discipline. In the six weeks following the March 24 restart of production at Goodyear, there were five sit-downs, four beatings of non-union workers, five murder threats, seven other acts of intimidation, and one bombing. One of the most publicized events of the sit-down movement occurred on May 19 and 20 at Goodyear. Union committeemen in the Plant 2 pit protested when a non-union worker was appointed to head the crew. Tire room workers joined the protest, and a union militant named Jimmy Jones took over the supervisor's desk. He and other strikers had clubs and knifelike tools as they ordered foremen and non-union workers into a "bullpen" area made from stock tables and racks. Jones issued passes when the "prisoners" wanted to go to the bathroom or cafeteria, and one pit worker who had been beaten reportedly was forced to stand for ten minutes before he was allowed to go to the hospital. The strikers kept the supervisors in the bullpen until noon the next day, when management canceled the appointment of the pit workers. After Goodyear attorneys questioned the hostages, the company took the reports to the county prosecutor, who charged thirty-one union men, including Jones and Chuck Lesley. Jones was tried first, and the prosecutor painted him as the leader of the ring. But after several bullpen victims also testified about talking and card games as well as threats and weapons, the jury deadlocked and never convicted any of the union militants. Nor did Goodyear executives attempt to discipline any of them. Litchfield said after already losing five weeks of production to the strike in February and March it was impossible for the company to take any action. "The strike showed the futility of attempting to act . . . while the forces of disorder are in the ascendancy," Litchfield said. "The policy of management, therefore, has been to avoid any further serious interruptions during this period." The pendulum of power clearly now leaned toward labor, with management powerless to act against even the most despicable of acts.

But union officials like Dalrymple found themselves caught in the middle. On one side they knew they would lose the long-term public good will they gained with the Goodyear strike if unions became known for calling a sit-down at the drop of a hat. On the other hand, they did not want to risk alienating the militants, whose support they needed. And the union leaders were not blind. They could see how employees flocked to join the union after a sit-down had given proof of the workers' collective power. Between March and December 1936, when the sit-down movement made national news because of the activity at General Motors Corp., no fewer than sixty-five sit-downs occurred in the Akron rubber plants, although many lasted just a few hours. Besides being a way to get their point of view heard, union militants also used the sit-down as a way to protest against the anti-union workers they were battling for more than just mere bragging rights within the plant. On June 2, several men in a car followed Lesley and two other unionists as they went to work. After a chase, the men fired a tear-gas shell into the vehicle carrying the union men, temporarily blinding the driver. About the same time, Boyle, another sit-down leader in the Goodyear plant, was abducted by several armed men and taken out to an Akron suburb, robbed, and thrown from the car. On June 10 several hundred of the Goodyear anti-union group formed a group called the Stahl-Mate Club as a potential successor to the company union that could be a threat to Local 2. The Stahl-Mate Club's main purpose, in fact, was to prevent the URW and Local 2 leaders from consolidating their gains and taking control of the plant.

The antagonism between the union and anti-union forces at the Goodyear plant in Akron came to a head July 13, when fourth-shift workers in several departments sat down for five hours to protest the presence of non-union men they claimed were starting trouble. Day-shift workers followed that with several brief sit-downs, and the fourth-shift mill room workers sat again July 14, when the sit-down spread to the pit and tire rooms, paralyzing the entire plant. Then Lesley and about fifty other union militants went throughout the plant ordering non-union employees out of the plant. They expelled seventy-five Plant 2 workers, and when Mayor Schroy learned of the incident he ordered the police to prevent any more expulsions and proclaimed the city to be done with sit-downs. Local 2 leaders, seeing how out of hand things had gotten, pledged to stop the sit-downs. More than three thousand Local 2 members adopted a resolution at a July 19 membership meeting promising action against any who violated the union constitution.

As with many other things in life, more of a good thing was not necessarily better. Akron was second only to New York City in the number of strikes during 1936. "We had plenty of sit-downs at General from 1934 to 1936," Murray said. "We didn't have arbitration, and this was how we had to settle our grievances." During 1936 and 1937 more than forty-two thousand workers in the rubber industry participated in sit-down strikes. The most common reason was the refusal of a company to grant union recognition. Rubber factories where unions were recognized and collective bargaining was in place had relatively few sit-downs. URW International officers even cautioned against the sit-down because they wanted members to use the existing methods for negotiating grievances. They also felt that overdoing sit-downs—especially in the case of settling minor grievances—impaired the chance to practice responsible unionism and thereby keep public support on the side of the workers. "Illegal stoppage of work is in strict violation of the constitution of your union," Dalrymple told delegates at the URW's 1936 convention. "We can no longer permit a condition of this kind to continue, and take this opportunity to advise all our members that they are required to take up their grievances in accordance to these laws and contracts. Only by respect and adherence to these laws and contractual obligations can we expect our union to grow in membership, influence and public esteem."

A GOOD MONTH FOR LABOR

In all of history, labor probably never had a better month than April 1937. More than ten thousand members of URW Local 7 had been on strike since March 3 against Firestone in Akron, demanding the company grant the union sole bargaining rights and abolish the company union. The URW also had been pushing to try to get NLRB votes at some of the other large tire plants, but the companies resisted. As it had with the NIRA, corporate America fought long and hard to try to have the Wagner Act declared unconstitutional. The moguls still thought organized labor had no business in their plants. And until the Supreme Court ruled one way or another, the rubber companies varied in how they dealt with the law, Dalrymple testified before the U.S. House of Representatives. "Some employers, believing that the act should be obeyed until it had been over-ruled by the courts, dealt fairly and justly with their employees," he testi-fied. "Some, opposed to the act and refusing to be bound by it, neverthe-less bargained with their employees in such a way as to avoid disputes. Still others, adhering to the old policies of industrial feudalism, bitterly fought the organization of their employees and collective bargaining with every weapon—legal and otherwise—at their command."

But then, on April 12, 1937, the Supreme Court ruled that the Wagner Act was indeed constitutional, that the large companies had to abide by its provisions, and that workers were indeed able to choose the bargaining agent of their choice. Chief Justice Evans Hughes wrote: "Employees have as clear a right to organize and select their representatives for lawful pur-poses as the respondent has to organize its business and select its own officers and agents. Discrimination and coercion to prevent the free exer-cise of the right of employees to self-organization and representation is a proper subject for condemnation by competent legislative authority." Those were the words labor had longed to hear.

On April 28 the URW and Firestone signed a labor contract, the first one between the union and any of the Big Four tire and rubber companies. Also on that date, B. F. Goodrich, Goodyear, and U.S. Rubber disbanded their company unions because the Supreme Court also ruled that these unions—which were favored and financially supported by companies— were not lawful under the Wagner Act. The contract at Firestone said that Local 7 would represent union workers and others "who desire their services." As Chrysler Corp. had done in an agreement reached several weeks earlier, Firestone agreed to suspend support for the company union. The URW in turn promised not to intimidate non-union workers or tolerate sit-down strikes. The pact also kept the six-hour day and thirty-six-hour week, overtime pay, existing piece rates, vacation and insurance coverage, and a seniority system. Though some workers were unhappy that the agreement did not explicitly provide for exclusive representation, the union leaders argued that in practice the URW would have that exclusivity. More than forty-five hundred voted for the contract with just about two hundred opposing it. The plant was back in operation on May 2.

Following the contract, local URW leaders turned their attention to Goodrich and Goodyear. By late May negotiators had come close to reaching agreements on wages and layoff procedure. But to resolve the issue of union recognition, the URW turned to the NLRB, which ordered employee elections in August. Although a new anti-union group—the Goodyear Employees Association, made up mainly of former company union members—appeared at Goodyear, Local 2 won that balloting by a vote of 8,464 to 3,193, with 89 percent of eligible workers voting. At Goodrich, Local 5 won handily, 8,212 to 834, with 75 percent of eligible employees casting ballots. Outside of Akron the URW made gains at key U.S. Rubber plants, especially in Detroit; Eau Claire, Wisconsin; Los Angeles; Indianapolis; and Mishawaka, Indiana. The URW faced an uphill battle but began to take hold at the Goodyear, Firestone, and Goodrich plants in California as well. The URW was beginning to flex its muscles as it looked to establish the union as a formidable force in the rubber industry.

BUILDING UP THE UNION

Building the United Rubber Workers into a formidable organization was not an easy task, but the numbers grew rapidly from a very humble beginning. President Dalrymple and Vice President Burns did much of the first organizing work themselves. Burns concentrated on his native New England and the Philadelphia and New Jersey areas. Salvatore Camelio also was hired, first on a part-time basis, to help organize in New England. He was paid ten dollars a week plus expenses and became full time in April 1936. George Roberts of the Goodrich local in Akron had been an AFL organizer for several years, and the AFL agreed to the URW's request to have him work full time with the Rubber Workers.

But growth did not come without a price. The early organizers had to be a tough, resilient breed. Tom Jenkins, retired from Local 2 in Akron, remembers his father being on a local organizing committee in Akron in 1935 and coming home beaten up. Jenkins's father even had both of his legs broken. "I really don't think he knew by who," said Jenkins, who did quite a bit of organizing himself during his URW career. "I'd see him come home kicked up and battered. That was part of organizing back in those days."

George Bass was sent to Memphis, Tennessee, in 1940 to organize the Firestone tire plant. On August 23 a Firestone supervisor and about twenty other men came to his room and threatened him with knives and clubs. Later about twenty men surrounded Bass and two other people in his car, overturned the car, broke the windows, jabbed at them through the windows with weapons, and tried to set the car on fire. Bass escaped by kicking the door open. When police arrived and an attorney who was with Bass in the car called the attackers a "bunch of SOBs," the police arrested the lawyer for profanity and put him in jail overnight. Three days later Bass—having requested police protection—distributed flyers at the plant, and he and another union man were beaten. And when Lesley was touring an open house of a new Goodyear factory in Jackson, Michigan, a number of Akron men recognized him. When he emerged with two officers from Local 101 in Detroit, several workers, including a Goodyear policeman, attacked the group and beat Lesley on the head and face. The local newspaper did not cover the assault, and Jackson city officials took no action because they were happy to have the new factory.

The workers had to beware as well, as not all the organizers were who they professed to be. George Freiberger recalled a story of how he and other workers at Inland Manufacturing Co. in Dayton, Ohio, got fleeced when trying to organize the plant—supposedly with the help of a United Auto Workers organizer. Freiberger went to work in the plant's running board department on March 12, 1934, at the age of sixteen. He was a high school sophomore at the time, but his father told him, as the oldest of six children, he had to go to work. So he went to the Inland factory. They were not supposed to hire kids that age, but Freiberger was a big strapping boy who played on an area semiprofessional football team called the Northridge Merchants. "We had big white 'N's' on our shirts," Freiberger said. "I went out there and they weren't doing any hiring at all, but when I went in and he saw that letter, he put me in the other room and they hired me."

Freiberger worked there for about three years before he and others started organizing activity. Freiberger was familiar with unionism as his father and uncle both were strong union members at the nearby Delco products plant in Dayton. Freiberger, Harold Beck—who would become the local's first president—and several other hourly employees were working with an organizer from the UAW. Or so they thought. Freiberger and the others worked throughout the plant, getting union cards signed and collecting dues for the first three months. But on the day of the first large group meeting, the organizer failed to show. "All at once we didn't have anybody there to lead us," Freiberger said. "We thought the best thing to do was to call Walter Reuther at the Solidarity House in Toledo, Ohio. Beck was on one line and I was on the other and we told him what was happening. We said, 'Your man is not here today to lead us in this meeting and we've been signing cards now for three months.' He said, 'Wait a minute, what's this man's name?' We told him his name so he got his files out and said, 'We don't even have an organizer by that name.' So I thought, 'Uh oh, somebody's run the gauntlet on us.' He had the money and our cards. It was our fault in a way, but we were green." Basically the man had just shown up and said he was an organizer, and the workers, who happened to be trying to organize—as were factory employees at most plants in the Midwest—took him at his word.

Reuther offered to make up the lost dues to the workers and send in an organizer with credentials. He also advised Freiberger and Beck to do all organizing work outside the plant—not to do anything in the plant. The two told Reuther they would get back to him when they were ready. They kept signing up workers but were having problems because of what had happened with the fake organizer. So they got in touch with nearby Dayton Rubber, which already had organized a URW local. Freiberger and Beck saw that much of the work at Inland—including running boards and steering wheels—were rubber products, so they decided to try to join the Rubber Workers union. They started by talking to URW President Dalrymple and told him what had happened and how the workers were scared to join up. Dalrymple said he would send down H. R. "Whitey" Lloyd. "He'll have his picture on, and he'll have United Rubber Worker credentials," Dalrymple told them. "When you find out who he is when he comes in, then you call me and let me know that you talked to him."

One of the events that helped push the organizing drive, according to

Freiberger, was the company's handling of bonuses. One week in the running board department the workers would make a 10 percent bonus, then another week they would get 7 percent even though they had produced seven hundred more boards than the other week. This angered Freiberger, who went to the general manager's office and questioned the bonus amount. "He said, 'Stop right there.' I said, 'What's the matter?' He said, 'George, there's the door. You can quit right now. Leave if you don't like the way we're handling things. There are guys standing right outside that door to get your job.' And at that time, it was a Depression. There were guys out there every day trying to get your job." Freiberger met with Beck and other workers that night. They went over to the union hall—actually a shack behind the Silver Tavern—and told Lloyd what was going on. "Lloyd said, 'Just keep signing up your cards, but keep your nose clean and keep your jobs. He ain't going to fire you. Don't worry about firing because we've got the [National Labor Relations] Board back of us.'" Lloyd convinced Freiberger and the others that he knew what he was doing. Sometime not long after that all the cards were signed, the union won the representation election hands down, and the workers at Inland became Local 87 of the URW.

And as the URW showed its mettle with the workers, the membership rolls started to grow, and Akron became one of the centers of organized labor in the United States. By late 1936 the URW had twenty-five thousand members in Summit County (which includes Akron) and about thirty-five thousand by late 1937. By the 1937 convention—the union's second anniversary—the URW counted 134 locals in good standing with total membership of seventy-five thousand. Of those, eighty locals worked under signed agreements covering hours, wages, working conditions, seniority, and some paid vacations.

By mid-1937, however, the Rubber Workers had organized most of the easy targets and needed to work on trying to organize the 60 percent of the rubber workers in the United States and Canada who remained outside the URW. The union's International officers asked the 1937 convention to increase the share of monthly dues that went to the International from 37 to 42 percent. As normally would happen over its history when the URW asked for more money or a higher share of revenue, the delegates balked. A number of strong locals in Akron did not want to put in jeopardy their organizations and related programs. More enlightened delegates saw how the Akron companies had threatened decentralization as a means to keep the Akron workers in line, so these delegates knew that to be successful the Rubber Workers would have to succeed outside of Akron to continue as a viable labor organization. After lengthy and vocal debate, 60 percent of the delegates favored the higher per capita tax—a majority, but less than the two-thirds vote required to amend the union's constitution. The leader of the opposition, after a quick caucus, broke the deadlock by agreeing to allow 40 percent of dues to go to the International.

A recession hit in the following months, and by the end of 1937 about 20 percent of URW members were unemployed, with that percentage climbing to 25 percent by February 1938. The URW had employed as many as sixteen organizers in early 1938, but that dropped to just ten by the end of the year. Dalrymple asked for another dues increase in 1939 as the union still could not mount a substantial wide-sweeping organizing campaign. The URW president was adamant that he wanted a permanent increase because he was tired of having to ask for donations from progressive members to fund the organizing effort while others refused to contribute anything. The opposition asked for a one-time assessment of one dollar per member to finance an organizing campaign. After two votes on permanent increases failed, the Executive Board asked for an assessment—or donations—to fund the organizing effort. That action netted just twenty thousand dollars, half from six U.S. Rubber locals and just thirty-five hundred dollars from the Akron locals, including a paltry six dollars from Local 2. The non-Akron locals also took this chance to fill a majority of the eight positions on the newly expanded Executive Board, showing that the rubber companies' decentralization plans and the economic recession had a direct impact on URW politics.

GOODYEAR, A TOUGH NUT TO CRACK

Despite success at many of the other major tire makers, the URW had trouble getting the union to take hold at Goodyear—mainly because of the continued resistance from the company. The union won NLRB elections at Goodyear plants in Akron and elsewhere, but it was clear the company just plain did not want the union in its shops. Litchfield would try to keep Goodyear within the letter of the law, but he clearly favored the company union he had helped craft nearly two decades earlier. This steadfast stand was bound to lead to more conflict with the Rubber Workers.

In 1938, violence broke out in Akron. A dispute that started in April centered around company plans to transfer employees to a new line of tires. While agreeing to consider seniority in making assignments, the firm selected men who were former supervisors, squadron members, company union officers, or former union members. The union claimed favoritism and met a number of times with Personnel Director Climer. At that time, Local 2 was in turmoil due to an outside group organized by former assembly members as the Goodyear Employees Association and also due to an activist group of committeemen led by C. V. Wheeler. Local 2 President House was leaving town May 25 for Cumberland, Maryland, where he and other Goodyear union leaders were to discuss the possibility of pushing for a national contract with Goodyear. House knew the situation at Local 2 was critical, but he urged his officers to do all in their power to keep the workers from going on strike. However, the will of the militant faction within the local that was angered by Goodyear's favoritism to the company union loyalists finally won out, and the workers walked off the job. While the 1936 walkout had been peaceful, this strike in 1938 erupted quickly into what would become the bloodiest battle in Akron labor history. "I learned later that almost immediately after I had left for Cumberland, the radical element began agitating for a showdown and that the effect of such agitation was heightened by management's removal of office equipment and personnel from the factory to be relocated at a downtown address," House said. "Responsible officers of Local 2 lost control of the situation and a chain picket line was marching up and down the broad sidewalk in front of the main entrance on Plant 1 on East Market Street just east of the Goodyear Avenue intersection when they were attacked by Goodyear plant protection police with clubs and tear gas, which the company had previously stored within the plant in anticipation of just such an event."

The picketing actually started peacefully enough. When police arrived in force about 9:00 P.M. there were only thirty-five or forty union members at Goodyear, while fifteen trucks, loaded with tires, waited inside the gate. But when police opened the gate about 10:00 P.M., picketers pelted the trucks with rocks. By 11:00 P.M. more than one thousand pickets and onlookers had gathered in front of Plant 1. At 11:30, plant guards out of sight of the crowd put on gas masks and readied guns and gas cartridges, while about one hundred union men formed a chain picket line and marched in a circle aiming to close the plant. The officer in charge then ordered his men to clear the area around the gate, and the police drew their night sticks and started to push back the crowd.

A narrative in the May 26 issue of the *Akron Beacon Journal* described the situation this way:

After two hours of increasing tension it suddenly broke, and in the twinkling of an eye grimfaced policemen were pouring a relentless rain of tear gas shells in to the milling mob they had been laughing and joking with a few short hours earlier. Through a cloud of tear gas we could see an officer suddenly go down to be mercilessly kicked and beaten by the crowd until rescued by brother officers. Squinting through steaming eyes we could see shell after shell burst into the faces of thousands of screaming and cursing men and women as the crowd, impeded by its own density, fought, clawed and stumbled in a mad dash to safety. . . . Leading the drive was the gas squad, ominous in their grotesque masks, firing a steady stream of tear gas shells from rapid-fire gas guns. Behind them came the 'mopping-up' squads clubbing and blackjacking the laggards, occasionally receiving a few blows in return from the more venturesome strikers.

The Local 2 office became the center of the conflict as up to one hundred workers hurling rocks and iron bolts kept officers at bay for nearly two hours. The police fired continuous volleys of tear gas through the first-floor windows. Eventually the union's attorney convinced police to allow him to escort the last dozen union men out of the damaged hall, and by early morning the violence subsided. Goodyear officials said they would keep the plant open and—with the police and National Guard on hand for the 6 A.M. shift change—there was no further violence.

When House arrived back in Akron he was met by a group of Local 2 members who still smelled of tear gas. "At least two gas bombs had come through the window of my office facing East Market Street and tore holes through a one-inch beaverboard on the opposite side of the room just above my desk," he said. Several union members were injured from being clubbed and hit by long-range tear gas shells; one bystander was hit by a police bullet; and two policemen were hit by shotgun pellets.

House and other Local 2 leaders knew another confrontation would be dangerous, and at a membership meeting May 30 an overwhelming majority voted to return to work and have the union try another time to negotiate a full contract. Talks with management began June 20; not so coincidentally as negotiations began, the company announced plans to lay off seventeen hundred workers to raise the workweek to twenty-four hours. Bargaining continued until December—with numerous company-inspired delays—when Climer said the company was unwilling to enter into a contract because it was starting a modernization program and did not want to tie its hands by signing a written agreement with the union. Harold Roberts in his 1944 book described the talks as the "process of negotiations of an employer who almost negotiated a union to death."

By 1940 the URW's main problem was trying to end the decline the union had been facing in the Goodyear plants. In May 1940 the CIO sent organizer Robert J. Davidson, who had directed union campaigns in the auto and glass industries, to try to reverse the downward trend at Local 2 in Akron. He completely changed strategies, scrapping the failed NLRB case and making no effort to negotiate a contract. Instead he focused on a reorganization campaign to bring members back into the fold. By appointing committees that represented both the militant factions and the more mainstream unionists, Davidson had plenty of volunteers to help smooth the effort, and by August about thirty to fifty workers daily were reinstating memberships.

Dalrymple was buoyed by the success and hoped to make a case for an expanded campaign financed by a dues increase. The International asked the locals not to instruct delegates to the convention, hoping to make a compelling case for raising the dues. Once again, delegates rejected an increase, but did vote to raise the International's share of dues revenues from 40 to 45 percent. Delegates also targeted Goodyear as the union's biggest problem, and the URW and CIO began a joint Goodyear campaign under Davidson. House, defeated as Local 2 president in November 1940, was hired as an extra CIO organizer for the initiative. Most of the campaigns succeeded. The first big breakthrough surprisingly came in overlooked Bowmanville, Ontario, where the Canadian workers were not happy with their wages, and by the end of 1940 had 90 percent of the plant's workers signed up. The Bowmanville local signed the first major Goodyear contract in February 1941.

The Goodyear campaign was quite successful with the exception of Gadsden, Alabama, and Windsor, Ontario. Davidson called a meeting of Goodyear local representatives in May 1941 to formulate contract demands to the company. The URW wanted a national contract with Goodyear similar to those won by the UAW and Steelworkers Organizing Committee with General Motors and U.S. Steel. The non-Akron plants especially wanted a national agreement because the Akron workers were paid more.

URW organizers pass out leaflets at the Goodyear gates in Akron as part of an organizational drive to get Goodyear workers to join the union. *(USWA/URW photo files)*

Gaining that equal standing also was important to the URW International because if the non-Akron facilities were not in line with the union, the rubber companies would continue decentralizing by moving work out of Akron. Conversely, if the URW could not improve the plight of these outlying workers, those newly joined members would have no reason to stick with the union.

The conference of Goodyear locals authorized Davidson and Dalrymple to open negotiations with Goodyear on a national agreement. Litchfield first wanted to dismiss the idea, but E. J. Thomas, by now Goodyear president, urged Litchfield to let him handle labor relations. Thomas said he would consider all options and not just agree to a contract. The

Goodyear executives told the URW leaders they would not go for joint negotiations but would start negotiations in all plants where the URW had won an NLRB election. Davidson and Dalrymple accepted, and Davidson instructed organizers in Akron, Los Angeles, Cumberland, Maryland, and Jackson, Michigan, to negotiate an immediate written wage increase as the first step toward a full contract.

Local 2 accepted a 7 to 8 percent increase on June 15. Negotiations resumed on the remainder of the contract on July 11 and continued through the summer. Points of contention included restoration of seniority for workers laid off in 1937, a union security clause, restrictions on the Flying Squadron, and a method of calculating overtime favorable to the workers. Local 2 members twice voted down contracts without these items. A compromise found the union abandoning some demands for concessions on overtime. Negotiators signed the agreement September 28, but the locals had agreed to take no ratification votes until bargaining at all locals was complete. The Cumberland and Los Angeles locals approved contracts in early October. So it was on October 28, 1941, that Goodyear became the last of the major tire and rubber companies to sign written contracts with the URW covering plants in the United States, finalizing the pacts with Local 2 in Akron, Local 131 in Los Angeles, and Local 26 in Cumberland. In addition, the Jackson local won an NLRB election September 11 and began contract talks in October.

While Goodyear President Thomas and Personnel Director Climer had become resigned to the fact that the company had to live with the union, Litchfield himself had trouble coming to terms with it. "When the time came to sign, Litchfield told Thomas and Climer he could not put his signature to the contract," Maurice O'Reilly wrote in a 1983 company history. "Although he recognized that the Industrial Assembly—one of his proudest achievements—could never return, he felt a great sense of loss and a certain disappointment in his factory boys, as he called them, whose team he had led for so long." Thomas signed the contract in Litchfield's place, as the URW's number one enemy during its early years could not bring himself to admit defeat—or to acknowledge the union's presence by putting his own signature to a contract.

CHAPTER 2

THE PROSPERITY OF WAR
THE URW MOVES FORWARD

As the United States became entangled in World War II, the companies and unions became involved as well. For most of the firms, it meant being retooled to make other goods for the war effort. During the eighteen months prior to the bombing of Pearl Harbor, all of the large rubber firms and many of the smaller shops became government contractors. By mid-1941, war production accounted for at least 25 percent of most of these firms' business. The plants made everything from gas masks and life rafts to linings for airplane fuel tanks and barrage balloons, as well as nonrubber products. Goodyear changed its old blimp plant in Akron into an aircraft factory while Firestone manufactured anti-aircraft guns and clips for machine gun bullets. Much of the rubber production shifted from tires to mechanical goods because the rubber shortage forced the government to discourage tire production for civilian use in 1940 and discontinue it entirely in 1941.

The URW also took advantage of the opportunity to add members and get the companies to agree to signed contracts and official recognition. Companies that had fought the URW at every turn found themselves forced to sign union contracts or risk losing lucrative government contracts. Traditional anti-union tactics that companies had employed for decades were frowned on by Franklin Delano Roosevelt's government. The war boom also helped the labor movement as a whole, with total union membership in the United States rising by more than one million members in 1940–41—an increase exceeded only during the sit-down periods of the 1930s. Between June 20, 1940, and June 30, 1941, the URW's membership grew from 55,000 to 75,000 members—or about half of the hourly rubber industry workers. By December 1941, the union boasted 93,000 members, or 63 percent of all rubber workers. Organizing victories were gained at many of the remaining Big Three plants. And by July 1944 the URW claimed total membership of more than 182,000. Women—stereotyped by the "Rosie the Riveter" character—were a big part of the increased industrial workforce, coming to factories in the rubber and other industries in record numbers to help out with the war production effort.

But not every aspect of labor relations turned into flag-waving patriotism. Shortly after the nation's formal declaration of war on December 8, 1941, business and labor leaders pledged to cease hostilities and avoid strikes for the duration of the war. In January 1942, President Roosevelt created the twelve-member War Labor Board, comprised equally of public, management, and labor representatives. The board was authorized to settle all labor disputes by using compulsory mediation and arbitration. The War Labor Board then attempted to stabilize wages by developing what became known as the "Little Steel formula," which arbitrarily limited raises for all workers to levels that supposedly existed in January 1941, with provisions for future cost-of-living increases. Labor argued that the guidelines were restrictive and unequal, saying that wage rates differed between industries and companies and that cost-of-living impact depended on a wide variety of factors. The War Labor Board tried to appease organized labor by allowing "maintenance of membership" clauses in contracts, which meant that workers who did not resign from the union within a fifteen-day escape window had to pay dues for the length of the contract. Thus unions were protected from large losses of members in what amounted to a practically closed shop, but in turn they granted a wage freeze, a no-strike pledge, and compulsory arbitration before the War Labor Board to settle grievances.

Rank-and-file members in many industries became disenchanted with the arrangement as the war moved forward: profits for businesses reached record highs, while consumer goods became scarcer and cost more; workers' wages were frozen, and mandatory overtime hurt them both physically and psychologically. Workers used different ways to express their unhappiness. Absenteeism rose precipitously, and the formal grievance procedures became jammed with thousands of complaints. At other times, more mutinous workers staged slowdowns or just disregarded the orders of superiors.

And despite the no-strike pledge by labor, wildcat—or unauthorized—strikes became commonplace in many industries, especially CIO unions.

The URW did not fit into this pattern, but was not exempt from the turmoil. URW Vice President Burns had taken a leave of absence from the union during the war to take a government job with the Office of Production Management. But as Burns remained on the union's International Executive Board, he submitted a resolution in April 1941 to support the defense effort and President Roosevelt's no-strike policy. He also sponsored a measure stating the URW International would not sanction any strike until an organizer and the Conciliation Center had failed in attempts to resolve the dispute. Despite the pledge, a number of URW locals staged work stoppages and wildcat strikes to protest the guaranteed profits companies received on government contracts while workers faced the wage freezes. Dalrymple spoke out at the union's 1943 convention against the unauthorized strikes, saying they "injure the morale of the membership, they tear down organizing efforts, they inflame the public mind against labor and they tend to break down the whole machine of vital war production."

Dalrymple particularly was at odds with Local 9 at the General Tire plant in Akron. Between August 1943 and January 1944, Local 9 staged twenty-four wildcat strikes. So when seventy-two workers in the band-building department again struck on January 5 and 6, 1944, Dalrymple expelled sixty-nine of the strikers for participating in the illegal work stoppage. After Local 9 members and officers protested vehemently, the URW on January 16 placed the local in receivership, and the union appointed a field representative as administrator of the local. After an eleven-day hearing in February and March, the URW Executive Board recommended the union try to get sixty-two of the strikers their jobs back. The Akron Industrial Union Council backed Local 9, and other Akron locals resented Dalrymple for taking such action. Local 5, Dalrymple's home local, even expelled him for his actions. It was not surprising that many locals were angered by Dalrymple's actions. As the union would show throughout its history, the URW rank and file preferred a decentralized governance, with most of the power residing in local unions. The URW president's involvement in a particular local was not something the union's members wanted to see from their top officers. These sorts of disputes, in fact, led to factionalism in the URW, which planted the seed of opposition against Dalrymple and eventually brought about the resignation of the URW's first president in September 1945, almost a decade from the date of the union's founding.

GADSDEN: MORE VIOLENCE FOLLOWED
BY VICTORY AT LAST

The URW particularly benefited from the tough stance of the U.S. government against awarding contracts for war goods to anti-union companies, like Goodyear at its plant in Gadsden, Alabama, the city where Dalrymple was savagely beaten. Unfortunately, it would still take a couple of years and one more vicious attack before Goodyear finally succumbed to pressure from the government and allowed the Rubber Workers to claim the coveted organizational victory.

House—the former Local 2 president who was among those attacked in 1936—returned to Gadsden in early January 1941. Alan S. Haywood, CIO director of organization, had appointed House as an organizer assigned to the joint URW/CIO campaign headed by Bob Davidson to organize Goodyear facilities. House was sent to work with Local 12 President C. S. Holmes to try to reorganize the URW local at the plant. Neither man had a car but they borrowed one from a farmer who previously had been president of Local 12 and was one of the group of members driven from the plant by the anti-union contingent in 1936. None of the Local 12 members at that time was still employed by Goodyear, but they maintained their membership. House and Holmes held a meeting January 10 attended by fifteen members, and the group realized their efforts would lead nowhere unless the NLRB did something to enforce its March 9, 1940, decision in which the company was found guilty of unfair labor practices and ordered to offer reinstatement and back pay to workers dismissed from May 1936 to August 3, 1937.

In his first report to Davidson on January 14, House had made it clear that any organizing campaign in Gadsden would be a difficult proposition. "I know you have a lot of experience and varied, but I doubt that you have ever seen a group of native-born Americans so beaten, so completely enslaved as most of these seem to be," House wrote. "I think this plant can be organized but it will take a long time and a lot of hard, painstaking endeavor to do it unless we can get some help from the board or the courts. I am not afraid of any violence here now."

At the time of this organizing drive, the Steelworkers had successfully signed up a good number of Gulf States Steel workers and arranged to hold an open meeting in a downtown Gadsden hall. When police learned that both white and black workers were at the same meeting, they raided the meeting, took all members present to the police station, and published their names in the *Gadsden Times* newspaper the next day to try to intimidate them and erode support for the union. But when none of the workers had been discharged after several weeks, as discharge would have been an obviously unfair labor practice, the news gave new life to the organizing campaigns at both Gulf States and Goodyear.

Holmes and House had signed up a considerable number of Goodyear employees, so they decided to try to hold a group meeting on January 29 at 7 P.M. Shortly after noon that day, Holmes said he had to meet a Goodyear worker who had expressed interest in joining the union. Holmes was to pick House up at the hotel just before the meeting but never showed up. So House walked to the meeting hall and, when he arrived, he saw first a group of thirty black men who, he later learned, were there to meet a CIO representative for the Construction Workers union. On the other side of the room were fifty white men, about four or five of whom he recognized as being members of the mob that had beaten the union contingent from Akron and run them out of town in June 1936. House did not know what to expect, but knew he could not show fear. So he sat down on a table facing the group and started to tell them what he was doing in Gadsden and what he hoped to accomplish. "Before I had completed more than two or three sentences I was interrupted by the obvious leader of the group who was one of those I had recognized as a member of the 1936 mob," House said. "He said they were not there to harm me but only to show me that I was not welcome in Gadsden; that they already had a union with which they were completely satisfied and did not welcome any outside interference. Having said his peace [*sic*] he walked out of the room followed by the entire group." House then took a taxi out to Holmes's residence and found him unconscious, apparently having been drugged by someone. From then on, the two vowed to stick together.

Unfortunately for House, the duo failed to keep that promise. On February 17, Holmes left their office for a dinner meeting with another Goodyear employee at a nearby restaurant. Within ten minutes a group of five men came in and stood just inside the door at the head of the stairway leading up from the street. One came forward to the table where House was working, placed both hands on the table, and asked if this was where he could sign up for the union. "I finished typing the line I had started when he approached and then looked up to him and started to answer him when I received a hard blow on the left side of my head which caused me by reflex action to stand up," House said. "I had failed to notice that the other members of the group had sneaked up behind me. They continued beating me with their weapons." The group apparently felt they had delivered their message and started to leave. House got to his feet to try to catch the last man, but then he saw former Local 12 President E. L. Gray enter the door from the street. He yelled to Gray to catch the last man, but Gray was so shaken by the sight of House (who needed eighty-six stitches to suture the deep gashes in his scalp) that he let the man get away. House gave the sheriff a fairly complete description of two of his attackers, but no arrests ever were made in connection with the assault. On February 19, Goodyear's Litchfield sent House a telegram expressing sympathy and wishing him a speedy recovery. "At the time I was feeling such deep resentment toward the company that I missed a golden opportunity by failing to acknowledge his telegram and tell him that I held him chiefly responsible for the attack by permitting his underlings to carry on such a vicious campaign against our union," House said.

When House left the hospital after a sixteen-day stay, he found he was unwelcome at all of the hotels in Gadsden. But he refused to leave town, instead boarding at the home of one of the workers discharged by Goodyear for his union membership and activities. On March 28, House, Holmes, and five other men were distributing handbills at the two Goodyear plant entrances. Those going to work on the second shift starting at 3 P.M. accepted the offerings, but House noticed a group of twenty or thirty men still in work clothes and armed with various tools start toward them in a menacing fashion. House's head was still sore from the previous beating so he headed for the car and called for Holmes and the others to follow. But Holmes waited until the gang physically drove him away. Holmes's brother was hit in the mouth and required hospital attention. When Holmes and a second man, "Slick" Freeman, reached House's car, Freeman faced the mob with his back to the car and a long-bladed knife open in his hand as he dared anyone to come closer. Holmes came around to the driver's side, reached in and took a 32-caliber gun that he carried in a briefcase, and then stood facing the mob gathered in front of the car. "Finally I persuaded Holmes and Freeman to get into the car— intending to run over any of the mob who refused to move out of the way," House said.

House and Holmes reported the affair to the Etowah County prosecutor, and in early May the county grand jury conducted hearings into the February 18 assault on House and the March 28 plant incident. Some members of the company union at the plant tried to get the grand jury to indict Holmes on a gun-carrying charge. They claimed they were at the window of the Goodyear plant cafeteria on the second floor of the building facing the parking area where the car was surrounded by the mob. But the jury foreman knew the area and took the grand jury there for a demonstration. He had them stand where the company union members testified they were when they saw Holmes with a gun. He then had someone stand where Holmes had been, holding a gun in his hand. The jury decided that no one could have seen a small handgun in a man's hand at that distance, so Holmes was not indicted. There also was no indictment handed down in the February 18 assault on House because of insufficient evidence. The workers named in the House and Holmes warrant for the March 29 incident were scheduled to be tried on assault and battery charges the following week, but they gained a continuance and never did stand trial—further evidence that Goodyear's anti-union actions had the full support of the area prosecutor and law enforcement agencies.

In his April 26 report to Davidson, House wrote: "Fear is the only thing that is holding up the program here. A vast majority of the men inside the plant realize they need a union and want to belong to the URW but they have been abused so long and have seen so little evidence that law enforcement agencies, both local and national, are able or willing to give them protection that only the most courageous, including those who had just as soon quit their jobs as not, are willing to take a chance."

In May, all Goodyear URW locals held a conference and developed the plan to pursue a national agreement with the company. By July, the URW and CIO were ready to throw in the towel at Gadsden once again. Davidson told House to leave Gadsden and go to the Goodyear plant in Jackson, Michigan, leaving Holmes to carry on by himself in Gadsden.

Finally, the following year, the Gadsden local—helped by the courts and federal government—began to make real headway. The Fifth Circuit Court of Appeals on July 6, 1942, upheld a 1940 NLRB order regarding Goodyear's Gadsden plant. Under this ruling, the union members fired in 1936 were rehired, the Etowah Rubber Workers Organization (the thinly veiled remnant of the company union at the plant) was disbanded, the Flying Squadron was prohibited from interfering with the employees' right to organize, and the company was ordered to provide its workers protection against violence. That spring, union organizer James W. Jones conducted a whirlwind sign-up drive. Community attitudes were softer then because the government had put Goodyear on a short leash, and many citizens also worried that the town's anti-labor reputation would prevent it from receiving its share of lucrative war contracts. When the NLRB held an election on April 7, 1943, the URW easily won by a count of 1,144 to 327. The first contract was signed August 25, with workers getting a three-cents-per-hour raise, bringing pay to seventy-eight cents an hour.

So after having been virtually driven into oblivion three times by anti-union forces during its decade of organizing efforts, the local at Gadsden finally was ready to take flight. And ironically, Local 12 would be led for most of the next three decades by E. K. Bowers, a man who promised when Goodyear hired him that he would never join the union. Bowers, though, was the stereotypical worker Goodyear searched for in staffing its Gadsden tire factory, and it took years for him to open his eyes to how the company treated the workers there. He was raised on Sand Mountain and worked on a farm until he was twenty-one. Back then, the farmers in the Sand Mountain area did not own tractors or modern equipment; Bowers and the others drove mules and plows. He got married on January 1, 1936, and he did not have a job. "I had a wife and $18, and I didn't have a home," Bowers said. "I didn't care. I had my wife." The newlyweds lived with Bowers's father for the first six months.

On July 1, 1936—just after the month of violence when Dalrymple and the other union organizers had been attacked—Bowers received word that he probably could get a job at Goodyear. His father was none too happy about the idea. "My daddy knew something about unions and I didn't," Bowers said. "I knew nothing. He knew they were having labor trouble down here, and he didn't want me to come down. I came anyway. I didn't have any money. The day before I started he gave my wife two dollars and said, 'Give that to the boy.' So I came down here with two one-dollar bills." Bowers had heard about the job opportunity from a highway patrolman named Ed Miller, who was a friend of his family. He took Bowers there to give him his personal recommendation. "From the front gate walking up to the main office, he said, 'Bowers, I want you to promise me two things.' Now, I'd have promised him the world for a job," Bowers said. "I said, 'What is it Ed?' He said, 'Well, if they want you to work, I want you to be here. I don't give a damn if it's Sunday or midnight. You be here. And the other is, leave the damn union alone.' So I made those two promises to Ed Miller, and he went up and talked to the personnel man and he hired me."

Bowers did not realize it at the time—and it would not have mattered anyway—but he was hired in the tire inspection area to replace one of the union men who had been run off their jobs by the anti-union forces. So Bowers lived up to his promise to Miller for seven years. But when Local 12 was resurrected with the NLRB election in 1943, Bowers became active. "I didn't know what we needed, but we needed help," Bowers said. "We were mistreated something terrible. We weren't allowed to talk to each other. We weren't allowed to show each other our paychecks. If they said jump, you didn't say how far, you just jumped."

Bowers described working conditions at the plant as a total dictatorship on the part of the company. Workers had no dignity whatsoever. Bowers did not help out on any of the organizing drives that occurred in Gadsden between 1936 and 1943, because, he said, "I had just come off the mountain, plowing and muling. And I didn't give a shit what happened. And I didn't know what the union was." His father told him that his mind would change. Bowers once went to a picnic given by the Etowah Rubber Workers Organization, the thinly veiled company union. To attend, the workers had to put the ERWO's streamer pin on. So Bowers put on the ribbon and went to the picnic. "I just wore it because everybody else was wearing it," he said. From there, Bowers went up to the mountain to his father's home, still sporting the ERWO ribbon. The elder Bowers asked what it was, and his son explained. His father told him, "Son, you add five years to your life and you'll be a union man." Bowers was unbelieving. "I thought he was crazy," the younger Bowers said.

Bowers credited Jones for much of the success leading to the 1943 NLRB vote, which Bowers had supported. "He was just as cocky as a game rooster," Bowers said of Jones. "So we all hung around Jimmy and Jimmy led the way. We all loved him. He was a football player and this was after all those other (organizers) had been beat up. He didn't think they could whoop him." Plant Manager Michaels and Personnel Director H. S. Cragmile led the anti-union fight for the company. Bowers said Michaels got his job because he had been an all-American football player at Ohio State

University. "He hated unions with a vengeance, and he did everything he could to get in our way," Bowers said. When it became apparent that the union was making headway, Goodyear sent Michaels back to Akron and brought in a plant manager from California who was more liberal and actually did some things to help the union effort. Michaels was brought back after World War II ended and made it tough on the workers even after Local 12 was established, Bowers said.

While Local 12 signed its first contract in 1943, it failed to get a renewal of the agreement until January 1946. During those three years, the local had a case pending before the War Labor Board, the last case to be heard. In the interim between contracts, the company had signed an agreement that when the War Labor Board made a ruling, that decision plus other items agreed to would be put in the contract. But Cragmile tried to back out of the deal, so Bowers and four other URW men drove to Akron to meet with Fred Climer, then Goodyear vice president in charge of labor relations. Climer asked if they had the agreement in writing, which they did. Climer told them to return to Gadsden and he would be there when they arrived. "He got on a plane and flew to Gadsden and stayed five days," Bowers said. "And we signed an agreement on January 21, 1946. Fred Climer was a decent man but he was working for an indecent company. They had some of the worst labor policies you'd ever seen." It was not until after this second contract that Bowers viewed Local 12 as a true union. "Until then we were nothing. We were on paper," he said.

Bowers became Local 12 president in November 1946. He served as president for three years and then was defeated by Virgil Thompson, a one-term president who lost a year later in a rematch with Bowers. This time, Bowers served until he was defeated in 1959, when he again sat out one term before retaking the seat during the next election. His final contest was in 1969, when he was defeated by C. V. Glassco. Since first being elected president, Bowers had won thirteen elections and lost three—ironically all in years ending in nine: 1949, 1959, and 1969.

After losing to Glassco, Bowers retired at the age of fifty-five, able to look back on a strong record of accomplishment for himself and Local 12. "We changed this whole community," he said. "We started from nothing until I was a candidate for mayor when I retired in 1969. . . . You see what had happened. We went from the time where we were afraid to walk down the alley to the time that we were a threat to becoming mayor of the city."

Over that relatively short period of history, Gadsden had gone from being described as the "toughest labor city in the United States" to being a strong union town. "It wasn't in the books," Bowers said. "It just happened."

BUCKMASTER TAKES OVER

It took ten years before the URW had its second leader. Leland S. Buckmaster became vice president of the URW in September 1941 when his predecessor, Thomas Burns, took a full-time position with the government, and served in the union's No. 2 position until taking over for Dalrymple in September 1945 when Dalrymple retired. Many say Buckmaster led the union in much the same honest manner as Dalrymple, believing that the union could gain much more at the bargaining table than through strikes. When he was president of Local 7 at Firestone in Akron, the plant had only two sit-down strikes in the summer and fall of 1936 when sit-downs were so prevalent at other factories. Not that Buckmaster would not take the union out on strike, as proven by the 1937 strike at Firestone while he was local president and by the multi-company strike during 1959 negotiations. But Buckmaster brought quite a different background to the job than his predecessor. Whereas Dalrymple had started factory work in his early teens, Buckmaster was born in Geneva, Indiana, in 1894, attended elementary and high school in Indiana, and majored in education at Tri-State College in Angola, Indiana. He worked as a teacher in the Indiana public schools for four years before joining the Army Air Service during World War I, spending thirteen months on active duty in France.

Upon returning to the United States after his discharge, Buckmaster went to work in 1919 at Firestone in Akron as a tire finisher and builder. "I worked at Firestone as a tire builder for one year," Buckmaster said. "I saw enough injustice to know that without a union we would never get fair treatment. When I was laid off during the 1920 depression I was making $1.25 an hour. When I came back seven months later I got 80 cents an hour for the same job. We didn't get a single raise in the eight or nine years before the big Depression—and then things got worse."

When the AFL established a Federal Labor Union at the plant, Buckmaster became a shop committeeman and later a member of the local's executive board. In November 1935 he was elected president of the newly chartered Local 7 of the United Rubber Workers. He became a URW Inter-

Leland Buckmaster became the second URW president nearly a decade after the union's founding.
(USWA/URW photo files)

national Executive Board member in May 1936 and stayed on the board until he was elected vice president of the union.

Local 12's Bowers was a personal friend of Buckmaster and his wife, and whenever the URW president came to Gadsden he always spent the night at the Bowers residence. Bowers described his friend as rather conservative—an old schoolmarm type—but exceptionally honest. "He believed in doing things by the book," Bowers said. Buckmaster never let a company off the hook because he was sorry for it, Bowers said, but only because Buckmaster always played by the rules. "He never played footsie with a company in his life, but he was honest. He was a man who could gain respect from his opponent. People who disagreed with him respected him."

Glenn Ellison marveled at the way Buckmaster could run a convention. "Buckmaster was very quiet and very controlled, but he was absolutely in control of it," Ellison said. "I can see Buck yet—he was a very tall, slender, dignified person. Of course in those days the three-piece suits were the thing and the URW was a lot bigger and had a lot more local union politicians that could take that convention floor and take the convention away from you if you weren't careful." But control was not a problem for Buckmaster, who had a simple way to deal with long-winded speakers, Ellison said. "We always had a convention rule you could only speak for five minutes. And Buck kept a stopwatch laying on the podium. When a guy started speaking he started that stopwatch. If it was somebody making one of those rabble-rousing speeches, instead of looking like he was flustered or worried, Buck very casually lit up a cigarette and strolled around up there and took a glance at that watch every now and then. And when five minutes was up, he just told him, 'Your time is up,' and he went on to the next one. You didn't get Buck flustered." Ellison also viewed Buckmaster as a master at parliamentary procedures, sometimes wondering if the old schoolteacher out of Indiana had missed his calling and instead should have been teaching parliamentary procedure at a university.

STEPPING UP TO THE BARGAINING TABLE

Besides electing Buckmaster as president at its 1945 convention, the URW—now officially renamed the United Rubber, Cork, Linoleum, and Plastic Workers of America as the union tried to widen its reach—made it clear it was ready to face the rubber industry giants at negotiations. With the war ending, the union had watched for years as large companies made big profits on guaranteed war production contracts while the workers toiled under government-mandated wage freezes. So the union put forth a seven-point wage-and-hour policy to present to the Big Four rubber plants. The goals included: a raise of thirty cents an hour; a basic thirty-hour week; time and a half for hours worked over six a day and thirty a week; time and a half for Saturdays; double time for Sundays and six designated holidays; straight-time pay for the six holidays when not worked; and ten cents an hour bonus for the night shift. Negotiations with the Big Four began February 19, 1946, and an agreement was reached March 2. The first postwar contract brought an 18.5-cent-an-hour raise, with twelve cents of that retroactive to the prior November. By the 1946 convention, 135 local unions outside the Big Four won agreements based on the seven-point policy.

At the 1946 convention, Buckmaster called for intensification of the efforts to bring about company-wide bargaining in the industry. The companies objected, except for U.S. Rubber, which began bargaining on a company-wide basis in December and reached an agreement in January 1947. Subsequent negotiations resulted in a company-wide agreement with Goodyear at the beginning of February 1947, while Firestone locals finally won a company-wide contract in June 1948.

It was the beginning of a pattern bargaining process that companies complained about for decades, but through the start of the twenty-first century had not been successful in replacing. Pattern bargaining obviously had its good and bad points. On the plus side, centralized bargaining allowed the company and union to come to terms on major financial issues in one set of negotiations, rather than having to deal with the same issues over and over at each plant, which in the 1950s and 1960s was a considerable number of facilities. Master contracts, as they became known, also served as a check-and-balance within the industry. With each company agreeing to basically the same set of economic terms, none could use its labor contract to gain an unfair competitive advantage over other firms. Competitive gains would have to come in other areas, such as technology and production efficiency. Having the industry players on a level playing field in the area of wages and benefits was particularly effective when the URW represented virtually all the plants at the major rubber product manufacturers, and before imports began to play a significant role in the domestic market.

As pattern bargaining became entrenched in the rubber industry over the years, give-and-take negotiating nuances began to take hold. And given the decentralized manner in which the URW operated, negotiators from the local unions took much of the responsibility for bargaining, even at the master contract level. That meant the Rubber Workers generally sent negotiators who had risen through the ranks from the plant floor without the benefit of a higher education to face company bargainers who often were college-educated negotiators, backed with all kinds of academic degrees.

But that did not necessarily mean the Rubber Workers were at a disadvantage. What they may have lacked in formal education, they made up for in experience and in knowing the needs of the membership. For example Bowers, the longtime president of Local 12 in Gadsden, came from the mountains of Alabama, but by the time he retired in 1969 he was looked upon as a expert in both negotiating and arbitration. "I did all I could," said Bowers, at first a bit bashful to tout his own attributes. "But let's give the devil his due. I'll admit to you that I was the man who could get the job done. I was born with that union. I grew up with that union. I knew that union like I knew the back of my hand. And nobody else did, so why shouldn't I do the better job?"

At the master contract level, the process started well before the company and union actually got to the bargaining table. "Every local has got their needs and their wants," said J. W. Battles, himself a former Local 12 president. Each local had a policy committee that set forth its goals. Then the URW held an overall bargaining policy committee to prioritize goals prior to the start of master contract negotiations. "Of course the company has their lists too," Battles said. "You go over each individual item until you reach the end. Some things you get, some you don't get and some fall through the cracks." Of course, it was often impossible for the union negotiators to please all their locals' members. "We knew what our people wanted, and a lot of times their wants weren't really what their needs were," he said. "You had to sift through that and come up with their needs instead of their wants. If their needs were different than their wants, that's when you got in trouble when you came back home with the contract."

During the actual bargaining, a certain protocol evolved, said Battles. The union and the company each had a main, three-man committee that did most of the talking. For the union, the representatives from the bigger locals sat on each side, while some of the policy committee members sat at a second table. "Each of the people at the company's back table is assigned to watch a union person on the other side of the table on any question or proposal to get the reaction of the individuals," Battles said. "And I'm sure at night they go over that. They evaluate those things daily. The union people got these poor old country boys trying to negotiate with those lawyers."

One thing that was vital was to have all your facts in line and the members of your local behind you, according to Gilbert Laws, from Local 286 at the Goodyear hose and belt plant in Lincoln, Nebraska. "When you make a proposal you have to know what you're going after and why the people need it, and if it's in fact what they really wanted. The people back you up a lot harder if they're directly involved." It never hurt matters when the company did something to upset the workers. During one round of negotiations, when the URW was trying to add dental coverage, Goodyear negotiators brought in toothbrushes for the union's negotiating committee and said, "Here's your dental plan." It likely was meant as a joke, but it also served to anger some of the union negotiators. "I was glad they did it because that made people so much more determined that we would have a dental plan," Laws said. "I still have my toothbrush. I never have used it but I look at it every time I go to the dentist every six months."

Every negotiator also has to have his own style. While some ranted and raved, that style was not for everybody. "Some like to come on tough and blustery. I never felt that way," Ellison said. "I'm a firm believer that the guy across the table—I don't want to talk to him any differently than I want him to talk to me. And if he sat down at the table and started giving me a cussing, I would do everything I could to defeat him."

One common problem for URW negotiators was trying to serve the varied interests of the different groups within any company or individual plant. While the theme of solidarity preached unity and "all for one and one for all," the URW negotiators knew that reality rarely worked out so easily. Different individuals had different wants and desires from any given set of negotiations, and somehow the negotiators had to come to terms with such differences. Laws always felt that during negotiations he had three different groups to try to satisfy. The group of workers who had just hired in were interested in wages and earnings and did not care about anything else. The second group had been at the plant for ten to fifteen years, were middle-aged with kids, and wanted things like time off and vacation and health benefits to take care of their families. And the third group were those nearing retirement. For them, pension gains were most important. "I try to explain it that there's only so much pie that you're going to get, and you try to divide it as equal as you can to where all people will benefit instead of just giving it all to one group," Laws said. "The longer they stay, the more they're benefiting from all areas."

George Freiberger told a similar story from his days of negotiating contracts for Local 87 at Inland Manufacturing Co. in Dayton, Ohio. During 1955 negotiations, Inland made its contract in the form of a wheel, with ten spokes, each standing for a different part of the proposal. One spoke was especially attractive. For every dollar an employee used to buy company stock, the company would put in two dollars. The only catch was that the union had to accept the whole wheel. They could not just pick and choose the spokes they wanted. At the time Freiberger worked in the tool room, where the employees made more money than the rest of the plant workers. Two of his fellow tool makers told Freiberger he was crazy not to jump at the chance to get that spoke with the stock match. But Freiberger knew that he was negotiating not just for the people in the tool room, but also for the pressman and the workers on the rubber steering wheel jobs that got laid off for two or three months every year. There was no way they could afford to buy stock. So Freiberger told his fellow tool makers, "We'll take that spoke when we get a closed shop and paid-up insurance. I'm bargaining for three thousand people. I have to look at what's best for three thousand people—not just the tool room and the maintenance department." So when the negotiating committee went in for the final bargaining session, they settled for the closed shop and the paid-up insurance. "Then I said, 'We'll take that stock deal if you'll throw that in with it.' They said, 'That wagon wheel's still there but you have to take the whole wagon wheel.' I said, 'Forget it. We're tickled to get the paid-up insurance.'" And in the end Freiberger knew he made the right choice. He later had two surgeries for colon cancer and his wife had a heart valve put in. The total cost of just those three surgeries exceeded $160,000. "Let me tell you, I'd have lost my home and everything if it weren't for the paid-up insurance," he said.

George Goebel remembered how one Local 73 member reacted when the Kitchener, Ontario, local negotiated health care coverage in the late 1950s. A young worker in his twenties got up and declared that he did not need the health care part of the contract—that he needed the money and he needed it right away. "I hadn't said a word up to that point," Goebel said. "But at that point I got up and said, 'You may not need it today, but you might tomorrow.'" As luck would have it, just a little while later the young worker drove into a horse and was in the hospital close to a month.

E. K. Bowers also said that when the union negotiated for pension and insurance programs, there were those in the plant—especially the younger workers—who strongly opposed them, but the majority backed him in the effort. Little did Bowers know that he himself would benefit so greatly from the very things he negotiated. By 1999, Bowers was eighty-four years old and lived in a nursing home. He had a hospital bed and oxygen machine in his room, paid for with the insurance. He had had surgery twice on his hand and once for a blood disease. "There ain't a man living who can make money enough to pay for that if he's working with his hands," said Bowers, who died in 2000. "When I was building this program, I didn't know I was working for myself."

INTERNAL STRIFE

The time from 1948 through 1949 was difficult for both Buckmaster and the URW, eventually leading the union's Executive Board to throw Buckmaster out of office. Dissension had been brewing within the URW, with differences centered on such issues as organizational methods and benefit goals. But what it really boiled down to was an old-fashioned power play: George Bass, known as the "champion of the Akron militants," wanted to run the union, and he had to dispose of Buckmaster to accomplish that goal. It was just one of numerous examples of how the URW treated its leaders poorly. As would be the case in later coups within the union, members of the opposition force had to find an issue that would catch on with the membership. In 1948, the rift occurred because Buckmaster had not reinstated Harry Eagle as the union's organizational director and the URW Executive Board refused to approve Buckmaster's appointments to replace Eagle. The trouble continued at the 1948 convention in Omaha, Nebraska, when Buckmaster narrowly defeated challenger Bass by a vote of 810 to 808.

House recalled the 1948 convention well. One of his friends—F. M. Dickenson—had tried to sway him to vote for Bass. House admitted he did harbor some hard feelings toward Buckmaster, although he refused to detail why. But he did not trust Bass either and questioned his qualifications to be the union's top leader. Each Local 2 delegate carried a total of five votes at the convention and House waited until the last minute to make his decision. "I approached the ballot box with one five-vote ballot marked for Buckmaster and another unmarked five-vote ballot," House said. "By this time I was fairly sure that the vote would be close and as I neared the ballot box I came to the conclusion that If I failed to cast my five votes for Buckmaster and Bass should thereby defeat Buckmaster, I would deeply regret it. So, reluctantly, I cast my five votes for Buckmaster." House was quite relieved when the tally of 810–808 in favor of Buckmaster was announced, knowing that if he had cast the blank ballot Bass would have won 808–805.

But Bass's two running mates were victorious. H. R. Lloyd, who had

George Bass tried mightily to wrest the URW presidency from Leland Buckmaster during 1948 and 1949, but failed both times. *(USWA/URW photo files)*

been vice president under Buckmaster since 1945 but by then supported Bass, beat Joe Childs of the General Tire local in Akron by an 811 to 807 margin. Charles Lanning was re-elected over Floyd Gartrell more convincingly for secretary/treasurer, by an 859 to 752 margin. Even worse for Buckmaster, the Bass slate gained the majority on the URW Executive Board. With the opposition holding such positions, Buckmaster knew that his difficulties were just beginning.

The worst trouble came in March 1949 when Buckmaster called a special meeting of Firestone Local 336 in Pottstown, Pennsylvania, for March 13 at the Eagles Auditorium in Pottstown. Buckmaster was going to inform the local about alleged abuses by Robert Garber, but Buckmaster did not forewarn Garber of the charges. While Buckmaster clearly was within his rights as president to call the meeting, he also was trying to throw his political weight around to get rid of someone viewed as a political opponent. Garber, though, called a meeting for the same time at the same location. As Buckmaster and the three men accompanying him walked to the speaker's platform, Garber already had possession of the public address system and was holding onto the microphone. Buckmaster tried to get Garber to give up the microphone, without success. When Buckmaster tried to wrest the mike from Garber's hands, Garber had two of his stalwarts physically force Buckmaster into a seat on the platform. Buckmaster and his aides made one more attempt to secure control of the meeting; the URW president walked to where Garber was talking into the microphone and tried to take the mike again. At this point Garber shoved Buckmaster off the platform, which stood about four feet above the floor of the auditorium, and one of Buckmaster's aides was knocked unconscious in the fracas that followed.

Buckmaster suspended Garber as president of Local 336, but the union's Executive Board—still stacked with Bass supporters—upheld Garber's appeal. Garber filed charges with the Executive Board that Buckmaster had illegally tried to take over the chair of the local union meeting. The Executive Board served as a trial board during hearings from April 25 to May 24 in Philadelphia. They backed Garber, and on May 24 sent Buckmaster a telegram informing him that he was being replaced as president by Vice President Lloyd, who named Dickenson vice president.

But in a union as democratic as the URW, where convention delegates reign as the union's supreme authority, that was not the end of the fight. Buckmaster immediately began his campaign for reinstatement by appeal-

H. R. Lloyd was part of George Bass's attempt to drive Buckmaster from office. Lloyd, in fact, was named interim URW president in 1949 when Buckmaster was temporarily removed from office. *(USWA/URW photo files)*

ing the Executive Board's action to the 1949 convention that fall in Toronto. The first good sign occurred when delegates reversed a Lloyd ruling from the chair and insisted that the controversy be aired on the floor of the convention rather than in committee. Each side was given three hours to present its case plus a half-hour for rebuttal. Buckmaster defended himself with a thirty-one-page brief of his position. After the seven-hour debate delegates voted 840 to 740 to reinstate Buckmaster to the presidency with full back pay, then later in the week elected him to a fourth term, again against Bass, by a more comfortable 867 to 727 count. This time Buckmaster's supporting cast and Executive Board nominees prevailed, with Childs beating Lloyd for vice president and Desmond Walker defeating Dickenson for secretary/treasurer.

When Lloyd went back to work January 6, 1950, at the Mohawk tire plant in Akron, he left no doubt about his disdain for Buckmaster. "After working with Buckmaster for ten years, it's a big relief and a great pleasure to again build tires." Lloyd remained as chairman of the Committee for Honest Unionism, which vowed to try to defeat Buckmaster during future elections.

Leland Buckmaster won reinstatement to his presidency during the 1949 URW convention. He then defeated George Bass for the second time in two years and remained URW president until 1960. *(USWA/URW photo files)*

As a footnote to the whole affair, Buckmaster shortly after the convention appointed both Bass and Garber as International representatives. Garber later left the URW and took a job for General Tire in charge of industrial relations for chemical plants. "I've negotiated with Bob," Ellison said, "and his word was absolutely good." After Buckmaster got through this 1949 battle, he, Childs, and Walker ran the union until 1960 with little opposition.

AKRON: STILL THE CENTER OF THE UNIVERSE

A lot of workers used to feel the same way about Akron as Clark Lantz did. He started working at Firestone in 1945 and considered himself the "luckiest guy in the world" to get the job. He went from job to job until 1950, when he went to the company's synthetic rubber plant, staying there for thirty years until Firestone shut down the latex facility in 1980. And during all that time he never hated having to go to work. "I mixed chemicals and made synthetic rubber. It was like being a cook," Lantz said. "It was not a dirty job. It was a really responsible job. You had to be on your toes. If you messed up, you were talking thousands of dollars."

When Matt Contessa was hired at Goodrich in 1950, Local 5 represented twelve thousand hourly workers, Firestone had fifteen thousand, and Goodyear seventeen thousand, not to mention another two thousand at General Tire. "They had a lot of clout within the city of Akron," he said. "Politicians always planned to go to the plant gates to pass out literature." When Doug Werstler was hired at Goodyear in 1965, the union presidents of the big chains were well-known power brokers in the city. "The politicians needed labor, because the numbers of the hourly workforce, obviously, outweighed the salaried people," Werstler said. "And the salaried people knew that what the hourly people gained at the bargaining table was passed down to them. Everybody watched and knew. The influence that we had on this town, it was just phenomenal," Werstler said.

Such a situation helped give rise to powerhouse local leaders, but none stronger than John Nardella, who reigned as Local 2 president for twenty-three years. There were two explanations for how John Nardella got the nickname "Big Slick." Nardella liked to say people called him that because he was so slick in negotiations. But more than likely it was because of the way he did his hair: it was slicked back and kept perfectly neat at all times. And he was always very well dressed, often in a jacket and tie. He wanted

An overhead view of the mammoth B. F. Goodrich Akron complex in 1948 when it was near its zenith, with more than sixty buildings in use. (*Rubber & Plastics News file photo. Copyright Crain Communications Inc.*)

the local president to garner respect, so he dressed the part. "John was an icon to our people," Werstler said, "although you could disagree with John. I disagreed with John in the past, but in the final say, when John said it was final, it was final. It was almost unheard of to challenge what John Nardella would say. The company would give him total respect. They were probably fearful, but they also knew that the people listened to John Nardella."

Besides his hair and dress, Nardella—who died January 22, 1999, on his 74th birthday—also became known for putting together some interesting phrasing. In Local 2 lore they are known fondly as "Nardellaisms," famous

John Nardella was president of URW Local 2 for twenty-three years, and if there was something going on with the union in Akron there was a good chance he was in the middle of it. *(USWA/URW photo files)*

lines such as "I need some questions to these answers." Werstler, later Local 2 president, kept a book of them in his office, and whenever he needed a laugh, he pulled them out and read a few. Gary Diceglio remembered many of them. His favorite was: "My eyes are as red as cucumbers from staying up all night thinking about all this."

Craig Hemsley said it was impossible to beat Nardella in Local 2, and the local also was a major force in the URW. When Hemsley was hired in 1965, the local had eight thousand members and was taking forty-four people to the conventions. "Some of us got more votes in some of these Local 2 elections than the mayoral contests in some cities," he said.

"Local 2 was a good place," said Diceglio. "When John Nardella was there, he had—and I mean no disrespect—a heckuva machine going there. There were a lot of people involved. We used to have two thousand or three thousand at union meetings. And with those numbers, the local could almost dictate the way things went within the Goodyear chain of master contract locals. At the time, they averaged 40 to 45 percent of the Goodyear employees covered by the master contract, so that went a long way toward getting half the members needed to pass an issue."

About the only thing negative Diceglio saw in Nardella was something he saw in presidents of locals elsewhere as well. "We had an old saying at Local 2 that we eat our young," he said. "There's a turf consciousness and I believe this is everywhere. They don't allow people to rise up like they should, because they're afraid of a political opponent." That was apparent with those who ran against Nardella and lost. They were rarely seen again, because Nardella was not the type of leader to try to win back enemies. "John was the old school: 'Either you're with me or against me, and if you're against me, that's the end of it,'" according to Diceglio. "He never turned his back on them personally, but in the shop world and the union world they were done, unless they came back and beat him. But nobody ever did."

Other large Akron locals acted much the same way. Within the Goodrich chain, the non-Akron plants thought the Akron local acted like the big brother, saying, "You do this or you do that," Contessa said. "There were times in the 1950s and 1960s when the Akron locals had enough membership that their vote would block anything. They used that power a lot."

The presidents of the locals in Akron generally got along and often banded together at conventions, according to Hemsley. "I don't want to say we were not well liked, but they kind of thought we thought we were the big shots coming out of Akron," Hemsley said. "We got a table of forty-four delegates and a lot of locals would have one or two people." Besides the Goodyear contingent, Firestone and Goodrich sent thirty to thirty-five delegates from Akron. There definitely was a feeling of jealousy, Hemsley said, and sometimes that played against the Akron group. At times, the locals outside the city would unite in order to beat the Akron locals on certain convention issues. Hemsley also remembered one convention at which a delegate from the South said: "Our guns are pointed North. We're going to take all your jobs." The delegate was ruled out of order, but in the end that pretty much happened; Southern plants ended up with most of the tire manufacturing jobs that once had been the heart of the Akron URW locals.

KITCHENER, ONTARIO: THE "AKRON OF CANADA"

While much emphasis during the URW's growth years in the 1940s and 1950s centered on the United States, the Rubber Workers also made a significant impact in Canada, especially in Kitchener, Ontario, a town affectionately known as the "Akron of Canada." Located less than an hour's drive from Toronto, the town once was a manufacturing center, fueled by the proliferation of so-called "subsidiary plants." Before the advent of free trade in the 1990s, many U.S.-based companies placed factories in Canada because high Canadian duties made the cost of exporting goods to Canada prohibitive. The facilities were miniature versions of larger complexes in the United States, making a full line of products mainly for sale in Canada. In the rubber industry, Kitchener therefore became home to two major tire plants and roughly a score of industrial rubber product factories.

Organization of Kitchener's rubber industry followed soon after the URW's formation in 1935. A year earlier, rubber workers from Kitchener, Toronto, and Hamilton, Ontario, had formed a Rubber Workers' Council to try to combine resources and organize workers in the region, but found little success. In 1936, a carload of Kitchener organizers attended the URW convention and asked for help in organizing the Canadian rubber industry. The convention granted the request and approved finances and staff for the organizing effort. The URW took to the task quickly, with the first URW charter in Canada granted on December 1, 1936, to Local 67 at the Dominion Rubber plant in Kitchener. Other charters in Kitchener were soon after granted to Local 73 at the B. F. Goodrich Co. of Canada operation; Local 80 at the Dominion Tire operation; and Local 88 at Kaufman Rubber, though that local had to be dropped and reinstated several times before finally winning a contract in the 1980s. By 1946, there were about twenty URW locals in Canada, representing 12,300 members.

Kitchener became a place where people like George Goebel came to work. Born and raised on a farm, he himself tried farming during the 1930s. He came from the west, in Saskatchewan, and the weather just would not cooperate. "It didn't rain—we had hail," Goebel said. "Anything bad we had. I couldn't raise anything." By the spring of 1941, Goebel—who was 30 at the time and had six children—knew it was time for a change. He bummed a ride on a freight train from Saskatchewan to Toronto, where his wife had a brother. But Toronto seemed a bit big for his taste. So the next day he took the streetcar out as far as he could and ended up by City Hall in Kitchener. He got a day job starting the next morning with a moving company. Then he worked a second day, during which he also stopped by the Goodrich plant. "They needed somebody for building tires," he said. "I'd never even seen a factory before. So any job in the factory is just like any other. It didn't matter a damn to me." When he got there he was told to go up to first aid. The woman there gave him a card to go see a doctor at two that afternoon. Now Goebel did not know his way around the city, and he was supposed to start work at three, but he decided to go find the street anyway. When he found the doctor's office was close to where he was staying, he stopped by and saw the doctor early. Goebel then went right back to Goodrich, and the nurse said, in a smart-aleck tone: "What time did I tell you to see the doctor?" Goebel explained how he had nothing to do and had found the office quickly so he got right in. Then she said something that Goebel remembered until the day he retired. "That's one thing you're going to learn here," the nurse said. "You're going to learn to do what you're told to do when you're told to do it." When Goebel retired on the last day of 1974, the first and only Canadian-born manager of the Goodrich plant in Kitchener asked him what he remembered about his career there, and Goebel told him the story of the nurse. "And he said, 'By God, you people helped change that, didn't you?' I said, 'I'd like to believe that.'"

Goebel joined the union almost immediately after landing his job in 1941. He was president of URW Local 73 in 1962 when Goodrich built a new tire plant in Kitchener, but he decided to stay at the non-tire facility rather than move to the new factory. When a labor relations person from the plant asked why he was not moving to the tire plant, he told him because he planned to work until he was sixty-five and he had seen no one retire at that age from tire building. The man said that Goebel had to be wrong. "I said, 'Tell me one,'" Goebel said. "So he mentioned a name and I told him where the man went before he retired. Then he mentioned another two and I told him where they went. I said, 'There wasn't one that retired off tire building since I've been here, and I'm not about to try to set a precedent.'"

One of the early major conflagrations for the URW's Canadian locals occurred during the strike of 1946. The union used the URW's Seven Point Program, adopted at the 1945 convention, as the cornerstone of its 1946 demands in Canada. When the companies all balked at an industry-wide agreement, all of the locals involved authorized strike action if needed. The various companies tried to stop the strikes by offering individual contracts to the locals, but none of these came close to matching the Seven Point Program. As bargaining extended into June—May 27 had been the original strike date—the URW's solidarity was threatened when Local 132 at the Dunlop Tire & Rubber Co. plant in Toronto and Local 88 at Kaufman Rubber in Kitchener accepted terms without going on strike.

More than ten thousand URW members at ten locals in Ontario, however, began the strike June 23, virtually shutting down the Ontario rubber industry. Other unions affiliated with the Canadian Congress of Labour also had walked off the jobs, so that by mid-July about sixty thousand Canadian workers were on strike. Progress in the strike was slow, with no contract offers made by the company until Dominion Rubber and Goodyear made offers on July 30 and August 7, respectively. Both were rejected. Local 292 at Barringham Rubber in Oakville, Ontario, did reach an agreement on August 22 against the advice of the URW's Strategy Committee. In September, Local 80 and Dominion Rubber were chosen as the pattern setter for the remainder of the rubber locals on strike. The union made a more modest wage proposal and the company offered a counter-proposal. Further bargaining brought an agreement on October 16—a week short of four months into the strike—with workers winning a one-year contract that included a thirteen-cent-an-hour raise across the board. By October 28, all locals had come to terms and were back on the job. While the economic gains may not seem that great on the surface, the union "made intangible gains with respect to its ascendancy in recognition, prestige, power and influence," according to Carlos Sousa, who wrote about the strike in 1986. "No longer could the URW simply be tolerated by the companies. The 1946 strike established the URW, once and for all, as a viable and permanent fixture in the Ontario rubber industry."

Leonard Bruder was around during the Rubber Workers' early days in Canada—including the 1946 strike. He got a job in March 1944 at Dominion Tire (later Uniroyal), where his father also worked. But he did not join the union right away. "They were collecting dues by hand—not off the payroll—and one little older fellow there came to me one day and he wanted to get my dues," Bruder said. "I told him I wasn't joining no union. He sat me down and gave me a good talking to, so I joined. He said to look at this plant and what we've had to put up with, the company working us long hours with no overtime and no paid lunches. He said, 'We've got to stick together, even just to get a raise.'"

Bruder worked just seven months before having to do a nearly two-year stint in the army starting in October 1944. He got back during the 1946 strike in Kitchener and became involved in union activity upon his return. He held the offices of steward and chief steward before being elected Local 80 vice president in 1952 and president from 1953 to 1957. During his time as president, he worked with the plant manager to stop the epidemic of wildcat strikes at the plant, which experienced as many as sixty such work stoppages in a single year. The manager was Wilson Martin, and he and Bruder did not get off to a good start. "He came to my machine and said, 'I'm going to get you for the wildcat strikes,'" Bruder said. "He didn't ask me if I caused any or not. I told him how to get the evidence. I said, 'I'll tell you what to do. If you want the evidence I'll give it to you and sign it. But I'll tell you there's one thing you don't do is tell me what to do as president of the union, because my membership does that. And I said as an employee of this company, you go through my supervisor.' And he was as red as a beet." Martin continued to press the issue until Bruder told him to go back to his office and the Local 80 president would come see him after his shift. "So I went down to his office on the way out and I said, 'Don't you ever come to my machine again and do that or you will have a wildcat strike right there. It's unsafe and I'm getting worked up and you weren't listening to me.'" With that out of the way, Bruder told him that all the company had to do to stop the wildcats was simply to follow the contract. Bruder told Martin of a violation that was occurring; the plant manager looked into it, found Bruder was right, and ordered the company to follow the contract. From then on, that was the way the two handled things. Dominion followed the written agreement, Bruder got his membership to listen to him, and the wildcat strikes stopped. "He kept his word, I kept my word with him and after we got working together we wouldn't look back," Bruder said. "That showed that management and labor can work together."

John Fuhrman started working at Dominion's non-tire rubber product operation in Kitchener in 1948, so he had an appreciation for the older workers who blazed the way for the union. "A lot of older guys knew where they came from," said Fuhrman, who served as URW Local 67 president at the plant from 1965 until 1988. "Some of them used to cut through the backyards so they wouldn't be seen going to a meeting. The company had their spies out and you would be fired." Having a tie to the older workers also helped Fuhrman appreciate the value of the benefits negotiated over the years by the Rubber Workers. "These guys now don't know what their benefits entail. They take it for granted," he said. "The old guys remember what it was like to pay the doctor. Some had to pay with a chicken or a jar of peaches."

All in all, Kitchener—much like Akron—had its time as a boom town. It differed from its sister city of Waterloo, Ontario, where white-collar workers, universities, insurance companies, and other businesses thrived. Kitchener, on the other hand, was the "lunch bucket" town, and income-wise both communities were thriving. "At one time you could get five good-paying jobs," said John Cunningham, former president of Local 677 at the Michelin-owned Uniroyal Goodrich tire plant in Kitchener. "You'd get hired at each one and report on Monday to the one you really wanted." Alan Turner, also from Local 677, said that in 1976 alone the company had to hire eight hundred new employees, and this at a time when the factory employed just 650 hourly workers. "Jobs were plentiful," Turner said. "I can remember one supervisor standing at a machine explaining to a new guy what the job was. He stopped on the way where there's a tire builder working away at the machine. And I walk by and I see the supervisor talking and I say, 'Hey Lou, who are you talking to.' And he said, 'This is . . .' and he turned around and the guy's walking down the hallway on his way out to the parking lot, thinking, 'No, I don't like that job.' But that's the way it was then."

The Rubber Workers were also well thought of in Kitchener. "Your doctors, your dentists; they really liked the union because of our health plans," said Reginald Duguay, who was a president of Local 80 and later URW district director in Canada. Turner said the rubber industry became so entrenched that generations of the same families ended up working in the industry. "You got a job in the rubber industry and you were pretty well set for life," Turner said. "You didn't have to go looking for any more work. And that's what made it much more difficult when places started to close down." The URW was respected as a union in Canada, achieving such cherished goals as cost-of-living escalator raises, thirty-and-out retirement, and top pensions, among other gains, said James Webber, who was president of Local 73 when the plant, then owned by Epton Industries, went out of business. "I would say the Rubber Workers were at the cutting edge," Webber said. "If you take a look at what the Rubber Workers achieved, I don't think there was any other labor organization in Canada that was ahead of us."

A NEW TEAM TAKES OVER

URW Vice President Joe Childs was widely thought to be the most popular of the URW's leaders during the union's 1958 convention. Many tried to get him to run for president that year, but that was not his way. He was loyal to President Buckmaster and wanted to let his leader serve his final term. Childs then would be the rightful successor and likely would win an easy victory. And that was the way it appeared things were going: Childs had the political machine put in place, and things appeared to be going well heading to the 1960 convention. But then the unexpected occurred—Childs died April 24, 1960, of a heart attack. His death left a void at the top of the ticket, and no recipient of all the work the "machine" already had done for Childs. Desmond Walker was left as the only incumbent running, and he tried to put a ticket together, but the machine had other ideas. The machine came up with a ticket headlined by George Burdon from Los Angeles, the URW's newly appointed organizational director, for president; up-and-coming Peter Bommarito from Detroit for vice president; and Ike Gold from Akron for secretary/treasurer. "No one had ever thought Burdon was the man to be president or Bommarito to be vice president," said E. K. Bowers. "They actually inherited Joe Childs' machine."

Buckmaster, though retiring, tried to get in on the politicking by supporting the Paul Bowers-led ticket that Walker put together. But the endorsement did not help Bowers, the union's pension and insurance director, according to Glenn Ellison. "The Rubber Workers have always been unique I think in that they have always resented an officer trying to name his successor," Ellison said. "They reserve for themselves the right to make that decision." Ellison supported the Burdon ticket. Paul Bowers asked for his support but Ellison thought that Bowers—while a master negotiator and an expert on pensions and investments—seemed interested

A chalkboard shows the results of the election the night George Burdon was elected URW president, along with his ticket of Vice President Peter Bommarito and Secretary/Treasurer Ike Gold. *(USWA/URW photo files)*

only in large locals. Not that Ellison knew Burdon all that well, but Kenneth Oldham was for Burdon and that was good enough for Ellison. "Kenny (later a URW vice president) was working on the URW staff at that time. He was a supporter of Burdon. Kenny could have swung my vote about anyway."

The election itself was not much of a contest, with Burdon—running on a campaign of "responsible militancy"—easily beating Bowers. Bommarito beat Jack Moye of Local 5 in Akron for vice president by an even larger margin, and Gold easily bested Walker for secretary/treasurer.

Burdon first made his mark in the URW out West, where he was founding president of Local 131 at the Goodyear plant in Los Angeles. He was named a part-time field representative in 1938 and in 1940 was named

URW education director for the West Coast. Burdon was named District 5 director in 1942, then was transferred later that year to the Midwest as a field representative in District 4. George Burdon's son, Jim, said his father was very close to Childs. Buckmaster and Childs had appointed Burdon organizational director in 1959, and the elder Burdon and Childs got to know each other quite well, with Childs asking Burdon to run for vice president on his slate. "Childs and my father just hit it off real well," Jim Burdon said. "They just personally liked each other, particularly because my dad lived [in Akron] for a year while my mom and the family were trying to move here." George Burdon never had aspirations to be an International officer of the union, let alone president, according to his son. "He was very content with being organizational director, probably believing he would never ascend to that height in the union. He had been an International field representative from 1941 to 1959."

Jim Burdon sees his father's greatest accomplishment in office as helping the URW workers maintain their income consistent with inflationary spirals without having to take the union out on a major strike. "There's two ways to negotiate," Jim Burdon said. "One is to say, 'You do it our way or we walk.' You start out with that real combative approach. All that does is really teach the management that there's not much that they're going to be able to do with you people, because all contract negotiations are some kind of give-and-take between both sides." George Burdon, on the other hand, took a different approach. He put together all sorts of facts and figures and knew what management was going to say. "They were always going to say they couldn't afford it," Jim Burdon said. "So he would put together a negotiating team that would have those facts and figures to demonstrate why management could do what they were asking for."

It would be easy to mistake George Burdon for a businessman, wearing a suit, with silver streaks in his hair and a mustache before it was popular, his son said. "He had a lot of energy," according to Jim Burdon. "When you talk about the days of the self-educated man, he was the classic example of that. I think he was just well-prepared and he had a reasonable negotiating approach. And he had advisers around him that all had a simple goal: Let's get what what we know we can get for these workers without putting them out on the street in a strike—knowing that he would do that if he had to, but it was never necessary because of the approach they used. And the workers still benefited."

Leland Buckmaster introduces George Burdon as the newly elected URW president in 1960 as Ike Gold, the new secretary/treasurer, congratulates Burdon. *(USWA/URW photo files)*

Looking at the record, URW members seemed to do fairly well at the bargaining table during Burdon's tenure. From 1961 to 1964, tire workers gained an average of 30.5 cents an hour in direct wage increases, 27.6 cents an hour in fringe benefit gains, and 2.1 cents an hour in average straight-time hourly earnings increase, for a total gain of 60.2 cents an hour. Non-tire URW members saw total compensation rise by 50.2 cents an hour, with 20.5 cents of that in direct raises and 27.6 cents in fringe benefit costs. Independents saw a total rise of 35.1 cents an hour, with 20 cents in general wage increases and 13.6 cents for fringe benefits.

George Burdon served
as URW president
from 1960 to 1966.
(USWA/URW photo files)

The URW also made some impressive organizing gains during Burdon's first two terms in office, chartering or reinstating ninety-eight local
unions during the four-year period. Some of the successful campaigns
included the U.S. Rubber tire plant in Opelika, Alabama; the Firestone tire
factories in Decatur, Illinois, and Salinas, California; Kelly-Springfield tire
plants in Freeport, Illinois, and Tyler, Texas; and the Armstrong tire facility in Hanford, California

When Burdon was first elected in 1960 he told delegates that organizing
the unorganized was the number one priority. Four years later in what
would be his third—and last—acceptance speech, he urged the delegates
to help him unionize the organized. "Too many of our members—young
and old alike—think that the union today is a slot machine," Burdon said.
"That you put your dues in one end and the wage increases and vacation

and pensions and insurance and seniority and job protection come out the other end. You and I know different. We know that the stuff of this union is the sweat and the dedication; the time away from home; the meetings and the arguments; the hours of preparation of cases; the abuse we take from an unhappy member; the days and weeks on the picket line. This is the human stuff that built this union and this is the blood and sweat and tears that it's going to take to keep this union great."

Burdon also asked for something else from the delegates at that 1964 convention: unity in the union. He said that as he began his third term as president he wanted the URW to show "unity of purpose in achieving goals we have set for ourselves at this convention; unity of cause in facing together, with an unbroken front, the companies with which we bargain; unity of dedication in bringing the message of unionism to those not yet under our banner; unity of brotherhood in creating, in our hearts and by our action, that full and free opportunity, which is the birthright of every American."

If Burdon had been able to peer into the future, he would have found he was asking just a bit too much.

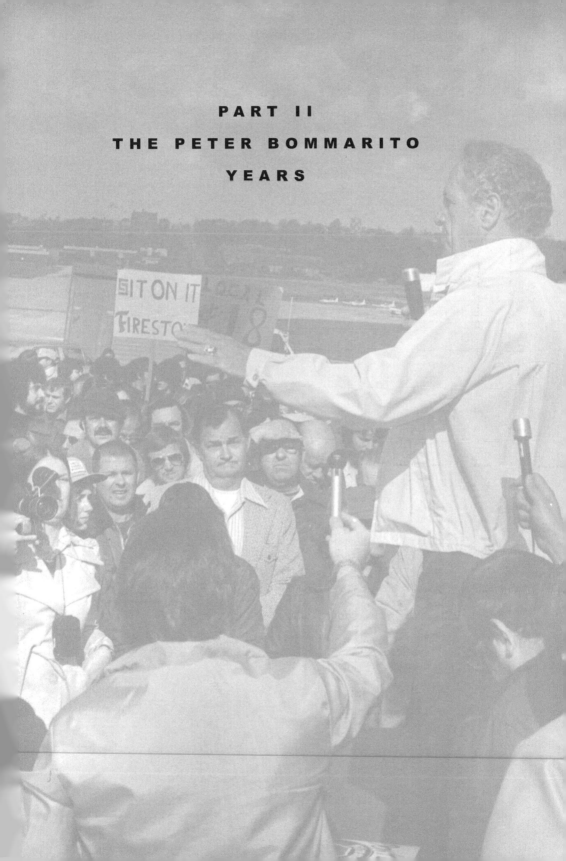

PART II
THE PETER BOMMARITO
YEARS

CHAPTER 3

THE BOMBER ALWAYS RISES TO THE TOP

Ask people about Peter Bommarito and several themes emerge. Nicknamed "The Bomber" from his days in the U.S. Marine Corps during World War II, he was the fighter that many in the URW felt President George Burdon refused to be. In Bommarito they saw someone who would take the fight to the rubber companies, but more importantly they saw a leader whom they would gladly and willingly follow into battle. "Charisma" was not just a word to describe Bommarito, it was the aura that followed him wherever he went. Just by walking into a room, he commanded attention. Just by speaking, he commanded awe and respect. Just by a handshake and a personal greeting, he commanded loyalty. There was no such thing as fear for the Bomber. He had, after all, earned his nickname during action at Guadalcanal, Cape Glouster, Peleilieu Islands, and a half-dozen other Pacific battle areas as a member of a sixty-man special weapons unit. With that kind of a resume, facing down a table full of company negotiators in suits and ties could not instill fear in Bommarito.

Of course, no man—or labor leader—is perfect, and not all URW members were loyalists. Some saw Bommarito for the human being he was, with flaws and insecurities. They saw him as one who had at times pushed too hard. They saw someone who sometimes downplayed the accomplishments of his allies and at times tried too hard to make his enemies into friends. The Goodyear locals as a group saw Bommarito as a leader not willing to treat them, as the largest faction within the union, with the respect they deserved.

Whichever side one leans toward, no one would argue that Bommarito towered over the United Rubber Workers as the dominant figure of the union throughout the second half of the URW's sixty-year lifespan. Beginning with his six-year term as vice president in 1960, followed by his fifteen-year run as president, Bommarito held one of the URW's top two offices for twenty-one consecutive years, and his long shadow hovered over his two successors to a degree neither would admit. Right up until the merger with the Steelworkers union in 1995, first Mike Stone and later Kenneth Coss had to hear the same criticisms over and over again: "That never would have happened under Pete Bommarito." Or "If Pete still was president, we would have gotten a better contract." And, "They just aren't as strong a leader as Pete."

Bommarito's ascent to this level of power no doubt started with the work ethic he gained as a youth. Born May 17, 1915, in Detroit, he was the youngest of Charles and Margaret Bommarito's twelve children. He learned early what hard work meant, having quit school at fifteen to clean the streets of Detroit because his father was ill and his family could not afford to lose the income. "So I went downtown and picked up the cart," Bommarito said. "I'll never forget this—I was sweeping away and I was right there in front of the University of Detroit . . . and all these young girls were out there and I felt ashamed, and I put my hat down over my eyes so they wouldn't see me. I did that for a few seconds and then I thought, 'Wait a minute, I'm making an honest living. What am I ashamed of? I'm a coward.' And I put my hat up and I'm sweeping away with gusto—I remember it so distinctly—I went up and started talking to those girls. As long as I'm making an honest living, I'm not going to be ashamed of it."

Bommarito went to work at the U.S. Rubber (later renamed Uniroyal) tire plant in Detroit in 1939 after working at several other factory jobs. He enlisted in the marines in 1942 and married Dorothy, his neighborhood sweetheart, on a short leave before going overseas. He was shipped stateside in 1945 and recovering from a bout of malaria in the Portsmouth Naval Hospital when the war ended. Returning to work at U.S. Rubber, he was elected to URW Local 101's executive board in 1948, later became the local's treasurer, and in 1955 was elected vice president. Bommarito was elected Local 101 president in 1957 and was in his second term as president of the then six thousand-member local when he was elected URW vice president on Burdon's ticket in 1960.

While Bommarito's resume outlines how quickly he rose through the ranks of one of the most political locals in the URW and landed in Akron at age forty-five as the No. 2 officer, it does nothing to show the mark he left on the union that was so close to his heart. For whether one was friend

Peter Bommarito first was vice president of the union, but won the presidency after
a successful coup in 1966. *(USWA/URW photo files)*

or foe, Bommarito left an indelible impression on everyone he dealt with. It is these tales that truly tell the story of what the Bomber meant to the United Rubber Workers.

"Pete was a piece of work," said Steve Clem, who was hired by Bommarito as the URW's assistant research director in 1969 and retired as research director in 1998. "Pete was a charger. Pete would get an idea and don't tell him it can't be done. He sued the government over the wage and price guidelines." While not the most eloquent guy in the world, Bommarito was a great communicator, according to Clem. "I guess you would say he was a man's man. People responded to him. He was a good communicator. He also had a knack of determining which way the crowd was going and getting out in front."

Mike Polovick entered the rubber industry in the 1970s as a negotiator for Firestone, and his one brief dealing with Bommarito during 1979 negotiations left a long-lasting impression. Bommarito simply came in to help present the pattern settlement, as Firestone that year had agreed to accept whatever the pattern was without question in exchange for a "no-strike" pledge from the URW. "That was my only real exposure to Peter Bommarito, but from just that one time, I could see just exactly why he had so much appeal," Polovick said. "He was incredibly arrogant, very confident and very handsome—a ruggedly handsome guy. He was just a real character, not afraid of anything."

Gary Diceglio was one who saw the personal way Bommarito dealt with the union members. Diceglio was from Goodyear Local 2 in Akron, while his father was a longtime Local 9 member at General Tire in Akron. Diceglio's father was in the hospital for a hip replacement, and Bommarito—and his ever-present tan—was at the same hospital for some tests. "He saw my dad there and he went over and asked my dad his name and said, 'Aren't you a member of the United Rubber Workers?' My dad said he was and Pete said, 'I'm Peter Bommarito, president of the URW.' So at some time or another Pete must have seen my dad at a union meeting or met him somewhere. But I'll bet Pete never saw my dad more than once or twice in his life, and he went over and did that," Diceglio said. "Pete was a leader and you would follow him. When he took everybody out in 1976, nobody even thought of going back or crossing the picket line, unlike today."

Others were amazed at how far Bommarito went without an advanced education, having quit school at fifteen. Carl Dimengo, retired URW assistant research director, told Bommarito how important it was to receive the two honorary doctorates the URW president received: one in 1979 from the Los Angeles College of Chiropractic and the other in 1980, an honorary Doctor of Laws degree from the University of North Carolina (UNC) in Chapel Hill. Bommarito had been instrumental in having chiropractic services covered under health care plans for URW members, and his bargaining also led to a health program at UNC. "I told Pete, 'Do you know how tough it is to get an honorary degree?'" Dimengo said. "I can't get one. You have to do something in life that meant something."

Dimengo also saw Bommarito's flair for the dramatic. One year the URW president was in charge of the Red Cross drive and did an hour-long film about the organization. That was a performance in which Bommarito ad-libbed much of it, sitting there talking about the Red Cross, the need for help in flooded areas, and all the needs that had to be met. "When he was doing the Red Cross movie, it was just like Cary Grant sitting there, saying 'Hi, how are you?' The guy just had it. Every time he gave a speech he got a standing ovation."

Kenneth Finley was another who loved to watch Bommarito. "When Pete would walk into a room, just his presence would demand attention," Finley said. "I mean, heads would turn. He just had a way about him. I especially enjoyed listening to his speeches because he always had a lot of material that really affected us. I used to sometimes sit and watch him from an angle. I was always fascinated how he would work his feet. He would pick one foot up and stand on one foot, and have just the toe of his other shoe back. Then he would switch them back and forth. It's just one of the little things you remember."

Finley also recalled vividly why he remained a Bommarito supporter throughout the years. Finley was the newly elected president of URW Local 196 at Faultless Rubber in Ashland, Ohio, and was attending his first meeting as a representative of the local. The meeting had recessed for lunch and Finley, young for a local president at twenty-seven, was waiting for the elevator so he could take his meeting material up to his room before going to have lunch. "I still remember, they had a couple of palm trees setting by the elevator, and I saw Pete come out of the convention by himself and walking up toward the elevator," Finley said. "I felt intimidated by it, just him coming up there. I thought, 'Is he going to speak to me or is he not going to speak to me? Or should I speak to him, or shouldn't I speak to him? Should I run?' So I kind of actually moved in close to this tree by the elevator. But Pete came over to the elevator and introduced himself to me, and asked who I was and where I was from. Then I said, 'Local 196,' and he said, 'I know this guy and this guy out of there,' and he started telling me about the program. He made me feel accepted and like I was an important part of being there at that meeting. He had a way of doing that. From that day on, as a local union president, I was in his corner."

Curt Brown, the longtime URW public relations director who was hired by Bommarito, said the membership adored their president like a celebrity—and Bommarito acted the part. When he went on a plane, all the stewardesses and everyone else would want to talk to him. "He would go in a room and he'd have little jokes and stories that he'd tell," Brown said. "He'd flirt with people. He was very charming and always an immaculate dresser. He had nice suits and good clothes, and shirts that fit him well. He always looked good and was well manicured. He was a good-looking guy." He had a good voice for delivering speeches, but Brown said even Bommarito had his off days. He was especially sensitive in his home district, which included Michigan, where he had worked in the U.S. Rubber plant, and in Ohio, where he spent much of his time as leader of the URW. "He would give his worst speeches there because he'd try too hard and deviate from the text and start ad-libbing," Brown said.

John Sellers said that speaking was not the only place where Bommarito made his mark—he could do it just going through a room. "If Pete decided to focus that considerable charm on you one on one, you were definitely impacted," Sellers said, "and I've seen him focus animosity one on one, and that was every bit as impressive." Bommarito definitely let people know where they stood with him, and it was not something he had to verbalize. "You just knew it," Sellers said. Of course the URW president was never afraid to verbalize it either. Sellers recalled once when Bommarito took a tour of the Voit plant in California where Sellers was local president. There had been problems with a shift supervisor who had been giving the women in the plant a hard time. "Pete had heard about that," Sellers said. "So we went on the tour, and went through the supervisor's department. This poor dumb guy came up and he wants to shake hands with Bommarito, and Bommarito says, 'Oh yes, I've heard about you. Let me tell you something. We're in negotiations right now and we have your ass on the table and we're looking at it with a magnifying glass.' And this guy just melted. But that was just vintage Pete."

Bommarito also had a sense of humor—a side of the Bomber witnessed by Dan Borelli. There was the time in 1981 when Bommarito, Borelli, and Phil Leonard were in Florida following a URW meeting. They were driving to see some Arabian horses—Bommarito loved horses—owned by one of the officials of the chiropractic association that had honored Bommarito. After stopping for breakfast, Leonard was driving on one of those Florida four-lane highways where the median is all bushes. "Pete says to Phil Leonard, 'You're going the wrong way, turn around here.' So Phil turned around, and Pete says, 'There's a cop right behind you.' Pete's laughing and the cop pulls him over," Borelli said.

Bommarito also liked being the center of attention at union gatherings. Borelli recalled a meeting in Phoenix for the Uniroyal Policy Committee. The hotel had an Olympic-size pool and Bommarito kept bragging about how well he could swim and how long he could stay under water. "He told this one guy, 'I can go the whole distance under water.' So he did," Borelli said. "He dove in and we're thinking, 'He's going to get killed.' Then he comes up and he's at the other end. The guy says, 'No, no you're not supposed to dive, you're supposed to go from the edge.' So Pete says, 'OK.' He takes a deep breath, goes under water and we're watching him. Johnny Izzard, a good friend of Pete's out of the same local, says, 'You know he will die before he comes up.' It's just the kind of a guy he was. Don't challenge him because he would kill himself trying to get something done."

Of course, not everything about Bommarito was positive. Local 12's E. K. Bowers, who played an instrumental role in Bommarito being elected URW president, saw two different sides of Bommarito. "He'd get the benefits for you if they were there and there was any way he could get them," Bowers said. "In a lot of ways he was a good president, but he was arrogant and sometimes inconsiderate, especially of his opponents." Bowers also said Bommarito was sometimes incongruous. He spent a week in Gadsden campaigning for Bowers when the then-retired Local 12 president made an unsuccessful bid for mayor. "But he also would cut your guts out if you went the wrong direction," Bowers said. That was particularly the case if you happened to be URW president and Bommarito wanted your job.

BRINGING DOWN BURDON

Jim Burdon pretty much had Peter Bommarito pegged when he first met him in 1960. It was in St. Louis, right after Burdon's father, George Burdon, had become the third elected president of the United Rubber Workers and Bommarito was elected his vice president. George Burdon was fifty years old at the time and under URW rules could have served as president for as long as fifteen years. Jim Burdon and his brother sized up Bommarito—just a few years younger than George Burdon—and decided he looked ambitious enough that they could never imagine him waiting for fifteen years to become the head man. Had Burdon served the maximum number of years possible as president, Bommarito could look forward to no more than five years or so as chief of the union.

"I remember that very clear impression," Jim Burdon said. "It was so clear that we told our dad about it and my dad wouldn't hear of it. In a way my dad was kind of upset with us that we mentioned it." Jim Burdon also could see the difference between his father and Bommarito. The newly elected vice president was charismatic. When he walked into a ballroom, everyone knew he was there—not because he was noisy but because he was so personable, going from person to person to make sure he greeted everyone. "My dad was never really like that. My dad wasn't really a politician. He couldn't shake hands. I mean he could do that but he couldn't do that very well. He was more interested in union business than in the things that you have to do to be in a position to make policy in a union—and that is get elected."

Bommarito's road to the presidency actually began not long after 1960, according to Jim Burdon. "Pete did a lot more traveling than the other officers did," the younger Burdon said. "Every time he would go to a local union there was politicking going on, not just servicing the local union. And my dad had no idea that was going on. That's because he wasn't much of a politician. My dad was a little naïve and he also was an intensely loyal guy. So he would never believe that someone who had been basically hand-selected by him to fulfill such an important role would ever turn on him. That would never have occurred to my dad because he applied his standards to other people, and not everybody is like that."

While it was Bommarito who would rise to the top slot, Secretary/Treasurer Ike Gold also was part of the planned coup by Bommarito at the

1966 convention. Gold, from Akron's Firestone Local 7, would keep his secretary/treasurer spot on the Bommarito ticket at the 1966 convention. Gold, in fact, probably took a more active role in attacking Burdon than even Bommarito. The true issue of the campaign was simple: Burdon was president and Bommarito wanted the job. Bommarito and Gold planned to take advantage of a bizarre aspect of URW politics: the union rank and file often treated its leaders poorly, both at the local and international levels. While Leland Buckmaster barely escaped with the URW presidency in 1948 and 1949, Bommarito and Gold worked hard to make sure Burdon suffered a different fate. "Pete kind of took the high road, but there wasn't anybody who knew Pete that didn't know it was Pete pulling the strings," Jim Burdon said. "Pete didn't do the public stuff, but at the cocktail parties inside the hotels he was very visible."

George Burdon never realized something was afoot until early 1966. Back then, URW conventions were held every two years and Burdon had been re-elected in 1962 and 1964 since first winning the office in 1960. By 1966 his assistant began telling him about the movement by Bommarito and Gold. At first he refused to believe it, but when other URW officials he trusted affirmed the story, he became convinced. "My impressions were that my dad was still a little bit naïve, thinking that hard work and loyalty and some of those things that are important to me and were to him would see him through that battle," Jim Burdon said. "But I think the people around him who were close to him were telling him the opposite: that Pete had built up an enormous relationship with particularly the larger local unions; that he had probably involved himself in the election of delegates from those locals; and that the convention was kind of stacked against my dad. It turned out all that was true."

Bommarito made his candidacy official on June 17, 1966, less than three months before the convention. He sent out letters to the four executive officers of each URW local union and a press release announcing his candidacy for International president and Ike Gold for re-election as secretary/treasurer. And many locals jumped on the bandwagon in a hurry. Several put forth resolutions to the convention denouncing Burdon in support of the Bommarito/Gold ticket.

The issue that broke Burdon was hardly one of enormous magnitude, but as many URW members explained, it was one that clearly could take hold with the rank and file. They claimed that Burdon had broken the union's rules by having his wife travel with him at URW expense. The union's International Executive Board had approved the expenses, but Burdon put the money in escrow when the issue was appealed to the 1966 convention. "The issue was [trivial] but it was something that resonated with the rank and file because it was presented in a way that suggested that my dad was actually taking money from the union for his personal travels," Jim Burdon said. "In fact, if you look at the minute details, the only time that my mother's expenses were paid for a trip was when there was an invitation given to him and his wife for some formal event. One good example was the inauguration of President Kennedy. You would expect that a president of the union would show up when given a formal invitation like that. There probably wasn't one other person who left his wife at home. And my dad's income then was something like $16,000, and he couldn't afford to take her and stay a few days in Washington, D.C. So he believed, and I think rightfully so, as did the union's auditor or comptroller, that it was all right under those circumstances to have my mother's expenses paid also."

As the convention opened on September 12, the button-counting vote appeared to be strongly favoring the two challengers. The white "Bommarito/Gold" buttons dominated, with the green "Burdon" buttons clearly at a disadvantage. Burdon did try to make an effort at changing some minds. His side put out a capsule comparison showing that on a total contract basis the URW was keeping up with the larger United Auto Workers union in terms of bargaining. And in his dramatic one-hour-and-forty-five-minute opening address to the convention, he tore into his opposition for what he called its "program of vilification," saying that he and his family had been threatened and harassed by obscene and disparaging calls and letters. "Either we will go forth from this convention in pride or we will tear ourselves apart in internal warfare," Burdon said in a last-ditch attempt to save his office. "How can people I loved and worked so hard for now join in this program of vilification? This is a sobering realization for me of what happens when men's minds become unhinged." He recounted accomplishments of his three terms in office and said he kept the promises he made when he first took office. "I yield to no man in dedication to the United Rubber Workers," Burdon said. Burdon said the revolt in the URW was "causing scars that will take years to erase."

Although the attack on George Burdon had its roots in Akron, the plan was to have someone outside of the URW's inner circle make the case at the convention. The man chosen was E. K. Bowers, who had been president of Local 12 in Gadsden, Alabama, and active in International politics. "I had no intention of supporting Burdon and I was vocal about it," Bowers said. During the campaign the *Akron Beacon Journal* had written an article about URW International politics, and the story mentioned how Bowers had come out openly supporting Bommarito. "They predicted Bommarito's victory based on what I had said, because they were recognizing me as a 'King Maker,'" Bowers said. "You see, I never ran for International office, but I always had somebody on the string I was supporting, so they called me the King Maker. They said if the King Maker is for Pete Bommarito, he will be elected."

While there were many reasons the pro-Bommarito group wanted Burdon replaced as president, the only thing they could technically and legally pin on the URW president was the issue regarding Mrs. Burdon's expenses. "Now that was a violation. He was guilty of that, so that's what we hung onto," Bowers said. The people running Bommarito's campaign were in Akron, and they supplied Bowers with the information to put together the appeal for the convention. The International Executive Board had upheld paying the expenses, so the group appealed the board's decision as being against the URW's constitution. "They violated all the rules and set them aside and put me up on the stage, and I presented my case," Bowers said. "I was given preferential treatment and time." Two Akron URW locals provided much of the research, but Bommarito definitely had his hand in it, according to Bowers. And what was Bommarito's main complaint with Burdon? "The fact that Bommarito wasn't president," Bowers said. "Bommarito was heartless. He was vicious. You'd best not cross him."

Glenn Ellison, later secretary/treasurer of the union, knew it was a ticky-tacky issue because of the small amount of money involved, but that was politics in the URW. "You get some attention-grabbing issue, where the real issue doesn't always come out at the convention," he said. "The real gut issue of 'How well is the guy doing his job?' doesn't get that much attention. If he goofs up and makes some blunder you can build a head of steam on, then that's what you do. Pete Bommarito was an astute politician and he was never happy being less than number one." And that was the only issue that mattered.

The debate on the appeal by Bowers and Local 12 took two and a half hours. They claimed that Burdon had charged nearly $1,500 for travel expenses for his wife when she accompanied him on trips from October 12, 1963, to October 2, 1965. The International Executive Board (IEB) had approved the expenses in December 1965, though Gold and Bommarito disagreed. Since the URW constitution was silent on the subject, they claimed the IEB incorrectly amended the constitution by allowing the expenses for Mrs. Burdon to be paid.

An estimated 600 of 750 delegates in attendance voted to overturn the Executive Board and make Burdon pay the money back. Those 600 votes were seen as likely votes for Bommarito in the election for president. While Bommarito did not begin his race for the presidency because of the money issue, it was clear that he would win because of it. There were other signs that Burdon's six-year reign as head of the URW was about to end. During caucuses to select running mates, 613 of the 780 delegates attended the Bommarito/Gold caucus, where Kenneth Oldham, the union's pensions and insurance director, was picked to fill the vice president slot on the ticket. The Bommarito/Gold slate had delegates pledged from nearly every URW local and had the endorsements of all seven URW district directors, nine of the twelve members of the International Executive Board, and the presidents of four of the five largest locals. Veteran delegates were predicting Burdon might take as few as three hundred total votes, a loss of major proportions for an incumbent president to suffer.

Burdon could count as well as anyone else. Instead of taking a beating of that magnitude, he instead declined the nomination in an emotion-packed speech to the convention, saying he did so to bring unity to the URW. "I will never do anything to harm this union and I will never let anyone do anything to hurt it," Burdon told the delegates. He said he was proud to have worked in the shop and eaten the lamp black and the zinc oxide prevalent in tire operations. "I was proud that I have the opportunity to do what I thought would help the union," he said. "You can't please everyone. A great Man tried to do that 1,966 years ago and was crucified. I'm not saying I'm being crucified, but evidently what I've had to offer hasn't been enough."

Tom Jenkins, a Local 2 member and later skilled trades director for the URW, was at the convention and supported Burdon, whom he described as a big man but soft-spoken. "I remember the speech that Burdon made," Jenkins said. "That place was full. He talked for about forty-five minutes, declining his nomination. There were a lot of grown men crying."

Burdon did not withdraw because he was afraid of losing—by that point the election actually was a foregone conclusion anyway. He withdrew because he wanted no public battle between the delegates to divide the union, according to his son, Jim. "He obviously wasn't happy, but he was probably less bitter than he was disappointed that they would do that," Jim Burdon said. "To him it wouldn't have been important enough to elevate himself in the union at somebody else's sake or at the sake of the union. That would never enter his mind."

Loyalty also was important to George Burdon, and that played a role in what he decided to do after losing the URW presidency. "I think he was crushed that he had lost the thing he cared the most about outside his family," his son said. "There was no place for him to go. Where could he go when he was the president? This is another telling story about my dad. He was offered all sorts of jobs by the companies that he had fought against all those years—lucrative jobs that would have paid him an awful lot more money than he ever made in the union. He turned all of them down because he felt it was disloyal to the United Rubber Workers to take the other side. And instead he found a lower-paying government job with the Department of Labor and that's what he did until he died." Burdon worked as a manpower development specialist for the Department of Labor and died June 17, 1972, after suffering a heart attack. He was sixty-three.

In the end, only one of the 780 delegates opposed a unanimous ballot for Bommarito. Burdon had found out that unlike many unions that were run from the top down, the officers of the URW truly were employees of the rank-and-file. "If Burdon is bitter at being sacked, he must remember that, after all, he was the employee of the men and women who work in the shops and who pay dues to the union and that they have the undisputed right to hire and fire their officers," the *Akron Beacon Journal* wrote in an editorial after the 1966 convention. "Peter Bommarito will do well to remember this fact. Also, it is extremely difficult to please 180,000 bosses and there are times when a union president must lead, rather than try to please everyone, even at the cost of his job."

The new team at the top of the URW was seen as a complementary trio, with Bommarito an expert in contract negotiations, Oldham an authority on fringe benefits, and Gold to continue as handler of the URW's purse strings. Bommarito, in his formal acceptance speech, declared that the "membership of the URW is entitled to receive, expects to receive and will receive a fair share of the profit pie." But the union must leave the conven-

Peter Bommarito (center) after winning election as URW president in 1966, along with Secretary/Treasurer Ike Gold (right) and new Vice President Kenneth Old-ham. *(USWA/URW photo files)*

tion united because the tire and rubber companies may see the disunity that the bitter race between Bommarito and Burdon brought as a golden opportunity to take advantage of the situation. "We cannot afford the luxury of complacency or the dangers inherent in disunity," he told delegates. The new leader also emphasized he would put his personal touch on the negotiations—something the rubber companies would have to look forward to for the next decade and a half. Bommarito particularly harped on the necessity for unity. "Unity is the reason for our existence," the new president said. "It is the very essence of unionism. Without unity we are all but powerless."

To George Burdon, that statement must have sounded a bit ironic coming from the vice president who had served under Burdon for six years, only to launch a bitter campaign to oust him from the presidency.

BOMMARITO THE NEGOTIATOR

It was at the bargaining table—and concurrently on the picket line—where Bommarito earned his reputation (table 3.1). At the opening of his first master contract negotiations in 1967, he moved quickly to make his presence felt. Meeting with Mike Reichow, a veteran negotiator for B. F. Goodrich, Bommarito started into a twenty-minute spiel on his ideals, the facts of the bargaining situation, and how that all related to those contract talks. But about halfway through Bommarito's round of volleys, it became apparent that Reichow was fiddling with something and not paying any

Table 3.1 Negotiating gains, 1967–78

Wage Increases
A total of $3.408 an hour.

Skilled Trades
Another 65 cents an hour above general raises.

COLA
Established in 1976 negotiations and then improved upon in 1979.

Supplemental Unemployment Benefits
Negotiated to equal 80 percent of gross pay in 1967 and then improved upon in 1976.

Pensions
Improved the benefit multiplier for future retirees by $9.25, going from $3.25 to $12.50 per month per year of service. Also negotiated an extra $3.75 per month per year of service for those already retired.

Plant Closure
Established preferential hiring in 1973 and gained 30 and out pension with improved insurance in 1976.

Safety and Health
Established Joint Occupational Health Program in 1970 and improved upon it in 1976.

Prescription Drugs
Established in 1971, attained for new retirees in 1973 and for past retirees in 1974.

Source: United Rubber Workers.

attention to the URW president. Bommarito slammed his hand down on the table and demanded to know what the BFG official was doing. Reichow looked up and said it was his hearing aid. The battery seemed to be getting weak and he wanted to replace it before the negotiations began. That being the case, he asked for a favor. He asked Bommarito to repeat everything he had just said. "He was testing to find out whether or not I'd get angry," Bommarito said. "Actually, what I did was to bust out laughing."

During his fifteen-year tenure, Bommarito and the companies had a mostly adversarial relationship—but that was expected in those days. Especially during Bommarito's early terms, both sides had roles to play and for the most part were comfortable with it. The major U.S. tire companies were doing well and had seemingly unending market share, so they could pass along higher labor costs to the consumers. The URW struck and struck often. Union members never were sure they had gotten the best possible settlement unless they hit the streets. And the companies stuck together, working much more in concert than in later years. "Their goal was to weaken the union, not so much to bust it," Bommarito said. The URW leader said negotiations could go smoothly or not, but in the end it was his job to get to the point where the company would give no more. "I can get to a rock bottom proposal," he said. "It's not hard to get there. I know what I'm going to ask for. I know what I'm going to do. I know where I'm at and I know where I'm going to end up. I can get there sooner or I can get there later."

Bommarito was an expert at putting the company negotiators on the defensive, according to Borelli. "Pete was well-respected by the Uniroyal group to the point that some of them were in awe of him, and that was surprising," Borelli said. "He was tough, very hard, not giving any. If he caught a weakness in them, he'd point it out to them, right at the table. He'd say, 'Dammit, I can't get nothing done with you. You're too weak. You can't make decisions.' And that's how he dealt with most corporate people. He was just pretty forceful."

Bommarito's endurance at the negotiating table also was legendary. "He could outlast anybody," Public Relations Director Brown said. "Those company guys couldn't stay up like he could. They'd recess or break off talks and go off and play cards for awhile; then they'd come back when they got good and ready to. I would have wanted him bargaining for me." Local 2's Jenkins witnessed some of Bommarito's marathon bargaining sessions. "Old Pete, he'd go into those negotiations and stay for twenty-four hours. He'd stay right in that room. He didn't care," Jenkins said. "He had been in this one room for, like, thirty hours, trying to get a contract. They took a recess, and the company negotiators sent this huge fruit basket in there. One of the staff guys took an apple and took a bite out of it. Pete said, 'Who the hell is eating the forbidden fruit?'"

Mike Polovick, who negotiated for three tire companies during his career, called Bommarito's negotiating a very personalized style of bargaining. "He was highly adversarial, although he apparently also was a guy who could make a deal," Polovick said. He heard a story of how Bommarito had wanted chiropractic coverage included in the 1976 master contract settlement. "The Goodyear guys told him, 'When hell freezes over,' and they didn't agree to it," Polovick said. "In 1979, the URW got that deal. It was part of the master package with B. F. Goodrich. So Bommarito kind of got right up in the guy's face at Goodyear, and said, 'Well, I guess hell just froze over.'"

Bommarito's style also brought strikes—lots of them. During each of the five master contract negotiations he oversaw, the URW struck one or more of the major tire and rubber companies. These work stoppages even had their own nicknames, being called, among other things, the "triennial passion plays," or "fun and games with the Bomber." Between 1965 and 1969, there were an average of 95 strikes in the rubber industry each year, about 30 percent more than the four years directly prior to that. That was far from the end, however. Between 1970 and 1974, the average grew to 117 strikes in the industry per year, with a high of 143 in 1973, the most in any year since 1951.

Bommarito wasted no time writing the script for the first of the "passion plays," as Rubber Workers struck three of the major tire companies for three months in 1967 and two others for less time, less than a year after Bommarito took the URW's top elected post. That number already surpassed the one notable strike during Burdon's entire time as president—a six-day strike against U.S. Rubber. During 1967 Bommarito also uncovered what he called the "unholy alliance." This setup was meant to blunt the effect of a URW strike against the target company in master contract talks. When one of the companies faced a work stoppage, the others, under this never-denied but never truly documented arrangement, would make the tires for the struck company so that firm would lose no business because of the strike. Bommarito decided the best counter to this effort was to strike more than one company at a time so none would be making tires.

So that was what the URW did in 1967. More than fifty-two thousand Rubber Workers struck Firestone, Goodrich, and Uniroyal for a little more than three months, from April 20 to July 24, with later walkouts of four weeks at General Tire and two weeks at Goodyear. At the beginning of bargaining in March, the URW said it would seek an increase in supplemental unemployment benefits, higher pay for skilled tradesmen, equal pay for tire and non-tire employees, and a "substantial wage increase." Prior to the strike, the average wage was between $3.25 to $3.35 an hour, with skilled tradesmen getting about $3.70 and tube employees about $3.65 an hour.

At the April 20 deadline, the companies had offered a raise of 23½ cents an hour over two years for tire employees, 18 cents an hour for non-tire workers, an additional 5 cents an hour for skilled tradesmen, and unspecified increases in the supplemental unemployment benefits program (SUB). Several weeks later the two sides agreed to include pensions in the negotiations—prior to that, bargaining on pensions and other benefits had been done later in the fall after contracts on the economic issues were settled. At this point the tire makers boosted the offer to a raise of thirty-eight cents an hour over three years for tire builders, thirty-one cents for non-tire employees, ten cents an hour extra for skilled tradesmen, granting SUB at 75 percent of average straight-time pay for laid-off workers, and an increase in the pension multiplier by two dollars to $5.25 per month per year of service. General Tire, which was not struck until June 2, then offered an even better package, with a raise of forty-three cents an hour in wages over three years, an 80 percent SUB package, a $5.50 pension multiplier, and an added paid holiday.

Fifty-two thousand striking members were receiving $25 a week in strike benefits, and the URW was spending about $1.5 million on these payments. At that rate the union expected to blow through its $6.5 million Strike and Defense Fund within five weeks. The URW also quickly went through a $3 million loan from the United Auto Workers union.

Bommarito called the company offers inadequate, citing a U.S. Department of Labor report that said wage settlements in major contracts were averaging a 5.8 percent increase, while the rubber company offers averaged just 3.7 percent. The companies countered by saying the pay raises exceeded most first-year increases in industrial settlements. They also defended the offers of raises of differing amounts for tire and non-tire workers because they recognized the different competitive situations of the various operations. The tire makers also pointed out that the companies offered to increase the pensions of those union workers who had retired since 1949, despite the "never, never" letter signed by the URW in 1958 saying that it would never again bargain for increased pensions for those already retired. Company negotiators argued that if the URW accepted the pact that contained the thirty-eight cents in hourly raises over three years, the union could claim its largest pay increases since 1946, when wartime price freezes were lifted and the Rubber Workers won an 18.5-cent general wage increase. The offer also was far better than the two-year contract of 1965, when the URW settled for a 7.5-cent raise the first year and 9 cents the second—a settlement that elated Burdon and other union leaders as the result of "responsible militancy."

Under the mutual aid pact—or "unholy alliance," as Bommarito dubbed it—Goodyear was building tires for the customers of Firestone, BFG, General, and Uniroyal up until the time the URW struck Goodyear as well. The five firms drafted a formula under which cash payments were delivered to the struck companies based on the number of tires involved. The Goodyear-made tires were credited to whichever struck firm held the original order, thus protecting those companies from losing customers to non-struck firms during the strike. It was not the first time the tire companies had made tires for customers of struck competitors, but it was the first time payment for the tires had gone to the companies on strike.

When it was over, the union basically won what amounted to the last offer by General Tire, taking the raise of forty-three cents an hour over three years, the $5.50 pension multiplier, an improved vacation schedule, and the 80 percent SUB plan, which would pay for as long as four years for those with twenty-five years of service. The SUB provision—in which companies put money into a fund from which laid-off workers were paid the difference between unemployment payments and 80 percent of their prior earnings—would prove to be important in ensuing years as the tire makers began laying off workers, especially at the older facilities in Akron and other parts of the United States. From July 1957 to July 1967, the Big Four tire makers paid a total of about $19.8 million in SUB benefits. But from August 1967, after it was strengthened in these negotiations, through December 1973, those same firms paid $59.8 million in benefits.

Although the gains in 1967 contract talks were substantial—hailed as the largest take to that point in the URW's thirty-one-year history—success failed to stop some from criticizing Bommarito during his first major set of master contract negotiations. "There's no question Pete is more aggressive than his predecessors, but whoever had been running the URW would have gotten this year's pattern of about 5 percent in gains set in other industry," said the head of one company bargaining team. "It's the trend of the times." The tire makers estimated that workers lost $85 million in wages during the strike. The *Akron Beacon Journal* estimated it would take the workers who had been on strike for thirteen weeks a total of twelve years to make up for the lost wages if the amount the URW had gained in the final contract were compared to the offer on the table the day the strike began. Bommarito countered the critics by noting that the newspaper did not take into account the extra $1.50 the union gained on the monthly pension multiplier for past retirees, meaning that a retiree with thirty years of service would have have his pension boosted by $45 a month. It also failed to mention the increase of $2.25 a month in the pension multiplier for future retirees, meaning an additional $67.50 a month in pension benefits for those with thirty years of service. The URW chief also said that wages in the rubber industry had not kept up with the increases in productivity. The U.S. Department of Commerce said the efficiency of the average tire worker rose more than 50 percent in the 1960s, while wages for those workers had gone up only 28 percent. During the same period, the big tire makers had seen after-tax profits jump by 63 percent.

The URW continued to make gains in 1970, this time with Rubber Workers striking target company Goodyear for fifty days and BFG for thirty-nine days. The workers received more than $1.35 an hour in increased wages and fringe benefits over the three-year contract. The wage package brought eighty-two cents an hour, with thirty cents the first year and twenty-six cents each of the remaining two years. On top of that skilled trades workers received an additional fifteen cents an hour the first year and another ten cents an hour the second. URW members also won an additional paid holiday, bringing them up to a total of ten per year, and the pension multiplier rose from $5.50 to $7.75 a month per year of service.

"The 1970 package settlement was by far the largest we have ever negotiated," Bommarito told delegates at the URW's 1970 convention later that year. "The wage increases alone amount to something over an 8 percent increase per year over the duration of the agreement and when you add in the gains made in fringe benefits, the first-year increase was over 12 percent." Bommarito also boasted about the pension gains, both for future retirees and URW members already retired. "In the last two sets of negotiations, covering a mere three-year span from 1967 to 1970, we have been successful in improving the normal pension amounts by $4.50 per month per year of service," Bommarito said. "In the period of time from 1950, when we first negotiated on pensions, up to the 1967 negotiations, we had only secured a total of $3.25 per month per year of service in that seventeen-year period." And past retirees, after seeing the monthly pension multiplier boosted $1.50 in 1967, received another increase of $1.25 in 1970. "In the last two sets of negotiations we more than doubled the pension amounts of some of our retirees," the URW president said. "We can hold our heads high with a record like this on pension benefits."

While the 1970 master contract strike against two firms was mild compared with the 1967 walkouts, the URW's militancy under Bommarito was far from over. At the time of the September 1970 convention, the union had twenty separate strike situations going on. From November 1968 until September 1970, there had been ninety-eight separate strikes initiated by URW local unions.

Bommarito, however, had a totally different battle in mind during 1970 negotiations, one that he hoped would be his legacy. In this fight, the URW chief turned his attention toward boosting the health and safety conditions in the rubber factory. In short, Bommarito hoped to find a cure for cancer.

CHAPTER 4

NEWS FLASH

BOMMARITO WANTS TO CURE CANCER

Pete Bommarito had a dream as president of the United Rubber Workers. He truly hoped that one day he would help find a cure for cancer. He had been around rubber and tire product manufacturing plants long enough to know that something was wrong. Workers were exposed to countless numbers of chemicals and made to toil in hot, unventilated factories. The URW president also noticed that Rubber Workers seemed to get cancer and other diseases—some he could not even pronounce—in disproportionate numbers. Bommarito had no data or hard facts to back up his assumption, but in his gut he knew it had something to do with their working environment.

He wanted to do something about it, not only for himself and future workers in the plants, but also for all the past workers who had died before their time. "As a young man, prior to World War II, I worked in conditions which were deplorable—heat, noise, exposures to solvents and chemicals," Bommarito said. "I felt these were conditions of employment that I had to tolerate—yes, tolerate and accept if I wanted a job. As an ex-Marine returning to the same plant after the war, I encountered the same conditions. I saw my fellow workers dismembered, seriously injured, completely disabled, unable to work to either support themselves or their families. I saw others with serious lung problems, who had difficulty breathing, skin problems that were disabling, and others who had serious health problems which forced them to either leave the plant or seek employment elsewhere if they were healthy enough to find a job. Those who were not able to work were literally out on the street."

URW members in both tire and non-tire plants alike can provide anecdote after anecdote about the horrendous conditions they faced at times. Don Weber started work in 1947 at the Goodyear tire plant in Topeka, Kansas, where his father was a foreman. In the curing room the tires came out of the old watch-case presses at three hundred degrees. When Goodyear built onto the facility, it cut off the air flow from the south to that area of the plant. "Under the union contract, with the safety and health clause, they're supposed to provide us with a safe place," Weber said. "They said they couldn't give us any more fans or any more relief. So I hung a thermometer around my neck and got several other guys to do it, to keep building a case. That was about 1953. We were working in 110, 115, 120 degrees. Over in the big pits—the truck and tractor tire areas—they were running 125, 130 degrees." Kansas can get hot in the summertime, with temperatures above 100 not unusual. Weber and URW Local 307 took all of their readings and filed a grievance through the normal process. The union won the case at arbitration, with the company told to put more fans in.

Patrick Warlow said the decades-long fight to organize Local 88 at Kaufman Footwear in Kitchener, Ontario, was worth it just for the gains made in health and safety alone. "People were breathing in chemicals there that no one knew what they were," Warlow said. He also saw workers washing off boots made at the plant with toluene, holding the rag in their bare hands. "It was going down their hair and down their face," he said. "And the carbon black! Guys would come to lunch to eat their sandwich and their sandwich was black from carbon black." After the URW local was in place, if someone had a complaint, rather than risk being fired if they brought it up, it went to a health and safety committee for investigation. "There are too many things that can happen without protection," Warlow said.

At the General Tire (later GenCorp) facility in Wabash, Indiana, it seemed that many of the workers died young of cancer, according to Annalee Benedict, who served twenty years as treasurer of Local 626 at the plant before retiring in 1996. "There were hundreds of people who had cancer," said Benedict of the local that at one time employed about fifteen hundred hourly workers. "We've always thought it had something to do with what we had to work with. There were times when the company—we called it Generous General Tire—would tear the labels off these barrels so we couldn't even check to see what was in there. They were big, round, heavy cardboard barrels. You could see where the labels were torn off. Had we known what we do today, we could have saved a lot of people's lives." Benedict herself developed an incurable lung disease that she had to live with for many years. "I know it came from there because I never smoked a pack of cigarettes in my entire life," she said.

Contractual language regarding health and safety issues was vague and broad in nature during the URW's early years. Often, the safety and health measures became items of concessions, given up for more tangible, short-term monetary gains. But Bommarito hoped to change that. During the 1970 master contract negotiations he got the companies to pay a half-cent an hour to fund a Joint Occupational Health and Safety Program. While that hardly sounded like much money (later negotiations boosted the amount per hour), when multiplied by all the hours worked by all the URW members covered by the master pact, it created enough money for the union and companies to start up the program, which had to be run through an established school of public health.

Besides negotiations for the funds and the program, the next important step Bommarito made with regard to improving health and safety was recruiting Louis Beliczky as the first full-time industrial hygienist hired by an industrial union in the United States. During the decade they worked together, Bommarito and Beliczky formed a mutual admiration society dedicated to one thing: improving the health and working conditions of URW members. "I was really in the trenches from the beginning of my involvement from 1971 when I officially joined the URW," Beliczky said. "I was involved in all negotiations with target companies. I wrote a lot of the language that was presented at the policy meeting for each of the negotiations." And he clearly was respectful of Bommarito, who over the years became more than an employer, a true friend of Beliczky's. "Pete Bommarito was one of the few men who I've ever met who were true leaders and recognized as such in the industry," he said.

Beliczky really did not come to the union as much as the union came to him. He had actually had some exposure to the rubber industry and the URW dating back to the mid-1960s. As president of the local section of the American Industrial Hygiene Association, he had paid a visit to local union members and toured a Firestone plant in Akron. "I thought to myself, 'These guys have a good union. They get paid eight hours for working seven hours and have all kinds of benefits,'" Beliczky said. He actually came very close to joining rubber company management in 1965. He was employed by a consulting group when he got calls from Firestone and B. F. Goodrich, both of which were looking for industrial hygienists.

Louis Beliczky, the URW's industrial hygienist, is sworn in as a member of the U.S. Department of Labor's Standards Advisory Committee on Hazardous Materials Labeling. Beliczky was the first full-time industrial hygienist hired by a union in the U.S. *(USWA/URW photo files)*

After interviewing with both companies, Beliczky received a call from the director of industrial medicine at the Euclid Clinic Foundation, a prestigious organization. "He called me at eight that night and said, 'Welcome, partner. You are now a partner at the Euclid Clinic Foundation.' I felt good about that. I was the only non-M.D. in the clinic setting." As it turned out, the foundation director called just in time. About forty-five minutes later, the BFG corporate director of industrial hygiene called to offer a job, but Beliczky had to turn him down.

Beliczky stayed at the clinic for five years, but found that working mainly for companies was not necessarily what he was looking for in his career. He especially saw what the working world was like during two consulting jobs that involved people exposed to asbestos. "When I was completed and finished my report and sent them my bill, they said, 'Okay, Mr. Beliczky, how about writing a report for the workers?' I said, 'What do you mean?' They replied, 'What you wrote here really says that these workers are at risk. But if you write another one, we'll pay you for that report too.' And I told them, 'There's no way I can do that. That's being unprofessional.' And at that point I decided that [for] all the studies I'd done for government, NASA, industry, and the Department of Defense, probably what really happens is that when I finish the report and I hand it to them they put it in a file and they lock it, and probably it never gets to the point of getting to the workers."

It was at this time that the URW had negotiated for the health and safety program and was looking for someone to head up the research programs. Beliczky got a call from the URW's safety director, who had been directed to Beliczky by a hygienist at the Industrial Commission of Ohio. Beliczky thought he might bring the program into the umbrella of the Euclid Clinic Foundation, so he and Dr. Otto Price from the foundation came to Akron to meet with the URW's three International officers: Bommarito, Vice President Kenneth Oldham and Secretary/Treasurer Ike Gold. At that meeting Dr. Price and Gold soon got into a discussion about company doctors. "Pete Bommarito, interestingly enough, had a tablet that was cross-hatched with squares," Beliczky said. "He was making X's. He was bored by this entire procedure and discussion."

It was at this point that Bommarito turned the discussion in another direction, and with it the direction of Beliczky's career. "Dr. Price, tell me about thrombocytopenia," Bommarito asked. Dr. Price had no answer for him, so the URW president turned to Beliczky. "Fortunately, I'd been involved in a project out in California," Beliczky said. "I said, 'It's a disease of idiopathic origin, which means they don't know what causes it. It can lead to damage of bone marrow and leukemia, and can affect the spleen.'" So Bommarito asked for Beliczky's home phone number and started a full-court press to hire the hygienist. This was just before Thanksgiving, and every week or two Bommarito called Beliczky and started negotiating on salary. Beliczky was no negotiator at the time, and thought he had no business haggling at the same table with one of labor's best-known negotiators. At Christmas, Bommarito called and talked about both money and benefits. Because of his large family, Beliczky especially was interested in the benefits. "The first week of January, he calls me and says, 'I want you in Akron next week,'" Beliczky said. "I said, 'Mr. Bommarito, I can't do that. I have contracts with industry. I have commitments. I can't leave and I won't be done until maybe March.' He said, 'I have to have you before then.'" Beliczky won, and started with the URW on March 20, 1971, after completing the projects to which he was already committed. Deep down, Beliczky could not quite figure out why Bommarito seemed so enamored with him. "I didn't know if he'd really interviewed anyone or not."

When Beliczky went to Akron, he went to Bommarito's office and the URW chief, sitting behind his big desk, dug into one of his drawers, pulled out a file about a foot thick, and told Beliczky, "Here, it's yours. This is what you have to do." The prime function at the time for the labor movement's first full-time industrial hygienist was to implement a program at a school of public health where an epidemiological study could be conducted. "That was a pretty big responsibility," Beliczky said. "Although I'd spent a good deal of time in industry, I was not fully aware of how they made rubber tires and rubber products. Nor did I really know what the state of the health of workers was in those plants."

Beliczky first put together a questionnaire that he sent to every URW local in the United States and Canada. He asked about their perception of health and safety problems, and about procedural things such as whether or not the local had a safety committee. The contract the union signed stipulated that the program had to be run through a "school of public health," so Beliczky also had to find prospective universities to house the study. Since he had graduated from the University of Pittsburgh's School of Public Health and worked with the school's Dr. Thomas Mancuso, who was director of the state board of health and in charge of occupational medicine, he went there first. It was Mancuso who had helped spark Bommarito's interest in occupational health through an epidemiological study of the rubber industry in 1965–66. Bommarito himself wanted to set up an Occupational Health Research Institute. "When (Bommarito) worked in Detroit, he knew that people became ill, and he was aware of some of the cancers that were there," Beliczky said. "In 1967, Bommarito had the URW send out its own questionnaire to all local unions. The results showed a lot of illnesses and diseases, cancers and leukemia." Armed with those survey results, Bommarito wanted to set up some kind of contract language to take to 1970 collective bargaining. Dr. Mancuso served as technical adviser. "When it came to the point where the rock and the hard place came together in bargaining, it was put in total stalemate because of this program," Beliczky said. "Dr. Mancuso sort of gave up" and told Bommarito he did not think he could sell the program and that he thought the union was going about it the wrong way. "Pete said, 'I'll handle this by myself.' Pete learned to pronounce big words, like thrombocytopenia. He really educated himself." During negotiations—where Uniroyal was the target— Bommarito spoke with the firm's corporate medical director, who convinced Uniroyal that the program had merit.

Despite this background, Beliczky still wanted to be loyal to his alma mater and met with Dr. Mancuso. He spent a lot of time with Mancuso and asked if Mancuso would share some of the information he had learned during the epidemiological study of the rubber industry. "He said, 'Only if I'm in charge of the project. Otherwise, I will not share my information,'" according to Beliczky. "I said, 'Dr. Mancuso, will you please repeat that?' And he did. And I shook his hand and walked out."

Beliczky therefore had to look elsewhere for a place to house the joint URW/rubber company program. Two candidates were the University of North Carolina's School of Public Health and the Harvard School of Public Health. Beliczky had worked with people from both schools. "There always had been an adversarial relationship in corporate management between Goodyear and BFG," Beliczky said. "Each company visited both places. Goodyear decided that they liked UNC. BFG decided that if Goodyear's going to be there, they were going to go to Harvard." So BFG signed a memorandum of understanding between the URW and Harvard. They were joined in that program by Armstrong Rubber Co. and Mansfield Tire & Rubber. Meanwhile, Goodyear, Uniroyal, Firestone, and General Tire went to UNC.

"One of the things that was nice about Pete Bommarito was, he assigned me this big stack of information and outlined my responsibility," Beliczky said. "But more or less, he let me do my own thing." From then on Beliczky spent a lot of time working with both universities. Each school conducted a walk-through study of the rubber industry. "They familiarized themselves with potential health risks and began an epidemiological study," Beliczky said. "They also went through all the data available from

Social Security records, death certificates, and autopsies to find causes of death."

From 1971 to 1975, each university put together formal studies and began publishing technical papers in prestigious journals. All information was shared with the local unions and the companies, with the URW not allowed to release anything to the press without approval of the corporations. "Nothing at this level had ever been conducted anywhere, involving not just one company but the six or seven big companies in the rubber industry that were organized by the URW," Beliczky said. "From it came the world's largest depository of information that related to the health of workers in the rubber industry. And not only about mortality, but also morbidity." The universities also evaluated in-plant conditions, taking air samples and finding out what was in some of the chemicals.

The studies found a high and significant incidence of cancer. They showed that rubber workers were at high risk for many types of cancer— gastrointestinal, pancreatic, lung, prostate, bladder, skin, brain, lymphatic, and leukemia. The researchers were able to relate incidents of illness or cancer to a particular operation or department. But what became trickier was that in the rubber industry, like other industries, the workers had exposure not just to a single chemical in their lifetime of exposure. Instead, they had multiple exposure over twenty or more years of employment, and the chemicals in use also changed over time. "Pete Bommarito felt very strongly that what this study was going to do was find out what the causes of cancer were," Beliczky said. "And maybe from that point exactly which chemical produced what cancers."

By 1979 it was apparent that the next step of the Joint Occupational Health & Safety Program had to be the implementation of a personal health surveillance program. Beliczky was given the full authority by the locals and the URW advisory board to handle that aspect of the contract negotiations. Goodyear locals were the only chain in the union that refused to participate in the surveillance program. "There was an internal problem or something political as it related to Pete Bommarito and the Goodyear locals," Beliczky said. "When I joined the URW and sat in negotiations with Goodyear, they felt that I was Pete's representative. I wasn't treated with the same understanding by Goodyear locals as I was by all the other locals."

Besides the programs that were put into place, Beliczky said the URW was also helpful in writing standards on specific chemicals such as benzene and vinyl chloride. He went to Washington, D.C., two or three times a month for several years, helping to work on these issues. After the union was successful in negotiating for a full-time health and safety representative to be paid by the major companies in each local, Beliczky was also able to develop a group of well-trained local union people who worked hard to learn as much as possible. "Some of them certainly were better informed than their counterparts at the local plant management level," he said. "The URW recognized that health and safety was a big issue. If the URW is recognized for anything among its leadership, it's not only the economic issues."

While Beliczky spent much of his time with the universities developing the program or in Washington working on new standards, he may have made his biggest impact at the plant level. He tried to spend as much time as possible helping the smaller locals. If they had a problem they could not resolve or did not understand, Beliczky would visit the facility and try to find answers by working with the local management and local union. "We got a lot of situations resolved that may otherwise not have been," he said. One of his first plant visits was to a rubber factory in Massachusetts. When he was finished, Beliczky made it a point to visit with the plant manager or a corporate representative. At this particular facility, the manager asked a question Beliczky would hear more than once in his career: "'Well Mr. Beliczky, are you going to shut me down?' I would say, 'That's not my responsibility to close a plant. It's my responsibility to keep the plant open and protect the health and safety of the worker.'"

Beliczky always tried to go through the proper channels. He did not want companies to think he was trying to pull a fast one on them or catch them just for the sake of punishment. To him, the goal of worker safety was a noble one, and both labor and management should work together in achieving a safe working environment. But if a firm refused to cooperate, he could play a little hardball of his own. For example, on his trip to the former Firestone tire plant in Los Angeles, he and Julian "Spike" Evans, president of the local, were supposed to tour the facility together. Beliczky had received permission from corporate headquarters to visit the factory, but the corporate director of safety was not at the plant. "I went in with this little camera and said, 'You wouldn't mind if I took pictures in your plant?' That's when it all broke loose." The company personnel man told him that no one was to take unapproved photographs, and Beliczky was denied entrance. Beliczky and Evans drove to the federal office of the Occupational Safety & Health Administration and requested an inspection. "I told them I had been refused entry into the plant," Beliczky said. "OSHA spent one month at that plant. After that, I was never kept from going into a facility."

With the coming of OSHA, Beliczky did see improvements. Plants with a mixing or compounding area had proper ventilation, and there were changes in the kinds of chemicals used. He also saw a definite shift in attitude among the more enlightened plant managers. Beliczky also was pleased at how seriously the URW health and safety representatives at each facility took their jobs. "These guys were self-trained and self-educated. Some of them went to schools, some went on to get degrees," he said. "Now some work for the federal government. It was a dedication on their part."

For Beliczky personally, joining the URW worked out more than well. "I knew I was helping someone and I could motivate people to initiate change." And it was gratifying to see other industrial unions following the URW's lead by hiring professionally trained hygienists. Of course, the companies never cooperated on all levels. Whenever a new federal standard was proposed on a specific chemical, the companies' normal game plan included putting up a tough wall of resistance. "In order to fight a federal standard, like the one on benzene, millions of dollars were spent on lobbying," Beliczky said. "If (companies) spent that on prevention, they probably wouldn't have had the problems that face them today."

Eagle-Picher Industries even tried to sue Beliczky and the URW after an article in the *United Rubber Worker* newspaper said that the firm had no health and safety programs in place at its Joplin, Missouri, plant and that the company did not care. The facility made lead, which at one time was an ingredient in the manufacture of rubber. He said the concentrations of lead in the factory were so high it was unbelievable. But what was more incredible to Beliczky was that the workers did not want to do anything about it because they were afraid to lose their pension and medical benefits. "That fear of losing their job and the pension that they worked so hard for (was so great) that they didn't want to rock the boat," he said. "Their ventilation was such that if they did have any it would go out the stack and circle as red compounds. The roofs of all the plants there, the sidewalks, and the streets were all red from the lead that they had."

Although Beliczky continued to work for the URW under Mike Stone and Kenneth Coss after Bommarito retired, the hygienist never felt the program had the impact or received the same priority it did during the early years under Bommarito. "We were very close friends," Beliczky said of the man who hired him. "There was a special trust between us. I recognized his ability. I was sort of his protégé. I respected him for what he did and what he was trying to do. It was a good opportunity for someone with a good background and who was objective—and I was always objective. I was criticized for not being objective, but I was." He also dismissed suggestions by others that he could have made more money elsewhere and that he would have done things differently. "I could never prostitute myself," he said. "As an industrial hygienist you are supposed to be ethical and not look at the signature at the bottom of the paycheck."

One thing that bothered Beliczky to some degree was that he and Bommarito did not complete the task they started. "We can isolate certain chemicals," he said. "We know that they produce the disease. We can isolate additives that go into the manufacture of rubber and know that they're cancer producers." But they did not know enough about the effect of adding temperature, steam, water, heat and other variables into the equation. And what happened when the individual chemicals were used in a mixing operation to develop a totally different compound? "Pete really felt that you would find a cause for cancer, and he really felt you'd find a cure for cancer," Beliczky said.

Jim Frederick tried to pick up where Beliczky left off. He was hired in August 1994, a little more than a year after Beliczky retired, and stayed on with the United Steelworkers after the merger. He observed that the health and safety improvements made in plants over the past two to three decades had been significant. "Certainly the employers have done a lot of the work to make improvements in the conditions," Frederick said. "Who knows what the speed of those changes would have been if it weren't for what the URW had done over the last thirty years?" He also found it interesting that some of the questions that existed in 1970 when the Rubber Workers made its initial push still remained unanswered. "What's causing cancer to the membership? Are our members at a higher risk of disease than the general population? Those couple of questions still exist today and although they have been partially answered by some of the research, those questions that remain are a real concern," he said. "As those conditions changed over those thirty years, a lot of the chemicals and compounds in the plants have changed, as well as the exposure to the workers. There are things we use now that we don't have a lot of information about. Lou and the URW and the local unions got some of the companies to get rid of some of the bad actors, but they brought in some things that we don't have a good idea what kind of actor they are."

EXTERNAL BATTLES: FIGHTING MULTINATIONALS AND IMPORTS

During the first half of the 1970s, both the union and the North American companies began coming to a realization: the world of business was changing forever. No longer could the domestic tire firms that had always dominated the U.S. and Canadian markets count on the region as theirs and theirs alone. No longer could those companies fall back on their normal business practice of giving up large labor settlements and just passing those costs on to consumers. Many of the top-tier tire and rubber companies—and most of the second- and lower-tier tire firms—had operated their tire businesses as cash cows. They had reaped the profits but failed to reinvest enough back into existing operations.

Much of the problem with the tire and rubber product trade deficit can be traced to two factors: the radial tire and the rise of multinational corporations. As foreign tire makers began to make some inroads into U.S. markets with the higher-technology radial tires, most of the U.S. producers initially held steadfastly to the soon-to-be disappearing bias-belt tire. Even when BFG tried to push the radial tire in the United States, Goodyear and others instead opted for an intermediate product: the belted bias tire, which could be made on existing tire-building machinery, thus delaying the tremendous capital outlay needed to change to radial technology.

"The problem of foreign imports is indeed a complex one—it often involves more than one country exporting to or importing from another," Bommarito said. "In many cases today the problem we are facing arises from the activity of what are called 'multinational firms,'" or huge enterprises with offices and plants in many parts of the world. Many companies will have parts produced in low-wage countries, ship the components to another country to be assembled, and then export the finished product to the United States and sell it at a large profit. "The result for the firm is higher profits; for the foreign countries higher employment and accompanying prosperity; and for some American workers the result is unemployment," Bommarito said. Compounding the problem, the United States for years had been lowering its tariffs while other countries during this period placed restrictions on the importation of American goods. Bommarito quoted Secretary of Commerce Maurice Stans, who said, "in many respects we have been Uncle Sucker to the rest of the world."

The shifts in trade patterns also caused a shift in the views of labor leaders on international trade. Trade unions traditionally had favored a trade policy along the lines of free trade. But as the unionists saw unemployment rise and as they perceived that multinationals were exporting jobs rather than products, the unions became more and more protectionist in nature. Protection included supporting such legislation as the Burke-Hartke trade legislation of 1972, a liberal package of protectionist measures that attempted to establish quotas that would have rolled back imports by 40 percent and increased the tax burdens of the overseas operations of U.S. corporations. Sponsored by Rep. James Burke (D-Mass.) and Sen. Vance Hartke (D-Ind.), the extremist measure had little chance of passing Congress, but URW President Bommarito still jumped into the middle of the fray, battling corporate leaders on a different playing field. In an Akron Area Chamber of Commerce survey of seventeen multinational companies in the Akron area, the firms claimed Burke-Hartke would cause them to eliminate sixty-five hundred area jobs, 10.6 percent of their combined workforce. The area's Big Four tire makers—Goodyear, Firestone, BFG and General Tire—would account for roughly half of the lost area jobs. The URW countered with a study published by the AFL-CIO, which alleged foreign trade between 1966 and 1969 had produced the equivalent of a net loss of five hundred thousand American jobs. Labor could see that the situation was only likely to get worse. In 1971, the year prior to Burke-Hartke, the United States suffered a $2 billion trade deficit, its first shortfall in decades. The news was even worse for the first four months of 1972, when the nation's trade deficit reached $2.2 billion, already surpassing the mark for the entire previous year.

Bommarito and the Rubber Workers also volunteered to hold the first of what was to be a nationwide series of "Save Our Jobs" rallies aimed at pushing for passage of the Burke-Hartke legislation. Bommarito and other labor leaders railed against the trade policies of the United States and the business practices of the multinationals. "The United States stands almost alone as a free trade nation," Bommarito said. "Other nations have set up barriers to block U.S. goods. This is not free trade, nor is it fair trade. Why is it that only in the U.S. is it considered unfriendly to set up some import standards to protect our jobs here at home?" He detailed how in the past ten years more than thirty-two thousand rubber-related jobs had been lost, with ten thousand of those in Akron. "The very real threat of rising imports means fewer U.S. facilities and fewer jobs," Bommarito said. "The worker is, of course, the one who takes the brunt of these actions. So many U.S. corporations are multinational firms interested largely in profit, and they can, have, and will move their facilities. The average worker cannot do this."

Everything went well with the rally except for one small detail: hardly anyone showed up. Organizers had expected all the members from around the Akron area—a city already hurting from rubber industry job losses—to fill the four-thousand-seat gymnasium hosting the event. But published reports estimated the actual attendance at just five hundred, and many of those left as the speeches dragged on. It was clear that the working man's attention was not captured by a legislative issue that would go nowhere.

Despite this apathy, the problems for the URW involving international trade and multinationals would only get worse, as became clear by studying the trade track record of two areas where URW workers lost jobs: tires and footwear.

The domestic tire industry had long been the personal playground of U.S. manufacturers. While U.S. tire companies for years had been building plants abroad in an effort to increase their share of the world tire market, they had not seen such an assault on their home field. In 1963, for example, imports accounted for less than 2 percent of the domestic tire market and by 1965 the imports still held just a 3 percent market share. But then the foreign tire makers started making inroads. Imports held almost 8 percent of the U.S. market in 1965 and 9 percent in 1970. In terms of value, the total value of all imported tires in 1960 was just $10 million, but a decade later that figure had grown to roughly $300 million (tables 4.1 and 4.2).

The URW viewed each imported tire as a lost job opportunity. The union used a formula developed by a Goodyear director of corporate business planning and research, who determined that each million auto and truck tires imported into the United States from abroad meant a corresponding loss of 457 U.S. tire industry jobs. According to the URW, the

Table 4.1 Passenger Tire Imports, 1971–81

| (figures in thousands of units) | | | | |
Year	Domestic Shipments	Imports	U.S. Market	% Imports
1971	135,009	7,974	142,983	5.6
1972	141,295	10,397	151,692	6.9
1973	142,002	12,229	154,231	7.9
1974	123,460	11,637	135,097	8.6
1975	122,956	9,940	132,896	7.5
1976	123,000	12,643	135,643	9.3
1977	129,283	13,078	142,361	9.2
1978	135,211	12,925	148,136	8.7
1979	121,922	15,160	137,082	11.1
1980	106,912	13,743	120,655	11.4
1981	125,263	17,487	142,750	12.3

Sources: U.S. General Imports, Schedule A (FT135), Dept. of Commerce; Rubber Manufacturers Association; U.S. Dept. of Commerce Report No. IM-146.

19.4 million tires imported in 1970 accounted for 8,900 lost job opportunities. And when 23 million tires were imported in 1971, that represented 10,600 lost job opportunities. And as imports began taking a larger share of the North American tire market, France's Groupe Michelin did what the top U.S. companies had started years earlier—it brought production to where the business was. With the U.S. tire producers negligent in switching to radials, Michelin—the worldwide leader in radial technology at the time—first built plants in Nova Scotia in Canada, then in the mid-1970s began production in the southern United States. While Bommarito expressed delight that it would now be U.S. workers making the Michelin tires, neither the URW nor other unions in Canada were ever successful in organizing any of the Michelin factories in North America.

By 1975 the URW was starting to see the increase in imports truly translated into job layoffs. In 1973, imports had captured nearly 11 percent of the domestic tire market. Worse yet, from 1965 to 1973 imports had skyrocketed at an average annual rate of 26 percent, while domestic shipments rose by only 5 percent a year. Even in 1975, when a recession had taken hold and domestic shipments of automotive tires had dropped 14.6 percent, imports still ran 2 percent ahead of 1973 totals. The major exporters of tires to the United States were West Germany, France, Italy, Spain, Canada

Table 4.2 Truck/Bus Tire Imports, 1971–81

| (figures in thousands of units) | | | | |
Year	Domestic Shipments	Imports	U.S. Market	% Imports
1971	18,358	1,516	19,874	7.6
1972	20,102	1,945	22,047	8.8
1973	22,866	2,478	25,344	9.8
1974	21,299	2,097	23,396	9.0
1975	19,751	1,686	21,437	7.9
1976	22,282	3,562	25,844	13.8
1977	25,912	4,093	30,005	13.6
1978	29,982	4,259	34,241	12.4
1979	28,859	4,772	33,631	14.2
1980	24,359	4,255	28,614	14.9
1981	28,453	3,908	32,361	12.1

Sources: U.S. General Imports, Schedule A (FT135), Dept. of Commerce; Rubber Manufacturers Association; U.S. Dept. of Commerce Report No. IM-146.

and Japan, nations that all had much higher duties on tires than the 4 percent tariff the United States charged at the time.

By 1975, about 20 percent of the URW's U.S. membership was laid off, with others working short workweeks or living through extended plant shutdowns because of lack of work. URW members at the five Uniroyal tire plants were hit hardest. At the time of the 1973 negotiations, these locals had about nine thousand members, but by 1975 more than thirty-three hundred of the hourly workers were laid off, including one thousand of twenty-six hundred at Local 101 in Detroit, Bommarito's home local. Other major tire makers were not hit quite as hard as Uniroyal, which was more dependent than the others on the automotive business in Detroit, but they still made substantial cutbacks. Firestone had about two thousand, or 12 percent, of its seventeen thousand production workers on layoff. Goodyear was about the same overall, but laid off 27 percent of its workers at Local 131 in Los Angeles and 18 percent at Local 878 in Union City, Tennessee. Goodrich had heavy layoffs at three factories. "The U.S., weakened by the deepest economic crisis since the 1930s and suffering massive unemployment, is in no position to cut its tariffs," the URW told the International Trade Commission (ITC). "The U.S. now has a tariff structure generally lower than that of our trading partners, the result of which has been an influx of imports. For the U.S. to seek out additional tariff cutting will only increase the stream of imported goods and feed on the recession at a time when the country is struggling with programs aimed at reversing the decline."

By 1980, the URW had filed twelve petitions for Federal Trade Adjustment Assistance under the Trade Act of 1974 for workers in the Akron area alone. Trade Adjustment Assistance was a federal program to help U.S. workers who became totally or partially unemployed as a result of increased imports. It provided eligible workers with trade readjustment allowances during periods of unemployment or underemployment. At that point, Firestone had gone from having 3,011 active production employees in Akron in December 1976 to about 200 after the company announced in October 1980 that it was closing Akron's Plant 1, making 1,345 workers jobless. Goodyear dropped from 5,255 active production workers in December 1975 to fewer than 3,500 in September 1980, with another 770 on layoff. And General Tire went from 1,533 hourly employees in Akron in November 1978 to just 1,042 active workers in June 1980, with 487 on layoff.

While URW members in tire plants were hit hard by the impact of international trade and offshore production, union members at footwear factories fared even worse. Footwear production workers never made up a large percentage of URW members. With tire locals dominating the URW for most of its history, locals at footwear plants represented a smaller niche of workers. But footwear plants meant something from a historical, symbolic standpoint. Before the automotive industry took off and brought the tire business with it to the land of prosperity, footwear was one of the dominant products for the rubber industry, made in factories in New Jersey, Rhode Island, Connecticut, and other states. The eastern region of the country dominated rubber production before the industry discovered Akron. It was in the East that many footwear operations flourished until companies found that the labor-intensive products were prime targets for manufacture in low-wage countries.

The URW believed that multinational corporations helped destroy the U.S. footwear industry. The companies that shuttered plants in the United States were mainly the same firms that began dumping their products into the domestic market from low-wage countries. In 1955 imports of shoes held a 5 percent share of the U.S. market. By 1970 the market share for

Table 4.3 Footwear Trade Deficit

(thousands of pairs of rubber-soled, canvas-upper footwear)

Year	Domestic Shipments	Imports	Exports	% Imports of U.S. Market
1964	162,151	29,063	225	15.2
1965	165,741	33,363	195	16.8
1966	157,491	35,060	167	18.2
1967	153,656	44,659	211	22.5
1968	152,257	49,200	239	24.5
1969	140,575	44,463	195	24.5
1970	145,865	49,726	129	25.4
1971	156,489	62,872	112	28.7
1972	159,399	58,020	105	26.7
1973	148,575	66,291	29	30.9
1974	144,496	67,352	*	31.8
1975	129,002	73,083	*	36.2
1976	119,726	115,399	*	49.1
1977	91,230	105,610	*	53.7

Sources: U.S. Bureau of the Census; U.S. Department of Commerce; Rubber Manufacturers Association.
  *RMA no longer collected data because number was too small.

imports jumped to 36 percent and by 1971 surpassed half the market. At the same time, exports of shoes dropped from 4.6 million pairs in 1955 to 2 million pairs in 1971. From 1966 to 1971, 250 shoe factories shut down in the United States. Of 240,000 jobs in the industry in 1968, by 1974 roughly two-thirds had moved to other countries. Hourly wages in the countries that received the work averaged twenty-three cents in Taiwan, sixty cents in Japan, fifty-six cents in Spain, and $1.25 in Italy, compared to the $2.95 an hour the shoe workers made in the United States. In early 1970 the URW prepared a petition on behalf of the workers of URW Local 224 at the Uniroyal footwear plant in Woonsocket, Rhode Island, for Federal Trade Adjustment Assistance. It was the first such petition granted in the footwear industry, but it would not be the last. More than twenty URW-organized footwear factories were certified for assistance by 1978.

One group that typified the plight of footwear production workers was URW Local 45 in Naugatuck, Connecticut. The plant struggled and struggled to hold onto the operation, but in the end it was of no use. Located in a town of fewer than twenty-five thousand, the facility had long been a mainstay of the Naugatuck Valley. At one point the footwear plant employed six thousand workers. Local 45 President James T. Nardello was the fourth generation of his family to work at the Uniroyal operation there. The local took a moratorium on wage increases in both 1970 and 1973 negotiations, and while their wages remained stagnant, the cost-of-living jumped by 36 percent from 1970 to 1975. They also elected not to take any fringe benefit improvements in 1973 negotiations. It was clear the operation was in trouble. In 1965, when imports controlled just 17 percent of the domestic footwear markets, there were more than forty-four hundred production employees in Naugatuck. A decade later that number had dropped to twenty-seven hundred.

Nardello made every effort to save jobs in his local. In testimony before a committee conducting hearings on trade negotiations, Nardello stressed that government assistance was not the answer. "We are willing to compete with anybody on the market, calling an apple an apple, or a tennis shoe a tennis shoe, but we can't compete with these shoes that are coming in from the Far East when they are selling for probably three or four dollars less a pair," Nardello said. "We don't feel that assistance is the answer. We feel jobs are the answer. We come from a pretty proud area. We would rather work for our money. We don't feel that the government should be paying our bills. We figure, give us eight hours, we will make our own money." He also described how many of the workforce had very few options if they lost their jobs. About 30 percent were over forty-five years old, two-thirds were women, six hundred were black, and five hundred were Spanish-speaking—all groups that were having trouble finding jobs during the recession. Many at the plant had nearly thirty years of service or more.

Nardello even wrote a letter in December 1976 to President-elect Jimmy Carter. He explained how it was in Naugatuck that Charles Goodyear had first vulcanized rubber in the 1800s, thereby giving birth to the process that made the vast rubber industry possible. He told Carter how Local 45 had just been notified that Uniroyal planned to move boot production from Naugatuck to Scotland, meaning a loss of two hundred jobs. "We are not looking for programs or aid after we lose jobs," Nardello wrote to Carter. "We are not looking for unemployment compensation or welfare. All we want is to keep the work here and our jobs." Unfortunately, all of Nardello's efforts did nothing to prevent the inevitable. In April 1977 Uniroyal followed movement of the boot production with an announcement that it would lay off 45 percent of the Naugatuck employees, with some of that production moving overseas. A year later, in April 1978, Uniroyal notified workers it was closing all production in Naugatuck, leaving just a warehouse. The Naugatuck facility joined other shuttered Uniroyal footwear plants in Mishawaka, Indiana, and Woonsocket, Rhode Island, along with the scores of other footwear plants that had shut down in the past fifteen years.

Labor leaders, along with the workers who lost jobs, blamed imports for the death of a domestic industry. By 1972, imports accounted for about 27 percent of apparent U.S. footwear consumption. The foreign penetration grew to 31 percent in 1973, 32 percent in 1974, 36 percent in 1979, 49 percent in 1976, and a whopping 54 percent in 1977 (table 4.3). And no help was forthcoming from the federal government. In February 1976, the U.S. ITC unanimously found that imports had caused substantial injury to the domestic shoe industry, but President Gerald Ford decided against imposing restrictions on imports. He said restraints on foreign footwear would be contrary to the U.S. policy of promoting an open, fair world economic system. Apparently Ford had no policy on trying to keep jobs in the United States.

INTERNAL BATTLES: FIGHTING WITHIN THE URW

While Bommarito and the URW struggled with the trade problem, the URW president also faced problems within his own union from those who began to doubt the Bomber's abilities. The problems showed yet another time how the Rubber Workers were tough on their leaders, even those loved and admired as much as Bommarito.

One battle was with the union's own 116-member URW Staff Representation Association. The association represented members of the URW staff, including field representatives, assistant department heads, time study engineers, auditors, education representatives, and special representatives, in its bargaining with the URW International. During this 1972 dispute, Bommarito butted heads with Leonard Bruder and Gilbert Laws, president and vice president, respectively, of the staff union. The disagreement got so heated that the staff union actually filed unfair labor practices charges against the URW with the National Labor Relations Board (NLRB) in the United States and the Office of Conciliation Services in Canada. The charges stemmed from bargaining limits contained within the URW constitution. Under URW bylaws, such things as salary and expenses for staff association members were set by delegates to the union's conventions. The constitution also provided for a mandatory twelve-month probationary period and allowed no final and binding arbitration of grievances—something the URW demanded from the companies it negotiated with. During the September 1972 URW Convention, delegates narrowly defeated an amendment that would have given the staff associa-tion the authority to negotiate directly with the URW officers concerning issues contained in the unfair labor practice charges filed by the staff union. Field representatives at the time earned $13,000 a year, with addi-tional expenses averaging $3,000 annually.

"Salaries and expenses aren't necessarily the problem," Bruder said. "It's the right to bargain on all issues. We can bargain, but only within limits. The charges were filed only after a lot of frustration. It's frustrating to be fighting for things for members of the URW and not be able to get them for ourselves." Bommarito acknowledged the staff union's right to file the NLRB charges, but said he wished the matter had been resolved in-house. "We still feel that this can be accomplished if the give-and-take principle of collective bargaining would be given an opportunity to function."

But Bruder said the URW president had no desire to follow that princi-ple of give-and-take when it came to dealing with the staff association. "We were in negotiations and [Bommarito] said, 'We're going to make a final offer,'" Bruder said. "I said, 'I don't want a final offer. I want a final agreement negotiated.' And he said, 'Well, we'll get you a final offer.'" At that point, there was not much holding the two sides apart. Bommarito and his team left for a bit, and then the URW president came back with Secretary/Treasurer Gold and Vice President Oldham. "Bommarito came in and said, 'This is our final offer.' I had told the committee, 'When you see me fold up my books, you fold up your books,'" Bruder said. "And I folded up my books and said, 'The meeting's over and we're going home.' He said, 'What do you mean?' I said, 'I told you, you don't come in here with a final offer. It has to be a negotiated settlement. There's no one-sided settlements with me.'"

Things then got a bit personal. Bruder had the staff union members give the negotiators strike authorization to strike their very own union, and the unfair labor charges were filed. Laws said he did not really want to strike the International, but felt the URW should be treated just like any other employer. "We were working for them and we had the right," Laws said. "All we wanted to do was negotiate on wages and they said we couldn't. The convention set the wages; therefore they couldn't [negotiate]. I said, 'Well hell, the company could say that too, that the stockholders set the wages and they can't give you any more than that.'"

Bruder said Bommarito sent a letter to all the staff union members making disparaging remarks about him. Bommarito also issued a news release in which he basically hid behind the URW constitution and asked if the staff association officers—who were also URW members—had overlooked their obligation to uphold the constitution. "It is not my purpose to debate the issues involved in this dispute in the press, but suffice it to say that the equity of our offers to the staff association has been unanimously supported by the URW International Executive Board, which incidentally is made up of rank-and-file members," Bommarito said. Laws was right in his assertion that if a company executive had made such a statement, the URW president would have attacked the executive mercilessly.

In the end, the matter was settled between Bommarito and Bruder. According to Bruder, Bommarito asked him how they could straighten out the matter. Bruder told him it had to be a negotiated settlement, and that the URW president had to apologize in the press and by letter to the staff union members. "He did and that ended that," Bruder said. "Then we went in and settled the damn thing in half an hour."

Laws especially disliked the way the whole situation was handled, including the resolution. He felt that Bommarito and the URW leaders then took some actions of retribution against him. For example, the International cut back on educational representatives, sending Laws back to organizing. "They sent me out organizing in South Dakota," Laws said. After a few months, Laws quit the URW staff and returned to Local 286 at Goodyear's hose and belt factory in Lincoln, Nebraska. Once he got re-elected president of his local, Laws set his sights even higher—running against Bommarito himself at the 1975 URW convention. Since his election in 1966, Bommarito had been re-elected in 1968, 1970, and 1972, facing either no or token opposition at each convention. And the issue Laws based his campaign on was winning a cost-of-living allowance during 1976 master contract talks. "Every time we would go into negotiations and the biggest thing is, 'We're going for a cost-of-living increase,'" Laws said. "Then the first thing we give up was the cost-of-living increase. I figured that if I got elected there would be a COLA [cost-of-living increase] or there wouldn't be a contract, because I thought it was important enough."

Laws figured he had little chance of winning, but thought that Bommarito needed some competition anyway. "It's pretty hard to run against the incumbent," Laws acknowledged. "As president, you can promise jobs and do things for people." He also campaigned with sparse funding, just whatever donations he received. Laws had no running mates for vice president or secretary/treasurer on his ticket, just himself running for the presidency. At one time, Laws had been a big Bommarito supporter. He was one of the Bomber's first supporters in 1966 in his race against Burdon. "I was the first man in 1966 that Pete appointed to the International union," Laws said. "I thought he had a lot of good qualities."

The issues at the convention dealt mainly with the URW's performance at the bargaining table. "We used to be on a par with the United Auto Workers. Now we are way behind, about $1.25 an hour behind," Laws said. The challenger did not get much reception at the convention. "It didn't feel very heart-warming—about as welcome as a skunk at a picnic, I guess," he said. "People didn't really say all that much to me about running against him. They thought it was ridiculous about anybody trying to beat Bommarito."

While Bommarito handily defeated Laws by a five-to-one margin, perhaps Laws did do something toward accomplishing his original goal, as Bommarito made a strong declaration toward going for COLA in 1976. "The 1976 round of master bargaining has the very real potential of being one of the toughest we have ever encountered as we will be seeking one of the most meaningful and sizable packages in recent years," Bommarito said in his acceptance speech. "Therefore, we have a lot of challenging work ahead of us as we must prepare ourselves and our entire membership for the commitment and determination which will be required to make our 1976 bargaining objectives in both the U.S. and Canada became a reality."

It was a call to arms that led to the rubber industry strike of 1976, one of the epic labor struggles of the 1970s. And in that battle, Bommarito would be right where he wanted to be—at center stage.

CHAPTER 5

THE STRIKE OF 1976
THE BOMBER HOLDS COURT

When negotiations began on the 1976 master contracts with the Big Four tire makers, Peter Bommarito was still seething over what had happened in 1973 bargaining. Under the specter of government wage and price controls of the Nixon Administration, Bommarito had declared in 1973 that the URW wanted a raise in excess of the 5.5 percent maximum under the guidelines. Despite strikes of twenty-four days at B. F. Goodrich and three days at Firestone, the URW basically settled for the maximum allowed, and they definitely took a financial hit in the months to come. Shortly after the contract agreement, the wage and price controls were lifted and inflation reached 12.3 percent, easily erasing the buying power of the 5.5 percent raise. Tire prices were jumping by about 16 percent a year, and corporate profits—not under a freeze—soared. Bommarito, in fact, had been an alternate on the Pay Board under the Nixon Administration's Phase II price-wage control programs but was one of four of the labor members who resigned from the board in 1972 because they claimed the rules hurt the working class. "While the administration permits this rising tide of price increases, its Pay Board persists in holding down workers' wages," Bommarito said upon quitting the board. "And profits are free to rise—and have been doing so—without even the pretense of controls."

Bommarito had asked the master contract firms to reopen negotiations based on economic conditions. It was not an unprecedented request. A number of smaller firms had granted extra raises or bonuses to try to make up what workers had lost. But not the big companies. When the URW president made the request, the reply was a polite but firm "No." The position was that the Rubber Workers had signed the contract and they had to live with it for three years. There was little the URW could do. They had agreed to the pact, and if the Big Four rubber companies refused to return to the bargaining table the union had to live up to its word—and to the signed agreement. To members it meant their earning power kept dropping as the cost of living kept rising. The Rubber Workers could only wait. So when contract talks opened in 1976 the union vowed not to make the same mistake twice. URW members had indeed fallen behind other unions that reached agreements after the wage freeze guidelines had been lifted. So the coveted cost-of-living allowance—COLA for short—would be a must for the URW's master contract in 1976. Other unions such as the United Auto Workers had won COLAs. Even the major tire and rubber URW locals in Canada had paved the way two years earlier by staging a long strike and winning a cost-of-living escalator clause. This success proved to Bommarito and the U.S. URW locals that the tire makers would yield on this most important issue.

"Pete had made a good effort to get them to voluntarily reopen the agreement on the theory of the contract being a living document," said Glenn Ellison, who was on the URW International staff in 1976. "Since the rules of the game had changed so drastically because of rapid inflation, the industry should sit down and negotiate a make-up wage increase because the companies' profits were going up like crazy. The worker was really getting hit hard. Nineteen seventy-six was one of those things that just had to be. I think the people were justified basically in their positions on protection against inflation. It would have been interesting to speculate what would have happened if the rubber industry would have granted Pete's request to negotiate a wage increase prior to that, whether the [strike] would have ever taken place. It's strictly speculation, but you never know."

It was clear the Rubber Workers' assertion that their wages had fallen behind had validity. The President's Council on Wage and Price Stability in early 1976 singled out tire workers as one of just two major groups negotiating that year whose earnings had not kept up with the cost of living during the prior decade. Using data from the Rubber Manufacturers Association, the council said wages for tire workers at Goodyear, B. F. Goodrich, Firestone, Uniroyal, and General Tire had risen from $3.65 an hour in 1965 to $5.81 in 1974. Combined with fringe benefits, total average hourly compensation increased from $4.77 in 1965 to $8.72 in 1974. The workers at these companies had seen wages rise roughly 60 percent over the decade, while the cost of living—measured by the government's consumer price index (CPI)—jumped 71.2 percent over the same period. Only the URW and the apparel workers failed to keep up with the CPI. By comparison, pay to the United Auto Workers climbed 99.4 percent, construction workers 98.9 percent, truckers 108.3 percent, electrical equipment workers 78 percent, meat packers 89.2 percent, and retail food workers 94.1 percent.

These figures, especially the gains made by the UAW, no doubt weighed heavily on the minds of the Rubber Workers as they met in January to develop bargaining policies for the coming year. One of the first ideas to surface was to strike two or more of the major rubber companies at the same time. The URW had made it a practice to target one company at a time if master contracts expired and settlements could not be reached. The union had last deliberately aimed at shutting down more than one major rubber firm in 1967, in Bommarito's first set of master bargaining as URW chief. Staging a major work stoppage at the entire Big Four, with contracts covering sixty thousand workers expiring April 20, would blunt the effectiveness of the tire makers' "unholy alliance." If the URW struck all the companies at once, then none of the majors would have production to aid their competitors through a work stoppage. Bommarito and the URW would have taken a large step in shutting down the industry, and taken a step up in the all-important game of leverage.

With its strike fund nearing $6 million, the URW was not shy with its goals. The URW Policy Committee devised goals that would boost total worker compensation by an estimated 50 percent or more. The union did not officially compute the cost of its requests, but some committee members estimated the cost at $4 an hour or more. The "wish list" included gaining parity with the United Auto Workers, with an immediate catch-up raise of $1.65 an hour for production workers and $2 an hour for skilled trades employees; a COLA clause even better than the UAW had; further wage increases in later contract years; and a whole range of fringe benefit gains. Among the benefits the URW put on its first list of demands included a "twenty-five and out" plan whereby any Rubber Worker could retire on a full pension after twenty-five years of service, regardless of age; guaranteed pensions after five years of service rather than ten years; a raise in life insurance and accidental death and dismemberment insurance; a raise in benefits for workers off the job because of sickness or accident; company payment of all employees' prescriptions without the $1 co-pay; recognition of chiropractors as doctors for company insurance payment purposes; and company payment for annual physicals and treatment for mental illness, alcoholism, and drug addiction problems.

While the URW was busy making its demands known, the companies made it clear before negotiations began that they would not be pushovers. Goodyear, after hearing the union's high demands, hinted that it might have to close some of its Akron non-tire facilities if the URW insisted on high wage settlements. Goodyear Vice President O. M. Sherman said the firm faced an "extremely serious" problem in non-tire production because of the URW's refusal to allow lower pay raises for workers making non-tire products. "We've reached the point where we can't continue the kinds of settlements we have had. If there's any further movement in this direction, those plants may have to close their doors," Sherman said in the company's weekly newspaper, the *Wingfoot Clan*. He said higher UAW wages had cost jobs in the auto industry and the rubber industry should learn a lesson from that. URW Local 2 President John Nardella said Sherman was trying to put the "fear of God" in workers before negotiations. "He's saying to bow down or you might not have jobs," Nardella said.

Negotiations started in early March, with Goodyear bargaining taking place in Cincinnati, Ohio; Firestone in Cleveland; Goodrich in Columbus, Ohio; and Uniroyal in New York City. Although URW membership at master contract plants still represented a real threat, the total rolls at the locals in the Big Four chains symbolized a warning of things to come. As talks opened in 1976, the URW represented about sixty thousand workers at Big Four locals under the master contract, down from nearly seventy thousand during the 1973 talks.

THE STRIKE BEGINS

The Big Four tire makers made their first offer on economic portions of the master contract in early April, but made no offers to non-tire plant workers. They suggested instead that the non-tire factories negotiate their contracts at the local level, in effect removing them from national master contract talks. The URW rejected the offer. As the April 20 expiration of contracts neared, the union picked Firestone as the target for negotiations to reach a contract and for a worldwide boycott. Bommarito also accused Goodyear of leading the other companies into making inadequate contract offers. As the deadline approached, Senator Edward M. Kennedy—a longtime friend of labor—even asked the Antitrust Division of the Justice Department to investigate the mutual aid pact of the Big Four rubber companies. Kennedy's letter asked the U.S. assistant attorney general to find out whether an informal pact existed and whether the practices violated antitrust statutes.

In the end the inevitable occurred. About sixty thousand URW members struck forty-seven plants in twenty-one states, with roughly eleven thousand Rubber Workers walking off the job in Akron alone. Bommarito and the URW had followed through with their threat of striking all Big Four tire and rubber companies at once. The strike idled most of the nation's tire manufacturing and a good portion of the non-tire rubber product output as well. After pickets prevented an estimated 15,500 white-collar and other nonstriking employees from entering Akron plants, Goodyear, BFG, and Firestone moved quickly to get an Akron judge to issue temporary restraining orders limiting the number of pickets at each gate. Uniroyal sought similar court injunctions in New York, where it was headquartered. The only real violence at the beginning of the strike came at the Goodyear conveyor belt plant in Marysville, Ohio, where workers set fires outside the gates of the plant, threw a firebomb at a gatehouse, and cut a telephone cable to the facility. Although the $6 million in the URW strike fund sounded like a substantial amount, with sixty thousand members drawing $35 a week in benefit payments the fund could not last more than three payments. As URW members were apt to say, however, strikes are won with planning, commitment, and determination—not with a few dollars in strike pay. For the Rubber Workers, it looked more and more as though it was going to be a long, hot summer.

As the target firm, the Firestone talks were the key to a strike settlement, but the two sides remained miles apart as the old contract expired. At a news conference at 3:00 A.M. on April 21, just three hours after the deadline passed, Bommarito called Firestone's latest offer a "slap in the face." The URW tried to frame an agreement with the overall increase of about 39 percent in wages and benefits predicted earlier in April by a securities analyst. After that forecast, the union had cut its original demands, which included $1.65 in first-year wage increases alone. By then, the union indicated it would accept a three-year wage increase package of $1.52 for production workers and $2 for skilled trades if the COLA formula demand were met. As of the April 20 contract expiration, Firestone had offered wage increases of sixty cents an hour the first year, thirty cents the second, and twenty-five cents the third. Those increases would add about $100 to the monthly pay of Firestone workers the first year and over the three years would cost Firestone an extra $40 million in pay raises alone. The company also said it offered a COLA clause without a cap or limitations, but patterned it after its current Canadian URW COLA provision—a clause that granted increases only when the criteria of a complex formula were met. Bommarito said the total wage offer was inadequate even as a first-year catch-up offer, and that the COLA offer would net a wage increase of less than than eight cents an hour if inflation occurred at the 7 percent rate predicted by government economists. "We can in no way accept this substandard approach to cost of living, but the company will attempt to mislead our members and the public by calling it uncapped," Bommarito said. The URW president also said the company made an insulting pension offer, no offer to increase benefits for current retirees, inadequate wage increases for skilled tradesmen, no dental or health insurance offers, and no proposal to protect against plant closings or to increase worker health study funds and supplemental unemployment benefits.

The hardball negotiations started quickly on both sides. The URW announced plans to kick off its boycott against Firestone tires in Akron and seven other U.S. and Canadian cities. Besides Akron, May 8 demonstrations were slated for Dayton, Ohio; New Haven, Connecticut; Des Moines, Iowa; Long Beach, California; Pottstown, Pennsylvania; Memphis, Tennessee; and Toronto, Ontario. Not to be outdone, Goodyear and Firestone made the unprecedented move of suspending supplemental unemployment benefit (SUB) payments to about fourteen hundred workers who were laid off before the URW strike began. The SUB fund guaranteed laid-off workers 80 percent of their pay, with unemployment compensation supplemented with SUB payments. BFG followed suit a couple of days later, while Uniroyal's SUB fund was depleted, so no formal suspension of payments was necessary for the one thousand laid-off Uniroyal workers. Bommarito made the SUB pay a strike issue and said URW members would not return to work until the firms agreed to pay the benefits retroactively to the laid-off workers. A Goodyear spokesman acknowledged that the suspension of SUB payments was a pressure tactic. "But so is a strike," he said.

Bommarito even flew to Geneva, Switzerland, to try to gain support from worldwide labor organizations and to try to impose severe international hardships on Firestone, its negotiating target. The foreign union

Bommarito addresses a crowd of about one thousand outside the Akron Rubber Bowl during a rally at the start of the 1976 strike. (Rubber & Plastics News *photo. Copyright Crain Communications Inc.*)

leaders pledged to support the URW's boycott against Firestone and also promised to urge their workers to refuse overtime at Firestone or Goodyear plants to keep the firms from boosting overseas production to ship the tires to U.S. markets.

About one thousand URW members and supporters attended the May 8 rally at the Akron Rubber Bowl to kick off the Firestone boycott. "We're not going to step back," Bommarito told the crowd. "We're going to suffer a little. We want an equitable settlement the United Rubber Workers can be proud of." He told the strikers they would see movement by the company on contract offers by June, if not sooner, because of an expected shortage of tires available to the auto industry. Not all of the planned URW rallies in other cities ended up as successful as the one in Akron, which, in all fairness, was boosted by Bommarito's presence. The other top rally was in Des Moines, with a crowd of about one thousand. Only about one hundred fifty attended a rally in New Haven and three hundred in Pottstown; about two hundred people picketed in the Memphis area, which ended up having no rally. Planned gatherings in Dayton and Toronto were scratched.

For Bommarito, the strike was the perfect stage for a labor leader who had made his name on the battlefield, both in military combat and on the picket line. And it was not just the URW president who seemed to enjoy the competitive nature of a strike. "There were people on both sides that needed that aggressive combat," said Kenneth Coss, who was one of the coordinators of the Firestone boycott. "Many times it was a contest of wills, a feeling that you held your own against the other side as much as negotiating an equitable contract." Glenn Ellison said most tire industry management in 1976 still felt they had unending market share. "You went after whatever you could get because the company was able to pass the costs on," Ellison said. Michael Polovick, on the Firestone labor relations staff at the time, said, "at that point in time, the union was trying to fight with the companies and the companies were trying to fight with the unions. And both sides were good at it."

In 1976 times were different and there was a a different code of ethics, according to Coss. "It was a bitter struggle, but it was not in anyone's mind to destroy the other party," he said. "Pete was dynamic and charismatic, but human too. He had the same doubts and fears as everyone else. Certain people have a certain presence. For the times and what the demands were, he was a good president. It was a 'fight to the finish' type thing with Firestone. It was an especially bitter situation, and no one ever doubted the strike. But no matter what people say publicly, everyone hates strikes. When people say they love strikes, you have to doubt it. It's a major upheaval in people's lives. Everyone figures it's a last resort. That's why they're so bitter. People feel they did what they can to avoid it, so they're upset and angry. But because of the times, because of the employer coalition and the attitude of the people, you were never sure you got everything you could have unless you went on strike."

Bommarito also thought it important that the Rubber Workers were as willing to sacrifice for the cause as were the union's founding fathers four decades earlier. "Pete considered himself an old marine. You sacrificed.

You did what you had to do. He even had stomach trouble he worried so much. He figured we had do do it," Coss said. "If we hadn't, people would still be working ten-hour days and get Wednesday night off if you promised to go to church. That was part of our business. I think Pete was really motivated by 'I'm the leader and I'm going to get out there in the front and we're going to fight this thing no matter what.' I didn't disagree with that at times. Sometimes you have to step back and take a look, but most of the time that was what established unions. I think we're getting into a different age now, but when Pete was president that was still how you had to do it. And the companies certainly asked for it."

With the national media focusing on the URW strike, Bommarito was at his best during the conflict, said Curt Brown, the URW PR director. "He was driven. He was like Patton. He kept the forces rallied," Brown said. "He was good with the media. He talked to them. He knew how to put the best image forward. He was not a perfect politician but he was pretty adept. The imperfection would be that he was almost a little too effusive sometimes—he was almost a little too much. People wouldn't see that in the first few contacts but if you were around him all the time, it was like, 'Come on Pete, calm down,' which you didn't say to him." Brown himself got a taste of just how far-reaching the media coverage was at the beginning of the strike. "We were up in Cleveland and we were doing a national interview," Brown said. "Pete was standing there and I was behind him. I wasn't trying to pose. I was just there because it was my job. That night my secretary's aunt called from Florida and said, 'I saw your big boss [Bommarito] on TV, but who was that mafia guy behind him?' which was me."

BFG and Firestone attempted to get their side of the strike out to the people as well, taking out full-page newspaper advertisements. In its ad BFG noted that the company faced the fourth URW strike in the last decade and that on each working day the Goodrich strikers in Akron alone lost $111,000 in wages. The firm said it made two economic proposals prior to April 20, including the offer on the table at the time of the strike that called for general wage increases of 40 cents an hour in 1976, 25 cents an hour in 1977, and 20 cents in 1978. BFG also proposed an additional 25 cents an hour over the first two years of the pact for skilled tradesmen and a COLA formula that could add an additional 8 cents an hour for all workers. Lower wage increases were offered to Akron BFG employees because the Akron plants did not make passenger tires but non-automotive-related products that must compete with other firms producing other types of rubber products, many of whom had lower labor costs than BFG. "The wage proposal by B. F. Goodrich represents an offer which is greater than any agreement negotiated in the past," the company said. "BFG will continue to seek a settlement which will be in the best interests of its employees, its customers, the company, and the communities where its facilities are located."

Firestone took out advertisements titled "Nobody Wins" in eleven newspapers, saying that its offer had gone as far as it could without causing real inflation. "Every day the rubber strike goes on, the industry loses another day's production, the strikers lose another day's pay, their families lose another day's security and consumers face the prospect of higher prices from an inflation-pressured settlement," the firm's ad said. Firestone also outlined its offer of an average increase of $100 per month the first year and another $100 a month over the following two years; COLA as protection against inflation; improvements in pensions, life insurance, survivor income, and disability benefits; more liberal payments for outpatient hospital care and medical diagnostic services; and additional monthly payments for present retirees and their spouses to reflect the cost of Medicare.

Goodyear Chairman Charles J. Pilliod Jr. wrote to striking employees, warning that layoffs were certain to occur at the Windsor, Vermont, shoe products factory. He said in his late May letter that 100 of the 350 URW members at the factory would be laid off even if the strike ended immediately. Pilliod wrote that Goodyear had lost $1 million in customer orders at the plant, much of that to non-union facilities.

A SUMMER ON THE STREETS

The feeling of going on strike is hard to describe to someone who has never had the experience. "When you first go out, in the back of your mind you have fear," said Doug Werstler of Local 2 in Akron. "Am I going to make it through? Am I going to have a job? Is the company going to shut down the plant? But when you finally walk out the door, in the beginning it's elation that, 'I'm standing up and I'm making this stand. I'm not going to be kicked around and things in my life are important enough for me to withhold my labor.' And that's what a strike is: the withholding of your labor. You are not doing your job and you're letting the company know just how valuable an asset you are."

The child of a striker takes part in picketing to show his support for his father during the 1976 strike. (Rubber & Plastics News *photo. Copyright Crain Communications Inc.*)

Werstler had a much better handle on the strike in 1976 than he did in 1970, when the Goodyear locals struck for about forty days. "I got married when I was in the military. I came back and I'm starting a family, so I need to get a house," Werstler said. "I started building a house in the fall of 1969 and the day that we moved in, in 1970, was the day that we went on strike. So I had a house payment and I didn't have a job. I went out and got a job the next day pumping gas." But 1976 was different. Although the strike lasted much longer for the Goodyear workers than in 1970, Werstler has fond memories of '76. "I hate to say it but that was probably the best summer of my life," he said. "I spent time with my family. The city of Akron was shut down as a result of that strike. Other people who weren't prepared I'm sure lost homes, lost wives, lost husbands. I mean that was a pretty critical time in the labor movement. I did home repair and built picnic tables. In fact, I was doing pretty good. Another fellow craftsman and I, we worked fixing garages, rewiring houses, plumbing, siding. We were doing really good. We contemplated not going back and going into business for ourselves. But the benefits are hard to give up."

When the time came in 1976 to hit the streets, the Rubber Workers were ready. "We knew we were going to go for the cost of living," said Craig Hemsley, also of Local 2, who served as a gate captain for the strike. "It was that simple. I don't think anybody I worked with at Plant 2 didn't think that we would strike that night. I think we did a heckuva job. We stayed unified at all four major union chains throughout that strike. It was tough. That was a long one, but we always had the gates manned. We had a kitchen and soup room at the union hall."

But no matter how much a union prepares, there will be many individuals with problems ranging from minor financial difficulties to personal ruin. Local 2's Tom Jenkins did not suffer personally but knew plenty who did. "That strike was hell," he said. "There were a lot of people who became destitute over that strike. People would lose their cars, they couldn't pay their rent, and they had to get on food stamps or welfare—anything that could help you survive. If you didn't save any money of any kind, those were the people who were hurt." Jenkins himself was active during the strike, picketing every day. When he was called to court on a charge of disturbing the peace, a judge told him, "I have enough pictures of your vehicle I could wallpaper my whole office."

While nearly 20 percent of the URW members on strike were walking the picket lines in Akron, the 1976 strike involved Rubber Workers in twenty-one states. The Goodyear local in Union City, Tennessee, was especially active, according to J. Michael Stanley, onetime president of Local 878 and later International vice president. The tire plant was completed in early 1969, so it was still relatively new in 1976. "I really have to commend our membership," Stanley said. "They stuck together real good. We manned the picket line twenty-four hours a day. We always had a good ten to fifteen people out there. A lot of times people would come up and walk when it wasn't their turn." Stanley found a job with a company called Mid-

Ten Electric. He helped install traffic lights, putting electric wires in the pavement. "I was running one of those pavement saws. I was working evening shifts and walked the picket line during the day. I pretty much walked it every day." Stanley and his wife had been saving up money to buy a house, but quickly ran through whatever savings they had. Between the two of them, they still managed to get through it. "We really had good morale," Stanley said. "I don't think anybody regretted the strike. I spent all the money I had for the house, but through the cost-of-living raises, I more than got that back. I can't even count the many times over I got that back."

The strikers in Union City had their moments of levity on the picket line, a necessity when a strike goes on so long. For instance, there was the time someone brought a goat out to the picket line. "It stayed out there with us for two or three days and the next thing we knew the rascal was gone," Stanley said. "Some of the guys used to poke a little fun at me because I told them a story one time about how my granddad used to kill goats and we used to barbecue them. Somebody said, 'Stanley must have gotten that goat and used it for barbecue.' I still get ribbed for that."

Bob Bianchi was a division chairman of Local 310 at the Firestone plant in Des Moines, Iowa, in 1976, and he was responsible for running the boycott against the tire firm in the area. Bianchi organized informational pickets at filling stations and the local Montgomery Ward service center. At the time, Firestone sold a goodly number of tires through both distribution channels. "We just wrapped those filling stations up," Bianchi said. "I had groups of people walking around them constantly." Bianchi, who later served as Local 310 president, recalled how the manager at the Montgomery Ward service store told him the one day he was going fishing and would not be able to be reached. "He said, 'Please, just don't have [the picketers] stop. Keep them moving.' So I just wrapped their service department up. I must have had 250 or 300 people there that day. They just kept walking around and around it. We shut it clear down that day. There was no business there at all."

Bianchi was a big supporter of shutting down all the Big Four firms at once. "In those days the corporations were very much together," Bianchi said. "Whichever company we chose as leaders, they would coordinate with each other and say, 'I don't know if we can afford it.' They would crunch numbers. So Pete just said, 'Hey, let's shut them all down.'"

At each of the striking locals, workers scrambled to get odd jobs where they could and get help when needed. But most of all they did what they had to do to get by. "Everybody was gung-ho to start with," said Tony Smith, a member of Local 12 at the Goodyear plant in Gadsden, Alabama. "After we were out a couple of months, we got a bit of the empty pockets. Everybody was wanting to go back to work. Everybody was getting depressed." Smith was one of the smart ones, having put money back for the strike and having a working wife. "I just told her we would do the best we could. We just didn't get to do a whole lot while we were on strike. We just got by." Smith and his family also were lucky in that both he and his wife had understanding parents who were willing to have them over for meals. "We didn't have to buy many groceries."

Dan Baldwin, also in Local 12, went out of state looking for jobs during the strike. First he went to Mississippi as a crane operator. Goodyear had given him a driver's license to operate a portable crane. When Baldwin went to the Mississippi plant to get a job as a millright, for which he was qualified, he found that they had hired all the millrights they needed. "They said they needed a crane operator so I just pulled out that little license, so they put me on a job running a stationary crane," Baldwin said. "I'm telling you that boom was a long son of a gun. It took me two days to get the hang of it. I worked it a month, then got fed up with it."

Two others in Local 12, Bill Willard and Ronnie Reed, also had jobs to tide them over, Willard as a bartender and Reed painting houses. "I made out well," Willard said. "The county had just gone wet and I worked as a bartender. My wife was glad to see me come back to work. It was not unusual for me to have a paycheck and end up paying a little bit more to cover my bar tab." Reed hated painting, but did what he had to do. "I was able to pay all my bills," he said. "I thought I was really doing well until we got back to work and all my money was gone."

Willard was happy about the general lack of violence during the strike, far different from the URW attempts to organize in Gadsden in the 1930s and 1940s. Willard recalled how his father was involved in a strike years earlier and was beaten up. A sheriff's deputy who knew him had to bring him home. "You can put it in perspective. I was out in 1976 for four and a half months and nobody tried to bodily harm me."

TROUBLE WITHIN THE URW

The URW strike started April 20 with the sixty thousand members striking the Big Four master contract plants. If the work stoppage lasted into late spring and summer, Bommarito counted on those ranks growing when contracts at smaller tire and rubber product makers expired. Many of the locals and companies involved in those contracts normally followed the economic portions of the master contracts, with many having "me too" agreements. The URW president expected these locals to honor the national strike, putting even more pressure on the companies to settle. But the plan did not always go as Bommarito had hoped. General Tire was the fifth largest domestic tire manufacturer at the time, and contracts covering 2,700 URW members at the firm's tire plants in Akron and Waco, Texas, expired in mid-May. But instead of joining their union brothers and sisters on the picket line, the two locals reached a last-minute agreement to keep the plants open on a day-to-day basis under the terms of the old contract. Bommarito said that the General Tire locals' decision to stay on the job was not "in the best interests" of the URW, as the General Tire talks were no closer to settlement than those at the Big Four. He said General's current contract offer was roughly equal to Firestone's.

Local 310's Bianchi said it was important to try to get the other URW locals to strike when their contracts were up. "When it came time for their deadline, we expected them to go out," he said. "We expected them to have something on the table that the company couldn't give them so they'd strike. So we had to encourage sometimes because the companies at that time were willing to give more for them not to go out. It was a great, opportune time for smaller organizations like Cooper (Tire & Rubber Co.) to pick up a lot of replacement market business. They were willing to give a little more."

URW members did not want to pay extra dues to replenish the strike fund to help the more than one-third of URW members off the job. In late May the International Executive Board (IEB) called a special convention in Chicago to "take action on a proposed amendment to the URW constitution which would provide for a monthly dues supplement to go to the strike fund." The strike fund disappeared after two full payments of the $35 a week benefit to strikers, with a third payment of $25 made after the URW transferred $1.35 million from other union funds to the strike fund. In the transfer, the URW used all its building fund, which was supposed to help construct a new headquarters. But right before the special convention, the fifteen-member IEB proposed there be no dues increase to replenish the strike fund. The IEB gave three reasons to the 465 convention delegates, representing 244 of the URW's 560 locals, for leaving the dues as they were. They said it would be an "unreasonable burden and unjust onus" upon one hundred thousand non-striking members to support the sixty thousand members striking the Big Four because it would cost $100 a month per member to continue the $35 weekly benefit checks; because they wanted to impress upon the companies that the existence or nonexistence of strike benefits would have no effect on the union's determination in achieving its demands; and because URW members had suffered enough from inflation and other factors, and a dues supplement would be an additional burden.

Presidents of most of the locals involved in the strike said at the convention that a dues increase at that time would not come in time or be large enough to make a difference in the current strike anyway. Most of the speechmaking in support of keeping the status quo relived the old days when the union struck without any weekly benefits. "We'll win the strike because we're Rubber Workers, not because of $2 or $35 a week," said Ray Wiseman, president of the BFG local in Fort Wayne, Ind. In the end, delegates voted overwhelmingly to leave the dues structure alone and continue the strike with an empty strike fund.

Another blow to URW solidarity came in early June, when nineteen hundred members of Local 26 at the Kelly-Springfield plant in Cumberland, Maryland, reached a tentative agreement on a three-year contract agreement just before the old contract expired. Bommarito had predicted the Local 26 members would strike the Goodyear subsidiary, joining the sixty thousand other URW members already off the job. Several other locals also stayed on the job rather than join the walkout, including those at Dunlop Tire Corp. in Buffalo and Mohawk Tire & Rubber in Helena, Arkansas, along with the General Tire locals.

More than one thousand members of Local 17 at the Mansfield Tire & Rubber Co. in Mansfield, Ohio, put some glitter back in the union's solidarity by joining the strike on June 16 and taking another twelve thousand tires a day from the market. At a unity rally in Akron three days later, Bommarito told the two-thousand-member crowd he was assured that the Mansfield local would stay on the streets, "because otherwise it would be like crossing a picket line." But before the day was over, the Rubber Workers did not even have the small consolation of having Local 17 off the job. As soon as the local struck the sixty-year-old plant in Mansfield, the company's board of directors threatened to close the factory. Just two days after the Mansfield local began its strike, the workers agreed to return to work on a day-to-day basis with a promise that the company would leave the plant open and give Local 17 a percentage of whatever the Big Four locals won in negotiations.

While the return of Mansfield Tire to work disappointed URW members, much more wrath was aimed at the General Tire locals in Akron and Waco. At the June 19 rally in Akron, a ten-year-old boy carried a sign referring to the Akron local that read "Judas' price was 30 pieces of silver. Local 9, What is Your Price?" Two days later, on June 21, about two hundred picketers from the other struck rubber firms in Akron gathered just before midnight at the General Tire gate to shut down the firm's plant. Though the number of pickets dropped to about twenty-five by 8:00 A.M. it still was enough to keep the next shift off its jobs as well. The demonstration kept about fourteen hundred Local 9 members off the job that day. The pickets took out their frustrations on their working union brothers verbally, if not physically, with one Local 7 member shouting into the face of some General workers, "You're either with us or against us. It's time to stand up and be counted."

What confounded many of the URW members about the dispute was the fact that Local 9 President Nate Trachsel, prior to the 1976 strike, had been Bommarito's "fair-haired boy," as Matt Contessa, president of Local 5 at BFG in Akron, put it. "He wasn't his fair-haired boy after that." Bommarito even had been grooming Trachsel for International office, having named the Local 9 president as chairman of Bommarito's political caucus at the past two URW conventions and having given him other choice assignments. "Nate Trachsel was the right-hand man of Pete Bommarito," said Bianchi. "He was slotted to be the next president of the Rubber Workers. He was going to move him up and bring him in the fold. Of course that all ended. That was the end of Nate Trachsel. I wasn't in his camp so I don't know why he did it. It just didn't make any sense. Either that or he thought Pete was wrong."

Trachsel came under a lot of criticism from labor for not striking and, ironically, later was double-crossed by General Tire. Local 9 had agreed to let the company keep a portion of a raise to be put into a fund for building a new tire facility in Akron. It would have been the first such construction in the Rubber Capital of the World in decades. Local 2's Werstler said that Trachsel probably saw Goodyear and others moving plants or shutting down Akron production and thought maybe this was the way he could save jobs for his members. "I think he saw it coming and thought, 'I'm going to do what I can to keep work for my people right here in Akron,'" Werstler said. "If they built the plant and expanded and kept the jobs he would have been a labor hero." Instead General never built the plant and gave Local 9 members back their money without interest.

Some smaller locals did join the national strike later, including 3,300 URW members at five Armstrong Rubber Co. tire plants; 475 workers at General Tire's Logansport, Indiana, non-tire facility; and 700 workers at four Richardson Co. factories. At one point the total number of workers on strike approached 70,000.

The companies continued to put economic pressure on the strikers when their health care coverage lapsed by terms of the old agreement ninety days into the strike. The firms said the only way the striking Rubber Workers could keep up their expiring medical coverage was to pay the premiums to the company. Goodyear did continue free coverage to those hospitalized, retired, or pregnant before the ninety-day extension period ended. "We haven't been totally heartless," said Goodyear Assistant Treasurer Bennett Shaver. The companies, however, said a couple of weeks later that they would extend the medical and life insurance benefits to strikers on a "pay later" basis. The firms said they would deduct the cost from the employees' salaries after they returned to work. Bommarito had made a major issue of the medical coverage cutoff. Even after the firms agreed to extend the coverage and deduct the premiums after the strike, the URW president said he would ask the companies when the strike was settled not to deduct the costs from workers' pay.

Goodyear and Firestone also rubbed the URW's face in the situation somewhat by granting raises to some of its white-collar workforce. Goodyear gave a $130-a-month raise effective July 1 to all its non-union white-collar workers making less than $2,000 a month, amounting to about thirteen thousand employees nationwide, including six thousand at its headquarters in Akron. The firm said the raise equaled an increase of seventy-five cents an hour, the exact amount the striking Rubber Workers rejected as a first-year wage settlement. Firestone gave unspecified increases to its white-collar employees on June 1, adding that it would institute a cost-of-living escalator clause in 1977 for its salaried staff. The COLA would be payable to 27,500 white-collar workers in the United States, with 4,400 of those in Akron. BFG later said it was considering several changes in its merit raise program for white-collar employees, and that its salaried employees—under the merit program—had been paid raises averaging 24 percent over the last three years, compared with 16 percent for URW members.

More dissension surfaced within the URW when the Goodyear bargaining team tried to start economic bargaining with the company in opposition to the union's policy of concentrating its efforts only on the target firm. Goodyear's Pilliod sent another letter to strikers, saying that the company wanted to bargain with its own union employees but had been prohibited from doing so. He wrote that there is no "lack of desire on the company's part to discuss Goodyear issues with Goodyear representatives, but there are no Goodyear representatives authorized to meet to bargain these matters." Company negotiators in late June had voted to try to start their own economic bargaining with Goodyear locals, but Bommarito sent a telegram telling them that doing so would be against the URW's rules and regulations. Union leaders outside the Goodyear chain were worried that Goodyear locals would settle for less than the other groups within the master contracts. Just three years earlier, Goodyear locals had settled first as the target firm, but Firestone and BFG locals then struck because they felt the Goodyear settlement was not acceptable. By doing so, the Firestone and BFG URW members received a better settlement, particularly on pensions. "I was always led to understand that prior to 1990, that the feeling was at the International that the Goodyear system would settle for less than Firestone or Uniroyal," said Local 2's Hemsley. "That in turn incensed a lot of the Goodyear local presidents because they wanted to be the master contract target company. Personally, I'm from Goodyear but I think we got better settlements when we took the other companies as targets."

On July 30 Goodyear, BFG, and Uniroyal filed charges of unfair labor practices against the Rubber Workers with the NLRB after negotiations broke off as the strike passed the hundred-day mark. The companies claimed the union was not bargaining in good faith because it targeted Firestone and allowed economic bargaining only with Firestone, although strikes were called against all four firms. By this time, the union had eased off on its original request for an immediate $1.65 "catch-up" general wage increase and was asking for a little more than $1 an hour in the first year. The tire firms were offering $1.30 an hour over the three years, including seventy-five cents in the first year. On COLA, the URW wanted the UAW's model of a one-cent-an-hour raise for each rise of three-tenths of a point in the federal consumer price index. The companies offered one cent for each rise of four-tenths of a point in the index, but only during the last year and a half of the contract. On pensions, the companies offered to increase the monthly multiplier by seventy-five cents per month in each year of the contract, but only for service after age forty-five. The URW wanted a larger increase without age limitations.

AT LAST: A SETTLEMENT

U.S. Secretary of Labor William J. Usery Jr. played a key role in bringing a close to the longest strike in the history of the tire industry at that time. The federal government took a great interest in the work stoppage. Not only did the Big Four carry a certain amount of clout in Washington, but in the back of everyone's mind was the potential impact upon the automotive industry. Bommarito, in choosing to strike the four largest tire makers at once, had hoped all along to reach a settlement by cutting the supply of original equipment tires to Detroit. He figured that if the automakers did not get the tires they needed, they would pressure the tire manufacturers into settling the strike by giving the union close to what it demanded. But the situation in Detroit never quite reached crisis level. Some of the auto firms took to delivering cars without a spare tire—to be replaced after the strike—but the supply of tires to car makers was never seriously in jeopardy.

Nevertheless, Usery was interested in resolving the URW strike. He brought the parties to Washington for bargaining on July 27, for a brief round of talks. After just six hours of talks, Bommarito said the rift was larger than ever. Talks broke down on July 29 after just three days as each side blamed the other for not budging. On August 5 Usery, undaunted, called for negotiations to resume August 7 and told both sides to come prepared for continuous bargaining until an agreement was reached. When bargaining reconvened, the two sides remained more than $1 an hour apart from settling the strike. And when Usery said to come prepared to bargain, he meant it. The union and company teams negotiated into the wee hours of the morning four of five days, with little time allotted for sleep. Just after midnight on August 12, a Usery aide told reporters keeping a vigil in the office that a settlement was near. An hour later he said he miscalculated. Just before 2:00 A.M., the negotiators sent out for twenty-four McDonald's hamburgers. At 3:15 A.M., the aide declared the negotiators had entered a final round of chit-chat "that we call death rattles in the business." Ten minutes later, the parties were celebrating an agreement by having drinks in Usery's office.

The Washington agreement covered the main economic portions of the master contract, including wages, COLAs, and pensions. Although the target bargaining was with Firestone, the pact also was endorsed by Goodyear, BFG, and Uniroyal. It increased the total compensation package by about 35 percent and was the largest gain negotiated in 1976 by any union, eclipsing the 32 percent increase won by the Teamsters in April. "We recognize that this economic package is more expensive than other settlements negotiated this year," Usery said. "At the same time, we recognize that the members of the URW were caught in the restrictions of wage controls when they agreed to their last contract three years ago. URW members were among the few in major industries who received no cost-of-living clause protection during the time when inflation was at its worst."

During the last set of marathon negotiations in Washington, URW negotiators won more than 50 cents an hour in wages, fringe benefits, and projected COLA raises than the Big Four had previously offered. They got general wage increases of 80 cents an hour the first year, 30 cents the second, and 25 cents the third, plus an additional 8.8 cents an hour for Firestone workers, who had given up that amount in the 1973 contract in exchange for other benefits. The URW also came through on its chief goal of COLAs, where it won full coverage for three years, ending with a formula as generous as the one that the Auto Workers gained—the exact formula the URW sought. The pension multiplier was raised from $10 a month per year of service to $12.50 in the last year of the contract. Goodyear workers, who had been behind in their pension multiplier since 1973, were brought back even with the other chains. Bommarito also followed through on his vow to have the companies pay for hospital and medical insurance premiums and bills that strikers had paid themselves since July 19. In addition, current retirees received an immediate $1 increase in their monthly pension multiplier.

The URW did not prevail on all points, though. The union failed to get the "30 and out" pension plan, where workers would receive full pension benefits after thirty years of service regardless of age. The URW also failed to gain comprehensive dental insurance, a plan to try to keep SUB funds from running dry, and raises in other benefit areas. Each company also designated certain plants as distressed, with these plants to receive something less than the final contract. Firestone designated just one plant, BFG two, Goodyear four, and Uniroyal five.

It was estimated the sixty thousand workers lost about $300 million in wages, but would gain back about $180 million in first-year wage and benefit increases alone. Having the COLA at a strong formula—it was improved even more in 1979—gained workers untold millions of dollars over the following decades, as that portion of pay (as of 2000 workers' paychecks still broke down base earnings and COLA earnings) accounted for more than half of wages for URW members under the master contract. "Some say you never get back what you lose in a strike," Coss said. "It turns out they got many times over what they lost in that strike." And despite the economic hardship on the companies, stock prices of the Big Four pretty much held their own during the strike and earnings projections were stronger than expected.

The only thing left to end the marquee rubber industry strike was to come to agreement with the Big Four firms on noneconomic items not covered under the Usery agreement. Goodyear and the URW reached a tentative agreement first for the twenty-two thousand Rubber Workers in that chain covered by the master pact. Employees at Goodyear plants in New Bedford, Massachusetts, and Windsor, Vermont—both labeled as financially distressed—received smaller raises, though the company still declined to promise to keep jobs at the two plants. Firestone and the URW came up with their agreement next. Firestone Vice President Joseph Cairns declared that the new pact eventually would cost jobs in Akron and elsewhere, especially at the non-tire plant in Noblesville, Indiana.

Goodrich was the last to settle, reaching terms on September 6, the 139th day of the strike. It was the end of the longest summer in URW history and would be the source of debate more than two decades later. Had Bommarito finally gone too far? Was this the "Last stand" for the URW? For the time being, though, the strikers for the most part reveled in what was viewed as a landmark victory for the union. But the Rubber Workers knew they had been through a battle. One had to look no further than the strike T-shirt worn by one striker, who had scratched out the "Catch" on his URW strike shirt and replaced it with "Beat," so the shirt read "Beat up in '76."

"That was a heckuva contract," said Local 2's Hemsley. "I think we got more in that one contract than we did my whole life at Goodyear. We paid for it by going on strike, but we really gained: wages, pension, COLA. We would have never got it if we didn't strike. And I don't think we would have got it if you just took one company out. I think you had to take them all out. Pete knew that." Dan Baldwin of Local 12 concurred. When he hired in as an apprentice in 1967 he earned $2.08 an hour, and it took four years to get to full rate. By 1999, with COLA, he was making about $18.50 an hour, with workers at some plants making close to $20 an hour. "If we didn't have COLA, we'd be making chicken feed," he said.

And as the tens of thousands of Rubber Workers filtered back to work across the country, they also were happy to be earning a paycheck—money that was dearly needed, no matter how much preparation a striker had made. "Some people really had it tough," said Jimmy Palmer, a member of Local 12 in Gadsden, Alabama. "I remember this one guy I worked with, O. D. Hope. He was a good guy. We had just come back to work after the strike and gotten our first check. Some guy hollered out, 'I'm going to frame this check.' O. D. Hope looked up at me and this other guy and said, 'I might frame the stub.'"

Of course, even some union members saw the toll that such a large URW victory took on the companies that needed to prosper in order for the Rubber Workers to continue to have jobs. "I've really got a lot of mixed emotions about it," said Mickey Williams, who was a Local 12 department representative in 1976 and became the local's president in 1995. "We probably made some of the gains that we currently think the most of in our labor agreement during that strike. At the same time, maybe we opened the door to a lot of foreign competition in America that might not have been open for a few more years. It seemed like following the 1976 strike we started to lose jobs en masse to foreign competition."

It would be an issue that opponents of Bommarito within the URW—particularly from the Goodyear chain—would focus on as the union went forward toward its 1978 convention.

CHAPTER 6

BOMMARITO'S SWAN SONG

During Peter Bommarito's first twelve years as URW president, he never faced a serious threat for his job. But all that changed in 1978. Local 12 and other southern locals were adamantly opposed to Bommarito in the latter part of the URW leader's tenure in office. "In 1976, we were told that, especially at the Goodyear locals, we had an opportunity to settle the strike much earlier than it was settled," said Local 12's Mickey Williams. "The story was that Bommarito was interested in settling with another company before he settled with anyone else. He just really wouldn't make himself available. I'm not sure how much truth was in that. It left kind of a bad taste in a lot of folks' mouths about the 1976 strike."

Gilbert Laws, Bommarito's opponent in 1975, felt the same way. "It seemed to me that he didn't think we had the ability in Goodyear locals that some of the other locals did," Laws said. "That was the impression he left with me. It was probably because he couldn't control us. He couldn't just come in and say, 'This is what we're going to do and that's it.' We must have done something right, because all the other companies sold out to foreign investors."

The animosity between Bommarito and Goodyear was left over from the 1973 negotiations, when Goodyear locals reached a contract first but then BFG and Firestone locals struck to get a better deal. Bommarito had told the press he opposed the settlement and repeated the sentiment at that year's District 1 council meeting. Those statements did not sit well with Charles R. Denny, who was president of Local 831 at Goodyear's Danville, Virginia, tire plant. "You said you told the committee and made it plain to them that the Goodyear settlement did not meet the needs of their members, but the Goodyear committee and membership made a decision to accept the contract," Denny wrote in a 1973 letter to Bommarito. "You said you objected strongly and was so disgusted with the committee that you walked out of the meeting. Brother Bommarito, I ask

Bommarito presents an award to Bob Long during happier times, before Long unsuccessfully ran against Bommarito for the URW presidency in 1978. (*USWA/URW photo files*)

you to tell me, just when in the hell did you object?" Denny wrote that he recalled Bommarito telling the Goodyear committee to accept the company's offer prior to the committee vote. "At that time you told the committee you thought the committee had done real good and had a good contract offer but any decisions made would be ours, but we had better take a close look at Goodyear's offer and not take our people out on strike to get something the government might take away later," he wrote. After more discussions the Goodyear committee voted to reject Goodyear's offer unless there was movement in three areas. After Goodyear agreed to move, Denny said he had no recollection of Bommarito's voicing any objection.

"I realize that in any organization of this type there is a certain amount of politics but I will not stand quietly by and take abuse and be belittled for the job the Goodyear Policy Committee did during these negotiations," Denny wrote.

Thus came the so-called "Reform Group" in 1978, which put forth the most unlikely of candidates. Bob Long had been a top Bommarito confidant from 1971 to 1977 and at one point seemed destined to be picked as an eventual successor to Bommarito. Long joined the URW in 1947 at the BFG tire plant in Miami, Oklahoma. He became Local 318 president there in 1955, holding the post for six years. He joined the URW International staff in 1962 as a field representative and over the years served in various staff posts, including assistant to the district director, special representative in the pensions and insurance department, coordinator for Armstrong Rubber and Uniroyal negotiations, and assistant to the president. "Bobby had been an insider," said John Sellers, a URW staff member at the time. "People seem to get impatient, waiting their turn. I guess Bobby wanted to be president and a lot of people convinced him that he could be, so Bobby became the figurehead for the reform movement."

Another one who was surprised at Long's candidacy was Curt Brown. "It amused me because I started to work at the URW in 1974, and Long, the first thing he said about Bommarito was, 'Isn't he great, isn't he great?'" Brown said. Kenneth Coss remembered the same thing about Long, having been subjected to a number of Long's pep talks on the many attributes of Bommarito. "He couldn't tell you enough about Pete," Coss said of Long. "Pete was wonderful. He couldn't keep up with Pete. Pete is a superhuman person with endurance. He would just go on and on." Coss said he thought that some Bommarito supporters may have set Long up, and that when Long said something against Bommarito, the organizing director was shoved out there where he had no choice but to run for president. "If you can pick your opponent you're a lucky man, and Bob never had a chance from day one," Coss said. "I think he was a handpicked opponent by Pete. I kind of felt sorry for Bob at the time. Bob had his quirks and was an unusual person, but I kind of felt a little empathy for him because he was shoved out there."

"Bobby was Pete's organizational director, and wherever Pete went, Bobby went," Dan Borelli said. "Back in those days, everybody felt he was the heir apparent to Bommarito. I was not in on what happened between them. In this business, I think a lot of people will build you up, tell you their support is there, and it looked like he had a heckuva lot of support. Bobby was a very good worker. As a pension and insurance guy, you couldn't beat him. Would he have made a good International president? I don't think he would have. That's not a knock on him. It's just some people can and some people can't."

Shortly after Long became International organizing director in February 1977, a post he had held in a dual capacity since 1975, the relationship between Long and Bommarito started to sour. Bommarito contended that the bad blood between the two stemmed from Bommarito's selection of Mike Stone as vice president in 1977. Long, however, said the two had an earlier conflict over the role of union professionals. Early in 1977 he said he became concerned that the professionals—staffers hired from outside the URW rank and file—were stepping beyond their job assignments into the URW decision-making process. While the number of such professionals was relatively low, Long said they actively recruited support among URW nonprofessional staffers, hence giving the professionals more power.

Long, who died in 1999, said he first tried to speak to Bommarito about the situation as a friend. "Nobody had fought harder for him—to elevate him to his position—than I had, but as a member of the URW for more than thirty years, I had the right to express my opinion." He said Bommarito responded to his inquiries by stripping him of much of his authority. Long contended that Bommarito hampered his performance as organizational director by refusing to furnish Long with the field representatives' weekly activity reports; limiting his travel by requiring he get advance written approval before making travel arrangements; denying his request to attend the URW district organizational directors meeting; hiring and assigning temporary and permanent organizational staffers without Long's knowledge; and sending him on out-of-town assignments normally handled by field representatives to impede Long's presidential campaign.

"The union becomes almost a religion to some of us," Long said. "If you believe in something strongly enough to devote years of your life to it and to serve in its various positions, then you must also be willing to fight for it." The challenger said he deplored tactics by Bommarito that he claimed were turning the election into a race based on personalities rather than issues. "The union is too important to get into such name-calling," Long said. "It only belittles him to attack me on a personal level after my many years of service to him and the URW." Long also claimed that Bommarito eagerly took credit for membership gains made through Long's efforts as organizational director. In the August 1978 issue of the *United Rubber Worker* newspaper, a banner story proclaimed that nearly eight thousand workers became URW members in representation elections in Canada and the United States from 1975 to 1977. "At a time when anti-labor, anti-people sentiment seems to run strong in these two countries, the United Rubber Workers has done a credible good job in organizing," Bommarito was quoted as saying in the story.

The reform group focused on five controversial points in trying to draw support away from the incumbent. First, they claimed that Bommarito should not be eligible for re-election under the URW's constitution because he had officially retired from Uniroyal on May 1, 1977. The group said that Bommarito had consistently ruled that local union officers and members of the International Executive Board must retire from office at the end of their term following the time they retired from their respective companies. Long also accused Bommarito of improperly accepting more than $2,000 in pay taken in lieu of vacation, which the challenger also claimed was against the union's constitution. Long noted that Bommarito's campaign against George Burdon in 1966 had centered around Burdon having his wife travel at URW expense. "It was wrong in '66 and it's wrong now. Bommarito is more guilty because there's more money involved," Long said.

Another rallying point for Long and the reform group involved the URW's purchase of an old cigar store, which was adjacent to the URW's headquarters building on High Street in Akron. Long and his supporters said the International officers purchased the building with $90,000 in funds earmarked for the construction of a new International headquarters. The reform group also was upset about a $500 retirement gift given on behalf of the union to Joseph Cairns, Firestone vice president of labor relations and a longtime adversary of the URW. Because of the controversy, Bommarito and the other two International officers reimbursed the union's treasury for the full amount. Reform group supporters also accused Bommarito and the International officers of trying to cover up irregularities discovered by a committee studying discrepancies between money collected for the URW's political education fund and the amount turned in to the URW secretary/treasurer. The reform group claimed that

Bommarito convinced the Executive Board to delete from the committee's report all references to these shortages.

Long also was critical of Bommarito's handling of the 1976 strike and contended that, while the URW had made gains in bargaining, the union actually had a poor record in comparison with other international unions. He specifically complained that Goodyear locals were never allowed to try to reach an agreement after the strike started, with Bommarito still insisting that negotiations be focused solely on target company Firestone. Long pledged to be "militant" but credible in contract negotiations. His ten-point campaign platform placed the number one priority on improvements in organizing and the number two priority as merger or affiliation with another union. He ran his campaign on $30,000 donated by rank-and-file members and said he would make sure it was the union members who were in charge of the URW. "Every dollar of my campaign has come from the rank and file. And my campaign has been completely run by local union volunteers," Long said. "[If elected], I will return control to the rank and file. They own it. They bought it. They maintain it. And I intend to be fully attuned to their needs and desires."

Bommarito was quick to dismiss Long's allegations, saying that he had not changed since he was first elected a committeeman at the U.S. Rubber plant in Detroit. "I have always been concerned for my fellow man, trying to work for the best interest of the working person," Bommarito said. "Nothing is of value unless it's related to people. The essence of the struggle is how do you relate technical progress to human progress? How do you translate material wealth into human values? The struggle in our union is to assert the sovereignty of people over things, of human rights over property rights, of people over profits." Bommarito also called Long's contention that professionals had taken over the union as an "idiotic statement," noting that the URW had just seven such professionals on staff. The URW president insisted that his problems with Long did, in fact, stem from Bommarito's choice of Stone from a pool of ten to twelve candidates to replace Oldham as URW vice president. "After a thorough study of the qualifications of each, I found Long was impulsive, often made hasty decisions, didn't use horse sense, had a bad temper, and I even questioned his truthfulness," Bommarito said. "For these reasons, I decided he could not serve in the best interest of the URW." Bommarito said the chief goal for 1979 negotiations would be job security, which was tied closely with the

growing problem of plant closings. He said workers must have early warning of factory shutdowns to allow them to react and perhaps influence the
decision to keep the operation open or to enable them to have some input
into how the plant-closure plan was carried out. "The way to do this is to
make plant closure a heavy financial burden on the company, thus giving
reason for them to modernize old plants," Bommarito said. "If this option
is taken, jobs will be preserved and perhaps created. If the company
decides to close anyway, the people's welfare will be protected through
substantial benefits."

Both sides made numerous attacks—both public and private—during
the campaign. And both Bommarito and Long had plenty of lieutenants
willing to go to battle, with all seven district directors for the incumbent
and the International Executive Board split with eleven for Bommarito
and six for Long. The presidents of the five Acme Boot Co. locals wrote a
letter to convention delegates detailing the role Long had played in their
eighteen-week strike in 1977. After twelve weeks on strike the Federal
Mediation and Conciliation Service in Washington told Long there would
be no contract with Acme Boot as long as field representative Prentis
Lewis continued to head up negotiations for the union. "Mr. Long told
them that was no problem, that he would pull Prentis Lewis off the negotiations," the presidents wrote. "This would have happened, except we
called President Bommarito and he stopped this move. Brothers and sisters, we in the Acme Boot plants were fighting for our very lives and Mr.
Long was willing to take away from us the only chance that we had to win
this strike."

Bommarito's re-election committee also sent a letter to all URW members explaining why Long was sent out on an organizational assignment at
Aeroquip Corp. in Nebraska during the campaign. Long supporters complained he had been sent to "Siberia," but the Bommarito committee
countered that Long had previously said these campaigns were a top priority and that, as organizational director, the assignment was squarely
within his area of responsibility. "In fact, Long himself suggested someone
be assigned there as soon as manpower was available," the committee
wrote. "Despite his campaign rhetoric about the importance of organizing, he formally protested his assignment to this campaign. Apparently he
feels organizing is everyone else's job."

Others said the action of sending Long to Nebraska should have been expected. "In retrospect, it was a big waste of money, but that was when we had plenty of money," said Steve Clem, URW research director at the time. "That was not unexpected. It had been done to other people before. Bobby was Pete's assistant and ran against him. You have to do something. Pete put him out somewhere where it becomes difficult to politick." Stone, who got the vice president nod that Long had wanted, concurred. "Long was in a spot where he should have resigned the spot as organizational director, quite frankly, because that was really pretty much a political appointment of the International president," Stone said. "If you can't support the president, you shouldn't stay at that job. He tried to use it as a springboard."

The reform group even criticized the *United Rubber Worker* newspaper, published by the URW and mailed monthly to members and retirees, for running too many pictures of Bommarito. During the first eight issues of 1978, the URW president's photo had appeared a total of seventy-six times—fifty-seven in the May and June issues alone—while Long's photo had appeared just twice. Curt Brown, the union's PR director and editor of the paper, said Bommarito's picture was used so often because of the newspaper's emphasis on coverage of local union events, district council meetings, picnics, and presentation of service awards. "Peter Bommarito is an active president and he spends a lot of time with the rank and file," Brown said. "Since we stress local coverage, there will naturally be a lot of pictures of him at local events."

As the October convention neared, the lines of support began to form. Bommarito was endorsed by Local 87 in Dayton, the biggest URW local, with all sixteen of the local's delegates pledging to cast Local 87's sixty-four convention votes for the URW president. Long, though, received much support from the Goodyear locals that still were upset with Bommarito. Local 2 at Goodyear in Akron, the union's second largest local at the time, was firmly behind Long, though several of the local's delegates stayed with Bommarito. About a month before the election, Bommarito claimed he had 1,139 delegates pledged to him with 532 for Long, while Long said his count gave him 931 delegates to fewer than 500 for Bommarito.

Local 7 at Firestone in Akron found itself at the middle of the controversy regarding the selection of delegates. About twenty dissident members of Local 7 picketed the local's headquarters at the end of August because they claimed Local President Joe Daniele had violated the union's constitution regarding how Daniele planned to allocate the local's votes at the convention. Local 7 carried thirty votes at the convention, but elected just fourteen delegates to attend, with Daniele automatically selected as the fifteenth voting delegate. While Daniele openly supported Bommarito, Local 7 members elected ten delegates pledged to support Long and just four delegates pledged to Bommarito. In May, however, the local membership had voted to let Daniele allocate the thirty votes among the fifteen delegates as he deemed appropriate. Rather than allocating each delegate two votes, he granted the five Bommarito delegates, including himself, four votes apiece, meaning that Bommarito would get twenty of Local 7's thirty votes. Daniele allocated one vote each to the ten delegates pledged to Long. Daniele did call a monthly membership meeting and gave the Long backers a chance to take away his vote allocation power, but Daniele easily won that vote. "They wanted to make a fight of it and we won," Daniele said. "They lost and that is what they are going to get."

As the convention opened in Toronto, both sides still claimed to have a substantial lead and worked hard for position at the convention hotel's front door to furnish arriving delegates with campaign buttons. Bommarito supporters wore white nylon jackets with "Bommarito, dedicated to the worker" printed on the back. Long had bedsheet-size campaign posters on most floors of the hotel and his supporters' shirts had Long's name on the front and "Bye, bye Pete" on the back.

Bommarito recommended to the Rules Committee that appeals concerning his eligibility to run for re-election and charges that he illegally accepted money in lieu of taking vacation be heard by the convention prior to the presidential election. Appeals traditionally were heard later in the week, after the voting process. Regarding his eligibility for election, Bommarito had retired from Uniroyal two years earlier and was collecting a $500 monthly pension on top of his URW salary. Local 746 President John Nash appealed Bommarito's eligibility to run for another term based on previous rulings that union officers may finish a term after retiring but were not eligible to run for re-election. The International Executive Board voted 10 to 6 that Bommarito could run again. The president argued that he had continued to pay dues to his local union in Detroit and the constitution allowed retired, dues-paying members to be employees of the International and that he, as president, should be considered an employee of the union. The IEB ruled that Bommarito, sixty-three in 1978, was eligible to run for office until he reached the union's mandatory retirement age of

Ike Gold retired from the URW at the 1978 convention, but not before raising hell one more time. *(USWA/URW photo files)*

sixty-five. URW convention delegates upheld the IEB ruling when the issue hit the convention floor.

The split within the Bommarito and Long camps clearly surfaced during the debate on the so-called "Ginty Appeal." Edward Ginty, of Local 895 in Waterbury, Connecticut, argued that the URW constitution prohibited the top three officers from accepting pay in lieu of taking vacation even though staff members were allowed to do so. The delegates decided it was not proper for the convention to rule on the appeal because it had not first been submitted to the IEB, as required by the constitution. Then, amid boisterous protests from Long supporters, Bommarito called Secretary/Treasurer Ike Gold to the podium to clear the record. As Gold began to speak, about 150 members of Long's delegation left the convention to protest Bommarito's handling of the situation.

For Gold, it was one last time to take center stage at a URW convention.

After the convention, Gold was retiring, following eighteen years as a Rubber Workers International officer. Gold had been elected along with Burdon and Bommarito in 1960, and it was he who helped engineer much of the controversy that led him and Bommarito to oust Burdon in 1966. Though he and Bommarito did not always agree, there was no question the two formed as tough and powerful a duo as the URW had seen. And in his final convention, Gold would not be denied the chance to speak. The issue Gold spoke on was not much different from the one used to oust Burdon twelve years earlier. Now, as then, the question centered more on principle than on the few thousand dollars involved in either case. Gold and Bommarito said that Burdon had gone against the URW constitution by allowing his wife to travel with him on URW business at the union's expense. Similarly, Long and his supporters said the URW constitution established executive officer compensation and that the maximum approved for president was $36,000 a year. By taking pay in lieu of vacation time, they argued that Bommarito and the other officers circumvented the constitution to receive an amount in excess of that.

Just as Local 12's E. K. Bowers said that in 1966 he had been given information from those in Akron with which to form his appeal against Burdon, Gold said that two URW insiders had indeed written Ginty's appeal for him. Gold told convention delegates that when he was packing the appeal material for shipment to Canada, he examined each file to make sure nothing was missing. While examining Ginty's material, the secretary/treasurer found a letter to Ginty signed by URW Comptroller Howard Ligon and Manuel Jones, assistant to the International vice president. "Ed, attached is the appeal to the convention," the letter said. "We have also included a covering letter you can retype on your local union stationery." The letter also outlined the exhibits included, when the appeal was due, and that it must be sent by certified mail. Gold assumed that Ginty must have attached the letter to his appeal by mistake. "I am not opposed to political maneuvers," Gold said at the convention. "We Rubber Workers always take our electioneering seriously. But whenever we electioneer and we say things publicly and we put things down in writing for the public to see that could be harmful to the Rubber Workers and could be used against them in the future in organizing and across the bargaining table, then I say those people cannot be considered good union men and women, nor can they be considered good Rubber Workers."

Gold had the union's bookkeeping department prepare a document showing who had taken vacation pay in lieu of time off. Bommarito had taken just twenty-seven days total in his eighteen years in office, or $3,081, while Gold over the same period had taken sixty-four days or $6,500. Gold said former Vice President Oldham, who had retired earlier and was supporting the reform group, took ninety-nine days for $9,926. Gold said the opposition conveniently overlooked the fact that Bommarito received no pay for 177 days of vacation not taken before the IEB voted to allow officers to take the pay. "Ike Gold lost 331 days of vacation because he had too much work to do," Gold said of himself. "I felt service to the membership came first, vacations came last." The secretary/treasurer said he always took his vacation as a member of Local 7, except that then he had a union protecting him. In closing, Gold asked the delegates, "I want you when I leave here—when I leave here finally—I want you, for the record, to tell me I'm still leaving here as a first-class citizen."

While the Long backers criticized Bommarito for the way he handled the gavel, the URW president's supporters marveled at the way he chaired a convention, and said he was at his best in 1978. "It was fun to sit back and watch the convention work and to watch different issues, how they would be processed through from the time you were there," said Kenneth Finley, a former Local 196 president who was on the URW staff by the 1978 convention. Finley was a good friend of Long's, but still supported Bommarito in 1978. "I think Pete was great for our union," he said. "Pete could control a convention, which is a good thing for a leader. He would call for a vote and as soon as that vote was over, 'The ayes got it,' he'd yell. People would be screaming, 'Wait a minute,' and Pete would say, 'Next.' Sometimes you could force a split of the house, but on the ones that they did, they still came out the way Pete called it."

John Sellers had a great view of Bommarito during the convention. As a member of the busy Appeals Committee, he spent most of the convention on the stage. "It was really something to watch Bommarito work," Sellers said. "He loved it. He was just literally up on his toes through that whole convention. When he saw a floor fight coming, he'd just be up on the balls of his feet. He was just bouncing. He couldn't wait." Bommarito also was a master of handling the various microphones for delegates to speak, Sellers said. "From where I was sitting you could see which mikes were lit. Pete knew what buttons to press. When someone would raise a point of order,

Pete would address that point of order and move to the next mike. There wasn't going to be any damn debate, not from that guy. It might come from somebody else but you had better be lined up at a mike. He certainly did not invite disaster. He was a master manipulator, and I mean that in the sense of being able to run a convention." Local 12's Larry Thrasher attended a couple of Bommarito conventions and marveled at his ability to lead the meetings. "Brother, that microphone's broke, you'll have to go over there," Bommarito would dictate from his position at the podium. "By the time you got over there," Thrasher said, "that one had quit and you had to move back. Only Bommarito's people spoke for any length of time. I saw the kill switch on the podium. And that's just another side of a good leader."

As the convention unfolded it became apparent that Bommarito likely would have enough strength left to win one more term in the job from which he had become such a dominating personality on the labor scene. Nearly 600 delegates attended the incumbent's "pro-administration" caucus with an estimated 450 delegates at Long's caucus. The number of delegates at a particular caucus did not necessarily translate into a certain number of votes as delegates can carry up to five convention votes, but it normally gave a fair measure of a candidate's strength. Bommarito's caucus chose Stone for the vice presidential slot on the ticket. He was unopposed after Donald Tucker withdrew at the last minute and opted to run for the secretary/treasurer spot on the ticket.

The Long caucus chose John Dawson, a URW staff member in Texas, for vice president on the ticket, and Local 2 President John Nardella for secretary/treasurer. Having Nardella on the ticket helped bring Long the lion's share of Local 2's forty-four votes, with only five or six of the delegates siding with Bommarito, including Craig Hemsley and his father, Tom, who had been a Local 2 officer under Nardella. "My dad would never, ever go against Pete Bommarito no matter what," said Hemsley, who shared his father's loyalty to the URW president. "I'm not criticizing Bobby Long, but I knew Pete Bommarito. I knew the Big Four feared him to death. . . . I don't think Bobby Long really had an issue." While most of the Local 2 delegates supported Long because of Nardella, some of them never supported Bommarito, according to Hemsley. "Local 2 had a reputation that they would be anti just to be anti," he said. While Craig Hemsley got a URW staff job the following year, largely because of his and his father's support for Bommarito, it hurt him politically in Local 2 circles. "I never got myself the votes after the election in Toronto that I had before," Hemsley said. "I know they literally cut me apart after that convention. I wore the white Bommarito jacket the day after the election when we came back to Local 2. I wanted them to know that I voted for him."

Doug Werstler attended his first convention as a Local 2 delegate in 1978 and dutifully backed Nardella as his local president. "I supported the reform basically because of John Nardella. I owed him that much." Although Werstler ended up backing the losing candidate, he did get a great lesson in convention politics. "It was my first convention, and they'd come around, take you aside and try to convince you that this is the best man," he said. "It was floor fights. Kicking a microphone off. You had microphones at each area and you'd get up to stand and they'd recognize the mike and if you started saying things that mike would go dead and it would go to another mike. There was hollering on the floor, walking out of the meeting. I mean it had it all. It was the good old days."

Bommarito used his opening speech during the convention as one last opportunity to tell delegates why they should stick with him, and why Long was the wrong man for the job. First, he reminded delegates of the gains the URW had made under him, and that they had all done it together. "All of these gains required sacrifices by every member of our union," Bommarito said. "Management has never said, 'Here's more. You deserve it.' But all of us—together—squared our shoulders and pursued these goals with determination because we believe in decent and fair wages and benefits for the work we do." He hailed the 1976 agreement as a triumph of solidarity that was a very costly strike, but worth it. "Now as prices continue to rise, most of our members are protected by some sort of cost-of-living clause," he said. "As a result of that 1976 victory, the number of COLA agreements held by URW local unions has tripled. In terms of membership, that means that over 70 percent of URW members are covered by some type of COLA clause." As of the convention, he said the Big Four already had paid out about $47 million in COLA to URW members.

Bommarito also took some shots at Long and his record as organizational director in his speech. "I propose expanding and improving the URW's organizing program," the URW president said. "The direction of our union's organizing program has grown stale, devoid of new ideas and initiative. Lately, I've gotten too many excuses and alibis regarding our organizing efforts. I've had to assume too much of the responsibility in directing the program." He proposed spending more money and hiring more organizers to bring the union's program up to date.

As for fighting, the convention was full of it—and not all on the convention floor. "We got on an elevator and these two guys got in a fistfight on this elevator," said Annalee Benedict, a onetime International Executive Board member. Benedict said she tried to get between them, but someone pulled her back. "I said, 'We're all in this for the same thing, now come on, shake his hand.' And you know what, he wouldn't do it. The one guy had the other guy down and I jerked the guy by the beard and said, 'Now get up off of him.' The guy wanted to hit me, but didn't. They had enough respect. Nowadays they would have broke my nose. They were just on opposite sides of the politics, and he was pounding him right there in the elevator. Solidarity? They thought solidarity was something they ate at the hospitality suite."

When the delegates voted, Bommarito retained enough support to beat Long 1,093 votes to 685, not that close a contest but still the closest race the URW had had for its top office in thirty years. Long said he was surprised by the loss. "I sincerely thought we had 900 votes," he said. "I think we had some slippage after the delegates arrived in Toronto." He said the "carry votes," which are cast by a delegate for locals that could not afford to send a delegate, went heavily in Bommarito's favor. Long said he congratulated Bommarito after the election but did not ask his backers to forget their differences and support Bommarito. "If I did not agree with him before the election, I cannot agree with him afterwards," Long said. "I think our people will support the leadership when the leaders are right, and I've encouraged them to question it when they think there is something wrong."

Sellers said the outcome was almost exactly as Bommarito had predicted. "Pete told me six months before that convention—and I would imagine he told many people this—how many votes he had. I remember thinking about it at the time of the vote count, that he was only off by about a half-dozen votes. And he erred on the conservative. He actually had six more votes than he had told me six months before," Sellers said. "He was prepared there. There was nothing in that convention that took him by surprise. He was ready for every move." Some were surprised not by the outcome but by the fact that Long never addressed the convention, not even when he had the chance on the many issues the delegates decided.

"Long could have beat him if he got up there and did anything," said Local 2's Tom Jenkins, another of the several Bommarito supporters from that local. "I do believe if he would have got up and made any speeches of any kind that he could have beat Pete. I'll tell you what, that was a tough convention."

Bommarito acknowledged the battle in his acceptance speech and urged a return of unity. "I accept the position of president of the URW with humility and appreciation," he said. "The strongest desire in my heart right now is to see a spirit of unity replace the division we have experienced for much too long. It's a relief to see an end to the political struggle which has so occupied the time and attention of this convention." While the URW's democratic structure allows for such battles and the airing of differing viewpoints, in the end its members are all brothers and sisters, and what is best for the union must take precedence over any personal desires, he said. "We share a common cause that is certainly more encompassing than any one of us."

Though the delegates gave Bommarito the nod for one last term, they also rejected an IEB proposed amendment designed to make the URW's constitution conform to the federal mandatory retirement age, which recently had been raised to seventy. Although URW General Counsel Chuck Armstrong said federal law would overrule the union's mandatory retirement age of sixty-five, it was the delegates' way of telling Bommarito he had better think twice if he wanted to go against their wishes and run again in 1981 at age sixty-six.

Despite Bommarito's appeal for unity in his acceptance speech and in a letter in the December 1978 edition of the *United Rubber Worker,* he also used his letter to take a parting shot at Long. He said that when future political battles come, the URW members must not become involved in half-truths and must put the welfare of the union above individual desires. For example, he said that although the reform group filed no fewer than four appeals scheduled to be heard at the convention, "their candidate spoke not a single word about them or any other issue pending before the convention," Bommarito wrote. "In fact, his only words to the convention were, 'I accept.' . . . In my opinion, this demonstrates not only a lack of leadership but a willingness to let one's friends go down without striking a blow in their defense."

ONE LAST TIME AT THE BARGAINING TABLE

The tire industry master contract bargaining of 1979 was like no other during Bommarito's time as president. For starters, there was no industry-wide strike such as the one in 1976, with the only work stoppage involving Uniroyal. That did not mean negotiations were boring. Among the happenings, BFG proposed a no-strike plan to the URW; Bommarito allowed Firestone to agree to a "me-too" status, ensuring that the union would not name the struggling company as target; Bommarito set one of the union's main bargaining goals basically on a whim; one tire company negotiator agreed to a potentially controversial contract clause just to make trouble for his competitors, who he knew would be hurt more than his firm; and the URW tried to sue the federal government. Of course, by far the most interesting activity of the negotiations was the infamous Uniroyal "renege," where first they had a tentative agreement with the URW and then they did not. When all was said and done, Bommarito insisted that Uniroyal apologize in writing for its actions, which the URW president said made him look like a liar. All this action took place against a backdrop of another round of government wage and price controls, as well as growing layoffs and rubber industry plant closings.

Well ahead of the 1979 contract talks, BFG on two occasions proposed a no-strike plan to the URW to try to avoid facing a strike for the fifth consecutive master contract negotiations. BFG offered its union employees at the six plants covered under the master contract prevailing wages and benefits, in addition to a $200 cash bonus, in exchange for a no-strike agreement from the URW. BFG's plan would have extended the contract expiration date of April 20 by ninety days, essentially removing the firm from the spotlight of the Big Four negotiations. The plan also would have required all disputes over application of the wage and fringe benefits package to be sent to binding arbitration. Because B. F. Goodrich was the smallest of the Big Four tire firms, the company believed separate bargaining was necessary, said Peter J. Pestillo, vice president of employee relations for BFG. "We are trying to have our own identity and participate in establishing our own destiny," he said.

Pestillo himself said he felt labor relations had improved to the point where he was optimistic the company "might have a better experience than in 1976." Pestillo, who later moved on to Ford Motor Co., was well regarded by those on both sides of the bargaining table as one who was willing to look at labor relations in a different way and not necessarily seeking to take everything out of the hides of the workers. "Hiring Pete Pestillo brought a new era of labor relations between the URW and Goodrich," said Matt Contessa, a onetime Local 5 president at BFG in Akron. "I think history will show that after the 1976 strike, the parties felt there had to be a better way."

Even Bommarito was showing signs of adapting to the times. The union was concentrating on winning a job security provision in the 1979 contract. By then, the Rubber Workers were seeing the beginning of what became massive layoffs and plant closings. Unemployment benefits and severance pay plans were written into all the agreements, and the union concentrated on trying to preserve existing jobs and encouraging the rubber companies to create more. "The doors are being shut, and our job, for a company that still has a plant, would be to see that the company expands that plant and invests in renovation and new equipment rather than simply allowing it to run down, as so many companies have done," he said. Bommarito also was quick to see that Firestone—then in dire financial shape largely because of the recall of the Firestone 500 radial tire—was not in the position to face a strike or to set a proper pattern settlement for the rest of the industry. So the URW chief got Firestone to abide by a "me-too" agreement, whereby the tire maker would accept whatever the industry pattern was and the Rubber Workers would not target the firm in contract talks or strike the company. Firestone also agreed to get out of the so-called unholy alliance that Bommarito had fought against for much of his presidential tenure. That agreement effectively broke the mutual aid arrangement and meant that if the URW struck, it would not need to go out against the whole industry as in 1976.

Bommarito and Pestillo even granted a first-ever joint interview to the company's internal newspaper, *BFG Today,* prior to the 1979 contract talks. The two talked about a seemingly new spirit of cooperation between the company and union, how the institution of interim meetings helped, and how the changes in attitude on both sides might show up at the bargaining table. "What has been done by B. F. Goodrich and our own committees should help us approach the bargaining table in a reasonable manner," Bommarito said. "I honestly believe we can avoid the multitude of problems that we had in 1976. A realistic approach to the matter, especially job security, can produce, in my estimation, a settlement." Pestillo said he believed 1979 was different because there were no overwhelming issues facing the two sides as there had been three years earlier. "I believe we understand each other better, that we can communicate in quicker ways, and that we have enough good faith to agree to work some matters out later," Pestillo said. Bommarito and Pestillo also touched on the URW's refusal to accept Goodrich's offer of a no-strike agreement and whether that might impact negotiations. "I don't think the Rubber Workers are ready for arbitration," Bommarito said. "It wasn't the time and it wasn't the place." Pestillo said that while the plan was rejected, it was not a total failure because it was a clear showing of good faith by the company. "The first thing President Bommarito said was, 'I don't think we'll agree to that, but we appreciate your offer. In Goodrich plants, we've had four strikes in four times. We don't want that anymore, and know Goodrich doesn't want that anymore.' Therefore, if nothing else succeeds but a good contract concluded, then our offer played a constructive role," Pestillo said.

Bommarito still had a trick or two up his sleeve: a spur-of-the-moment thought helped to develop one of the URW's main bargaining goals for 1979. The place was the union's Policy Committee Meeting in Cincinnati, where the URW decided what it would seek in that year's master contract talks. The COLA formula won in 1976 granted a one cent raise for each three-tenth point rise in the CPI, but Bommarito wanted even better protection. "Pete looked at me and said, 'What would it take for us to have 100 percent coverage on COLA, given the wage rates we're at?'" said then-URW Research Director Steve Clem. "So I did some quick calculations and said a penny for each 0.26? Now I had no idea what he was going to do next. When it came his turn to get back up, he got up and said we're going after a 0.26 COLA. It was an odd number. That drew a few calls to my office. The UAW and others were saying, 'Where in the hell did you guys come up with 0.26. It's always an even number.' I said, 'Hey, the man asked a question and I gave him an answer.' I didn't know what he was going to do with it, but we got it. No one's ever gotten one any better in major industry." But that was vintage Bommarito, Clem said. "If something popped into his head, 'We're going to get it,' he'd say. He was a charger. That's just the best description I can think of. He went straight ahead."

Because Uniroyal had substantial pension program problems, the URW held early and confidential bargaining with the company beginning in late December 1978, well ahead of the normal start of negotiations. The two sides apparently—at least in Bommarito's mind—reached an agreement during bargaining in New York City on April 18, and the URW president was eager to present it to the rest of the industry. "With a brand new settlement in hand, we flew immediately to the Firestone table in Cleveland, laid out the package to the company, then drove to Columbus to do the same thing with BFG. Both companies accepted the agreement," Bommarito said. But the next day, as the URW prepared to take the pact before its Big Four Advisory Committee for approval, Uniroyal reneged and denied any agreement had been reached. "Labor relations in our industry were never a model, but nobody ever reneged before," Bommarito said. "The difficulties with Uniroyal were a result of federal government interference in the process of free collective bargaining, bolstered by the urgings of the Rubber Manufacturers Association, southern industrial interests, and General Motors that Uniroyal back off its agreement. The guidelines had already been bent by the Teamsters' settlement. But when it was suspected that we broke the [government-mandated] guidelines, they stepped in and torpedoed our agreement."

This action placed the URW in a situation it had never seen before. It had two companies ready to agree to a pattern contract that apparently did not exist. Some in the URW wanted an immediate strike against Uniroyal, but the union held off for nearly three weeks to meet with the company and the Federal Mediation & Conciliation Service (FMCS). Despite these efforts, the URW finally struck Uniroyal on May 9. With those talks nowhere near resolution, the FMCS brought the URW and BFG to Washington and the two sides—basically renegotiating what already had been talked out—reached an agreement within a week. "The agreement exceeded the [government] guidelines, no matter what kind of math you use," Bommarito said. The URW estimated the pact would increase total compensation by 42 percent over three years assuming 10 percent inflation, an assumption that proved conservative as inflation grew 13.4 percent in 1979 and 12.5 percent in 1980. The main gain in the pact was a strengthened COLA, with the one cent an hour raise for each 0.26 increase in the CPI. The union also received a boost in wages, pensions for future and present retirees, vacations, insurance, and plant closure protection.

The agreement also brought a neutrality pact that pledged the compa-

President Carter and Bommarito may be smiling here, but the URW president sued the president during 1979 negotiations because of Carter's wage control program. *(USWA/URW photo files)*

ny to a position of neutrality in URW organizing campaigns at their tire plants.

It was this organizing neutrality clause for tire plants that Pestillo agreed to that always caused Clem to chuckle. "B. F. Goodrich was the only one [of the Big Four] that didn't have any unorganized tire plants," Clem said. "Our assistant counsel at the time was asked to come to Washington, D.C., for some sort of meeting. He was asked to get up and tell everybody about the organizing neutrality agreement we negotiated with Goodrich. They wanted to know, 'Just how were you able to negotiate this organizing neutrality agreement? What special tactics did you use to negotiate it?' He said, 'All their plants are already organized. They stuck it to the rest of the industry.'" The URW did, in fact, organize Firestone plants in Oklahoma City and LaVergne, Tennessee, after the neutrality clause was put into effect, although no one can say for sure how much, if any, importance the clause played in these campaigns.

Settlement with the other major rubber companies followed shortly. "In Uniroyal, in addition to the pattern, we demanded and got a letter of apology from the company, a letter confirming the existence of an agreement on April 18," Bommarito said.

While all that was going on, the URW—later joined by several other AFL-CIO unions—filed suit against the government charging that the guidelines were actually mandatory and that the president had not been given authority to implement such mandatory controls. U.S. District Judge Barrington D. Parker actually granted a summary judgment for the plaintiffs against the government. "President Carter has exceeded the authority conferred on him by the constitution by seeking to control incomes and thereby prices through the procurement power," Barrington wrote in his ruling. "The program established a mandatory system of wage and price controls, unsupported by law. The court, therefore, reluctantly concludes that the president's anti-inflation program cannot be sustained." The victory was short-lived, however, as the Appeals Court later reversed the ruling and the Supreme Court declined to hear the case, letting the Appeals Court decision stand.

WHY DID RUBBER PLANTS LEAVE AKRON?

One of the longest debated questions in Akron is this: "Was the militancy of the URW locals in Akron and the union's reluctance to accept concessions and changes in work rules responsible for rubber and tire jobs leaving Akron?" In 1950 Akron locals had nearly thirty-eight thousand members. By 1975, that number dropped to fewer than fifteen thousand and continued falling until no tires were made in the city except for racing tires. By 1986, the number was down to thirty-six hundred, more than 90 percent less than the 1950 total. By the 1970s, management claimed that restrictive work rules made the Akron plants 10 to 30 percent less productive than non-Akron plants using the same equipment to build the same tires. Consequently, the last passenger tire was made in Akron in 1977, the last truck tire was manufactured in 1981, and the last aircraft tire in 1988. By 1980, Southern plants accounted for 75 percent of the industry's passenger and truck tire production.

The question does not have an easy answer, but one former Goodyear chairman said the union was at least partially responsible because of the URW's lack of cooperation. "We told them the only thing that would give them job security was to be part of a successful operation," said Charles Pilliod Jr., chairman when Goodyear closed its Plant 1 in Akron in 1975 and Plant 2 in 1978. Goodyear was building a new facility in Lawton, Oklahoma, that would be its "model" radial tire facility when it opened in 1978. The machinery would be far better than anything the company had in its other factories, and much less dependent on labor to make a quality finished product. When the radial technology was perfected at Lawton, Goodyear planned to take what was learned and use it elsewhere, and the firm offered Akron's Local 2 the chance for the second phase. During negotiations, the company wanted work rule changes to get rid of featherbedding that had found its way into contracts over the years. "We let them know we would shut down [the Akron plants] if we didn't get it," Pilliod said. "At negotiations, they made it clear they were not ready to accept work rule changes."

Pilliod felt some obligation to Akron and spearheaded a $75 million investment to convert the old Plant 2 into the company's Technical Center and to build an adjacent test track as well. But Goodyear sent the coveted radial tire plant investment to its Gadsden, Alabama, factory, a move Gadsden unionists said was the reason their operation was still in existence in 2001. For that, Local 12 had former Local President Ernie Hayes to thank. After the Akron local rejected Goodyear's proposal, Gadsden was next in line and Local 12 did not say no. "There is no doubt as far as labor was concerned, Ernie Hayes was the responsible person for a radial plant being built in Gadsden, Alabama, in 1978," said Mickey Williams, who was elected Local 12 president in 1995. "He saw what a lot of folks didn't see in America: He saw the demise of the bias tire. He knew sooner or later we would not have jobs if we didn't have some radial technology come into Gadsden." Membership was not too happy to accept the changes, but Hayes convinced the workers that the alterations were necessary. "Ernie Hayes was dominant in those discussions," Williams said. "We thought they were major changes at the time. Compared to some of the things we have to do today, they were probably pretty minor. If it hadn't been for that, we would have been closed a long, long time ago."

Gary Diceglio thought that Nardella, Local 2 president when most of the Goodyear Akron plants shut down, took the closings personally, feel-

Demolition starts in 1980 at Firestone Plant 2 in Akron. *(USWA/URW photo files)*

ing that he had been back-stabbed by the company. "We did some work rule changes, and no matter what we did, it never seemed to help," Diceglio said. "If you look around Akron at that time, every company asked for concessions or work rule changes, and all they did was buy a little bit of time." Diceglio also accused Goodyear of not playing straight with the Akron workers, recalling how Local 2 members read about plans to shut down Plant 2 in the paper. "The company was absolutely terrible to us back then. I felt that there were a lot of outright lies." For example, the company told the union if Plant 2 got to a certain rate, everything would be fine and the facility was safe. The workers got to the standard right away, but six months later Goodyear still shut down the factory.

Diceglio also disagreed with Goodyear Chairman Pilliod's statement that the union was to blame for Goodyear moving jobs from Akron and the role the multistory factories played in the closings. "I'd say there's enough blame on that for both sides to go around," Diceglio said. "It wasn't the union who made the decision not to get into radial tires until years after everyone else was in them." Much was made about the inefficiency inherent in the multistory plants, built in the early decades of the 1900s, when compared with the new, expansive single-story facilities the tire industry turned to in later years. "They can talk about that all they want, but with the conveyor system in there, I don't think the conveyor cares if it goes upstairs or downstairs or flat," Diceglio said. "A conveyor's a conveyor. If it played a part in it, it was a very small part."

Local 2's Hemsley also discounted the union's role in rubber jobs leaving Akron. The city's plants did not build radial tires, but rather the bias-ply tires that began to lose favor in the 1970s. Hemsley did not think the Akron locals should be blamed for that. "If anything, it's the hindsight of the company for not putting radials in Akron—not us," Hemsley said. "We tried to tell them to build radial plants here."

Curt Brown said industry always has tried to blame unions for everything. "I don't know how the industry makes decisions," Brown said. "Obviously they sometimes don't make very good decisions because Akron was a great place to manufacture. We had experienced people, we had transportation, we had water." And the companies did nothing to help keep the Akron factories up to date. "I virtually didn't see a cent put into these old multistory plants," he said. "My opinion is that the Akron plants were milked and that the new plants were already in place, and they tried to go to union-free environments where we weren't organized."

Tom Jenkins, however, was one Local 2 member who believed that Nardella's politics cost the Goodyear local jobs in Akron on more than one occasion. He gave three separate examples where he believed the longtime Local 2 president was responsible for the loss of jobs. The first was when Goodyear threatened to move production of crash pads out of Plant 3, affecting nine hundred to twelve hundred jobs, mostly held by women. "John's position was, 'They won't do anything about it.' Everyone was telling him, 'John, we've got to get involved in it.' We didn't and consequently we lost all the jobs." Next was tire manufacturing at Plant 2. Jenkins said the company had posted countless rates over a number of years, and the union challenged virtually every one of them. "I think the company just got disgusted with that and shut it down," he said.

The third situation Jenkins cited was the company's industrial tire business. He said a Goodyear executive told Nardella the cost of the operation was way too high. "I can't wrap three one dollar bills around every tire we build, John," the executive said, alluding to how much extra each tire cost to build there. "All I want these people to do is work while they were there." The workers were on piecework and often would meet their quota in four hours and take the rest of the shift off. Goodyear wanted the machinery to run, saying that as long as it's producing tires the workers were making money and so was the company. But Nardella did not want to touch that situation either, because of the politics involved, according to Jenkins. After one meeting, the executive told Nardella: "You see all those big holes in the wall where we bring in machinery? We can take it right back out those same holes." Nardella maintained that Goodyear was bluffing and did nothing about it. Three months later Goodyear shut down the industrial tire unit, affecting twelve hundred workers, and moved all the work to Madisonville, Kentucky.

And Goodyear was far from the only tire and rubber company moving jobs from Akron. Goodrich, Firestone, and lower-tier firms such as General Tire and Mohawk all shut down major tire operations in the city. A critical turning point for the B. F. Goodrich operations in Akron came in 1972, when the company came out with its "Hey MAC" program, standing for "Make Akron Competitive." It was supposed to save the plant and save a lot of jobs. But it actually ended up being the undoing of Local 5 President George Cunningham, who supported the program, according to Matt Contessa, the successor to Cunningham as Local 5 president in 1974. "As it turned out, we think the company was not truly honest with us because after we did a lot of things to save jobs, there were a lot of jobs that left," Contessa said. Braided hose production went to Tennessee, then, in 1975, BFG shut down the last of its passenger tire manufacturing in Akron. A total of eighteen hundred Akron jobs were transferred or eliminated over the following eighteen months.

Some Akron labor leaders other than Jenkins also believed the unions had to take some of the blame. Local 7's Clark Lantz said in hindsight he thought the unions could have done more. He cited an agreement Local 7 made with Firestone while he was president in 1988 that led to the building of tire machinery and racing tires in Akron, keeping at least a couple of hundred hourly jobs in town. "But if you're not up in a position of being a president or an International official, they're the only ones who can do that," he said. "They dictate how things are going to go. There was always politics in the union."

Contessa also said the URW definitely played a role in the loss of jobs, with politics one of the key reasons. He said union politics at that time were like no other form of politics, featuring a "no holds barred" format much like a street fight. "The sad part about union politics is that a lot of times it cost jobs," Contessa said. "I've said publicly that in a lot of cases, because of union politics, people were reluctant to make a decision to save jobs, and as a result jobs went." For instance, there were the 1985 negotiations when Goodrich asked that Local 5 forego a forty-three-cent raise the other BFG locals in the master contract received. The firm said if the local did not accept the raise it would guarantee a certain number of jobs in certain product lines—roughly five hundred to six hundred jobs—for the three-year term of the contract. "The union membership chose not to forego the raise and as a result during that three-year period everything left," Contessa said.

Despite the actions of the unions, Contessa also said there was plenty of blame—and other factors—for the loss of Akron rubber jobs. One factor in particular was failure to pay attention to the threat that foreign competition would pose to the North American tire industry. "I can remember at the 1970 convention in Miami, Florida, when the president of a local from the East Coast—a Uniroyal footwear plant—got up and made a lengthy speech about jobs going overseas," Contessa said. "He said, 'You guys in these tire plants, it may not affect you now but it's going to affect you later.'" And so, during the 1960s and early 1970s, when the URW was working to get its "pound of flesh," so to speak, these foreign tire companies began making their move. "While we were being adversarial with the rubber companies, these foreign firms were basically eating our lunch," he said. "I guess it didn't dawn on us until after the 1976 strike that there had to be a better way."

Jobs also left Akron because some of the myriad products once made in the city no longer had a viable market, and because smaller companies elsewhere started making many of the lower-volume goods that had become unprofitable for a large firm because of production inefficiencies. Contessa also pointed out that the URW did do a number of things to try to save jobs, both in Akron and elsewhere. He referred to the decision first of Local 5 at BFG and then of Local 7 at Firestone to go to eight-hour days. Then there was an agreement by Local 5 to combine two rubber band departments into one for seniority purposes. And finally, there were a number of actions by Bommarito to save jobs. Bommarito persuaded Local 2 to vote again to allow master contract changes to keep Goodyear's Topeka, Kansas, tire plant operating, and also told Firestone the union would not target the firm in 1979 negotiations because the company was reeling from the Firestone 500 tire recall.

It was common for labor and management to look at the same situation and come to opposite conclusions. One Firestone executive told a congressional committee in 1975 of a situation three years earlier in which the company wanted to begin making radial truck tires at its Akron plant. "We had every intention to produce that in our Akron facility, and we addressed ourselves to meeting with the representatives of the labor bargaining unit to see if we could find a way to change some of the work practices," testified Mario DiFederico, a Firestone executive vice president at the time. He said that over a period of several months Firestone undertook a program of continually talking with the employees, trying to point out the problems the company faced. The firm even put a setup of the new equipment in the Akron plant to try to demonstrate it was serious about putting the new radial production in Akron. But the union local turned them down. "It's not a matter of not wanting to do something," DiFederico said. "It is a matter that if we cannot produce at a cost that lets us compete in the marketplace, we are not going to produce it at all." But Local 7 President William Jones told the same committee quite a different story. He said that from 1946 to 1975, the company had cut six thousand hourly jobs in Akron through moves to other plants and attrition due to automation. Jones said at times the firm said certain machinery was being taken out for repair, never to reappear at the factory. He also said Firestone never gave the union much real chance to get the radial tire production brought to Akron. He testified the company wanted the workers to take a 50 percent cut for its rates on this type of tire. In the end, Firestone built a new radial truck tire facility in LaVergne, Tennessee, near Nashville, a factory later sold to Japan's Bridgestone Corp.

Charles Jeszeck, a staff economist with the U.S. General Accounting Office, wrote that the conflict between management and labor was a contributing factor to the rubber decline in Akron—but not the determining one. He said America's manufacturing woes in the 1980s often were blamed on workers and unions, with the criticism being that unions had eroded employer competitiveness through high wages and restrictive work rules. Jeszeck maintained that this was not the case in the tire industry in Akron. Instead, tire production left mainly because of developments that were outside the power of the workers and the unions that represented them. He blamed corporate shortsightedness, complacency, and slowness to react to new competitive forces in the industry. "Popular accounts of Akron's decline notwithstanding, unauthorized work stoppages and restrictive work rules did not destroy the city's tire industry, and concession agreements by Akron local unions did not and could not have saved the industry locally," Jeszeck wrote in *Grand Designs: The Impact of Corporate Strategies on Workers, Unions, and Communities*. The only thing that could have saved Akron's tire operations, he said, was timely and proficient radial tire production. He believed that even if locals had met every concession demand, domestic tire makers already had dismissed Akron as a potential site for substantial investment, despite the experience and skill of the Akron workforce, which was unionized and historically militant. "Because investment and location decisions were beyond the range of union bargaining rights, organized labor in Akron was reduced to a single choice in its response to deindustrialization: capitulate or resist in an adversarial relationship," Jeszeck said. "Either way it had to lose."

TOUGH GOING OUT WEST

While Akron definitely felt the brunt of tire and rubber plant closings, another area that was hard hit were the many tire factories located around Los Angeles. These plants also had been built earlier in the 1900s to serve the western United States because of the prohibitive cost of transport at the time. The URW and other unions had faced nearly as much opposition organizing industrial sites in Los Angeles as they had in Akron. If it were possible, the California city was viewed as even more of an "open shop" town than Akron. Still, after many years of struggles, the URW made significant inroads in organizing the tire plants most of the majors had constructed in Los Angeles. Local 43 leaders won a formal contract that included the six-hour day following a three-week strike in early 1939. Local 131 at the Goodyear plant was among the Goodyear locals that signed their first contracts in October 1941. And Local 100 won a May 1940 NLRB election and negotiated an agreement after a March 1940 NLRB decision that ordered the company to withdraw recognition from an independent union and reinstate six discharged URW members.

At one point the URW had about thirty-five thousand members in what was then the union's District 5, which included the eleven western states, according to John Sellers, who once was president of Local 639 at the Voit plant near Los Angeles. All the major tire makers had plants in the Los Angeles area. Mattel had three plants in the area that brought the URW more than seven thousand members total. The unions also organized two big plants in Denver, at Gates Rubber Co. and Samsonite Corp.

But some of the same factors—such as cheaper imports—that closed plants in Akron and elsewhere also negatively impacted plants in Los Angeles. "It was a lot like Akron," Sellers said. "The tire plants were (almost) all bias-ply plants. They were never replaced. They just simply ceased to exist. The cost to retool those plants—they were all multistory—was far more than the cost to build a new plant, certainly with all the incentives that a company gets to build a new plant." Also like Akron, there was a certain amount of expectation that the Los Angeles tire facilities would close, but it was still a shock when it happened. "When you talk about plant closures, people know that it's coming," Sellers said. "They expect it, but reality is far different than the prospect of it. When the Goodrich plant shut down in Los Angeles, within weeks they demolished that building and you really couldn't tell where it had been. There was nothing left."

END OF AN ERA: BOMMARITO DEALS WITH ADVERSITY

Peter Bommarito was at his best when the industry was prosperous and there was potential for a lucrative bounty for his Rubber Workers. The tire and rubber companies worked closely together and the fighter in Bommarito loved to go against the big boys of industry. He took over a union that was looked upon as solid but timid at the bargaining table, and he appealed to the militant side of this group of unionists who felt they were not getting their fair share and were ready to rise up and be counted. Many URW members a full two decades after the Bomber's retirement still pointed to him as the best leader in the union's nearly sixty-year history. And his record at the bargaining table clearly shows that Bommarito delivered on a lot of the things he promised.

But as he served the last term of his fifteen-year tenure as URW president, the landscape of the tire and rubber industry was changing, and so too was the way labor and management dealt with each other. Imports were making greater and greater inroads in the North American market, to the point where many of the foreign firms began looking for domestic production. Groupe Michelin of France had already established manufacturing beachheads in Nova Scotia and the southern United States and was going to great lengths to ensure these plants remained non-union. In the decade that followed, all of the top five U.S. tire makers except Goodyear would be foreign-owned. Plant closings escalated as the industry moved from bias-ply to radials and, consequently, the URW membership rolls began to plummet. Clearly, the proverbial pendulum that had favored labor for much of the time Bommarito reigned in the URW began a swift swing away from the working class and toward management. And the question that lingered over Bommarito was how would he operate in such a changed environment? Would he be shackled to his old ways of fighting every three years or would he be able to evolve and reinvent himself as a labor leader who could thrive under such drastically different circumstances? The point remains a debatable one because, while Bommarito did lead the union through the beginnings of what would be a catastrophic time, it would be Mike Stone, his successor, who faced the most difficult decisions.

"In the Bommarito era, there was no such thing as global competition," said Mike Polovick, who negotiated during his career for Firestone, Pirelli Armstrong Tire Corp., and Continental General Tire. "It's probably good that Bommarito left when he did because, as bright as he was, he probably just by virtue of his personality and who he was would have destroyed the industry because he couldn't understand the need for change. He was just there during the growth era and when it was a U.S. ball game. When the world started playing a major part in tire sales, I think he would have ignored that fact and could have led to the absolute demise of tire manufacturing in the United States just because of his lack of understanding."

Ken Coss expressed similar sentiments. "He was a great president for his time," Coss said. "Probably the only drawback I could see was when things really started to go the other way, when things weren't just there for the asking and the taking, it was tough for Pete to realize that you couldn't always exceed what you did before. And that was one of his goals. He always wanted—whatever we had done before—he wanted to do better."

As much as Sellers respected Bommarito, he too was uncertain how the

Bomber would have reacted as conditions in the industry and union deteriorated. Sellers had been on the URW International staff just a short
while when Bommarito had to lay off a number of staff members, including Sellers. "The fact that he had to lay off staff, I think Pete took very personally," Sellers said. "I know that he called me and told me we were going
to have to do this. He didn't insulate himself from it. We got into an era
where it called for doing some agreements that gave back some things.
That was just not Pete's style. Pete could not have done that. I don't want
that to sound as if Pete wouldn't have done it and others did. I just don't
know if Pete could have dealt with that."

Local 2's Gary Diceglio, however, was one who believed Bommarito
could have adapted. "I think Pete could very easily have changed with the
times," he said. "I think he was that intelligent. I think he would have
changed."

There was no debating one thing: Bommarito did get a taste of the difficulty in dealing with plant closing after plant closing during his final term
in office (tables 6.1 and 6.2). Membership in 1978, the year of his last election, was nearly 178,000, according to URW statistics. By 1981, when Bommarito's reign ended, the rolls already had dropped to 140,056 and were
down to 132,141 in 1982, the year after he left office. And like everything else,
Bommarito faced it head on. He testified at hearings on prospective legislation. He spoke at rallies. He worked toward getting members compensation under the Trade Adjustment Act. And he fought to keep plants open
when he thought there was some chance to save a factory—and a few times
when he probably knew it would do no good anyway.

And it was not just at the big tire factories that URW members lost
jobs. In testimony before one congressional subcommittee, Bommarito
told how three Mattel locals in southern California employed about forty-
six hundred URW members in 1967. But between 1969 and 1971 Mattel
moved between two thousand and three thousand jobs to Mexicali, Mexico, to make Barbie dolls. He also told the story of Hewit-Robin, a division
of Litton Industries in Buffalo, New York. The plant employed about 715
members of URW Local 188. In 1963, the workers had pulled together to
increase production and keep the factory from relocating. In 1973, Local
188 helped out again, allowing the company to defer a pay raise. That April
the company said it would invest $5 million in a modernization and
expansion project. Yet the facility closed on May 31, 1974, while Local 188

Table 6.1 Summary of Tire Plant Closings, 1973–81

1973
Gates Rubber Co.: Local 154 in Denver and Littleton, Colo.; 800 employees

1975
B. F. Goodrich Co.: Local 43 in Los Angeles; 732 employees

B. F. Goodrich Co.: Local 5 in Akron (partial closing); 200 employees.

Goodyear: Local 2 at Plant 1 in Akron (partial closing); 1,300 employees

1976
McCreary Tire & Rubber Co.: Local 293 in Baltimore, Md.; 85 employees

1978
Goodyear: Local 2 at Plant 2 in Akron; 1,200 employees

Firestone: Local 7 at Plant 2 in Akron; 1,000 employees

Mansfield Tire Co.: Local 17 in Mansfield, Ohio; 750 employees

Mohawk Rubber Co.: Local 6 in Akron; 300 employees

Uniroyal: Local 44 in Los Angeles; 500 employees

1979
Mohawk Rubber Co.: Local 539 in West Helena, Ark.; 470 employees

Pennsylvania Tire (owned by Mansfield Tire): Local 845 in Tupelo, Miss.; 700 employees

IRI: Unorganized plant in Louisville, Ky.; 300 employees

1980
Goodyear: Local 131 in Los Angeles; 1,100 employees

Lee Tire (owned by Goodyear): Local 785 in Conshohocken, Pa.; 850 employees

Uniroyal: Local 11 in Chicopee Falls, Mass.; 1,300 employees

Uniroyal: Local 101 in Detroit; 1,600 employees

Firestone: Local 100 in Los Angeles; 1,205 employees

Firestone: Local 726 in Salinas, Calif.; 1,290 employees

Firestone: Local 336 in Pottstown, Pa.; 1,980 employees

Dayton Tire (owned by Firestone): Local 178 in Dayton, Ohio; 1,240 employees

Seiberling Tire (owned by Firestone): Local 18 in Barberton, Ohio; 840 employees

1981
Firestone: Local 7 at Plant 1 in Akron; 1,345 employees

Armstrong Rubber Co.: Local 93 in West Haven, Conn.; 650 employees

Source: United Rubber Workers.

Table 6.2 Non-Tire Plant Closings, 1980

AGP Corp.: Local 897 in Peru, Ind.

Barrday Division of Wheelabrator Corp. of Canada Ltd.: Local 1052 in Cambridge, Ontario.

Canadian Urethane Soles Ltd.: Local 977 in Hamilton, Ontario.

H. O. Canfield Co. of Indiana Inc.: Local 863 in London, Ohio.

Cart Manufacturing Inc.: Local 646 in Columbus, Ohio.

Champion Rubber Co.: Local 864 in McAlester, Okla.

Flintkote Co.: Local 950 in Chicago Heights, Ill.

Goodyear: Local 532 in North Chicago, Ill.

Healthways subsidiary of Eldon Industries Inc.: Local 451 in Los Angeles.

Killian Manufacturing Division of Akwell Industries Inc.: Local 20 in Akron.

National Fibrit Division of Mansfield Tire Co.: Local 1009 in Springfield, Tenn.

New Jersey Rubber Co. and Luzerne Rubber & Plastics Co.: Local 575 in Taunton, Mass.

Nosco Plastics Inc.: Local 319 in Erie, Pa.

Oliver Tire & Rubber Co.: Local 676 in Flemington, N.J.

Seiberling Latex Products Inc.: Local 842 in Oklahoma City.

Structurlite Plastics Inc.: Local 1058 in Lebanon, Ohio.

United Foam Corp.: Local 1038 in Shawnee, Okla.

Source: United Rubber Workers Research Department.

was on strike, although community and union leaders believed that Litton had planned to close the plant all along and the strike gave them a welcome excuse. "People who have given many years of faithful service to a company find themselves suddenly without a job, often with little hope of finding other or equivalent employment because of age, because of community dependence on the dislocated plant, or because of a tight job market," Bommarito said. "And unless they were covered by a union contract, it is unlikely the employees will get any benefits from the employer."

But workers at the tire plants took the major blow. As radials took over more and more of the U.S. market, many of the antiquated, high-cost bias factories shut down. And as globalization began to take hold, many of the smaller tire manufacturers closed shop or sold out. From 1973 to 1981, twenty-five tire manufacturing facilities in the United States either partially or completely closed. Twenty of those shut down from 1978 to 1981 as the nation suffered through a tough recession. Bommarito was quick to blame the government and tire manufacturers, but never seemed to want the union to take any of the heat. "The closures were mainly caused by the failure of the government to address the flood of automobile imports—and thusly millions of tires—from foreign countries, and that is still true today," he said in 1981. "It is also true that some of the tire companies were using such antiquated machinery and were so mismanaged that nothing could overcome their ineptness."

During the 1979 negotiations, the URW was successful in negotiating a six-month advance notice of plant closure that gave the union the right to negotiate to save a facility and, where that was not feasible, to negotiate on how the closing would be carried out. The union also gained special pension programs, severance benefits, extended medical coverage, preferential hiring rights, and life insurance protection. "We did what the legislators couldn't do," Bommarito said. "The URW's plant-closure clause has become a model for other unions to follow."

The URW and rubber industry management sparred again in 1978 over the proposed National Employment Priorities Act, which was first introduced in 1973 and would have amended the Fair Labor Standards Act of 1938. The legislation would have required companies to provide advance notice of and justification for all plant shutdowns or relocations; provide federal support to communities and individuals suffering hardships as a result of such corporate action; and discourage plant moves through government assistance and penalties. "While there is nothing wrong with states actively competing with one another to lure new industry to their areas, in this contest the cost to the losers—the former employees—is tragically high," Bommarito said.

Industry sentiment toward the bill was universally negative. Companies contended the measure would impair management's ability to make judgments on plant closings and relocations in the same manner as other economic questions; allow the entry of the federal government into a fundamental business decision; inject clearly noneconomic factors into situations where economics should be the overriding concern; encourage industrial immobility; and cause a serious defect in the American free enterprise system. "If there is a real sociological problem involving plant closings, then it does need to be addressed, but companies are not insurers on social welfare," said BFG's Pestillo. "We still operate on the theory that strong companies survive and weak ones die."

Often the URW and others tried to find ways to keep plants open, but most of those efforts failed. Bommarito worked closely with Detroit city officials in 1980 to try to save the seventy-five-year-old Uniroyal tire factory where the URW president began his rubber industry career. Bommarito also held futile discussions with a group of West Coast investors reportedly interested in purchasing plants to be closed by Firestone and Uniroyal. One of the most publicized attempts to save a tire plant during this period was when publisher Beurt SerVaas was asked to consider becoming part of a local effort to save the Uniroyal Tire plant in Chicopee Falls, Massachusetts. SerVaas earlier had helped save nearly six hundred jobs for URW Local 110 members when he bought and revived a Uniroyal inner tube plant in Indianapolis, Indiana, that was slated to close. But the same magic did not happen, as Uniroyal, while offering an attractive sales price, could not provide suitable tire molds, and increased price competition in the industry kept away potential customers.

While plant closings in the tire and rubber industry were widespread, one day stood out above all others. On March 19, 1980, Firestone in one announcement detailed the closing of six U.S. factories, including five tire factories and its Akron synthetic latex plant. The largest one-day plant closing in rubber industry history permanently put eighty-five hundred people out of work. The tire factories primarily made bias tires, with the exception of a Salinas, California, facility that did make some radials.

Mike Stone, Bommarito's vice president during his last term, was there at the Pittsburgh airport when Bommarito got the news about Firestone. "We were waiting between planes and Pete got paged," Stone said. "We kidded that he paged someone to page him, so he went and took the call. It was early in the morning, about 8 o'clock. He came back and said, 'You guys better sit down.' It was Firestone calling to tell him about the move to shut down all those plants in one fell swoop." Bommarito reacted tough, trying to make use of the distressed plant language in the union's contract with Firestone. "We were supposed to meet and try to save the plants,"

Stone said. "But Leon Brodeur, number two in the chain of command, said, 'There's nothing to talk about.' He said, 'It's gone too far.' Pete raised hell in the newspaper and everything else about not living up to the contract because they pledged they would try to save plants."

Though Bommarito did change near the end of his tenure, fear still was never an option, according to Stone. "They didn't make Pete run scared. I don't know that anyone could make him run scared. It wasn't in his make-up," Stone said. "He was an ex-Marine and a Golden Glove boxer. When he got in a battle he battled to win. There was no backing down."

But he mellowed at the end of his term, because the union was starting to make concessions. Bommarito faced the facts in some cases that something had to be done or plants would close. One was the Goodyear tire plant in Topeka, Kansas. Local 2 also made some concessions in Akron that allowed for the construction of a mold plant and an air springs facility. "He recognized that some things had to be done as well," Stone said. "He didn't like to admit it, but his actions spoke louder than words. He was still pretty vocal on the outside, but he acted responsibly. No one usually gives Pete much credit for acting responsibly, but the fact is that he did."

Matt Contessa was one who saw evidence of Bommarito's ability to change and play it smart. Contessa, on the URW staff at the time, was assigned to help negotiate a contract that expired in October 1979 at Local 18 at Firestone's Seiberling Tire unit in Barberton, Ohio, a suburb of Akron. The tire firm traditionally followed the master contract pattern agreement, but during these particular negotiations, the local just could not get the company to agree to anything. Some of the Local 18 members were upset and wanted to strike. "Pete told me, whatever you do, don't let them strike," Contessa said. Bommarito had received word that Firestone was planning to close a number of factories, and one likely to be on the block was the old Seiberling plant. Contessa told Local 18 President Joe Albanese to inform the company that the employees would work day-to-day under the terms of the old contract. "We worked that way until Firestone announced it would close six plants, and that was one of them," Contessa said. "After that the workers got all the benefits that went with plant closing rights. Had they gone on strike, the company would have blamed that closure on them going on strike."

Bommarito—who died September 25, 1989, at age 74 after battling cancer—left his last official impression on the Rubber Workers at the 1981 URW Convention, where he sadly had to hand over the mantle of leadership. In his final report to delegates, Bommarito showed he knew he was leaving the union at a critical time. "Not since the middle of the 1930s, when by law we were given the right to organize without coercion and management interference, has the assault on organized labor been stronger," he said. "The public relations attorneys and consulting firms that are set up to show companies how to violate the law are the fastest growing businesses in the United States and Canada."

The URW president also touched on how difficult it would be to give up "what has been the driving force in my life," but that he would respect the union's constitution and retire as it dictated. "I hope that I have left a strong legacy to the URW," he said. "But while one man can make a difference, no man is an island. Whatever has been accomplished during my tenure has been the result of the efforts of a lot of good people. Once again I thank you all for your support in the past. We made a good team. We made the Rubber Workers a better union. That's what really counts the most."

And that was pretty much what others still thought about the Bomber two decades after he left office.

PART III

THE ONCE AND FUTURE UNION

CHAPTER 7

THE URW IN TRANSITION
THE MIKE STONE YEARS

Milan Stone—known to most everyone as Mike—vividly remembers his introduction to the labor movement. He was working at the U.S. Rubber (later Uniroyal) tire plant in Eau Claire, Wisconsin, a small but well-organized union town. Besides the tire factory, a paper mill and a pressure cooker factory were the primary employers in Eau Claire. Along with the United Rubber Workers Local 19, there were the barber union, the bartender union, and numerous other labor organizations in town.

Sometime during 1947, Stone was working the night shift in the Banbury Department at U.S. Rubber. His task of dumping carbon black was among the filthiest in the plant, and he was showering in the morning when one of his co-workers told Stone the Packinghouse Workers union needed help on the picket line over at Drumm Packing House, a local slaughterhouse. Stone recalls the Packinghouse Workers as a pretty militant gang, and they were striking over health and safety issues. "It got to be a pretty violent strike," Stone said. "The workers tipped cars over, but they didn't hurt anybody."

When they recruited volunteers, Stone was quick to jump in. He had never been on a picket line before and, after all, it was something to do. So after showering he went to the packing house, arriving just as the union members prepared to stop a train from entering. Supervisors in the slaughterhouse had loaded refrigerated boxcars, and the company was trying to send a train engine inside to pull the cars out. "So our job was to get on the railroad track and stop that train from going in," Stone said. The railroad men jumped off the engine because in those days it was unthinkable for a union man to cross a picket line. The strikers formed three circles and started singing "Solidarity Forever" and other union songs. A supervisor took control of the train engine and tried to scare the strikers off. "That guy would come within a quarter inch of you. He'd nudge that train up," Stone said, "and we wouldn't budge. Finally they backed away. So I've always said that my introduction to the labor movement was to prove that I had a face that would stop a freight train."

Stone said there really was nothing extraordinary in his background that would foretell his career as a union leader and fifth president of the United Rubber Workers. "It just sort of happened," Stone recalled. "I didn't have any sort of union background. My mother and father were farmers, and I didn't really have feelings one way or another about unions."

Born June 11, 1927, Stone was raised on a dairy farm in Rock Falls, Wisconsin, about twenty miles from Eau Claire. He joined the navy when he was seventeen and served in World War II from 1944 to 1946. After the war he worked as a section hand on a railroad and then polished pressure cooker kettles at National Presto in Eau Claire while still living in Rock Falls. Stone rode in a car pool with some U.S. Rubber employees. He noticed that while their paychecks were the same size as his, the tire workers got twice as many, being paid weekly instead of bi-weekly, as he was. So he kept checking at the tire plant for openings, finally landing a job later in 1946 dumping lamp black. It was dirty work, and Stone got laid off often in the early days.

After the first layoff, Stone tried to get his old job back. "The guy said, 'You left us to go to the rubber company. Just stay there.' He did me the biggest favor he ever could have done." In those early days, Stone really wanted to work in the tire room. But he had to do heavy-duty bagging and curing first. And dumping lamp black—a filler ingredient in tire compounds—was where he started. "It wasn't a very desirable job but I needed one real bad. I was newly married, so I said I'll take it. Well, it was dumping fifty-pound bags of lamp black through this big hopper up on the roof of the building, up on the fifth floor. That was pretty modern at that time. It went through the big hoppers to all the floors of the building and then was weighed automatically with automatic scales."

Although he hoped to move to the tire room, Stone spent the next seventeen years in the Banbury Department, not dumping lamp black but in compounding and just about every other job there was. It was also in this department that he received his first contact with the United Rubber Workers, on his very first day of work. It was Marlin Hammond who showed Stone the ropes on his new job and introduced him to all the union stewards. "I haven't seen him for forty-some years but I'll never for-

Mike Stone was the
URW's fifth president,
serving in a time of
industry globalization
and downsizing.
(USWA/URW photo files)

get his name," Stone said. "And he told me if you ever have any problems, you go see these guys. I've always said that really made an impression on me that he did that." In fact, had it been a supervisor who approached Stone, his career might have taken a different course. "If the supervisor had been the first guy to come to me, and told me all the great things the company was doing for me, who knows—I might have been a plant supervisor instead," he said.

During his time at U.S. Rubber, Stone was active in Local 19 virtually from the beginning, but again there was nothing to forecast his eventual ascension to the top of URW hierarchy. He first served as a shift steward, then moved to chairman of his division and a spot on the Local 19 executive board. From 1956 to 1963, Stone was a time-study engineer, helping to determine how much time individual jobs should take. From 1959 to 1961 Stone was Local 19 vice president, but he never became president of his home local.

Local 19, especially in the mid-1950s, struck at the drop of a hat. "If they raised the weight of a tire half a pound, well, there was a strike. It was overdone some," Stone said. Finally, by the end of the decade, U.S. Rubber instituted a labor policy union workers called "three, six, and twenty." It meant a worker was suspended three days the first time he was involved in an unsanctioned wildcat strike. That was followed by a six-day suspension the second time, twenty days the third, and dismissal for the fourth wildcat strike. "It really is a pretty liberal policy, but man, we thought it was terrible," Stone said. "But it pretty much put a stop to that."

Stone joined the staff of the URW International in 1963 as an International field representative in District 4, serving URW locals in the north-central states. From 1964 until December 1972 he was assigned as an International time-study engineer. He then came to URW headquarters in Akron as a special representative in the Pensions & Insurance Department, and also served as the coordinator for the Uniroyal locals during 1973 master contract negotiations. Stone moved back to his home District 4 at the end of 1973 as assistant district director, before being named district director just two months later. District 4 was the URW's second-largest district with more than 40,000 members in eleven states at the time.

In 1977 Stone's career within the URW took an unexpected upward turn. Kenneth Oldham retired mid-term as URW vice president and an immense lobbying effort ensued to sway Bommarito's appointment of his successor. Donald Tucker, who would be elected secretary/treasurer in 1978, wanted the vice presidential slot. And Bob Long, who would run against Bommarito on a reform ticket in 1978 after not getting the VP nod, really wanted it. Stone, though, had no designs on the job. "I didn't lobby for it or anything else. In fact, I was supporting Don Tucker. But Bommarito didn't really give me any inkling that he had me in mind."

Bommarito did send out a couple of signals. Whether it was naïveté or tunnel vision, Stone just did not read them. First there had been the assumption that Stone did not hail from Akron and preferred his home territory. He had, after all, transferred back to District 4 just a year after getting his first Akron-based position. That led to a discussion with Tony Campos, then a director on the East Coast. At first it seemed like a benign talk, two friends just playing a game of "what if," and Campos's question to Stone was: "Would you ever go back to Akron." Stone said he would if the job was right.

Following that was a strange conversation with Bommarito. "He called me up and said, 'Don't pledge your support to anyone,'" Stone said. "I said, 'I'm kind of leaning toward Don Tucker.' He repeated, 'Don't pledge your support to anybody.'" So Stone just figured Bommarito had another candidate in mind outside of those lobbying for the post, and the URW president was warning Stone not to burn any bridges by supporting a losing candidate. "Then Pete called me up and said he was going to appoint me, but keep it quiet." Looking back, the signs seem so clear. Campos was acting as the "fisherman," testing the waters to see if Stone was amenable to the switch. The top officer would never make such an offer without being certain of an affirmative answer. "I had no idea what [Campos] was talking about," Stone said. "Afterward he told me he was assigned to talk to me like that."

At this point, however, having Bommarito's blessing did not necessarily make Stone a shoo-in. There was a split on the URW's Executive Board, with a faction still supporting Long. "I had some real good friends who voted against me," Stone said. "They weren't really voting against me. They were voting against Pete." Bommarito still had enough support on the board to bring about Stone's appointment to vice president, thereby surpassing any expectations the new number two URW officer had ever set for himself. "I never had even set my goals for anything like that, to be honest with you," Stone said. "I thought maybe when Bommarito retired that I might have a shot at being one of the three officers. But not of being president. I hadn't thought about that. I really kind of thought that Don Tucker was the likely guy to move up in that spot, and so did [Tucker]." Tucker, in fact, intended to run against Stone for the vice presidential slot on Bommarito's ticket at the 1978 URW convention. But when Ike Gold retired as secretary/treasurer, Tucker ran for that office instead. "[Tucker] campaigned right up until the convention," Stone said. "He didn't have the votes. So when we had our caucus, Tucker decided he'd run for secretary/treasurer. That avoided a battle in that instance."

So Stone was on his way to taking the United Rubber Workers through most of the 1980s, a decade that saw the rubber industry, the URW, and all of labor in transition. How Stone's leadership is viewed depends on who is asked. Detractors characterize Stone's nine-year tenure as "caretaker leadership," while supporters credit him for acting sensibly and being open to new ideas. One thing was clear: he was not Bommarito. That was a plus for supporters and a minus for detractors.

"I remember being in a negotiating session as a minute-taker in 1979. Bommarito walked into a negotiating session, but before he walked in, everybody from the union walked in. Then, as Bommarito was walking in, I could have sworn I heard a drum roll," said Mike Polovick, then a negotiator for Firestone. "Then contrast that three years later when Stone came in. He was in the room fifteen minutes before I even realized he was there. That was the difference: Peter Bommarito played all the avenues and took full advantage of all the qualities of being a leader."

But the times dictated Stone's actions, and he did not get the credit he deserved for keeping a number of plants open, Polovick said. "If you would have put Peter Bommarito in Mike Stone's era, I'm not sure Bommarito would have been successful." Longtime tire industry analyst Harry Millis agreed: "Mike Stone was the right guy at the right time. There are always going to be people on both sides who feel they could have gotten more or given less. It got to the point where everyone came to realize you had to sit and talk about what's doable, not what's desirable."

Steve Clem worked for both Bommarito and Stone, and he said both were leaders for their times. "Pete was a charger, but you needed a charger and the industry and the country could afford it. I don't say that facetiously, but we didn't run into real competition from overseas and down south [Michelin] until pushing the latter part of Pete's tenure," Clem said. "Pete could not have done in the '80s what he did in the '70s because the times were different."

Stone, though, never enjoyed the luxury of having 180,000 members behind him. Tire companies had already started closing plants, and the URW lost literally half its membership during the latter part of Bommarito's tenure and Stone's term of office. "We didn't have the clout that we used to have, so you had to go at it a different way," Clem said. "And Mike

Stone was a guy who could go at it a different way." Clem never felt Stone received proper credit for all of his accomplishments, probably because Stone had some stances that were not popular in labor circles. For example, Stone espoused the philosophy of working a full eight hours for eight hours of pay. Many tire industry workers traditionally were paid on a piecework system, meaning they had a certain quota to meet per shift. When that production was met, the worker was free to relax or leave and still receive a full day's pay. Stone saw domestic tire makers struggling to remain competitive and felt some practices must evolve for both tire firms and his membership to thrive, Clem said. "And I think to his credit he recognized that there was enough blame to go around. That was pretty much Mike's philosophy. He tried to get some of these unreasonably strict work rules changed. For a labor leader that's pretty gutsy stuff in a lot of respects."

Curt Brown also liked Stone. "He tried to do things with diplomacy. He was intelligent, and we never wrote a speech for him," Brown said, adding that Stone mainly would speak from some notes. "He gave the best speeches and he never had a written speech. He made sense and he'd get to the point, and he knew what he was trying to do." On the rare occasions someone would present him with some "good fighting language"—a speech that Bommarito would relish—Stone invariably would reply, "Sounds a little scratchy." Brown said Stone did not want to insult the companies or anyone involved with them in the press. "He wanted to work cooperatively and I think he was a very statesmanlike International president," Brown said.

Stone lacked, however, in the areas Bommarito excelled, according to the PR director. "Stone had a good sense of humor, but he did not press the flesh. He'd go out to a district meeting and see the people, and give a cordial and friendly speech. He was just a little more reserved. He would shake hands with [meeting attendees] and greet them. Bommarito worked the room and so did Ken Coss. But Mike didn't work the room very well." Stone, however, shined in other areas, such as working better than Bommarito both in the URW's relations with Goodyear and in the International's dealings with local unions representing Goodyear workers. "He was a really good president in what he did. I just don't know if URW members knew how good he was because he was so undemonstrative."

Stone seemed almost surprised by his success, Clem said. He recalled a time right after Stone had been elected URW president and several union officials were still in Florida. "We were out on a small yacht going for an evening cruise on the intercoastal waterway," Clem said. "Mike and I and [URW General Counsel] Chuck Armstrong were standing on the back of the boat, looking out at the wake that we were leaving. Somebody said, 'I guess we'll get a good look at where we've been.' And Mike replied, 'Yeah, but I still don't know how I got here.'"

Despite his success, Stone never forgot his roots. He kept a picture in his office of himself and a group of coworkers from the carbon black department at the U.S. Rubber plant back in Wisconsin. "He was just covered in carbon black," Clem said. "He said, 'I keep that up there to remind me of where I was.' He was a union man through and through."

BRINGING THE UNION CLOSER TOGETHER

The URW entered its 1981 convention anything but united. At this gathering in Bal Harbour, Florida, delegates faced the task of selecting a successor to Bommarito, who had reigned over the union for a tumultuous fifteen years. It was widely assumed Stone would stroll easily into office, carrying the weight of the vice president's office and, more importantly, a strong endorsement from Bommarito. But things are never that simple. Bommarito had faced a tough fight from the reform group at the 1978 convention, and some of that bitterness remained. In addition, URW members came to the 1981 convention worried about their jobs. Membership had fallen to 140,000 members from 190,000 just seven years earlier, and more plant closings were expected.

Glenn Ellison, District 1 director since January 1979, provided the competition. By all accounts, he and Stone ran a civil campaign, something that could not be said about the Bommarito-Long battle three years earlier. "Mike Stone and Glenn Ellison conducted the most gentlemanly campaigns I'd ever seen in a labor union," Clem said. "They just both focused on what they felt they could bring. Even in the caucuses and hospitality suites, there was not a lot of character assassination going on."

Ellison said that his candidacy had more to do with keeping Bommarito from running rather than any thoughts Ellison himself had of rising to the URW's top office. "I believe that after winning the 1978 election, Pete almost felt he was superhuman," Ellison said. He told of a spring 1980 meeting of district directors and department heads in Florida at which

Bommarito tested the waters. "I was beginning to get the feeling—and I don't think it was all bluster—that if Pete could convince himself that he could jump that age factor that he would run for president again," Ellison said. While the URW constitution's provision mandating retirement at age sixty-five arguably was illegal, Bommarito in 1978 had unsuccessfully attempted to have the decree lifted. The only way to really get around the mandate, Ellison thought, was to have the clear support of all URW leaders for a further candidacy.

So at the Florida meeting Bommarito polled the directors and department heads on the question: "If I ran again, what would be your position?" Ellison said everyone, including Stone, pledged their support to Bommarito until it was Ellison's turn. Rather than toe the party line, Ellison spoke his mind. "I told Pete, 'Number One, I've supported you since 1960 when you went in as vice president. I've voted for you at every convention that I attended. But if you try to run in 1981, that age question is going to be an overwhelming factor and I don't think it will go.' Pete got visibly—I thought—upset, and he said something to the effect, 'Well I enjoy a good fight and you've just said enough to almost make me run.' I said, 'If you want to run that's your business, but I will not make a commitment to support you.'" When the polling got to Tucker, he told Bommarito, "You better listen to what Glenn is telling you." From that point on, Ellison said, there was no love lost between himself and Bommarito, or Bommarito and Tucker, for that matter. Because of that, Ellison said he took it upon himself to oppose Stone for URW president in the 1981 campaign. "I had no illusion that I could beat Mike," Ellison said. "And it wasn't an ego trip, believe it or not, but I felt unless there were at least some token opposition, that Pete was going to run again."

Stone held most of the cards, and Ellison had trouble gaining support. Stone even used the opening on his ticket to gain additional backing. He and Tucker ran unopposed in the pro-administration caucus, but nine candidates contended for the vice presidential slot on the ticket, including two local union presidents who had backed Long in 1978. Stone, Tucker, and Bommarito played no favorites, allowing the pro-administration caucus to choose. The tactic, whether intentional or not, served to bring supporters to the camp. Unofficial tallies showed attendance at Stone's caucus outnumbering Ellison's by a six-to-one total. In the end, District 2 Director Joseph Johnston won the number two spot on Stone's ticket.

Bommarito passes the gavel to Mike Stone in 1981 as Stone is elected the fifth URW president, along with Vice President Joe Johnston (right) and Secretary/Treasurer Donald Tucker. *(USWA/URW photo files)*

"There is no question that the strategy brought a tremendous number of delegates into the pro-administration caucus," Ellison said. "That's politics." Stone acknowledged that politics played a role in the selection process. "The only thing we said was if you're going to run for vice president in our caucus, then you have to pledge to support Stone and Tucker and whoever comes out of that caucus," he said. Stone remembers talking about the strategy with an *Akron Beacon Journal* reporter covering the convention. The reporter remarked the tack was a good way to keep all those people in line. Kidding with the reporter, Stone said, "Oh, is that it? I just thought all those people were really for me."

In the wake of his victory, Stone did make some promises he would find impossible to keep. "Michelin will belong to our union some day. The other tire companies were tough, too, but we got them," Stone said. But what URW insiders remembered was one promise Stone did keep: helping to unify a fractured union badly in need of a dose of solidarity. "That's what we had to do after the convention," Stone said. "There was bitterness and so on. Even though Ellison didn't get that many votes, there were still people out there who were ticked off from the previous convention. So I used people according to their qualifications and not their political allegiance."

Clem said Stone was effective in healing fractures developed in the Bommarito years. "Mike's acceptance speech was something like: 'We've been split. Let's become a *United* Rubber Workers.' He held out the olive branch and put some reform people on staff in important positions. Mike did a lot for the URW. He was almost like President Eisenhower. We needed somebody to calm things down a little bit, and Mike did that."

TOUGH TIME TO BE PRESIDENT

It is said the best leaders adapt to the times in which they lead. Most leaders probably would rather have it the other way around, and be able to make the times adapt to them, but normally that is not an option, particularly if you are president of an industrial union. Stone, unfortunately for him, had little say in the state of the tire industry—or for that matter the U.S. economy or political environment—when he took office. By all measures it was not a good time to be a labor chief. Had Stone been given the choice to select when he wanted to be president of the United Rubber Workers, he would have chosen the selection marked "any time but the 1980s." But that is not the way things work.

For Stone that meant at any particular time during his tenure having to deal with any number of potentially catastrophic events. First there were tire plant closings, both before his presidency and, to a lesser degree, during his first two terms in office (table 7.1). These closings caused declining membership rolls, which translated into fewer dues making their way into the union's coffers. That in turn meant the union had to keep its staffing levels lower, so URW locals began feeling that URW International was not serving them well. It also meant less clout at the bargaining table and on the political scene. The U.S. Department of Labor reported that the URW was among fifteen labor organizations reporting membership drops of more than 25,000 between 1978 and 1980. And with a gross decrease of 27,000 members, the URW actually posted the biggest percentage drop, at 15.2 percent of its members.

If that were not enough, Stone and the URW had to contend with foreign tire makers taking a growing share of the North American replacement tire market. The trade imbalance, along with the growing globalization of the industry, helped weaken many of the U.S.-based tire producers to the point where foreign manufacturers came in for strategic acquisitions. In the 1980s alone:

Japan's Sumitomo Rubber Industries purchased Dunlop Tire Corp., with two U.S. tire factories;

Germany's Continental A.G. bought GenCorp's General Tire operations and its four tire plants;

B. F. Goodrich and Uniroyal merged their ailing tire businesses, forming Uniroyal Goodrich Tire Co., which later was purchased by Michelin of France;

Japan's Yokohama Rubber Industries bought Mohawk, which came with just one tire facility;

Italy's Pirelli S.p.A. scooped up Armstrong Tire Co. and its three tire plants; and

In the biggest deal of all, Japan's Bridgestone Corp. purchased Firestone. Still the second-largest American tire maker, Firestone had gone through a disastrous recall and made wholesale plant closings, and Bridgestone gained a coveted North American presence in its bid to become the world's number one tire manufacturer.

All the wheeling and dealing left Goodyear and smaller Cooper Tire as the only U.S.-owned firms among the world's ten largest tire producers. It also left Stone's URW having to negotiate increasingly with companies where the first priority was in a country on some other continent. When it came time for cutbacks it largely was assumed—especially by the Japanese-owned firms—that the axe would fall on U.S. workers before the company would make the politically tough choice of slicing the workforce back home.

The 1980s also were the time of corporate takeovers and a "Greed is good" mentality on Wall Street. The rubber and tire industry did not go unscathed. Goodyear faced a takeover bid from corporate raider Sir James Goldsmith, who took more than $90 million in profits, leaving the leading U.S. rubber company saddled with billions of dollars of debt and forcing it to close at least two plants and sell various other businesses. Uniroyal

Table 7.1 Plant Closings, 1982–87

1982

General Tire: Local 9 in Akron; 1,018 employees

1983

Firestone: Local 186 in Memphis, Tenn.; 1,680 employees

1984

Goodyear: Local 185 in Jackson, Mich.; 300 employees

1986

B. F. Goodrich: Local 318 in Miami, Okla.; 1,600 employees

Firestone: Local 887 in Albany, Ga.; 1,650 employees

B. F. Goodrich: Local 281 in Oaks, Pa.; 882 employees

General Tire: Local 312 in Waco, Texas; 1,229 employees

1987

Armstrong Rubber: Local 303 in Natchez, Miss.; 440 employees

Kelly-Springfield (owned by Goodyear): Local 26 in Cumberland, Md.;
     1,028 employees

Source: United Rubber Workers Research Department.

and General Tire parent GenCorp also faced hostile takeover bids, in both cases helping to lead to divestiture of their respective tire operations. "It was the worst time. It wasn't just us, but for everybody—steel and auto and everybody," Stone said. "The attitude of management was to get concessions. In a lot of cases maybe they really needed them, but in some cases they just went after them because it was the possible thing to do at the time." Clem saw firsthand what a difficult period it was, as his department compiled the figures on everything from plant closings to loss of members to trade deficits. "Mike presided over the URW during a period when we lost a lot of membership, but it had nothing to do with Mike," Clem said. "The die was cast and Mike tried mightily and did what he could to stave off some of that. And I can't give you a bunch of successes but once a company makes a decision to close a plant, they're usually going to close that sucker."

Table 7.2 URW Loses Strength

1975: Of the sixty-five tire plants in the United States, the URW had organized fifty-seven, leaving just eight unorganized.

1986: Of the forty tire plants operating by this time, just thirty-one were organized by the URW and nine were unorganized.

Lost members: All but one of the U.S. tire plants closed from 1975 to 1986 were organized by the URW, costing the union about thirty thousand members.

Source: United Rubber Workers Research Department.

A quick look at the numbers Clem and his department compiled paints a bleak picture of exactly what Stone and the other URW leaders faced (table 7.2). From 1975 to 1986, tire makers closed thirty of the sixty-five tire plants in the United States, and constructed just five new factories. Of the shuttered plants, the URW had represented workers at all but one (several URW plants closed in Canada as well). Conversely, the Rubber Workers union organized none of the new tire factories. At the end of the decade of shutdowns, the URW represented just thirty-one of the remaining forty U.S. plants, just two more URW shops than the total shut down since 1975. Nineteen of the twenty-nine closings occurred in the four years prior to Stone's taking office, marring the final years of Bommarito's reign. There were 89,900 U.S. tire production workers in 1975, and an estimated 54,000 by 1986. By 1987, the URW represented just 75 percent of tire-making capacity in the United States, a share that dropped steadily over a ten-year period.

Most of the closed facilities were older units making the outdated bias-ply tires that had been replaced by the longer-lasting, technically superior radial tire. While radial tires were more labor-intensive than bias-ply, the new radials lasted several times longer, delaying the need for consumers to buy replacement tires and taking a huge bite out of the aftermarket. In addition, U.S. companies were well behind their foreign counterparts in switching to radials, and the overseas firms took advantage by taking a larger and larger percentage of the U.S. tire market. Not surprisingly, total

URW membership took a free fall during this period. From the high of 190,000 in 1974, the union's roster had already dropped to 140,000 in the year Stone took office. By 1987, membership totaled fewer than 109,000, before stabilizing between 104,000 and 105,000 during Stone's last term.

Plant closings told only part of the story. Besides losing members to closings, many other URW locals suffered losses in membership as numerous companies scaled back operations without making full-blown shutdowns. The voting strength of locals declined sharply from the union's 1972 convention to the 1981 gathering when Stone was elected president. Each local gets a vote for every one hundred members, and during that period sixteen locals lost five votes or more, representing a loss of membership of at least five hundred workers in each local. Several lost many more, especially in Akron. There, Local 2 at Goodyear dropped a whopping twenty-eight votes from 1972 to 1981 (and lost another seventeen votes during Stone's tenure, leaving it at nineteen votes); Local 5 at B. F. Goodrich fell by fifteen votes (and lost another twenty in Stone's years, dropping it to two votes); and Local 7 at Firestone lost twenty-four votes (before dropping fourteen of its remaining sixteen votes under Stone). The sixteen locals lost an aggregate 179 votes, and dropped another ninety-one votes during Stone's three terms of office, representing an approximate loss of 27,000 members at those locals alone. By comparison, just six locals gained at least five votes from 1972 to 1981, rising a total of just forty-two votes. Those locals gained another eighteen votes with Stone in office, not even coming close to neutralizing the losses.

One thing that kept the URW, as well as other industrial unions, from replacing lost membership was the sheer number of laid-off workers. Every closed plant that sent a thousand or more workers packing would take several successful organizing campaigns at non-tire factories to replace the lost membership. Tire plants became less and less an opportunity for organizers. Just nine U.S. plants remained unorganized after the rash of closings, and four of those were owned by Michelin, famous for its anti-union stance. Of the remaining five, four were located in right-to-work southern states, where union membership was optional and the companies worked hard to guard the facilities' non-union status. Stone and other URW officials did become adept at giving speeches on plant closings, getting plenty of practice in telling the reasons, the effects, what needed to be done, and so on. There was the radial tire, the economic recession brought on by the Reagan administration, the virtual depression in the auto and housing industries, and many other factors. One thing Stone always tried to impress upon audiences was the impact of plant closings.

"Today, many of our workers who have given years of service to a company find themselves suddenly without a job, too often with little prospect of finding other or equivalent employment because of age and a tight job market," Stone said in one speech before the Economic Policy Task Force shortly after he was elected. "Today, the rubber worker, as well as workers in other industries, is facing a different situation. In previous recessions, people viewed layoffs as temporary, but with the current economic situation the worker fears permanent job loss. Many Rubber Workers currently on layoff see little hope that they will be back to work in the near future." Throughout the unpleasant period, Stone handled himself better than anyone could expect, said John Sellers, who was a staff representative out west during most of Stone's tenure. "Mike agonized over the decisions that had to be made. Mike really cared," Sellers said. "Who would want to be the steward of a union through a period like that? If you had a crystal ball and could see that coming, would anybody really want that job? But Mike did it and he did it with dignity."

The URW actually found itself in a bit better shape than some of its counterpart unions because of contract language gained in 1979 master contract negotiations. Since that pact, unionized tire plants had to give the URW a six-month notice of a plant shutdown and negotiate with the union to try to avert the closing. These two features—advance notice and consultation—were featured in plant closing legislation that the U.S. House of Representative considered but did not pass. Other URW contract protection included unreduced pensions for those with twenty-five years of service or those age fifty-five or older with five years of service. Workers not eligible for pensions received continued health care and life insurance coverage for two years.

Cities frequently were decimated by the closings. Often the plants had been the major employer for decades, creating a ripple effect on city population, school enrollment, and tax bases. The effect on Akron—the longtime "Rubber Capital of the World"—has been well documented. Eight tire plants closed in Akron alone from 1975 to 1982, affecting more than seven thousand workers, ending large-scale tire manufacturing in the city.

Back in the 1940s and 1950s, between fifty thousand and sixty thousand workers—known as shop rats—toiled in Akron's rubber plants. By the time General Tire shut down the last major tire unit in Akron in 1982, fewer than seven thousand hourly employees worked in the city's factories.

Other cities, though, felt pain as well. Places like Conshohocken, Pennsylvania, where a Goodyear closing left 850 people jobless in 1980. Or Chicopee Falls, Massachusetts, where Uniroyal furloughed 1,300, also in 1980. Or any number of West Coast cities, where all but one tire plant closed. Miami, Oklahoma, was typical of a small town where the tire plant was king. Workers at the Goodrich factory had been the highest paid workers in the town since 1945, making more than $20 an hour in wages and benefits when BFG pulled the plug on the two-thousand-employee plant in 1985. Often, the closing notice came with no forewarning. For example, General Tire workers at Local 312 in Waco, Texas, had ratified a three-year contract in May 1985. The company even gave the facility business projections reaching into 1989. But six months later came word that General Tire would shut down the factory the following spring, blaming the declining market for the bias tires made in Waco. "All we got was a statement from the company that came as a complete surprise," said Local 312 President John Dawson. "There were some concessions put in the contract and that's all a matter of record. But we thought they put in what they needed to stay in the market."

What made the closings even harder to accept were the stories behind the headlines. It was not difficult to become desensitized to tales of hardship and cutbacks. When it happens again and again, it is easy to lose the perspective that behind every layoff is a face, someone likely trying to pay off a mortgage and put children through school. The blue-collar middle-class workers could not even get the one thing they wanted most: hope. "The best message to give them may be that they're lucky they did so well for so long. For a lot of these people it really *is* over," said Dennis Ahlburg, then a professor of industrial relations at the University of Minnesota.

KITCHENER: NO LONGER A BOOM TOWN

On a Friday night at the labor hall on King Street East in Kitchener, Ontario, it was hard to imagine that the city had once been a labor mecca. At one time there had been thirty-three locals affiliated with the labor hall, including a number with several thousand members. But by the end of the twentieth century that number had dwindled to fifteen locals, with just one of those boasting more than a thousand members. So now, at 7:30 P.M. on a Friday in March, the only people to be found were the bartender and the president of one of the Kitchener locals. Big parties thrown by the locals used to be the norm. Union members used to have to be there by 1:00 P.M. on a Saturday just to get a seat for the ever-present card games, the bartender said. Now the hall is lucky to do $60 in business on a Saturday. The hall used to employ three full-time bartenders; by 1999 it had just one. "What keeps us going is the dart leagues," the bartender said, pointing to the fifteen dart boards that decorated the walls.

And closings by rubber plants were a big part of the decline. Kitchener once boasted more than seven thousand URW members, a number that fell to fifty-five hundred by the time of the 1995 merger with USWA and fell further to fewer than three thousand by 1999. John Fuhrman was president for twenty-three years of Local 67 at Dominion's non-tire rubber product operation in Kitchener. He served from 1965 until 1988, when he lost by a vote; then he sat out a term and was elected the next time as vice president for the guy who beat him. "At one time we had twenty-two hundred people there, not counting the salaried help or people in the lab," he said. The plant at one time was predominantly a footwear plant, then it made a wide range of products such as crash pads, geo cells, sponge rug underlay, and, for a short period of time, floor mats for cars and plastic bumpers. By 1999, though, the operation had gone through several ownership changes and the workforce had dwindled to just 250 or so workers following a decade or so of decline. Fuhrman said that what happened was not all that different than what happened in Akron. "I can remember when I was in Akron, I went to see some of the plants that were closed up already," Fuhrman said. "I never thought that it would happen to us, but it was quite a few years later that the closures started to come. I remember I did a survey of the labor hall here when I was president. I wanted to find out how many members the other locals had. We had lost about five thousand members then through plant closures." He motioned to the main street through Kitchener. "This street was a bustling street at one time. Now the only time I come down here is once a year to pay my taxes, and I kind of regret that because it's not that safe. They don't have anything here downtown."

James Webber knew just how tough it was when the plants closed through personal experience. He was the president of Local 73 when Epton Industries went out of business, putting Webber's members out of work. Goodrich had still owned the plant when Webber started working there. "You had this false sense of security that if you worked for that corporation you had lifetime employment," Webber said. "And things pretty well stayed the same until the mid- or late 1970s." But then a recession hit in the early 1980s, and Goodrich made the strategic decision to diversify away from tires and rubber products into chemicals. The company as they knew it would never be the same. BFG made the decision either to sell or close the non-tire rubber product plant in Kitchener. The operation was sold to the so-called "whiz kids"—former BFG Canada Treasurer Michael Wheaton and his partner, James Aylward. They named the business Epton Industries. Local 73 accepted a 23 percent cut in wages and benefits to ensure the deal went through, Webber said. The local struck the plant in 1986, but in the late 1980s, Webber said, the union and workers acted responsibly. "We as a union went to management because we had concern as to what we had seen," he said. "Basically we saw some very stupid business decisions." Webber cited Epton's plan to concentrate not on rubber but on plastics, in which the firm had no expertise in technology.

Epton eventually filed for Canada's version of Chapter 11 bankruptcy protection from creditors. Just prior to the URW's merger convention with the USWA in 1995, it appeared that the business was going to be sold. "In a period of one month's time, that deal basically fell apart," Webber said. The buyers had met with Local 73 to negotiate an agreement, and it looked like the deal was all set. "Then the new government came in and that was the end of it," he said. "Everyone in this community knows what the Rubber Workers did (to try to get the sale approved). It was sold, but management pulled the plug on it." It was during this time of need that Webber saw—as did the many other local union leaders when their plants had closed—the true value of being part of the URW. "No matter where you went, if you requested anything, help was only a phone call away," he said. "It was right here in town. That's what made the Rubber Workers union, in my opinion. There will never be another union like it. Never."

While many of the Kitchener locals were shrinking or disappearing, one local finally broke through after decades of trying. If perseverance counted for anything, then the members of Local 88 at the Kaufman Footwear plant in Kitchener would have qualified for a grand prize of some sort. It took fifty years from the time the workers first voted to join the United Rubber Workers union to the time when Local 88 finally got a signed contract and received its URW charter in 1988. It took at least four organizing campaigns, a couple of failed strike attempts, and a great deal of persistence to receive that coveted charter. At times the union won the representation election but could never get the Kaufman owners to agree to a contract. Local 88 had such a low local number because the Local 88 designation was saved from when the workers first voted to go URW. One reason Kaufman was so difficult to negotiate with was because the footwear maker actually was a Kitchener-owned business, unlike the many U.S. subsidiaries that popped up in town. "It's a one-man owner and always has been. He seems to own the town," said Local 88 President Patrick Warlow. "They definitely do not like unions, someone telling them how to run their business."

Warlow said it was not a lot of drastic items the union sought in its contract, just things like respect and dignity for the people who worked there. One area in which he hoped the union actually could help the business was in employee turnover, which went as high as 80 percent annually at the plant. "We would sit around the lunch room and if there were ten of us, there'd probably be only two left by the end of the year," he said. One reason for the high turnover was that pay varied from employee to employee. "The merit raise system was ridiculous," Warlow said. "You would go up as long as you got along with your foreman." But then there were cases where some workers who had been at the plant for thirty years still made the base rate. "Finally, we were able to negotiate that out of the contract," he said. Some other gains in the decade after getting that first contract included such items as bumping and seniority rights, and job postings—"just things other people take for granted that they've had at other places for years."

Albeit slowly, Warlow acknowledged that Kaufman did start making progress in dealing with the union. "There's a lot of things that have been straightened out," he said in 1999. "They're coming out of the '30s and starting to work toward the '60s now." Health and safety conditions improved markedly. The two sides started out with one-year contracts for the first three or four years, before going to the more traditional three-year pacts.

Even in 1999, however, Warlow saw signs that bad times were ahead for the maker of footwear products. During the previous year or two a lot of the plant's work had gone to factories in China and Mexico. Employment at Kaufman had dropped from about fourteen hundred in 1996 to just more than eight hundred three years later. A number of industrial plants around town had shut down, making workers at Kaufmann wonder when they would hit the chopping block. Unfortunately, it was just a year later, in 2000, that the Kaufman workers received the bad news: the company went into receivership and its assets were sold off. After fighting for a union contract for five decades, the workers had only twelve years to enjoy the benefits of its coverage.

As Kaufman went the way of so many other Kitchener businesses, so too did the closing leave still fewer union workers to tell the stories of early URW pioneers like George Goebel—the "martyrs," as Warlow liked to call them. "Those guys went through tough times," Warlow said. "They didn't do it for themselves. They did it to benefit somebody like their children and me. And I've got a lot of respect for that."

URW NOT ALONE IN ITS TRAVAILS

Stone and the United Rubber Workers could take one consolation from the trouble the union was having in the first half of the 1980s: the labor organization was far from the only union experiencing such ills. By 1983, 10.7 million people were unemployed, translating into an official unemployment rate of 9.6 percent of the domestic workforce looking for jobs. The unofficial rate likely would have been several points higher if it included those who had become discouraged and given up hope of finding jobs. While the nation supposedly was in an economic recovery at the time, studies showed that the gap between the rich and poor widened, the standard of living for the middle class remained stagnant, and the poverty rate in the United States rose above 15 percent in 1983, the highest since President Lyndon Johnson started his "Great Society Programs" in 1965. About thirty-five million Americans lived in poverty, six million more than in 1980. "The most unfortunate aspect of this statistic is that today roughly one child in four under the age of six lives in poverty. A great nation does not stand tall when it leaves the poor behind," the URW stated in its 1985 Collective Bargaining Policy. In that policy, the URW clearly blamed one person for the state of the nation's working class: Ronald Reagan. "Reaganomics hasn't worked for labor," the URW said. "It hasn't worked for the industrial sector. It has helped only the affluent. This nation needs new economic policies that will benefit all the people, not just a fortunate few."

To give a clear picture of the effect of domestic plant closings and job cutbacks, the U.S. Department of Labor's Bureau of Labor Statistics conducted a special study of workers whose jobs were abolished or factories shut down between January 1979 and January 1984. The study identified 11.5 million workers age twenty or older who lost their jobs for one of three reasons: closing down or moving of a plant or company, slack work, or the termination of a position or a shift. The Labor Department concentrated on the 5.1 million who had been at their jobs at least three years, assuming those workers had developed a relatively firm attachment to their work. Of that group, 60 percent (3.1 million) were re-employed in January 1984, 25 percent (1.3 million) were looking for work, and the rest (700,000) had left the workforce. But among those who had jobs, about 360,000 were able to find only part-time jobs, and about 45 percent were earning less in their new job. Age and geography also played a significant role in the ability to find work. While 70 percent of those age twenty to twenty-four had new jobs, just 41 percent of those fifty-five to sixty-four were working. The hardest hit area was the East North Central Region (Illinois, Indiana, Michigan, Ohio, and Wisconsin), with 1.2 million displaced workers. This area, where many of the closed rubber plants were located, also had the highest rate of unemployment, with nearly one-third of the workers still searching for jobs.

The power and numbers of labor definitely declined as more and more workers lost jobs, with many manufacturing employees having to choose jobs in the nation's growing service sector. The percentage of non-farm workers in the United States belonging to unions took a corresponding plunge. In 1970, 27.3 percent of non-farm workers were unionized; by 1980 that percentage dropped to 23 percent, and to just 18.8 percent by 1984. Union ranks fell from 20.1 million to 17.3 million members from 1980 to 1984 alone. Unions still represented a larger percentage of manufacturing workers, but even that slid to 26 percent in 1984 from 32.3 percent in 1980. Overall union membership stabilized later in the decade, as did the URW's, with 17 million total union members in the United States in 1989, a number that was virtually unchanged since 1985. But as overall employment in the nation increased, the unionized portion of the workforce declined from 18 percent in 1985 to 16.4 percent in 1989. The URW needed to look no further than its eventual merger partner, the United Steelworkers of America, to find a union suffering similar losses—but on a much grander scale. The USWA lost half its membership in the first half of the 1980s—dropping it to 740,000 members—as major steel producers felt the impact of the recession and increasing market penetration by foreign and domestic non-union competition.

Both labor leaders and company heads looked at the U.S. trade deficit as one reason for the dire straits of the domestic industrial economy. The nation suffered a record trade shortfall of $40 billion in 1981, but that was nothing compared to what would follow. The deficit reached $70 billion in 1983, $123 billion in 1984, and approached $200 billion by 1985. The rubber and plastics industry pretty much followed suit. The deficit for rubber and plastics products was $1.87 billion in 1983, $3.25 billion in 1984, and headed for $4 billion in 1985. Tires and footwear were the main culprits, accounting for 75 percent of the rubber and plastic trade shortfall for 1984. The trade deficit in tires was $1.45 billion, and in footwear nearly $1 billion.

Imports of car, truck, and bus tires reached nearly 49 million units in 1987, representing an all-time-high 26 percent of the U.S. replacement tire market. To make matters worse, 3 million automobiles equipped with 15 million tires and 900,000 new trucks and buses with 4.5 million tires were imported in 1987, meaning that the United States that year absorbed nearly 69 million imported tires in these segments. In market sectors such as radial truck and off-the-road tires (for such things as earthmovers), imports held closer to 60 percent of the market, with tires coming from South Korea, Mexico, Brazil, and Taiwan, among other countries. It was easy to draw a correlation between rising imports and falling U.S. jobs. In 1973, tire and tube imports totaled $500 million and there were 115,000 American jobs in the industry. By 1985 imports had soared to $2 billion, and domestic jobs in the sector had plummeted to 66,500.

Stone was vocal in his cry for "fair trade" rather than "free trade," a concept he said existed only in theory. "The labor movement does not consider itself to be protectionist, although some have put that label on us," he said. "Instead, we regard ourselves as supporting fair trade and being realistic enough to recognize that the United States, the biggest market in the world, cannot indefinitely continue to absorb the rest of the world's goods at the expense of our own domestic industries. We simply don't live in a

Fair trade was a rallying cry for years for the URW. Here, Local 12 President J. R. Countryman shows off a bumper sticker in his office in Gadsden, Ala., that sets forth his message that buying foreign cars puts Americans out of work. (*USWA/URW photo files*)

free trade world. We never have. We've got to stop kidding ourselves and realize what is happening to the industrial base of the American economy. And we've got to do it soon, while we still have an industrial base to save."

The URW leader said that while Americans had the right to buy whatever product they want, wherever it was made, they had to live with the consequences to the U.S. economy. As imports captured 30 percent of a slumping U.S. automotive market, more than 1 million jobs were lost in the auto and auto-related businesses. "Please don't get the impression that I am blaming imports for all of America's unemployment problem—only for part of it," Stone said. "But the fact remains that high levels of imports at a time of high domestic unemployment definitely do not mix." Stone argued that the United States must realize there was no free and open "world market," and adopt such measures as domestic content legislation for the automotive industry. "This is a world in which nations, some more than others, have protected their markets and pursued what they view as their national interest. They do not apologize for it, but we do," he said. "We need to negotiate fair trade with the rest of the world. We need access to their markets just as they have access to ours. . . . The bottom line really is this: If we don't support our own domestic industries that employ our friends and neighbors, the cost later on will be astronomical."

It was against this economic backdrop that Stone found himself in a difficult position when representing his membership where it counted most: at the bargaining table.

CHAPTER 8

A FOUR-LETTER WORD
CONCESSIONS

Had Mike Stone ever dreamed he might breeze through his first set of master contract negotiations without a hitch, Uniroyal squelched that hope shortly after Stone took office. The rubber company faced financial doom, and came to the URW in late 1981 seeking company-wide financial concessions. It was rare that such givebacks took place on such an extensive level; normally companies sought contract modifications from individual facilities that were in jeopardy of extensive cutbacks or permanent shutdown. But Uniroyal's financial ills called for drastic action, and Stone and the URW recognized that fact and granted the company relief to the tune of $18.3 million a year in cost-of-living allowance and wage and benefit cuts for the next three years. In turn, Uniroyal agreed to accept the master pattern contract as long as those concessions were applied to the pact. "I told Uniroyal, you guys can sure pick the time if you need that right before we go into negotiations," Stone said. "We did make some concessions because they were screwed up. It wasn't our making though, it was management's, really, and they needed the concessions they got."

Stone, as the new kid on the block, wanted to make sure the other companies in the master contract process—Goodyear, Firestone and B. F. Goodrich—did not try to capitalize on the Uniroyal concessionary agreement. "I thought negotiations were going to be tough, but when we got to Goodyear, I just told the company: 'Don't use what we did with Uniroyal as some sort of pattern, because it isn't going to be that way. If you want to open up your books and show us you're in the same shape as Uniroyal is we'll talk to you. Otherwise, forget that Uniroyal had any dealings with us.' And to Goodyear's credit, they never mentioned it." The URW president also told Goodyear that how the company treated the union in bad times, which 1982 definitely was, would be how the Rubber Workers would treat Goodyear in good times. Stone pointed to those negotiations as a turning point at which labor relations with Goodyear—traditionally stormy and confrontational—started to improve. "Goodyear was an honorable group of people to deal with, I found. Pete (Bommarito) used to battle with Goodyear all the time," Stone said. "I'm not sure if he did some of that for political reasons or not. I found them to be honorable. You didn't need to have it in writing with Goodyear. If you had their word that was good enough."

STONE'S MASTER CONTRACT NEGOTIATIONS

The tenor of comments leading up to the 1982 contract talks made it clear that reaching a peaceful settlement indeed was possible during that round of negotiations. For most of the previous fifteen years it had been common—almost expected—that Bommarito would lead the URW on strike against one or all of the major tire manufacturers. Numerous factors made such a stance unlikely in 1982. President Reagan was in office and set an undeniable anti-union tone in his policies, with the crushing of the air traffic controllers union a case in point. The nation was in a deep recession. Domestic tire shipments slumped to their lowest levels since 1967, and tire companies' financial fortunes were at a low point. New URW president or not, 1982 did not look like the year for the URW to draw a line in the sand. Cooperation had improved dramatically over the past three years, and it was obvious both sides had a definite understanding of each other's needs.

Not that Stone's URW would lie down and be a patsy. He and other union leaders said there were certain provisions of the contract—particularly COLA during that inflationary time—that were untouchable. "We want to give them fair warning that if they have any ideas to do anything with those provisions of our agreement, that we'll have a problem," Stone said.

The 1982 talks went pretty much as projected. The agreement contained no general wage increase but did maintain the current COLA formula. Most importantly, it was the first set of master negotiations without a strike against one of the top-tier tire firms in more than fifteen years, although there was a short strike later that summer against second-tier firm Armstrong Rubber.

Times were better for the industry going into 1985 talks, and the URW's tone and bargaining goals reflected that. Profits had been good for the Big

Four tire companies covered by the pattern bargaining. After earning just $6 million in 1982, Firestone posted profits of $111 million in 1983 and $102 million in 1984. B. F. Goodrich tripled earnings to $60.6 million in 1984, while Goodyear and Uniroyal both posted record profits in '84, at $411 million and $77.1 million, respectively. Aggregate profits for the four rubber companies exceeded $1.1 billion for the two years leading to 1985 talks. "The rubber industry has done rather well since we last met and they are expected to do well in 1985," Stone said. "We realize the industry still has some problems. However, I think it is only right and proper that we get a fair slice of the economic pie. We recognized the industry's situation in 1982 and settled without a general wage increase. That situation has changed. Rubber Workers deserve a general wage increase in this set of negotiations."

The talks, while unspectacular, did take a few strange twists. Firestone started early by trying to abort the pattern settlement process, telling negotiators it planned to close its Des Moines, Iowa, tire plant (concessions later saved the operation) and it would not abide by the pattern settlement. "An agreement by Firestone will have to be tailored to Firestone's particular demographics and cost measurements," said William Rusak, Firestone vice president for labor relations. "The tire companies in this industry are more diverse than in any time in history. The historical practice for a pattern settlement regardless of content is over."

The URW selected Goodyear as the target company with which to set a pattern contract, but switched to B. F. Goodrich after Goodyear locals turned down a tentative agreement. Goodyear warned workers that if they went on strike only ten of the twelve U.S. facilities covered by the master agreement would reopen after the walkout ended. The company, of course, did not say which two plants were targeted for shutdown. BFG and the URW then came to an agreement that kept COLAs and boosted the pension multiplier for future retirees from $16.50 to $20 per month per year of service (meaning a worker with thirty years of service would receive a pension of $600 a month). More importantly from the workers' standpoint, they did get a general wage hike above and beyond COLA, albeit only forty-three cents an hour over the life of the contract. The pact was adopted as the pattern and was accepted by the other companies, including Firestone, despite the firm's earlier threats. "The pattern strategy is fair and reasonable for the parties involved," Stone said. "The union has

Mike Stone wears an old-style organizing cap. (*USWA/URW photo files*)

demonstrated its cooperation if a company has special needs but the profitable tire industry must share with those employees who have built these companies, including our retirees."

Observers noted that the conditions leading to 1985 contract talks were similar to those of 1976—company profits were high and the union was coming off below-average results from the previous negotiations—but the bargaining outcomes were quite different. Nine years earlier the URW had staged its historic strike and won a large settlement, but the 1985 talks ended peacefully and with a relatively low-cost contract for the companies to deal with. One difference, though, was that in 1976 the URW shut down an estimated 60 percent of industry capacity at the strike's peak and conceivably could have closed 75 percent. But by 1985 the union, still reeling from a decade of plant closings, probably could have shut off no more than 40 percent of domestic tire-making capability.

The 1988 talks had a little bit of everything. One company settled early. Firestone again tried to break the philosophy of solidarity behind the master contract process. Locals at Goodyear rejected a tentative agreement. Workers at Firestone struck for a week. One local president resigned when he felt he no longer had the pulse of his membership. Goodyear's chairman made an unprecedented appeal at one plant. A federal mediator was called in to help. Some cracks in unity within the URW ranks began to show. And former URW President Bommarito even put in his two-cents worth at one point.

The process began innocently enough in late January when the URW put out its negotiating policy and goals for the year, as it always did prior to master contract negotiations. The goals included the usual laundry list such as a general wage increase, maintenance of COLAs, and improved pensions. But this time the union stated job security as its number one goal, asking for a guarantee of no plant closings during the three-year contract; a company commitment to improve or maintain existing plants; layoffs limited to specific situations; and worker protection and retraining when technological changes were made at factories. Job security always had been important to the URW, but the 1988 Negotiating Policy covered the subject in much more depth than in the past. The URW also wanted guarantees that the manufacturers would invest in existing facilities to maintain and improve competitiveness.

Firestone was quick to address the URW's stated desire for job security—but not in the manner the union had hoped. The company went public with a plan that did guarantee jobs at three of its tire plants. "Each employee working at a facility covered by this agreement will be guaranteed employment," said Peter Schofield, Firestone director of labor relations. "During this period the plant will not be closed and no one will be laid off. We must mutually pursue new approaches to more effectively operate our business." Some of the terms, though, were not likely to meet worker approval. During the three-year moratorium on plant closings and layoffs, workers also had to agree to a freeze on wage and COLA increases, and on other employee benefit costs such as pensions, insurance, and supplemental unemployment benefits. Firestone's plan struck at the heart of solidarity, saying that any contractual matters whatsoever that are agreed to at the local plant level would not require the approval of any other local union. As a matter of course, any changes at the local level that affected items covered by the master contract had to be okayed not only by the individual locals, but also by the URW International's Executive Committee and a majority of other master contract locals in that company's chain. The reason behind the approval process is simple: to avoid allowing companies to isolate individual locals and strong-arm them into approving concessions, or to play one local against another to see which was willing to give up the most. Since 1985, five of the six Firestone locals involved in master contract bargaining (three locals were at non-tire facilities) had, in fact, granted concessions. In 1987 Firestone threatened to close both its Des Moines, Iowa, and Oklahoma City tire factories, but reconsidered after union locals offered concessions. The locals, however, had to battle with other Firestone locals and the URW Executive Committee before the agreements were approved.

URW officials never publicly commented on the merits of Firestone's proposal. They did call Firestone's statement inappropriate because it violated the traditional agreement to keep negotiations private until a tentative agreement was reached. Firestone's Schofield said the firm just wanted to inform the locals of the company's position. Nothing ever came of the proposal, and the talks proceeded as normal—or as normally as they could in 1988. By this time, Uniroyal and B. F. Goodrich had merged their tire operations as Uniroyal Goodrich Tire Co., so they were represented as one company in the now "Big Three" of U.S. tire manufacturers covered by the pattern bargaining. In mid-February, more than two months before

the expiration of the old contract, the two sides reached a three-year economic agreement that emphasized job security and cost containment. The
agreement was reached early because BFG already had announced plans
to sell its 50 percent stake in the company, creating a need for Uniroyal
Goodrich to recapitalize. The URW and Uniroyal Goodrich still had to
resolve the noneconomic portions of the contract and emphasized that
the pact was not intended as a pattern settlement for the rest of the industry. The contract called for no general wage increase and put a restriction
on the COLA formula for the first year of the contract; increased the pension multiplier by $2 per month per year of service; and called for workers
to receive equity units in the firm based on its performance. Most importantly, from the union's side, Uniroyal Goodrich guaranteed that the firm
would keep open its tire plants in Fort Wayne, Indiana, and Opelika and
Tuscaloosa, Alabama, during the life of the contract. At the fourth plant in
the chain—Stone's old factory in Eau Claire—the two sides agreed to discuss measures to keep the facility open.

That left the URW with just Goodyear and Firestone from which to
choose a target company for the rest of negotiations. Given Firestone's
earlier stance, along with the fact that Japan's Bridgestone was in the
process of acquiring the company, it came as no surprise the union selected Goodyear to set the pattern. The URW and Goodyear had little problem coming up with an initial tentative agreement that called for no general wage increase, maintenance of COLA, and a $3.50 increase in the
pension multiplier to $23.50 a month per year of service. The only men-
tion of job security was an agreement that the two sides would meet to
discuss job security, plus a continuation clause that assured the pact would
carry over if a facility was sold.

As Goodyear locals prepared to vote, the URW tried to sell Firestone on
the "pattern." But Goodyear locals were not receptive to the contract, and
divisions within the URW ranks began to show. The rank and file were
irked at the lack of a pay raise, and they vehemently despised "Letter 19,"
which they felt struck at the core of solidarity. The clause stated that if an
individual local agreed to financial concessions, only the URW International Executive Committee need approve, eliminating the need for ratification by the Goodyear locals' policy committee and membership of other
Goodyear locals.

Although six of eleven Goodyear locals ratified the contract, the pact was rejected because the five locals voting "no" represented a majority of the fifteen thousand Goodyear workers covered under the pact. The URW's method of contract ratification was another check-and-balance process aimed at safeguarding solidarity. Under URW rules a master contract had to be approved by a majority of locals representing a majority of the members covered under the pact. This method attempted to divide the power among smaller and larger locals. In practice, several small locals could not push a vote through because they did not represent a majority of members, but on the flip side neither could a couple of large locals, because they failed to account for half the total number of locals involved. In that case, locals at three large Southern tire plants—in Union City; Danville, Virginia; and Gadsden—voted against ratification. Federal mediator David Thorley, who often worked on URW negotiations, was not surprised it was this so-called "Southern Coalition" that put up a roadblock. "They just couldn't get them to agree to anything," Thorley said. "Their locals were so political those guys were afraid to ratify almost anything. They couldn't get the membership to buy anything."

Stone ordered the locals to reconsider their votes, prompting Goodyear Chairman Robert Mercer to make his unprecedented personal appeal to workers in Danville. He met for more than an hour with fifteen members of the local's executive board to try to get them to sway the membership toward ratification. Mercer's visit aside, Danville and the other locals stood by their earlier vote against the agreement.

Meanwhile, forty-eight hundred URW members struck Firestone on May 15 when the company failed to make a proposal anywhere near what Goodyear had offered in the areas of COLAs, pension improvements, and fully paid hospital insurance. "These are the three issues that are very dear to our hearts, and we will fight to keep those, and that's why we're on strike," Stone said.

As Thorley stepped in to try to solve the Firestone disagreement, Goodyear locals threatened to walk out as well. But that was where solidarity began to erode. Five of the Goodyear locals said they would not honor a strike. Locals in the Midwest, representing more older workers, were more interested in job security and pension improvements, while the younger workers at Southern locals wanted higher wages. Local 2 President Bill Breslin resigned when the Akron local voted to honor any strike, after he vowed not to lead Local 2 on a strike he believed would gain the workers nothing. When Local 2 voted 725 to 691 to strike if needed, he wrote out a one-sentence resignation notice. Of the vote, he said: "They're going to destroy everything I tried to do here. I can't believe they're that stupid. I thought they were ready to be more realistic and keep more jobs here."

Local 12 in Gadsden was trying to recoup some of the concessions it had given just two years earlier in order to save its plant, but other locals in the chain would not help out, said J. W. Battles, president of the local at the time. When Battles tried to push the union's Goodyear Policy Committee to go for a general wage increase, an official from another Goodyear local told him: "Look, we don't have anything against you boys in Gadsden, but if you think we're going to strike to get you back some of the money you gave up, you're crazy."

Bommarito blamed his successor, Mike Stone, and a lack of leadership at the top for the problems the URW was experiencing. Bommarito said Stone should have been more in touch with the membership and that Stone, not Mercer, should have been making the direct appeal in Danville. "I think it just shows that Stone is a wimp, really," Bommarito said. Stone said the Danville trip was a reflection of Mercer's style, and that the solidarity problems in the union were no greater than usual.

Goodyear and the URW reached a second tentative accord the morning of May 17, beating a noon strike deadline by less than an hour. Goodyear retracted the Letter 19 proposal to ease the approval process for economic concessions; granted a twenty-five-cent-an-hour immediate advance in COLA payments to be made up as the cost of living rose; and offered a possible no-strike wage reopener in the third year of the contract. Goodyear showed it "has always been willing to do more to avert a strike than settle one," said Frank Tully, Goodyear vice president of human resources and the firm's chief negotiator. Said Stone: "It's a good agreement. I'm sure they [union locals] were looking for more. I'm convinced that there isn't any more and they should ratify this." This time the Goodyear locals listened as nine of the eleven locals representing 10,500 of the 15,000 members ratified the agreement. Only Gadsden and a smaller local in Madisonville, Kentucky, turned down the accord.

After just seven days, the Firestone locals ended their strike, as Firestone accepted a pact similar to the Goodyear agreement, but for reasons that were not made public at the time. Firestone had been willing to take a strike of two to three months to try to get contract changes that would get it away from pattern bargaining and make the company's union plants more competitive, according to Mike Polovick, at the time a negotiator for Firestone. But then several matters took precedence over Firestone's grand negotiating plan. Bridgestone and Italy's Pirelli Group made competing offers for Firestone, and General Motors Corp. dropped Firestone as an original equipment tire supplier except for its Saturn Corp. unit. Polovick himself was not sure exactly what happened. There was talk that Firestone did not want to risk losing original equipment business with Ford. By then, Ford employed former B. F. Goodrich Co. negotiator Peter Pestillo, who had promoted good and improved labor relations with the United Auto Workers union.

All Polovick knew was that top Firestone management changed its tune in a hurry. "All this determination that we were going to do what it takes to get what we needed to get went by the wayside and we had to come back and get a settlement and get back to work by the following Monday," Polovick said. That, of course, put the union in the driver's seat in bargaining, and the union quickly took advantage, according to Polovick. "We're sitting in there and say we want to deal," he said. "The union would say, 'Well we want this.' We'd say, 'OK.' Then they'd say, 'But now we want this.' It just kept going on."

So, thanks to the perseverance of Stone in pushing through the agreement at the Goodyear locals and a little bit of help from Firestone, the union—though not making great financial strides—was able to hold off changing the process by which concessions were approved and maintained at least the semblance of a pattern contract process.

OVERALL VIEW OF CONTRACTS

When discussing contract negotiations during his tenure, Stone made no apologies for not leading the URW on the long, confrontational strikes that Bommarito specialized in. "I never looked at that as a sign of weakness. It's a lot harder to stop a strike than it is to start one," Stone was fond of saying. It was during the '80s that President Reagan fired the air traffic controllers, setting the tone for companies to replace strikers. That alone was enough to dissuade most industrial unions from striking, and the decade saw fewer walkouts than the prior decade. "I always figured you were better off if you didn't have to strike," Stone said. "You never say never, but you have to weigh the consequences."

Firestone's Mike Polovick, in fact, said Stone was visibly affected when the Firestone locals struck in 1988. "I will never forget, Stone was at the table on the night of the deadline, almost at the verge of tears, telling the company something to the effect: 'I wanted my legacy to be that there would be no strikes during my tenure. I don't want this strike but it's obvious that you folks do.'" Polovick said. "Literally, it appeared to me like the man was on the verge of tears because he wanted a resolution and there wasn't going to be one."

Local 12's J. W. Battles said Stone's unwillingness to take the workers out on strike definitely hurt him with the rank and file. Stone was from the "old school," but realized there had to be changes. "I think he did make some changes, but he was on some ground that was awful unfamiliar for an International president, and change put him in a bad light with the membership," Battles said. And when Stone in 1988 brought the local leaders back to Akron rather than call for a strike, the stance definitely did not play well in Gadsden. "There's some change that shouldn't have taken place because if you shut the companies down you take everything," he said.

Analyst Harry Millis said relations between labor and management definitely softened during this period, if only by necessity. "Instead of being confrontational every three years, they became negotiators and communicators," Millis said. "To me, (Mike Stone) was just a realist. He had to face different times that required a different approach."

Stone also said the contract settlements stood up financially to what other industrial unions were getting during very difficult times. "You know the Auto Workers had a knack for making a nickel look like a quarter when they talked about it," he said. "We were always hearing at meetings, 'Why can't we get what the Auto Workers get?' But the settlements we were getting, when you took all the fluff out of [the Auto Workers' deals], our settlements were as good or better than the Auto Workers."

Clem recalled a Presidents Meeting in 1988, when he was charged with comparing the URW's settlement with what other unions received that year. The URW research director even surprised himself a bit when he realized that based on percentages and benefits, the URW's settlement looked pretty good. "We may not have had quite the PR selling job that some of your big unions did with their settlements, but ours was as good as theirs when you started really putting the pencil to it," Clem said. "So I gave my presentation and we were out having a coffee break and Mike came up and

Table 8.1 Rubber Industry Earnings, 1981–90

(Average weekly earnings in dollars for production workers in rubber & plastics industry)

Year	Rubber & Plastics	Tires	Fab. Rubber Products	Rubber Footwear	Reclaim, Hose & Belts
1981	280.95	459.68	269.07	178.40	321.31
1982	302.54	473.40	284.93	193.91	322.00
1983	329.60	531.05	313.03	196.08	335.79
1984	345.69	575.83	336.54	210.26	353.22
1985	350.99	560.10	342.36	214.70	350.69
1986	360.55	590.04	348.99	234.42	365.93
1987	369.41	617.32	356.04	251.45	379.06
1988	378.98	649.52	365.25	255.50	405.31
1989	390.83	658.94	366.20	266.99	405.83
1990	401.70	664.22	383.36	283.58	423.67

Source: Employment and Earnings.

said, 'Damn, we did negotiate a good agreement, didn't we?' He'd gotten a lot of grief on it because it didn't have a general wage increase. I pointed it out to the delegates there when you figure out what it's worth with COLA compared with what others got (without the COLA), and we got pension improvements that were much better than theirs."

A look at historical figures backed up the claims of those supporting Stone's performance in contract talks—and also pointed out the importance COLAs played in URW contracts throughout the 1980s (table 8.1). In 1980, overall hourly earnings for rubber and plastic industry workers averaged $6.52, with tire workers the top earners at $9.74 an hour. By 1987, although master contract talks in 1982 and 1985 brought just a small general wage increase in the latter negotiations, rubber and plastics hourly wages jumped to $8.90, with tire workers at $14.11 an hour. And as of October 1989, COLA had yielded $6.95 an hour in extra wages in the Big Three master contracts since its inception in 1976.

It also was true that URW wages were able to maintain parity with United Auto Workers' pay. The "tandem wage principle," whereby the Rubber Workers' pay kept pace with the UAW, had been something rubber companies long had wanted to end, but had been unable to. Tire workers actually made 6 percent more than Auto Workers in 1967, but saw their comparable level fall to just 88 percent of UAW wages by the end of 1975.

But bolstered by gaining COLAs in 1976, and winning the even more desirable COLA formula three years later, the URW regained parity by 1981 and moved 2.9 percent ahead of the UAW in 1984.

One place the URW failed to keep pace was in pension gains, especially for current retirees. URW retirees were covered by the contract in place when they retired, and only got raises if negotiated in future years; there were no automatic cost-of-living increases. And rubber companies, owing pensions to literally hundreds of thousands of retirees, did not jump to add higher costs to these pension liabilities. For example, in 1988 talks the URW was able to gain a measly fifty-cent addition to the pension multiplier for current Goodyear retirees, while Firestone agreed to just a $200 lump sum payment to each retiree. "We thought at the time we were doing a decent job," Stone said. "We've got a lot of people who are fortunate enough to still be living but they're only getting a $7 a month pension [multiplier], or $7.50. That's not much to live on."

Local 12's H. W. "Huddy" Hudson was one who felt the brunt of pensions being put on the back burner of bargaining. He felt the presidents of his local never fought hard enough to push for higher pensions. While raising the pension multipliers became a top priority in master contract bargaining during the 1990s, those increases came too late for workers like Hudson. Going into 1991 negotiations, the basic pension multiplier was $23.50 a month per year or service for plants covered under the master contract, but by the end of the 2000 talks the pension multiplier jumped to $50. That meant a worker with thirty-five years of service would get a basic pension of $1,750 a month, and many retirees also received an early retirement supplement of several hundred dollars more a month to last until they were eligible for Social Security benefits. The problem for many older retirees, however, was that most negotiated plans had no cost-of-living escalator clauses. Whatever the pension benefit was at the time of their retirement was what they received for life.

Where that left Hudson—and hundreds of thousands of retirees like him—was trying to make ends meet on a very fixed income. Instead of a monthly pension nearing $2,000, Hudson had received $750 monthly since his 1979 retirement for his forty years at Goodyear. "My retirement today barely pays my utilities," he said in 1999. "If it wasn't for my Social Security I guarantee you we'd have a tough road, my wife and I." Hudson said that through the years every time contract time came up, he would go to the Local 12 president and try to push for higher pensions. "They'd be on the floor in there and bring it up to the membership, and the young guys would hit the floor and say, 'Hell no, we want that money in our pockets.' Who do you think the presidents and the other people are going to support? The ones who were going to vote for them. That's precisely why we didn't get any more done toward our retirement than what was done." Hudson was glad to see some signs that attitudes had changed. In early 1999, he spoke to a group of still-active Local 12 members and told them stories about his efforts over the years to try to raise pensions and how the younger workers invariably opposed it. When they got through, one younger worker approached Hudson and told him: "Huddy, every word you just spoke a while ago is the damn truth." The man said he was one of those young guys who always fought for the higher raises rather than more for pensions. "And he said, 'I'm one of those guys who got the money in his pocket, but I'm not proud of it a damn bit.'"

CONCESSIONS ON THE RISE

While the URW appeared to hold its own at the master contract level, it was clear that a structural change was under way in the collective bargaining arena for the U.S. tire industry, and that shift manifested itself in the rise of concessionary agreements at the local level. In the mid-1980s, such a thesis was put forth by Charles Jeszeck, the staff economist with the U.S. General Accounting Office who also wrote about why the tire plants left Akron. Observers debated whether developments in labor-management relations during the time were cyclical or more permanent, structural changes. "I conclude that the recent developments in the tire industry bargaining mirror conditions in other organized manufacturing sectors and that, even as economic conditions improve, these factors will inhibit workers' ability to regain the bargaining initiative during the foreseeable future," Jeszeck wrote.

The economist said the structural changes included increased competition from foreign tire makers; dispersion of production to Southern states away from Ohio and the Midwest; the mass closings of plants, increasing the percentage of non-union capacity in the industry; the rise of the radial tire, giving imports more of an inroad to the U.S. market; and the emergence of anti-union Michelin as a major player in North America, adding even more non-union capacity. Management tried to take advantage of these structural changes, first by trying to win less expensive agreements and attempting, unsuccessfully, to sever the link between auto and tire worker wages. Companies were more successful in trying to win plant-level concessions, using the leverage of plant closings and the increase in non-union capacity to gain changes intended to make the facilities more competitive. Firms often concentrated radial tire production in non-union plants, leaving increasingly obsolete bias-ply production in the older, organized plants. "Local unions increasingly viewed plant closures as a real alternative for management," Jeszeck wrote.

Local concessions were rare before 1967, and between 1967 and 1970, just two plants signed such agreements covering tire-related production out of about fifty-five unionized tire facilities. From 1979 to 1982, local concessions were granted at twelve tire locals, and the number jumped to twenty-two concession agreements at eighteen tire plants—out of thirty-five tire plants then left organized after the rash of plant closings—during the 1982–85 time period. The concessions in the post-1979 period were negotiated at radial as well as bias plants and concentrated on major work-rule changes. Common givebacks included shifting departments from piecework to day-work pay and establishing seven-day continuous operations with reduced premium pay provisions. In the post-1979 agreements, all but two of the thirty-four pacts were negotiated under the threat of closure, and all thirty-four sought work-rule changes. Just six asked for explicit wage or COLA cuts, twenty-five wanted a switch to continuous operations, and thirteen sought the shift from piece- to day-work pay. A number of these later concessions, though, did promise investments in exchange for work rule modifications.

Just after this period, in 1986, Local 12 in Gadsden faced such a dilemma: give massive concessions that ate away at many of the gains the union had made over the years, or see Goodyear shut down the more than fifty-year-old factory. O. A. Garrard, as local president, was the union's lead negotiator in what became known as the "Boaz Agreement" in Local 12 lore. Goodyear in 1986 was under fire, fending off an attempted raid by financier Goldsmith. Under the restructuring necessary after it bought off the raider, it was clear that Goodyear would close at least one or more North American tire plants. Mickey Williams—elected later as Local 12 president—knew Gadsden was vulnerable. The decision came down to close either Gadsden or tire plants in Cumberland, Maryland, and New

Toronto, Ontario. So Local 12 officials, led by Garrard, and Goodyear negotiators, met in a hastily called retreat in Boaz, Alabama. In less than ten days, the two sides hammered out a pact that included about $30 million in concessions, according to Battles, who was vice president at the time of the Boaz summit. Workers agreed to a freeze on the cost-of-living allowance and an end to piecework, a move that cost some workers up to $3 an hour and $10,000 a year in wages. "Garrard no doubt told the people just as he was told, and he believed that if we don't do this, we're going to lose the plant," Williams said. "So we did it and sure enough, Cumberland and New Toronto were closed. I guess you might say that's whipsawing at its finest." The sweeping changes touched nearly every part of the agreement, so much so that workers continued to talk about it almost on a daily basis more than a decade later. "It's something I almost wish we could forget," Williams said. "We did it, and we had to do it. We didn't have a choice."

Clem for one found it interesting that the problems with work rules generally were blamed on labor, when it was management that instituted work rules in the first place. In the early days of American industry, many workers were craftsmen who did it all. As industry moved toward the need for greater quantity and mass production, the scientific management systems of the day decided to break jobs down into little parts: a worker would do one thing and nothing else. "Then later on they wanted to blame everything on the fact that their workers didn't want to do anything else than what they had been trained," Clem said. "It's just not a simple answer. There's plenty of blame to go around. Labor cannot accept the brunt of that. It's a whole lot of people's fault. You make decisions based on the information you had at the time."

Stone carried the rap throughout his tenure that the URW gave up far too many concessions. It was the main issue that would help defeat him in 1990. Lewis "Sonny" Milton was a longtime president of Local 703 at the Pirelli Armstrong Tire Corp. plant in Hanford, California, one of many tire factories that took concessions during Stone's URW presidency. Milton, whose plant survived until closing in 2001, was among the believers that Stone had, in fact, been far too conciliatory during negotiations. "Mike was a nice guy, period. That was one of the bad things Pete did," Milton said. "We all followed Pete's advice with him, and I don't think he was the man who should have been there. He was a good man to have, but not as International president. He'd let corporations just walk away with things. Mike just wasn't a fighter at all."

Bob Bianchi's plant also was forced to accept concessions during Stone's term, but the president of Local 310 at the Bridgestone/Firestone plant in Des Moines, Iowa, thanked, rather than blamed, Stone. "I thought Mike Stone did a helluva job based on what he had to deal with," Bianchi said. "We went under plant closure notice twice, once in 1982 and once in 1985. We took concessions and we survived."

PR Director Curt Brown agreed with Stone's position of trying to live to fight another day. Unfortunately, often the plants closed a couple of years after granting concessions. "I would much rather keep my job two more years than be out of work two more years," Brown said. "I think he was a good labor leader and that he served the URW well with very little recognition. He didn't demand to be the center of attention."

Federal mediator Thorley said those who derided Stone for making concessions did not know the whole story and were not privy to everything the company would tell the top URW officials. "Mike's in a different position. He can see it. He's got to weigh what he hears and sees and what he can develop," Thorley said. "The guy on the floor thinks, 'He gave it up. Why didn't he fight? They were snowballing or bluffing us.'" But looking at the economy and what was happening around the country, concessions the URW was forced into giving were a sign of the times, Thorley said, adding that he believed the tire companies did in fact need most of the givebacks they desired. Through it all, Thorley saw Stone as a true leader willing to put his neck on the line if he thought it was best for his membership. "They talk about how great Pete [Bommarito] was, but he had it when times were good," Thorley said. "It would have been interesting to see how Pete functioned when times were bad. Mike got caught in that. I'll give him credit, he didn't back down. He lived with what he said."

For his part, Stone called the issue of concessions a complex one for workers, especially when it was their plant threatened with shutdown. "You could be as militant as you want to be but the facts were when they gave you that threat to shut a plant down they were serious threats," he said. "I can't think of anywhere we made concessions where a company said they were going to close a plant where we went in under provision of the six-month notice that [companies] were pulling our leg."

Other factors included community pressures because of the debilitating effect a factory closing can have on a town. Stone recalled a time Firestone Chairman John Nevin threatened to close its Oklahoma City tire plant, but workers there agreed to givebacks totaling $8 an hour. The URW hierarchy vetoed the concessions, which covered master contract items. Oklahoma City community members came to Akron saying the URW should let the workers approve the concessions to save their jobs. "They had hugs and kisses for John Nevin. They didn't have hugs and kisses for us."

A number of plants were saved for at least a number of years with concessions, including, among others, Firestone's Oklahoma City and Des Moines, Iowa, factories; two Uniroyal Goodrich units in Alabama; Goodyear facilities in Gadsden, Alabama, and Topeka, Kansas; Armstrong Rubber in Hanford (later bought by Pirelli Group and closed in 2001) and Des Moines (later acquired by Titan Tire Corp.). "Anyone who votes for concessions doesn't like it," Stone said. "Would you like it if they told you you had to take a pay cut? Even though they did it to save their job, even after the vote and their job was saved, then you couldn't find anyone who supported it." That was one of the factors that would lead to his defeat, as most of the people who were at the 1990 convention because concessions had earlier saved their jobs ended up voting against Stone. "People hear what they want to hear, not always what they need to hear," Stone said.

WHIPSAWING AND PATTERN BARGAINING

From a union standpoint, perhaps the worst part of concessions was the process of "whipsawing," where the companies basically played their own game of "Let's Make a Deal." With whipsawing, the companies essentially played locals within a particular chain against each other. The practice took on a couple of different forms. As happened with Gadsden in 1986, workers at the Alabama plant agreed to concessions so that their plant stayed open while two other Goodyear tire factories shut down. At other times, the rubber companies held out investment as a carrot, where the local had to approve certain givebacks or work-rule changes in exchange for capital spending dollars. In the cruelest of whipsawing scenarios, once one local gave in, the companies would go to the next local and the next, asking for similar concessions. Once the company got through each of the locals, it was common to start the whole process again. Even after individual locals caved in, companies more than once were known to close the plants a year or two down the road, as was the case with Local 9 at General Tire in Akron.

Whipsawing especially cut at solidarity within the URW. C. V. Glassco, who served one term as Local 12 president, said the biggest mistake the union ever made was giving individual locals the right to give concessions to a master contract. "I think that the chain is only as strong as its weakest link, and if you make that link any weaker, you're going to bust," he said. Battles, also a onetime Local 12 president, agreed. "Up until that point in time, everybody was kind of as one," said Battles, who himself was Local 12 vice president during the 1986 Boaz negotiations. "But once this one over here makes a bit of concessions, then these locals are mad at them. Then another one makes a little concession. The company mastered playing one plant against another. They also mastered playing one individual employee against another individual employee. When I came to work here, if one tire builder had a problem, then every tire builder had a problem."

Battles recalled the 1988 negotiations when Goodyear proposed tying wage increases to the company's debt-to-equity ratio. The Goodyear locals had turned down the tentative agreement the first time through, but Mike Stanley, at the time president of the URW local at Union City, Tennessee, said he believed he could get his membership to approve the debt/equity formula. "Based on the formula they used, Goodyear would have never produced a wage increase," Battles said. "We voted against it the second time and Union City approved it. They got a ticket [production] increase and hiring. We got a ticket decrease and people laid off."

Of course, the jealousy easily ran both ways. Other Goodyear locals saw Local 12 as more willing to look at concessions for their plant alone in order to gain something, according to Local 2's Diceglio. He remembered one time when Bommarito was still URW president and Gadsden was going to give up some cost-of-living allowance money. Since it affected the overall master contract, it had to be approved by the other Goodyear master locals. "Local 2 was the last and deciding vote and we turned it down," Deciglio said. "They weren't going to be allowed to give their concessions. And Pete Bommarito came in and gave a real nice talk two weeks later. And we re-voted, which was kind of unheard of at the time, and it passed at that point." Then at later negotiations, in 1994, Gadsden tried unsuccessfully to get the money back, and that became a sticking point between the Goodyear locals. Deciglio wondered, "What's chain bargaining if someone can go back and cut their own deal after it's done?"

Some company negotiators defended their bargaining tactics. "We never took any concessions that were nonproductive," said Frank Tully, Goodyear chief negotiator from 1980 to 1993. "We spent a lot of money, but we didn't put it into things that were boondoggle kinds of things—duplication that would lead to inefficiency." He even told of a time when the workers at the Jackson, Michigan, plant wanted to give $4 an hour in concessions, but the company declined because the plant was beyond being saved at that point. "All we'd be doing is stealing money from them because the plant wasn't going to be competitive anyway," Tully said. "It was a decision that was being made in the marketplace, and it wasn't because we disliked anyone. We weren't going to ask them for concessions when they wouldn't benefit the people in the plant. It would be morally wrong, and it wouldn't help them in the end."

Tully also defended Goodyear against charges that it whipsawed the locals in the master contract by going from plant to plant to ask for individual concessions. About the only area where that might have applied was in citing plants that had continuous operations getting a larger production ticket over factories that did not operate continually. "You can cite that as a major issue," Tully said, "but it was based on an obvious, demonstrable fact. We could man it and cost it and there couldn't be a difference of opinion about the cost involved. You can say that was whipsawing, but I think that would extend the meaning." There were times, of course, when the company would tie investments to a certain amount of give-and-take from the union. "We have many times negotiated with a plant for an investment," he said. "That's a good, straightforward, honest kind of negotiations. I think it's a management responsibility to put capital investment where it can be most effective in a corporation."

The process of pattern bargaining also caused much debate between the URW and the companies it negotiated with. The URW—and the Steelworkers after them—defended the practice as a way to keep the playing field level between competitors. It established uniformity and set up rules with a degree of consistency. Most tire companies disagreed, saying master contracts attempted to apply a "one size fits all" mentality to a situation in which individual treatment was called for. Globalization also interfered with the intent of pattern bargaining, as most of the top players other than Goodyear became foreign-owned, according to Tully. "It was no longer the approach that should be used, but [the union] couldn't change," Tully said. "Part of the problem transcended the leadership even, because the leadership is elected rather than appointed. The company's side of the table is a bunch of salaried people like me who are hired guns, so to speak, who are appointed and served at the disposal of whoever they reported to. On the union side of the table, most of the people were elected by the membership, and that gives them a different set of problems. I'm not as critical of individuals in the URW and the URW leadership when I say that they failed to change. I'm more critical of the process."

Of course, Tully worked for a firm that, prior to the Mike Stone era, rarely was picked as the target company during rubber industry master contract talks, in part because of friction between Bommarito and the bargaining committee from the Goodyear locals. It was openly thought that Bommarito did not like to choose Goodyear as the target company in master talks because union leadership in the other chains thought the Goodyear locals would settle for a lesser contract. From a company standpoint, that was something that Tully did not like to see. "It benefited the company usually to be chosen as the target company and to make the settlement, because the settlement always reflected more the concerns of the settling company than it did the rest of the companies involved in the bargaining process," Tully said.

James Warren succeeded Tully as Goodyear's chief negotiator and agreed that pattern bargaining "stinks," but also believed that the process would stay for the foreseeable future. After one set of master negotiations, Warren, who retired in 1998, said that both labor and management talked about trying to come up with something better and discussed those ideas in a subsequent interim meeting. "We did some really soul-searching things and had some discussions," Warren said. "But no one came up with anything other than masters that looked doable. Different yes, but not better. It sucks, but here we are. So a lot of us said, 'Let's try to make it better instead of doing away with it.'" And he thought there were some improvements, including the six-year contract that Goodyear and the Steelworkers agreed to in 1997 instead of the normal three-year deal, and also breaking down the meetings into smaller groups so that each could tackle a specific part of the negotiations.

David Thorley, as a twenty-year mediator, looked at negotiating from a viewpoint different from either a union or company bargainer. He was always amazed at how much time was wasted in the master contract process. "They'd go three months prior to the expiration date to wherever they would stay, and nothing would happen for two months and three weeks," Thorley said. "They would sit around all day and do nothing. They would meet in the mornings for the big meeting at the big table, exchange pleasantries, and exchange a few proposals. Then they would go back to their separate rooms and make contact back and forth about things and do nothing." As mediator, Thorley said it was important to know how to maneuver without ever actually getting involved in the process. "They talk to you on the perimeters. They'd have discussions with you, but you were never allowed to go to the table."

Although Thorley came from a union background, it actually was the labor leaders who were more skeptical of him. "Unions are always so nervous that you could affect their political lifestyle," he said. "A lot of years union people thought mediation was just an extension of management. If you talk to management, they think completely opposite." Thorley did think his union background helped him understand the hidden agenda labor leaders sometimes had. "Companies aren't near as difficult to watch function because they've pretty much got a structure that's everywhere," he said. "Union people have to do things politically to keep them elected as officers. They just can't agree to certain things immediately at a table. That management guy can make that decision right there, but the union has to go back and talk to their committees."

Over his years of observation, Thorley said the union negotiators more than held their own at the table—some may say too well. "I always make the comment that they got all those things because the companies were making money and didn't care," he said. "They gave things away they never should have given away, because once you give it up, it's hell to get back." And normally it was not the wages that hurt the companies long term, but the work rules and other items in a contract. "I've always had a belief that the companies shouldn't have a problem paying people. It's the restrictions—the working conditions they allowed to get established. And the rubber companies gave away, in the early days, some terrible working conditions. You couldn't utilize a guy for eight hours. They'd make out on piece rates and be done the last two or three hours. I don't blame the union. The company didn't have to agree. You have a two-party system. Nobody forced them to do these things. They could have taken a stand. A lot of people say the Rubber Workers did it to themselves. I don't agree with that. I think two parties had to agree to those items."

THE ORGANIZING WELL RUNS DRY

Don Weber spent most of his time on the URW International staff as an organizer, working on campaigns in states like Illinois, Indiana, Nebraska, Kansas, Missouri, and Oklahoma—especially in Oklahoma. In that state he ran three campaigns, one in Stillwater, one in McAllister, and another in Wilberton. The URW also tried unsuccessfully to organize Goodyear's tire plant in Lawton, Oklahoma, and the Uniroyal tire factory in Ardmore, Oklahoma. But by far the most effort in the state was put into organizing Firestone's Dayton Tire plant in Oklahoma City, the URW's last successful traditional organizing campaign at a tire plant. At that plant, the Rubber Workers conducted seven NLRB representation elections in eleven years before finally winning in 1981, just before Bommarito left office. The only tire factory to come under the union's wing after that was the Bridgestone/Firestone facility in Warren County, Tennessee, where the company agreed to recognize the URW after a majority of employees signed union cards.

But Weber, who retired in 1986, remembered his time in Oklahoma well. The first election was headed up by Bob Long in April 1970. In 1974, the union came as close as it could without actually winning. The union trailed 451 to 455 with nine ballots challenged. After the challenged votes were counted, it ended up a tie vote, and in organizing, ties go to the company. The next election came in 1976. Weber wanted to have the election in August, but the URW was embroiled in its summer-long strike with Firestone as the target company. "I had the cards, I had the support," Weber said. "They thought they could win by getting a majority of the cards at the bargaining table. They wanted a majority of cards so they could present it. I told them, 'You can present them, but if they want they can force you to an election.'" So the election was pushed back to November 17. By that time General Motors Corp. had built a big assembly plant nearby for the Citation and Phoenix models. "One of the things that cost us was that a lot of the Dayton union supporters left and went to GM, because the URW waited too long," Weber said. Timing also was poor for the 1979 election. The director of that campaign brought in about ten to twelve representatives to help out and proclaimed he was going to give the URW a Christmas present with an organizing win in December. But Weber said a check of NLRB history would have told the director that December is one of the worst months to hold an election as far as union wins is concerned.

Weber was one of the main organizers in the 1981 campaign that finally brought the URW the victory that was more than a decade in the making. He said the URW used a different format and worked hard to build up the in-plant committee. And this time the URW had an issue to focus on. In the past, the company had basically given the Oklahoma City workers everything that the union had negotiated in the rubber industry. But this time the firm announced it was making changes that the employees did not have a say in. "So we capitalized on it," Weber said. "We had a good committee, and we thought we were going to win it." Not that the organizers expected to win easily. When the voting was completed, the union had challenged fifty-five or fifty-six ballots. Most of these were so-called clock-card supervisors, who were taken off supervision by the company right before the union election so they could vote. At this election they let the employees in as spectators, something that was not standard practice. "We would have our election observers and I would tell them who to challenge," Weber said. "If they felt they knew somebody in that category, they would challenge them." Before they did the actual vote count, they took a look again at the challenged ballots and some of the committee people convinced Weber to allow several votes to go through. In the end, the URW had won 564 to 513 with fifty ballots challenged, meaning the union had a clear-cut victory by one vote even if all the challenged votes went against the URW. "If I hadn't released five of those challenges, that means we likely would have won, but the company would have taken it into litigation past the master negotiations coming up the following April. By cutting the challenges down to fifty, we stayed out of litigation by one vote."

The Rubber Workers, however, never got close to success at either Ardmore or Lawton. Weber and Long tried to get something going in Ardmore, but found the company gave workers benefits that not even the URW had won for its members. "We just couldn't get the thing off the ground where we could have an election," Weber said. "There were just too many stumbling blocks."

Tom Jenkins also spent quite a bit of time organizing during his years on the URW staff, and the one thing he realized more than anything was that when an organizer went into a plant, he had to be able to offer the worker something concrete. He oversaw numerous organizing meetings, especially in the South, where somebody in the back would get up and yell, "What do you all got to offer me? I've already got all those things." Jenkins never knew how to answer. "What was I supposed to say?" he said. "The fact that I was going to take his union dues?"

Often it was not a matter of the union not putting enough effort into a campaign—it was just so hard to change long-held opinions. At organizational campaigns at three plants the URW never was able to conquer—in Wilson, North Carolina, and Lawton and Ardmore—the union would have ten to fifteen organizers in at a time. District directors would go in. Even the URW president would make appearances. "It wasn't like we didn't put a lot of effort into those things. It's just that once these guys make up their mind that they don't want to be in a union, it's tough to change it," Jenkins said. "Until the company provokes something, it has to be some mitigating circumstance where they say, 'OK, I've had enough of your crap. I'm going to join the union.'"

And danger was not out of the question. Jenkins worked on another unsuccessful campaign at a Goodrich non-tire plant in Thomaston, Georgia, with seven hundred to nine hundred workers. The URW, which did organize the plant in 1993, lost that election by something like two hundred votes, and when they came out of the plant lot at the end of the week in three cars, there was a group of workers who tried to turn over the organizers' cars. "If it hadn't been for the sheriff's department, we'd have probably been killed," Jenkins said. Another time, a women tried to run over Jenkins and others trying to organize a plant in Oklahoma. At other times, the cops would come out and arrest the organizers for menacing just to harass the unionists. "Organizing isn't an easy job," Jenkins said. "If you haven't done it, you don't know what you're going through."

John Sellers, a onetime URW organizational director, spent plenty of time on the front lines of organizing. He headed up a successful campaign at the Penn Athletic plant in Phoenix and was one of the first to volunteer to have a go at the General Tire plant in Mount Vernon, Illinois, another target the Rubber Workers never conquered. In organizing, he said, it was vital to tailor each campaign to the specific target; there were no "one size fits all" campaigns. But the most important thing in organizing was to build an in-plant committee that was representative of the whole workforce. That meant representatives from all departments and all shifts. He also preferred small meetings rather than large group meetings, because there can be much more communication with individuals, getting them to commit to work on the things that need to get done. "You can't organize a plant from the outside," Sellers said. "If I come in and tell you what your issues are, it doesn't strike quite the same chord as someone you work with telling you."

From an organizing standpoint, there has been no tougher nut to crack in the North American tire and rubber industry than Michelin North America, owned by Groupe Michelin of France. Michelin came to the United States and Canada, and was so successful in fending off attempts at unionization, because of its experiences at the firm's home factories in France as they were reconstructed after World War II. Those plants were staffed by very militant union workers who staged numerous wildcat strikes. Michelin knew that for political reasons it could never shut down its French facilities or even eliminate much capacity there. But as it entered the 1960s, Michelin started looking for ways to circumvent the ability of unions to close them down at any time for any reason.

So the company started looking for places to put new capacity closer to their global markets. Michelin sensed an opportunity in the United States to start selling more of its advanced radial tires—a product the U.S. tire makers picked up on too slowly—in the North American aftermarket and then to move into original equipment orders on new cars. It was no accident that the company picked Greenville, South Carolina, for its U.S. headquarters, a city in the least unionized county in the country. Not only was South Carolina willing to help Michelin financially, but the state's mindset clearly was anti-union. Michelin also located its other tire plants in the South, in towns where the firm would become one of, if not the biggest, employer in the area. That made it more difficult for the URW or other unions to stage a successful organizing drive.

Michelin took a similar course in Canada, where in the 1970s it opened three tire plants in Nova Scotia, an area of high unemployment at the time. "When you're out of a job and you now have a job, it's pretty hard, no matter what you say to somebody, to show them they're better off to join a union," said Alan Turner, a former URW member in Canada. Michelin also was careful when it hired people for the Nova Scotia facilities, in an area where mining and fishing had been the major industries and both were being downsized. Turner said he knew a friend who tried to get a job at Michelin, but was told they did not hire people who belonged to unions. "The people they hired were carefully screened in their hiring process," Turner said.

But that did not stop the URW—and other unions—from trying over the years. In fact, URW organizers truly believed they won elections at two of the three plants in 1979, but never got to count the votes. "We won the vote. We know we won the vote," said Reginald Duguay, a former URW district director in Canada. "We signed up enough cards and we had the election. We had votes at two of them. We were damn sure we had the vote and so was the company." But nobody will ever know for sure. Michelin got the election held up before the votes were counted at the Labor Ministry in Nova Scotia. The legislature was recalled for a special sitting between Christmas and New Year's Day, and a preferential piece of legislation was passed that became known as the "Michelin Bill." The measure was made retroactive—unheard of at the time—and basically said that when a company could prove that plants were interdependent, a union had to organize all as one bargaining unit. In this case, it meant that the URW or other unions had to have one simultaneous organizing election for all three Nova Scotia plants at once. There would be no picking or choosing. So the votes never were counted and a union victory that would have been historic within the North American tire industry never was to be. In subsequent years, unions made more than a dozen failed unionization attempts at the Michelin Canadian plants, including at least six by the Canadian Auto Workers.

At Michelin's U.S. plants, Jenkins worked on failed organizational attempts at all the plants Michelin constructed in the South. The URW had some good people on the in-plant organizing committees, but somebody would always bring up the question to which Jenkins had no answer: "What's in it for me?" Michelin was smart, Jenkins said. The company would give the workers virtually everything in wages and benefits that the Rubber Workers had. "They did it intentionally just to keep them from organizing." Michelin also took some subtle actions. Management would not get personally involved, but they made sure workers opposing the union attended the organizational meetings. They would also have meetings to inform employees about what the company thought was wrong with unions. And whenever there was a strike somewhere else, they would put up signs keeping a running total on how much the workers had lost. About the only thing the URW could offer the Michelin workers was a system to reward seniority, said Jenkins, who spent several weeks a year for six or seven years working on the Michelin plants. They could get it in a contract that the company could not just come in any day and move a worker to another job without notice. "The main theory was seniority and working conditions—they could change your working conditions every day of the week," Jenkins said. "There was no way to control it. They just do what they want to do. But that still wasn't enough to convince those people. We never got to a vote in Michelin (in the United States). We couldn't even get enough cards to take it to an election."

Although Goodyear in later years generally was not looked upon as an anti-union company like Michelin, the Canadian unionists said Goodyear did follow the same pattern as Michelin in setting up its tire plant in Napanee, Ontario, in 1990. It built in a rural, depressed area and used the same hiring practices, said James Webber, the former Local 73 president. And when mixed rubber was brought there from the unionized Goodyear plant in Bowmanville, Ontario, there was a special holding area for the trucks. "They took the rubber down there, they dropped the trailer off, and somebody would come with another tractor and take it up to the plant," Webber said. "They were not even allowed on the property in Napanee." Duguay claimed that the plant even had its own low-power radio station so management could warn incoming workers if union people were passing out leaflets.

Stone was familiar with all the things rubber companies did to keep plants from becoming unionized. On an airplane returning from England during his term as URW chief, the man sitting next to him asked what he did for a living. When Stone told him of his occupation, the man said, "You have that plant in Mount Vernon, Illinois." Stone replied that the General Tire facility was not union, but that the URW would like to have it some day. The man replied, "I don't think you'll ever get it." Apparently the airplane passenger was some sort of consultant, and Stone was never sure if he was on the level or not, but he told the URW president that General had hired him to determine where to build a plant that would never be organized. He told the company Mount Vernon was a good choice because a union staged a bloody strike in the city many years before, and the stigma remained. "The minute I heard General was going to build a plant in Mount Vernon, I thought, 'Oh man, we'll be able to organize that easy because the Mine Workers are big down there,'" Stone said. "Not true. Boy, that was a tough place." When the URW first tried an organizing drive at Mount Vernon, the union tried to give away turkeys at Thanksgiving. They could not get an employee list for the factory, so they handbilled the plant with a slip to fill out names and addresses and where to bring the forms to pick up the turkey. Exactly one person came for the free bird. "They were so scared that they wouldn't stop by to get a free turkey at Thanksgiving time, and the one who did stop was a janitor lady—an outside contractor," Stone said. The most recent USWA representation election at Mount Vernon was in 1998, when it received about 43 percent of the votes, by far its best showing.

Rubber industry industrial relations professionals agreed that there are benefits to having non-union facilities, and that they took certain steps to try to keep new factories union-free. Of course, that did not mean they always succeeded. Goodyear's Jim Warren said the company built its Kelly-Springfield plant in Tyler, Texas, with the intent of keeping it non-union, not because Goodyear was anti-union but because while the firm was changing to new equipment, the management also wanted to change the way they dealt with people. At the same time, the management also wanted to hire a more educated workforce than usual. So they put it in the guidelines that all workers needed to have at least a high school education, preferably with some college. Texas had a lot of two-year community colleges so they found a good nucleus for the hourly workforce at these junior colleges. Tyler therefore did not have the typical tire plant workforce, Warren said. They did not merely go home after work, drink a beer and watch TV, and then get up to go to work the next day and repeat the whole cycle. They did not attend junior college to be tire builders—they had much higher ambitions.

"Now they're building tires out in Tyler and they're not like all the sheep that follow the shepherd," Warren said. "They have their own minds, and suffice it to say they finally decided they could run the plant and they wanted those positions, and the way to do that was through a union." It was that simple, and once the workers got the union they were pretty bitter because the company—in what Warren said was probably a bad decision—hired a group out of Dallas to fight the organizational attempt. "And they said things to each other that they didn't really mean," said Warren, "but they had to say it to influence either getting the union or preventing the union. They came out of that with a lot of hard feelings."

And they came out of it with URW Local 746, which Warren described as a tough union led by a tough guy, John Nash, who remained president of the local even past the merger with the USWA in 1995. "He was a pretty bright guy, yet he had visions of the working class and where they should be in comparison to the rest of the folks," Warren said. "He committed himself to try to change things and he went about it in his own way." That way, however, sometimes meant that he would clash with Goodyear management, as for example in an incident shortly after Warren came to the Tyler plant: the workers walked out for several hours because Warren had not sought Nash's approval on the new schedule as had been done in the past. Or, in another example, there was the time that Nash took the local out over an alleged safety item that Warren claimed the union probably had rigged to use as an excuse to put pressure on the company. For that, Goodyear actually fired Nash, Warren said. And while the case was pending in arbitration, Warren actually had to negotiate across the table from a fired Nash—with the union on strike for thirty days. "They had some little issues," Warren said, "but the [real] issue was John's firing." In the end, the arbitrator reinstated Nash, telling Warren he "didn't really want to be known as the arbitrator who fired a union president."

That was not to say Warren had no respect for Nash, especially in the way he represented his workers. Nash was not a leader who just did a lot of talking. He backed talk up with his actions, Warren said. Nash was a good negotiator who would play every card; in arbitration cases he would show up in bib overalls and a red bandanna so the arbitrator would think he was just some poor country bumpkin. "He was a damn fox in sheep's clothing. He'd pull whatever he could to win for his membership," Warren said. "But I don't think John Nash ever did it just for John Nash. He had an ego like everyone else, but he truly represented his people. He truly fought for what he thought was their rights and what they wanted." But Warren did not want to make Nash—and leaders like him—out to be heroes, because the Goodyear executive maintained that Nash's actions did do damage in the plant, including the incident that got Nash temporarily fired. "It was so insignificant that I can't remember all the details of it," Warren said, "but we had a strike over that. That was the overkill that was typical of John Nash."

Goodyear did a good job in learning from its mistakes in places like Tyler and Union City, Tennessee (a city Warren would never have chosen to place a non-union plant, if only because of the name itself), when it built its tire plants in Lawton in the mid-1970s and in Napanee in 1990. Both remained non-union as of 2001, with no signs that the status would change any time soon. Warren said he believed Goodyear in Napanee came as close to the ideal environment of employee involvement as could exist in a tire plant. He was working as Goodyear's top human resources official in Canada when Goodyear chose Napanee as a tire plant site in 1988, and Warren had a good working relationship with the top URW officials in Canada. So he was surprised when two Goodyear engineers came up to Canada to pick a site for a union-free plant. When he picked them up from the airport, he gave the engineers this advice: "Why in the hell don't you get on a plane and go back to Akron. You do not want a union-free plant in Canada. Everybody's union. The people who carry your bags out at the store are union. The government's union." But somehow the company found Napanee, which had access to the Great Lakes, good water supply, cheap land, and a small community willing to give tax breaks. In addition, it was not a heavily industrialized area so unions had no stronghold. Warren did call the URW leaders in Canada to inform them of the plans, including Goodyear's desire to keep it non-union. Warren told them, "I'm going to be straight and tell you what we're doing, and if you can organize it, fine. If not, fine."

Warren said if Goodyear wrote a book on how it set up Napanee, it would be titled simply, "How the hell do you want to be treated and how do you treat people." And that was what the company did. They talked to the people, asked them for their views and ideas, and set up communications in order for that to happen. Warren denied Duguay's assertion that the company had an on-site radio station to warn workers when the union was around, but the Goodyear official never doubted that word got around quickly. "I'll tell you there was a network in that city. If there was a new face that showed up, everyone knew it," Warren said. He also believed that the plant stayed union-free because the workers wanted it that way. "I guarantee you, if those folks in that plant wanted a union, they'd have one. It's that simple."

There are two schools of thought on why industrial unions have had such trouble organizing in recent years, according to Daniel Nelson, a University of Akron professor emeritus of history and an author on labor topics. One theory is that they have not organized as much because they have not tried as hard. That explanation appealed to advocates of a more aggressive or radical union presence, and there was some evidence that the reason was plausible. For example, organizational expenditures generally declined from the 1950s on, so it was easy to argue that unions were complacent, relied too much on government, and got out of practice in organizing. The second explanation is that there have been longer-term shifts that were more difficult for unions to deal with, such as the changing character of the labor force and changes in the legal system and government policy. This evolution made it more difficult for traditional unions to use traditional appeals, and there's also evidence for this theory, the professor said. Nelson explained that the modern AFL-CIO subscribes to both theories to some degree; it is not necessary to be in one camp or the other. Presumably, industrial unions will need some type of serious unrest to make inroads. "Traditionally, unions have expanded in good times and declined in bad times, but that was at an earlier time," Nelson said. "A lot of techniques, like paying union wages to non-union workers, have been used by employers to deflect that tendency."

The URW was having problems organizing long before the union merged with the Steelworkers, especially at the main tire plant targets. The union was able to organize all of the twenty-one tire factories built in the United States during the 1960s. But of the roughly thirteen tire plants constructed in the United States since 1970 only two were organized, including the Bridgestone/Firestone facility in Warren County, Tennessee. To make matters worse, all of the twenty-two major tire plants closed during the 1970s were union plants, further diluting the percentage of tires made at union shops in North America.

Unions will continue to have trouble organizing as long as they promote an adversarial approach, according to Continental General negotiator Mike Polovick. With that strategy, he did not see unions succeeding unless a company did something wrong. "I think unions are trying to maintain a status quo in a changed world," he said. "They think the same old things that used to work are going to work today." Instead, they should stress what they can offer, such as the opportunity for leadership development that many employees never experience in a traditional company organization. "The old approach, I think, needs to change," he said. "I haven't seen a whole lot of New Age thinking in that regard."

Jenkins said there are any number of reasons workers refuse to sign union cards, including company meetings run by what he calls "briefcase assassins" who tell horror stories about unions and organizers. "This one plant had all of our pictures, where we came from, how long we'd been with the company, what our jobs were—all of this on slides," he said. "Anti-union guys aren't dummies. They know what they're doing."

After the merger with the USWA, Craig Hemsley went on staff with the Steelworkers and ended up as the union's director of organizing in Ohio.

He said the USWA organized more people in 1999 than they did in 1998, bringing in about nineteen thousand members with organizing campaigns. "That's not great but it's good; it's an improvement," he said. The USWA liked to focus on targets of at least two hundred employees or above, although the union would go into smaller facilities if contacted by the workers there. With that philosophy, the Steelworkers definitely will target the non-union tire plants in North America. Hemsley predicted the first tire factory to fall will be Mount Vernon, acknowledging that the Michelin facilities in the United States and Canada are "a different animal." Hemsley said he gets calls every day from employees inquiring about the union, and he remained optimistic that labor will organize more. "Labor laws haven't changed, it's just that companies got more sophisticated," he said. "We'll have to redo our approach." That means that when a firm sends a videotape to workers at home right before an election showing all the perceived negative aspects of unionism, then the unions will counter with a tape as well. Nothing negative, just positive things like the benefits of collective bargaining, the rights of workers to organize, and how unions get involved in the community.

Whatever the new tactics of the USWA, many feel they will have a hard time organizing the remaining non-union tire plants, including two new factories built in the South in the late 1990s—one by Bridgestone/Firestone in Aiken, South Carolina, and one by Titan Tire Corp. in Brownsville, Texas. "That's the reason for putting the Aiken plant down there," said Roger Gates, president of Local 713 at the Bridgestone/Firestone plant in Decatur, Illinois. "There's no hidden agenda there as far as the company's part. They thought it would be harder for us to organize down there." Titan Tire Chairman Morry Taylor said there was no way the Steelworkers will ever organize Brownsville. "With today's business climate, the days of the unions are over with," said Taylor. "All they do now is take dues after taxes." Taylor is one of the owners most hated by the USWA, because strikes that started at two Titan plants in 1998 were not resolved until late 2001.

Some observers feel unions have a tougher time organizing newer plants than old ones, because new facilities have a new workforce that does not know each other and because often it is the best steady employment the workers have had, according to Nelson Lichtenstein, a University of Virginia history professor. In his opinion, management also tends to violate the spirit of the labor laws. "The decision to form a union should be the decision of the workforce," Lichtenstein said. "As a historian of labor management relations, management should have nothing to do with whether workers join unions." As for organizing in the South, where a number of the non-union tire plant targets are, the USWA will have to overcome factors that have been deep-seated through generations. "The real issue is can people see it as a vehicle for hopes and aspirations," he said. "The union movement will succeed in the South when it has the same spirit, courage, and moral weight as the civil rights movement."

One labor attorney who represents companies involved in organizing campaigns said he had observed some change in union philosophy. "I think unions finally recognized that they can't compete simply by holding themselves up as an American institution," said James A. Matthews III, a Philadelphia labor attorney. "They can't just say, 'You're in a heavy industry, your father was union and you should be union.'" Unions have to recognize that they are a business selling a product, which is representation to the employer. And because the American workforce represented by unions dropped to roughly 14 percent by the end of the twentieth century, it became imperative that unions pick their targets carefully. The first fight they pick is where the employer has done something to alienate workers. "From a company's perspective, if the product the union is selling is representation, one of the principal reasons employees buy that product is if the prospect of trusting the union is more favorable than the prospect of trusting the employer," Matthews said. And while organizing campaigns still tend to be aggressive, workers now are more turned off by negative actions—both from the union and the company. "If you go negative and treat the union organizer like the organizers of the '50s, you lose credibility with employees and hand the union a market," he said.

Ken Coss said the best strategy for companies is what they have been doing: Act as if there is a union in there, paying the same wages, having the same benefits and some sort of procedure to address problems. "Then it's pretty darn difficult to get in there and appeal to their overall sense of fairness," he said. "All the workers think is, 'Yeah, it's going to cost me $40 or $50 a month [to join a union.]' And that's the way they look at it." Stone agreed that organizing was tough and getting tougher. "Companies have become so adept at fighting us, that they know how much they have to give the workers to keep them happy," he said. "You know, unions really do a lot for those who never paid a union dues in their life."

USWA President George Becker, who retired in 2001, said one thing that was imperative was to have a law in the United States banning permanent replacement workers. "The Supreme Court ruled they can't fire you without just cause, but they can permanently replace you, and they're one in the same," he said. Becker said there have been situations where at the first meeting the union has with a company, they show the workforce a stack of applications of people who would gladly take their jobs. Often the majority of workers in those places have signed cards asking for union representation, but when the company started working on them, threatening to shut down the plant or give their jobs away, then the majority started to dwindle. "The companies are very clever about it," he said. "And they fire people, even though it's illegal, to throw the fear of God into everybody else. Sure, the union can get the worker back after fighting six months to a year, but the organizing effort is gone. It's shot."

BOMMARITO BACK IN PICTURE

As Stone neared the end of his second term, having gone through six years of dwindling membership and rising contract concessions, an old friend showed up as an unwelcome nemesis. Stone had faced no competition for re-election at the 1984 URW convention, but early in 1987 none other than former President Bommarito, who a decade earlier had appointed Stone URW vice president, started floating the idea that he might run again. "I think the biggest mistake I made was putting him in office," Bommarito, by then seventy-two, told a reporter. "People in Akron and the vicinity—people in office—complain about the ability of [URW] International to command any respect."

Bommarito claimed Stone's lack of leadership had resulted in low staff morale and dissension from local unions. The former president said he had not gone hunting for support for a presidential run, but had been approached by southern URW leaders he declined to name. To run, Bommarito would have needed an amendment to the URW constitution, which mandated a retirement age of sixty-five and required that presidential candidates be working URW members and delegates from local unions.

There was no doubt Bommarito still would have been able to garner support. Local 2's Hemsley, who worked as a URW organizer in 1987, remembered a discussion he and four other organizers had in a Ramada Inn bar in Mount Vernon, Illinois, where they were attempting to organize the General Tire plant. The question they posed was this: If Bommarito could somehow overcome the mandatory retirement age, who would win a race between him and Stone? "We each took out the piece of paper where you put your drinks and wrote down our vote. It was 5 to 0 Bommarito over Mike, and that's the honest to God's truth," Hemsley said. "It's nothing against Mike, but I think Mike had a hard time replacing Pete because when you have a heckuva leader, he takes over." Hemsley, although he thought Pete would win the hypothetical election, did not appreciate Bommarito's bad-mouthing Stone. "What really pissed me off about that—and I like Pete—is that Pete cost us in organizing. You can't put that out. Every consultant in the country was using that against us. You've got to be careful when you put that out, that it doesn't come back to bite you."

Stone was nothing if not loyal. But he learned early in his presidency that he would have to distance himself from Bommarito to prove that he was his own leader, not just a stooge so that Bommarito could continue running the union. Shortly after the 1981 convention at which Stone was elected, when he was on his way home, the Uniroyal committee meeting in Clearwater, Florida, wanted to give Bommarito a gift. "So I stopped there too," Stone recalled, "and I was in the meeting and Pete was in the meeting and so on. And hell, he acted like he was still president. So I just let it go, but I made up my mind then that would be his last hurrah, because you can't let Pete be in there just a little bit. If you let his foot in the door, he was in the room."

So the 1987 surprise really did not surprise Stone one bit. At the time, an attorney from California had started a Tire Worker Litigation fund and was going to sue all the tire companies over asbestos exposure. The attorney was trying to sign up people for a class action lawsuit, and Bommarito was heavily involved. "Bommarito was into it with both feet," Stone said. "I even found out afterward that they had set up a separate lawsuit for him for a couple million dollars. That was going to be his payoff. He wasn't going to be in the class action."

Stone, though, openly discouraged the litigation. He received a call from one couple in their eighties who were getting pressure to sign up for the class action suit. Stone went over and talked to them, and they explained why they were upset. The woman had worked in the tire plant just three or four months; the man had worked all his life in the factory.

They were both in good health, yet people were still trying to force them to say they had been hurt by asbestos. "I told them what I thought of it, that I didn't believe you should sue someone for something if you didn't have it coming," Stone said. "There are people who really were affected by asbestos and they deserved something for it. But the way they were going about it was to sign everybody up and everybody benefits whether anything happened to you or not. I just don't believe in that."

Bommarito thought the guy was great as long as he was going after rubber companies. "That was Pete, he didn't care much how he got it," Stone said. "He wanted to get all he could from the companies. During most of the times when he was president that was fine, because we were on upswings in the '60s and '70s."

When Stone would have no part of the litigation fund, Bommarito got mad, and the next thing Stone knew his predecessor was looking to be his successor. Stone knew that the constitutional questions ultimately would short-circuit the actual bid, but rumors persisted right up until the convention that Bommarito had rented a suite at a nearby hotel and would make a dramatic entrance at the convention. In the end, nothing happened, and Stone faced just nominal opposition from Don Copass, the president of the local at the Armstrong Tire plant in Nashville. "Bommarito never showed up in Las Vegas because that year I didn't invite him and I felt bad about it [later] because that's the last one he could have attended [Bommarito died in 1989]," Stone said. "But hell, I wasn't going to pay the expenses for somebody to go out there and tear me apart. If he was going to do that he was going to do it on his own."

Although Stone dodged that bullet, it was clear the three-term president would be vulnerable when he ran for a fourth term in 1990; while he was looked upon as a man of honor, some URW members thought the organization should once again be a "fighting union."

CHAPTER 9

THE PERFECT CAMPAIGN
KEN COSS TAKES OVER

Kenneth Coss was in the office the night Mike Stone made the decision to run for president of the United Rubber Workers. Little did Stone know that he was confiding his secret to the man who nearly a decade later would try to wrest that job from him. It was after work hours in 1981, when the URW's headquarters was still in downtown Akron in its historic building on High Street. Stone was vice president at the time and Coss the assistant to Secretary/Treasurer Donald Tucker. Stone was in a tough position as the number one lieutenant to URW President Bommarito, because Bommarito was making overtures that he might try to buck URW tradition and try to stay on past the mandatory age sixty-five retirement. That was distressing to Stone, who on one hand wanted to remain loyal to the man who had appointed him to the union's vice presidency just four years earlier, but on the other hand felt he had earned his chance as URW president.

"I happened to be in the office the night he went around looking for somebody to talk to," Coss said. "Pete really didn't want to let go in a way. Mike made a determination. He said, 'I've decided that if Pete can change his mind, I can change my mind, and I'm going to run.' And I shook his hand and said, 'Well, you're going to be the next president then because as long as you take that kind of a stand, Pete doesn't want a confrontation. He just hates to give up, but he knows it's time also.'"

Coss himself had taken a route different from Stone's to a job in URW headquarters. Stone, like every other Rubber Workers president before him, had toiled for many long, dirty years in a tire factory. Coss, though, never worked in a tire plant, joining the URW through his job at the U.S. Rubber chemicals factory in Painesville, Ohio. But Coss knew long before then what unionism was all about, his grandfather having been an organizer for the Steelworkers union. "I knew what a scab was when I was five years old," he said. He even made one foray into management, but that was pretty much a disaster. It was an operation employing about three thousand people, and Coss had a different type of relationship with the people working for him. He generally gave them free rein as long as they got their work done, including the chance to sit down and rest when appropriate. One day his supervisor came in when the unloading crew was out by the shed. When the manager asked about the situation, Coss stepped forward and said those people worked for him. "The supervisor asked why they were not working," Coss recalled. "I told him they had done more work already than they used to do in a whole day. I said, 'Look at the place.' He said, 'Give them a broom and tell them to sweep the floor.' I said, 'No.' He said, 'You have to learn there's one thing that's most important and that's discipline.' I said, 'Look what they've done.' He said, 'That's not what matters. The only thing that matters is discipline.' As you can imagine, that was the end of my management career."

Before getting a job at the U.S. Rubber plant, Coss had worked at Industrial Rayon Corp. and was a member of the Textile Workers of America, serving on the local's executive board and as a department representative. He worked as an inspector in the assembly area of the plant, but the rate of pay at U.S. Rubber was so much higher that he took a job as a warehouseman in 1965 when the facility was expanding. When he joined the new facility, Coss told his wife, Carol, that he definitely was not going to be involved as a union representative at U.S. Rubber. He was quite adamant. "It's a thankless job and takes too much time and everybody's always kind of after you," he said. His resolve was short-lived. "I think I was only there about sixty or ninety days, and several of the people who had worked at the prior place worked over there. And we worked in a department that had a gung-ho guy who was just getting everybody in the department upset. Several of them asked me if I'd be a union representative already, so just about the time I got my probationary period over I got the job of representative again." In 1969, Coss was elected president of URW Local 553 and served five years in the office. While local president, he came to know the plant's personnel manager quite well, and they learned to trust and respect each other. The two, however, kept their close working relationship a secret. "It's just in that day and age you had to keep it kind of hidden from the corporate people that you were cooperating and working together because that wasn't a popular concept in those days," Coss said.

Kenneth Coss was the union's sixth and final president, winning the post from Stone following a bitter campaign in 1990. *(USWA/URW photo files)*

After five years, he was appointed in 1974 to the International staff by Bommarito. He served under Tucker, who was District 1 director at the time, and Coss's first assignment was organizing. He worked in southern Virginia, and was involved in several successful campaigns. "I was shipped out to Indiana with the idea that maybe some of the ways we were doing things were a little different than what had been done before," Coss said. "I believed it wasn't the International that organized people. People had to have that desire to organize themselves. We were there to help them and advise them." While normally it was older workers who had been around unions who would get involved in an organizing effort, Coss concentrated on getting involvement from younger workers. "I would get with a lot of the younger people and get them enthused and use their imagination." And Coss never concentrated just on bashing management, instead putting out material that often was humorous. "My position was the reason these people want a union is so they can cooperate with management; work with them and the place will prosper, but the workers want their share too."

The most notable victory Coss was involved with was at the Mohawk Rubber tire factory in Salem, Virginia. That was a perennial organizing effort that invariably failed. Coss got involved one day when he was back at the district office and noticed a field representative already getting ready for the following year's campaign. The colleague mentioned that there did not appear to be much chance of bringing the plant into the URW's fold that year. Coss talked to Tucker and offered to go and help out on the campaign for awhile. "Tucker said as long as we produced we basically had a free hand, so I went down and we took a look at things," Coss said. "I started meeting with an entirely different group of people than they'd been meeting with before." The effort apparently helped, as the URW finally was able to organize the lone tire plant in District 1 that was not in the union's fold at the time.

Coss got to play an important role during the 1976 strike as one of the coordinators of the Firestone boycott. He called it one of the more effective boycotts the URW ever implemented, although he admitted the company's performance had already been weakened by the Firestone 500 recall that nearly bankrupted the tire maker. Coss said he was always leery about boycotts because of the potential long-term effects. "You really don't want to permanently damage a company because when it's settled you have to go back to everyone and say, 'They're OK now.' It's pretty hard to have an effective one but once you do it's pretty hard to turn off."

His first headquarters job in Akron came as Tucker's assistant when the District 1 director was elected secretary/treasurer during the 1978 convention on the Bommarito/Stone ticket after Ike Gold retired following eighteen years in office. He remained an assistant to Tucker until early 1987, when Tucker retired and Stone appointed Coss as secretary/treasurer—but apparently not without some reluctance on Stone's part. "When he appointed me as secretary/treasurer he really didn't want to, and he more or less told me so," Coss said. "[Stone's people] came up with a scheme where if they put me up as interim secretary/treasurer I'd agree not to run for the job, and I wouldn't agree to that. Stone was worried, I guess. They didn't really want me in that arena."

Stone had fallen into the trap many leaders succumb to, Coss thought. Stone had surrounded himself with confidants who turned off many people in the union. Coss knew a couple of them had their eye on the secretary/treasurer job. "And they didn't trust me because they thought I had quite a following among the local unions," Coss said. "I guess their strategy was to shove me out there and beat me and get me out of the way where they didn't have to worry about me anymore; then he could have one of his right-hand guys in there as secretary/treasurer."

Coss said the URW Executive Board, however, refused to approve anybody else except him as secretary/treasurer. So Stone relented and put Coss in the position. In accepting the office, Coss made the following promise to the rank and file: "As long as you want me to be your secretary/treasurer I will be. I'll discharge the duties of the office the best I can. I'll never lie to you. And I won't be afraid to ask you for help."

Even at the URW convention later in 1987, rather than naming Coss as part of the pro-administration ticket, Stone mandated that Coss win the position in caucus—exactly as Bommarito had made Stone do nine years earlier after appointing him vice president. Coss said that at the convention Stone told him he was liable to pick another running mate. Coss retorted that if that were the case, he would just run against Stone for president, and that he believed he had the support to win. "Finally he told me that was the best thing I could have done; that he respected that kind of spirit and I was the man for the job," Coss said. "He went to the cooler in his suite and got me a beer. And even though we officially ran as a team, they had to hurry up the day before the election and go out and get stuff with all three of our names on it, because up to that point Mike and [Vice President Joe] Johnston were running, and I was running." Three years later that truly would be the case.

1990 CAMPAIGN: A BITTER BATTLE

Just as Coss was one of the first people to hear of Stone's plan to run for president in 1981, Coss said Stone was the first person he told when he decided to take on Stone nine years later. The decision was not an easy one, Coss said. "Honestly, I thought I had the best job in the organization when I was secretary/treasurer. I would have been perfectly happy to stay in that job. I tried to work out things with Mike at four different meetings because I kept telling him, 'Mike, I have no reason as long as the organization is heading in the right direction to even want your job,'" For one thing, the secretary/treasurer pay was not much less, and for another the stress level was several notches lower than for the president.

Despite the fact that the money was similar—and if he ran and lost he would take a big pay cut—Coss could not shake the nagging feeling that he truly could do a better job than Stone, whom he described as a "benign president." Coss thought the union should be doing more in education and practicing a different type of organizing. "We had an organizational director at that time who I just totally disagreed with," he said. "He had a very brusque approach. He was very overbearing and crude. He didn't go by intellect at all. It was all just bulldozing." Coss said the organizing tack was reflected in the URW's success rate. "We didn't have any success in organizing in those times. It was still the 1930's attitude. They're still the capitalists who are taking advantage of us and we've got to fight them because they're our enemy."

Coss, along with many others in the URW, also strongly disagreed with Stone's stance on giving up concessions on wages and benefits to try to keep plants from closing. "All we did was start a competition where we would try to save a plant," Coss said. "We would save a specific plant which in turn would put another plant in jeopardy because there were too many plants. There was just too much production at the time for the economy and so what we did, we kept shoving that right down the line until it affected everybody, and they still closed [plants] down." To Coss, the only way the union could be successful was if it worked with the companies and tried to make the tire and rubber industry successful in North America. "Basically I just thought the idea of giving wages and benefits back in most cases does absolutely no good," he said, "I don't think everything Mike Stone ever did was wrong. In his own way, Mike thought he was doing the right thing." For example, Stone made keeping his home factory operating in Eau Claire, Wisconsin, a personal issue. "He did not want that plant closing no matter what," Coss said. "That was his home plant and those people up there were good people. And they just kept that old plant going for years after it should have been shut down."

After much contemplation, Coss made the only determination he felt he could. The secretary/treasurer had told Stone he would inform him first if he ever decided to run against him. The climactic decision came during one of the discussions in which Coss tried to get his ideas across in several areas. "I remember Mike telling me, 'When you say I'm old-fashioned and I won't conform to any new ways and that I'm living in the 1930s, that's a compliment to me because to me that's the way unions should be.' That's when I said, 'Then I guess I might as well tell you right now I'll be running against you.' And that's kind of the way it happened," Coss said.

The race was on. Coss officially announced his candidacy in January 1990 and quickly had a campaign committee and treasurer in place. On March 12, seven of the eleven members of the URW International Executive Board put out a letter endorsing the challenger. "We feel if we are to grow and prosper in the '90s as an effective International labor union, we must have a leader with vision, a leader with intelligence and integrity, and a leader with the ability to easily establish a rapport with anyone he's called on to work with," their letter stated. Gilbert Laws, one of the four not signing the letter and Bommarito's 1975 opponent, kept his support behind Stone. "Nobody came out with why Ken Coss should be president and Mike Stone shouldn't," Laws said. "I think Mike Stone has done what he promised to do and kept the Rubber Workers together in tough times."

For Stone, the election year of 1990 was no fun at all. He said the campaign was one of whispered innuendos and unsubstantiated claims. "The whispers have been going on for a year or more, long before [Coss] was running for president," he said. "It's hard to combat when people tell a part of a story." Stone stood by his record, refusing to make excuses. He pointed to statistics showing the URW gained more in wages and pensions during the 1980s than the 1970s. He looked back at three master contract negotiations without a major strike. He took pride in maintaining full benefits and COLAs while nurturing the URW's strike fund from $2.5 million to $9.5 million in his nine-year tenure. He hated when others called him conciliatory or unwilling to call a strike. "No one in this union dislikes concessions more than I. If they try to say I like concessions, they're a liar." At the same time, Stone estimated that about ten thousand workers had been spared unemployment because of the union's willingness to grant relief in wages and/or benefits to various companies facing tough times. As for strikes, he said "the 1980s were not the time to put workers out on strike—we had seen these strikes come every time and each time . . . we'd see more plants close."

Stone also questioned why URW members moved quickly to accept Coss's assertion that it was so easy to get away from concessions. "I told them he has a program, but it's one of those Nixon Vietnam programs, where he says, 'I've got a secret but I'm not going to tell you what it is.' And they bought that bullshit from that guy," Stone said. Additionally, Coss irked Stone by his sudden opposition to contract settlements and concessions after not voicing displeasure at the time they were negotiated. "He always voted in favor of them, and all of a sudden none of the things were any good when he started running for president," Stone said. In addition, Coss made many promises the incumbent—having been in office for nine years—knew would be nearly impossible to deliver on. "They're going to have an education center," Stone said. "I knew it was crap, but he was kind of a personable guy and people believed him." And when a candidate jumps on a platform of "No concessions" following the period from which the URW had just emerged, the rank and file is going to get excited. The incumbent also derided Coss supporters' desire to "give the union back to the members" as nothing more than an old song. "It's so old, it's been around since before my opponent was dry behind the ears," Stone said. "Anytime you campaign against an officer, you say you want to give back to the union. It's a catch phrase that means absolutely nothing."

Stone acknowledged that his record was not the kind to fire up local unions. "They don't like those concessions," he said. "They thought it was great when their plant was ready to go down and it stopped it, but as soon as the ink was dry on the agreement, nobody was for it. And they didn't like the changes that they had to make. You can't blame them for that. I wouldn't like it either. The options were: You tell them to go to hell, and then they shut your plant down. Then you've got no concessions."

As the campaign took shape, it became clear that Coss's effort was not a mere token opposition to the incumbent. That was obvious from attendance counts at caucus meetings of candidates held at each of the district council sessions. For instance, at the District 1 meeting, 139 members attended the Coss caucus compared with just 16 at the Stone gathering. District 8 attendance was almost as lopsided, with 106 at the Coss meeting and 32 at Stone's. While such numbers do not directly translate into convention results—district caucus attendees will not necessarily be convention delegates—it was enough of an indication that Stone was in trouble. Craig Hemsley, who supported Stone, attended the District 1 meeting in July of that year and saw the huge disparity in attendance at the respective caucuses. Hemsley then talked by phone to Tommy Lynne, a Stone supporter in District 8, and heard similar results. "I said, 'What's it like down there, Tommy?' He said, 'Oh man, we're going to get smoked.'"

Coss tapped longtime friend Dan Borelli, who worked with him at the U.S. Rubber (by then Uniroyal) plant in Painesville, to run his campaign. Borelli was someone Coss could trust to be loyal to the cause, something that at times is hard to find in an organization as political as a labor union. And Borelli also was one who could help keep the campaign on the up and up, by trying to keep a rein on supporters who wanted to take the race down into the gutter. "I always liked Mike Stone," Borelli said. "I supported Mike when he first ran. I liked him as a vice president. He was a Uniroyal guy. He had some very good ideas. Mike was more serious than a lot of guys took him for as vice president." But Borelli could see that Stone had fallen prey to a pratfall that brings down many a leader. "One of the things that you say may have been Peter Bommarito's downfalls was: Pete became an institution," Borelli said. "Pete felt he could do whatever he wanted to do and people were going to just live by it. Mike felt like that was wrong coming in, but in a short time Mike was doing that. You can't say that it goes with the territory. You have to grow into it if you're going to do it at all."

If there was a true falling out between Coss and Stone, it was over financial considerations. "Kenny had the financial end of the organization," Borelli said. "He could see where it's going out but not coming in. We're not organizing, we're not educating, and we're not moving forward. All the unions were moving backward, but most of them had some place where they figured they would stop." Stone should have reduced the number of districts in the union, so the URW would have fewer highly paid directors and more field representatives servicing the locals, Borelli said. And travel should have been kept to a manageable dollar level, cutting down on representatives going to a local union picnic just for the sake of getting votes. Borelli also was irked at the $700,000 spent on refurbishing the URW headquarters building, a structure that was sold to the city of Akron and razed just a couple of years later.

And Coss's campaign manager agreed with Coss in his assessment of

Stone's associates. "I had a good view of it from being out in the local with some of the people he surrounded himself with," Borelli said. "They were arrogant. Let me be honest, I don't think they did an honest day's work. I think Mike was a hard-assed worker. As president, he put in a lot of hours." Stone also did not appear to take the challenge as seriously as he should, Borelli said, perhaps feeling comfortable that he would retain his office. "I think he surrounded himself with people who said what he wanted to hear, and some of the same people who were telling him that were the same people who turned the membership against him with their arrogance," Borelli said.

The Coss camp tried to keep the race sportsmanlike, he added, saying that any innuendos in the race did not come from anybody involved with putting together Coss's campaign. "You have to run on the job the guy's doing, and the kind of job you think you'll do. That's the way we kept it." Some things that did come out, such as allegations of credit card abuse, came from supporters and those on the executive board, Borelli said. Coss's camp did not make an effort to shut that down, knowing it would take months of a campaign just to prove or disprove each accusation, so on some things they just let the people think what they wanted to think. Borelli characterized the campaign as clean, stressing that Coss talked about direction, education, and building back up the URW's strength as a union. "We didn't want to go into negotiations where the first word that come out of the company and come out of us was concessions," he said. "We wanted to go forward. We'd taken enough concessions. If these companies couldn't afford to stay in business and pay a competitive wage and benefits, then they're going to have to open their books and show us and we'd look at them on an individual basis. We weren't going to have wholesale concessions in negotiations."

Coss said the campaign actually could have been a lot more bitter if some of the people supporting him had done some things they threatened to do. Coss declined to discuss details but said some of his supporters had gotten hold of material detrimental to Stone. "I told them I would withdraw as a candidate if they released it," Coss said. "I told them in the first place we don't need to use tactics like that. And if they did even accidentally print something like that I would withdraw as a candidate because I wouldn't have that as part of my campaign." Coss's actions were not altogether altruistic; they were practical as well. "That's the worst thing that can happen when you're way ahead to get into some of that stuff and make it look like you're raking up stuff or slinging mud or something. We felt that we were so far ahead from the get-go that anything that was controversial or looked like we were trying to get dirt on people would be detrimental to us more than to them."

Others in the union, however, viewed the campaign as very divisive at a time when the URW needed to be unified. "It was very bad in my opinion, and at a time when the union needed to be together," said Curt Brown, who served as public relations director under the last three URW presidents. "There were things said about Stone's character that I think were just plain lies. They were vicious accusations that were never proven. It was unnecessary to a political campaign." Stone's mistake, according to Brown, was appointing Coss as secretary/treasurer in the first place, putting a potential political challenger in a position where he could travel the country, press the flesh, and start his campaign. Once Coss began his challenge, Stone failed to react, Brown said. "I think Coss built an incredibly good political machine, and I'm not sure Stone could have beat it," the PR director said. "Mind you, I said I thought Stone was a good president, but I don't think he was a good self-promoter in that sense. Coss was a consummate self-promoter."

Despite Stone's assertion that he had done a commendable job leading the URW for nine years and that he deserved a chance to retire after one more term as the union's leader, Coss had no trouble finding allies. While the rank and file generally viewed Stone with respect, saying he did a credible job in tough times, many also characterized his tenure as "caretaker" leadership. The Rubber Workers were not satisfied with an "okay" union—they wanted more. They were looking for a leader who would energize them, activate them, and make them feel like a union again. They wanted a union that acted, rather than reacted. As United Mine Workers President Richard Trumka told URW delegates during that 1990 convention, "In the '90s we're through turning the other cheek. We can't and won't settle for less. It's time organized labor stopped working like some institution and put on the gloves."

For that renewed vision, there were plenty of URW members who turned to Coss, who seemed to bring an inner self-confidence to the job, as well as promises for more aggressive leadership and no concessions. Doug Werstler, a Local 2 executive board member in 1990, said at the time he was looking for a younger leader with more enthusiasm. He said he thought Stone had done a good job but had never been able to escape the shadow of Bommarito. "Stone had strength when needed, but he hasn't become his own leader," Werstler said. "Kenny doesn't have the same charisma as Bommarito, but he's believable, he gets people on their feet, and he hits the right buttons when he talks."

Kenneth Finley was a representative servicing more than twenty locals in Ohio and West Virginia, and he was strongly behind Coss. He felt that it was the challenger's ability to gather support from URW staff members that helped to turn the race decisively in his favor. "If you don't have the staff, you're not going to get elected, because the staff is the people who have the thumb on the pulse of the local union officers—not the International officers," Finley said. For staff representatives, especially, politicking was part of the job. "That's an intricate part of being a rep," he said. Finley said it was obvious the Stone-Coss race was going to be a good contest, if only because it was clear many URW members simply wanted a change. "You might be doing everything that you can and still you have to run on your record," Finley said. "Somebody's who's not there doesn't have to run on their record."

Some URW locals took the formal action requiring delegates to vote for Coss. For Local 12 in Gadsden it appeared that the mandate for Coss was better represented as a vote against Stone, according to Mickey Williams. "Gadsden at that point was a pretty militant union," Williams said, "and Stone made a lot of statements about how proud he was that he had never had a chain to strike during his tenure. Gadsden didn't want to be known as the one who wouldn't strike. They always wanted to be known as the one who took their part and did their thing and struck and did whatever else was necessary. They felt like Stone just wasn't militant enough to be leader of the URW, and they felt like Coss would be."

While Coss obviously had garnered a great deal of support—perhaps even to an insurmountable degree—Stone was not without his supporters. One of those, Patrick Glenn, actually had run against Stone on Glenn Ellison's ticket in the 1981 campaign. This time Glenn was one of three candidates to replace Coss as secretary/treasurer on Stone's pro-administration ticket. "Mike Stone established respect for the organization, using reasoned judgment," Glenn said. "We elect our friends and defeat our enemies. Mike Stone has been our friend."

Gary Diceglio could not get elected as a delegate from Local 2 in Akron after voicing his support for Stone. To show how hypocritical union politics can be, he told a story of how some Local 2 members had turned a seemingly gregarious gesture by Stone against the URW president. Diceglio and other Local 2 members had volunteered at an organizing phone bank effort to try to help organize a plant in Indiana. Afterward, Stone took the group out to eat at a local Brown Derby restaurant. Diceglio had a couple of drinks but had to leave before eating. "The rest of them had a good meal, and that was brought up at our union meeting how Stone wasted money for taking us out to eat," Diceglio said. "The same guys who were complaining about it were the ones who were there. If they felt that strongly about it, all they had to do was not go. They were there, they broke bread with him and had a nice time. Then they said it was a waste of money."

John Sellers, who was servicing locals out west at the time, favored Stone over Coss, though he liked them both and probably had a closer relationship with Coss. "I just did not think that it was time for a change," Sellers said. "I think Mike was going to serve one more term and beyond that Kenny was the heir apparent. I just didn't see the need for the change, and the need for the division the contest was going to cause. It wasn't anything personal. It was simply my view of what was good for the union at that time." Sellers was pretty active in the campaign, especially with the staff and the local unions he had contact with. But being based in California, Sellers was somewhat isolated from what was going on in Akron. "There certainly was a lot of bad information coming back about things like vote count, which certainly led to a false sense of security," he said. Any security Sellers and the Stone camp may have felt was quickly drenched upon arrival at the convention site in Hollywood, Florida. "When I walked in the door in Florida, I knew we were done," Sellers said. "You just get a sense of those things. I had certainly seen other campaigns. Kenny's message was out there. Kenny's people were working the convention already. He definitely had an organization. Quite frankly, we weren't that organized. When I walked in the hotel, I said, 'Uh oh, I don't think we're winning.'"

If there had been any doubt about whom delegates favored, it was apparent at each convention session who the likely winner would be. Coss walked into the sessions amidst a parade of flag-waving, T-shirt-clad supporters chanting, "KEN-NY, KEN-NY." Some of the shirts declared that it was time to "Come Out of the Stone Age." Coss took full advantage of his powers as secretary/treasurer to set up the convention as he saw fit, said one Stone supporter. That meant making sure locals supporting Coss sat up front, and all the hotel monitors carried Coss's message. "I could not believe that Mike gave Kenny free rein to set up that convention," the supporter said. "If I had been Mike I would have been damn sure I had somebody in the middle of that process. He set up everything from where the hospitality suites were to where Mike's suite was." The placing of the suites was typical of the convention and the campaign, according to Coss supporter John Cunningham of Local 677. "Stone was on the very top floor and everybody else was on the bottom," he said. "Coss was very accessible. Stone didn't really come out and mix all that much."

The convention was nothing if not political. There was the brochure put out by the Stone camp individually deriding each potential candidate on the Coss ticket. Comments in the brochure ran from the ludicrous ("Why Ellison and Coss even hired others into the building who drive foreign cars and motorcycles! IS THIS UNIONISM?") to the stupid ("Nothing else happened to Local 2 President Dan Kelly except he was a football player and a bench warmer at that") to the mean (Ray Wiseman's "against everything. First he's on one side, then he's on the other side . . . But he still can't convince anyone to give him a staff job!! There's probably a good reason"). They even were a little prophetic about Mike Stanley, president of Local 878 in Union City, Tennessee, and the eventual vice president under Coss. On Stanley, the brochure said: "He has voted against everything since he became active in the union! Pete Bommarito didn't satisfy him! Kenny Oldham didn't satisfy him! Mike Stone didn't satisfy him! Ten will get you one, Kenny Coss won't satisfy him either!"

The biggest order of business early in the convention was the caucuses to select the vice presidential and secretary/treasurer slots on the Coss ticket and a secretary/treasurer candidate to run with Stone and Joe Johnston, his vice president for all nine years of his presidency.

For the secretary/treasurer spot with Coss, Ellison faced one candidate, but won easily, having been considered pretty much a shoo-in from the start. But for vice president, Coss did much the same thing that Stone had done in 1981 by letting the caucus decide. That was how he ended up with presidents of five large URW locals running for vice president. Later Coss

Kenneth Coss (right) is paraded into the 1990 URW convention hall by Dan Borelli, his campaign manager. (Rubber & Plastics News *photo. Copyright Crain Communications Inc.*)

said it might have been easier for the union if his camp had handpicked a vice presidential candidate, as he and Stanley had a falling out in his second term. But Coss acknowledged it was politically beneficial to have a big group going for vice president. Of all those running for vice president in Coss's caucus at the convention, he least expected Stanley to come out of the pack.

Stanley was seen by some as a militant-type labor leader in charge of one of the locals forming the "Southern Coalition" among the Goodyear locals in the master contract. These locals often clashed with Goodyear, and many times did not see eye to eye with the other Goodyear locals when it came to contract goals and bargaining. Stanley's local in Union City could be so political that in 1983 Stanley and his uncle, Sam Odom, ran against each other for local president. Stanley ended up winning, but Odom came back and won later when Stanley left Union City. Like many URW leaders, Stanley had hired into the Union City plant young, at age nineteen, and quickly became involved in the union. Serving on committees and as steward, he was elected vice president of the local in 1980 and president three years later.

At the 1987 convention Stanley was elected to the URW's International Executive Board, so he had a close-up view of both Coss and Stone. "I felt that Mike just wasn't as strong as he could be with the tire companies in master negotiations," Stanley said. "We felt like we needed some new direction. We needed to be more aggressive at the bargaining table. I didn't feel like what was in place in his administration at that juncture was going to be the kind of leadership to get us where we needed to go." On the contrary, he and the majority of the board saw Coss talking about making the kind of changes they wanted, being more aggressive and being more militant—but what they called "measured militancy." Stanley actually announced late for the vice president race, not throwing his hat in the ring until July, just two months before the September election. During convention week, Stanley worked the campaign hard, going from one caucus group to the next.

When the final pro-Coss caucus came and it was time for the selection of running mates, everything seemed to fall into place for Stanley. Some of the other candidates faltered in one way or another, and Stanley headed to the microphone armed with a two-page speech he had written out. "When I got up there I pulled it out and laid it on the podium and didn't unfold it," Stanley said. "I just started talking and one thing kind of led to another, and I just kind of started speaking from the heart." He also got some help from the pro-Stone caucus next door. Delegates there were making a lot of noise, mostly normal rally-type clamor, but then they started pounding and making all kinds of racket. "I remember making the comment, it just came out, an old Tennessee folklore kind of chitter-chatter. I said, 'Well, you hear next door there's a lot of beating and bamming and yelling going on. We've got an old saying down in Tennessee. An empty wagon makes a lot of noise.' And I mean everybody just kind of came unglued. They were yelling and clapping. I can't even remember what I said after that point, but it just fired them up. I never even read from the speech. I just left there and folded it up and put it back in my pocket."

Stanley missed winning the nomination on the first ballot by just a few votes, but won the run-off against Ray Wiseman, president from the Uniroyal Goodrich local in Fort Wayne, Indiana, by a good margin. That put Stanley in position to be the first URW top officer to be elected from the rank and file—rather than a staff position—in thirty years, since Bommarito won the vice presidency in 1960.

Much convention debate centered on the question of imported paneling that supposedly had been installed at URW headquarters in Akron as part of a nearly $1 million refurbishing project. When the project was about two-thirds complete an uninstalled piece of paneling was discovered that had been marked "Made in Indonesia." It is a longstanding tradition of the URW—and all domestic trade unions—to buy only union-made material sourced from the United States or Canada, where the URW also represented a large number of workers. The project—directed by Ellison as assistant to Coss—was halted and Ellison questioned the contractor about the availability of union-made paneling. When told the size of paneling being used was unavailable in the United States, Coss, Ellison, and Stone then agreed to let the project continue. The paneling became a campaign issue when Stone supporters circulated literature about the project at the convention, including fliers touting Coss and Ellison as the "Import Candidates."

Coss said the paneling issue was about the dumbest thing for the Stone ticket to take on. When the piece of paneling marked "Make in Indonesia" was found, the refurbishing work was taking place on the second floor, where Stone's wife worked. Work in most of the rest of the building had been completed, and Coss and Ellison apprised Stone of the situation. Coss said that Stone replied: "Well you can't stop now. You've got to finish the second floor." Coss said the work continued, with all three of the officers knowing that the paneling might not be domestically produced by union labor. "Like I said before," Coss said, "if you can buy something in the U.S., you go ahead and do it. But we had all Sony equipment in our building. Our electronics and computers were all Japanese." Coss thought it made no sense to tear up work on three floors to the tune of several hundred thousand dollars. "It would have been better if they just kept quiet about it, because Stone was the guy who said 'Go ahead' with the little bit that had to be done," Coss said.

By the time the issue hit the convention floor, sentiment from supporters of both presidential candidates ran high in support of "ripping it out," especially after learning acceptable paneling was made in the United States. Even Stone, when asked his opinion, grabbed the microphone and yelled, "Rip it out," and delegates unanimously adopted a motion to replace the paneling. As a footnote to the debate, the union never actually had to reverse its error on the paneling as the city of Akron shortly thereafter bought the headquarters building and tore it down to make way for a new convention center.

When it came time for the actual voting, Coss's 658–370 victory—on September 27, his fifty-fifth birthday—was almost anticlimactic. With that margin, Coss had the clear mandate to push for the programs he said Stone refused to consider. "The day of the election when the result came in," Coss said, "I walked over to Mike and he said, 'Well, congratulations.' And I said to Mike, 'Wouldn't it have been easier to work things out?' and he said, 'I'll tell you what. You and I both know I had some pretty heavy baggage.' And I said, 'Yeah, that was part of the reason I ran.' He said, 'Yeah, I know.' We were talking about the people around him." Coss did not waste any time getting to work, having the new URW executive board one day after the election make its first course of action the redrawing of URW districts to reduce the number of district offices from five to four, an action that saved the union about $250,000 a year.

After the defeat, Stone did not retire right away, instead taking about a $30,000 pay cut from his $78,000 annual salary as president to return to the field as an International representative servicing locals and organizing non-union plants. Before the convention closed, though, he got one last chance to remind delegates they must never forget the old traditional values. His farewell address, which Stone wrote entirely himself, told chapters about the beliefs of the URW's fifth International president. "It isn't old-fashioned to be loyal," Stone told delegates. "It isn't old-fashioned to be honest. It isn't old-fashioned to be dedicated to a cause. It isn't old-fashioned to be respected by peers and adversaries alike. And it's not old-fashioned to love your union."

1991 MASTER CONTRACT NEGOTIATIONS

For a labor leader, the proof of the pudding is at the bargaining table. Fiery speeches can ignite the rank and file and possibly put fear into a company negotiator, and strikes make headlines. But in the end, for the

Kenneth Coss is flanked by his new officers, Vice President J. Michael Stanley (left) and Secretary/Treasurer Glenn Ellison after the trio was elected in 1991. (Rubber & Plastics News *photo. Copyright Crain Communications Inc.*)

worker as for the company, it is the bottom line that counts. And if you are the head of the United Rubber Workers, that meant taking a piece out of the hide of tire and rubber companies during triennial master contract talks. Coss's first chance to show his mettle came during 1991 master negotiations, pacts covering twenty-six thousand URW members at Goodyear, Bridgestone/Firestone, and Groupe Michelin-owned Uniroyal Goodrich that expired roughly six months after Coss took office.

True to his campaign promises, the new URW president quickly put the firms on notice about the union's views on concessions. "It's a last resort from now on," Coss said. "If we can help make things more efficient by working together, we're certainly there to do that. But to have it be the first thing we look at, we won't have that anymore." Coss and his newly elected vice president, Mike Stanley, also started meeting with top management people shortly after the 1990 convention to try to make sure everyone was on the same page. The URW hierarchy wanted to establish a rapport before starting negotiations, as they figured the companies had likely read excerpts of the convention, at which the new leaders had espoused such campaign rhetoric as wanting to "put all the fat cats on a diet."

Members of the URW Policy Committee, setting goals in January 1991 for the upcoming talks, also made it clear they wanted to move forward by gaining more than they had become accustomed to over the past decade. The goals for bargaining included a "meaningful general wage increase"; maintenance of COLA; improved pensions for active employees and a provision for automatic future increases through a cost-of-living escalator clause; improved job security from the effects of plant closings, mass layoffs, work relocation, and technological change; and initiation of employee education programs with the objective of enhancing occupational skills.

Bridgestone/Firestone helped make the March 11 opening day of negotiations interesting by announcing it would cut 340 production jobs at six North American tire plants and suspend hiring at its new truck tire unit to keep inventory levels in line with future sales projections. Although the layoffs coincided with the first day of master contract negotiations, both sides said they did not expect the cuts to affect bargaining, and from all outside appearances, it did not. During the ceremonial opening of talks with Bridgestone/Firestone, Coss looked to be all business, attired in a suit and tie. On the contrary, his counterpart, Samuel L. Torrence, Bridgestone/Firestone vice president of labor relations, showed up dressed more casually, wearing a sweater. At first glance it was hard to pick out who represented the company and who stood for the union. Both the URW and Bridgestone/Firestone had been involved since the 1989 contract talks in Partnership for Involvement, a program administered by the Federal Mediation and Conciliation Services. The 1991 master contract talks were the first chance to show off what the two sides had learned in the process, so Bridgestone/Firestone requested to be named the target company in negotiations and the union quickly agreed. On April 20 the two sides agreed in principle to a three-year contract that brought no general wage increase, but did maintain COLAs and raised the pension multiplier from $23.50 to $30 a month per year of service, although the workers shared a portion of the pension increase's cost in the second and third years of service. The overall package increased an estimated 18 percent in wages and benefits over the life of the contract for tire workers who made an average of $15.47 an hour in wages and $12.12 in benefits prior to the new agreement. Torrence emphasized that the hike in pensions "will enable us to provide an adequate increase for employees who retire while we are 'right-sizing' our facilities." The six Bridgestone/Firestone plants covered under the master agreement quickly ratified the pact, and the URW then reached agreements that closely mirrored the pact with Goodyear and Uniroyal Goodrich.

Coss said pensions were targeted because more downsizing was expected in the tire industry and the union found it more practical to boost the fortunes of those about to leave the workforce while protecting the jobs of younger people. He added that the URW was fortunate to have enough young people who understood the need to raise pensions in lieu of general wage increases. "This year we overcame the attitude that when things are bad you look to the unions to give back," Coss said. "We established that we would make gains and we did. We're giving people backbone. You can't be submissive. You can't lack respect."

Torrence called the agreement a "win-win settlement" based on principled negotiations that did away with the traditional system of demands, focusing instead on issues and options in order to conduct bargaining without a lot of the normal confrontation. He said employees must be receptive to new ways, and that if the process were to be successful, employees must believe in it and truly accept it because the relationship was founded on trust, integrity, and mutual interest in solving problems. The Bridgestone/Firestone chief negotiator also found Coss a good person to work with, saying the URW leader understood his role and the need to make sure the URW and management focused on what was needed for survival and growth. "He's open and candid and receptive to new approaches as long as it's consistent with what's important to his employees," Torrence said of Coss. "He's a fair person to deal with in negotiations and in the plant. That doesn't mean we agree on everything."

Coss eagerly returned the praise for his counterpart at Bridgestone/Firestone. "In my book he's one of the most honorable men I ever worked with," Coss said. If Torrence told you something—even if it turned out later that it was not advisable on his part—he would stick to his word unless released from the promise by the URW, according to Coss. "He knew that we wouldn't hang them unnecessarily if something didn't turn out the way you thought it would," the URW president said. Because of that close working relationship, Coss said the 1991 agreement was historical not only for what was gained, but for how it was accomplished. "We worked together on it the whole time instead of surprising the other side or letting the other side guess what it was we wanted to accomplish," Coss said. Having a non-traditional bargaining relationship such as this was not easy, Coss said, because some people on both sides continued to feel more comfortable with the traditional, antagonistic approach. "You do have to have unity and strength to be effective as a bargaining agent, but at the same time you can look at the other person's viewpoint and say, 'What is this going to do to the corporation?' and they can say, 'What is the positive effect if we do something for our people?'"

Vice President Stanley also admired Torrence, who was the reason he supported choosing Bridgestone/Firestone as the target company over the objections of his brothers from the Goodyear chain. "Torrence was refreshing to be around because of his philosophy, and he pretty well backed up what he was saying," Stanley said. "Sam truly wanted to see the URW and Bridgestone/Firestone have a true partnership."

Most observers gave Coss and his team high marks after a year in office, saying he helped win a credible package for his members, but still showed a deft understanding for the concerns of those on the other side of the table. "Everyone was guessing which way negotiations would go," industry analyst Harry Millis said. "The original wish list looked like it could be a severe problem. But the settlement actually negotiated looked extremely realistic. Perhaps the rhetoric turned out to be a little stronger than when reality set in." Mike Polovick, by then General Tire director of labor relations, said the master negotiations showed Coss could work to reach agreements that are fair and beneficial to both sides. "He's demonstrated that if management is willing, the union is capable of being beneficial to, rather than hindering, productivity and profitability as long as the union can share in it," Polovick said.

Sellers, a Stone supporter during the campaign, also thought Coss did a good job during his first term. "I think that Kenny had a positive impact," Sellers said. "The master contracts went well. Kenny really tried to get out and personally spend time with as many locals as he could. He damn sure worked long hours at it and most weekends. I think Kenny gets positive reviews for that first term." Even *Fortune* magazine heaped praise on the URW, citing the Rubber Workers as being in the vanguard of a union reform movement focusing on worker education, improved relations with management, and increased worker initiative and involvement in the workplace.

Some URW members, however, dismissed Coss's performance during his first master contract negotiations as Rubber Workers president. Bob Bianchi, who at the time was president of the Bridgestone/Firestone local in Des Moines, Iowa, said he had given Coss a message within hours of the 1990 convention election. "I told him point blank I knew where I was headed," Bianchi said. "I knew what I wanted, and we'd taken considerable beatings in 1985, and I'd already pre-negotiated a lot of things. I knew there was a $6.50 pension increase there. And I told him, 'You get in my way and it will be hell to pay.'" URW staff member Craig Hemsley also refused to praise Coss for the 1991 negotiations. "The history of this is, whenever you take over there's always that first and second year where you have a cushion of that former president," Hemsley said. "When Mike Stone took over for Pete Bommarito, he actually was still living off of Pete for the next year or two. That's why Kenny could live off of Mike for a year or two. Then he had to branch out. It's just like in marriage, the first year goes really smooth, then you find out what it's really like."

ORGANIZING SUCCESSES

In late 1992, the URW had its biggest organizing success in terms of numbers in nearly thirty years, bringing in eighteen hundred new members at Tyler Pipe Industries in Tyler, Texas. It was the largest new URW local union since the February 1964 victory at Mattel in Hawthorne, California, brought in twenty-four hundred new members. Coss said the Tyler Pipe campaign showed the importance of the "spheres of influence" approach, as members of URW Local 746 at the Kelly-Springfield plant in Tyler were highly involved in the effort. There had been more than a dozen attempts to organize the facility by various unions over the years. The URW first got permission from other internationals that had tried, wanting to make sure they did not step on the toes of a campaign from a union that already had pumped millions of dollars into an organizing effort. "They all laughed and said, 'Have a go at it,'" Coss said. "So we went down and got it organized the first time. What we did was go in and have educational programs and classes for the people. They formed a union structure before the election. They actually were operating like a union before they got organized." The URW also told the head of Tyler Pipe they would go through the plant with him and convince the people that the more prosperous the company was, the more successful the union would be.

A second big organizing victory during Coss's first term came at the Martha Mills plant in Thomaston, Georgia, another facility that had seen perennial failed organizing drives. By this time the company was doing poorly financially, Coss said, and he wanted to show the company how the URW actually could benefit the organization. Coss talked to a member of the firm's board of directors, someone he had known years before from Uniroyal, and they agreed on the parameters of what the URW would do if Martha Mills did not actively oppose the organizing campaign. "We told them we would use everything we had to come in and make it a more efficient operation," Coss said. "It was too destructive to everybody to keep having these fights every year."

Easily the most significant organizing victory—but in a very nontraditional way—was at Bridgestone/Firestone's newly built truck tire plant in Warren County, Tennessee. It was there that Mike Stone and Bridgestone/Firestone management agreed that when the truck tire plant reached a certain level of employment, the company would recognize the URW as the workers' bargaining agent if the union was able to get the majority of workers to sign cards. But when Coss took office, he said the effort was not moving forward, and Bridgestone/Firestone's Torrence was afraid the plan was falling through. So Coss and Torrence, along with other union and company officials, made a joint visit to the facility to try to salvage the historic organizing plan that had been loosely patterned after the Saturn agreement between General Motors and the United Auto Workers. "Sam would walk up and say, 'This is Ken Coss, he's president of the URW and he'd like to talk to you about trying to accomplish something that hasn't been accomplished anywhere in the U.S. We'd like to talk to you about the advisability of having a bargaining unit with the idea that we're going to work together to make this the most modern and efficient truck and bus tire plant in the world.'"

The duo talked to groups and individuals on all three shifts. At one point Bridgestone/Firestone even froze hiring at a certain level because just as the URW would get close to meeting the required percentage, the company would hire more people and keep the union from reaching the needed level. "We talked to everybody," Coss said, "and shortly thereafter they opted to be represented. We had an umpire come in and make sure a majority had signed the cards, and the company accepted that. There was never any challenge to it." It was the first tire plant organized since Bridgestone/Firestone's Oklahoma City factory in 1981, just before Stone took office as URW president. "What Warren County should be is an example of what can happen when labor and management work together," said a negotiator from another tire firm. "With that kind of arrangement, the plant may well be in a competitive advantage." As of 2001, no tire plants had since been organized by the URW or USWA.

WOMEN IN THE URW

There was no denying that the United Rubber Workers, like most industrial unions, was a male-dominated organization. No woman ever served as a URW International officer, and only a handful ever served on the International Executive Board. In the last directory issued by the URW in January 1994, a little more than a year before the merger with the United Steelworkers of America, with Coss as president, no women served on that term's Executive Board. None of the eight rank-and-file members holding positions at the Akron headquarters—such as assistants to the officers, organizing director, and pensions and investment director—was female. All four district directors were male. And just two of the forty-two staff field representatives were women: Shelby McLaughlin, who previously had been the first woman elected to the International Executive Board, and Rose Marie Jones.

Women fared better on the local union level, but their numbers still paled in comparison to the men holding positions. Of the 366 locals listed in that 1994 directory, a total of 341 women held one of the four elected offices at each local. About a fourth of those came from one of the 22 locals where each of the four officers were women. A total of 54 of the women holding local offices were presidents. The total number of female local union officers was somewhat deceptive, however. Many of the women in the leading positions were at the smaller locals, with women taking less of a leadership role at most of the larger locals. For example, at the thirty-one tire locals listed in the 1994 directory, only five of the possible 124 offices were held by women and none of the five was president.

Annalee Benedict was one woman who did make her mark on the

URW, both on the local and national levels. She served for eighteen years as treasurer of Local 626 at the GenCorp plant in Wabash, Indiana, was treasurer of the District 4 Council for fifteen years, and was elected to the union's International Executive Board. She took her union work seriously—she said it even helped wreck her marriage—and she was never afraid to let her opinions be known, whether or not the men wanted to hear them. Benedict also saw some of the barriers women faced in the URW, as she was turned down in several attempts to be hired to the union staff as a field representative. "The men were always very domineering in the early rubber years," said Benedict, who joined the union in 1961 and retired in October 1996. "[The men felt] women should be seen and not heard and if you did go somewhere you should stay in the background and be nice. I was never like that."

It was not just the men of the URW, however, that gave Benedict problems. Many outsiders questioned her beliefs. "I've been looked down on my entire life because I'm a strong believer in unions," she said. "I think the unions could be so much better if we could get more people involved—and I mean really get them all involved—because it's for their betterment." Benedict even made the union a family affair. "I started going to the union meetings. And every Sunday my boys would say, 'Mom, do we have a union meeting today?' We'd give four door prizes away every month and they would usually choose one of the boys. Those boys grew up in the union."

Benedict had a hard time making people in her local listen at first because she was a woman. "It's kind of hard to make them listen when they walk off while you're still talking," she said. "We had a lot of women, but the women were there just to earn a living, the same way I was. But I said to them, 'You know, if we get together and be strong, we've got to be a part of it or those bosses will rule us like animals.' And they *would* have." Benedict recalled a story about one boss while she was a coil packer at the factory. They were on piecework then and made pretty good money for the time. The more they accomplished the more they got paid. "I was a coil packer in Department 236 and the roof leaked and it had rained," Benedict said. "We were standing in water and we worked where there were electrical boxes. The boss said to get over there and catch that coil coming down the line. I said, 'I'm not going to get over there because I'll get shocked.' The boss threw a big piece of cardboard box [on the floor] and said for me to get over there to catch the coil. I said, 'I'm not going to do it.' He said, 'Are you refusing me?' I said, 'Yes I am. My mother never raised no fool.' And you know he stepped over there to grab that stock and that shock hit him and knocked him flat. It would have killed me because I didn't weigh a hundred pounds. You know he got up off that floor and he was white as a ghost. It could have killed him." The supervisor never apologized. Benedict told him she did not care if he fired her, she would not do it. "A lot of women would have jumped over there and done it."

Benedict was first elected as Local 626's treasurer in 1978, but that was not her first choice. She did not relish the thought of doing all the financial and tax reports. "I didn't want the treasurer's job any more than the man on the moon," she said. "I wanted to run for vice president. But we had no one who would run for treasurer on our slate. I had to drop out at the last minute and I ran for treasurer against this woman who was in there. She had said it would take an act of Congress to get her out of that position. She was good for the books, but she didn't know how to handle people. So I said, 'Well, I'm going to run against you.' And I beat her by five to one." Benedict received no opposition at all for the next two or three elections. Then people started running against her when they thought she was trying to run the union hall. Many of the older members wanted to save the local's money, while she thought the dues should be used to educate the members. "I was educated through the Rubber Workers," she said. "I got an education that I couldn't have gotten if I went to college for four years."

Benedict said that other women, such as Caroline Devine, made contributions at her local, but when the URW merged with the Steelworkers it was just getting to the point where some more women were going to make an impact at the URW International, she said. "That's when the women were coming around," Benedict said. "They were there not just to be on a man's arm. They were there for their duties. If we could have hung in a few more years, I really think we would have had a women president." When it came to speaking her mind, she was very good at it. "Our men in the Rubber Workers were afraid of women like me. That's why they disliked me so much," she said. "They were afraid because they knew that I would say anything to anybody. I didn't care what kind of power they had. I think they were all intimidated. I felt they were thinking in those days that women shouldn't be in those positions. I'd been through the ropes. I graduated from the school of hard knocks. So I know. I've been there—out on the strike lines and the front lines. And I just felt like I think God put me on this earth to do what I did." Her union work, though, did not sit well at home. "My husband thought I should be home. That's why we were divorced. And that's why I've been single for twenty-two years."

When Benedict did get elected to the International Executive Board, she said there were numerous occasions where she felt discriminated against. One such time was in a board meeting right after Bill Clinton was elected president. "Kenny [Coss] let something slip about going to Clinton's inauguration," Benedict said. "I heard it and I said, 'Oh, who's going?' Coss said, 'The board's not going to go.' And I said, 'I beg your pardon. If you're good enough to go, we are too. After all, it's our dollar.' He said, 'We can't take everybody.'" URW Secretary/Treasurer Glenn Ellison, who by that time was at odds with Coss, then offered his tickets to Benedict if he could not go. A couple of weeks later Ellison called and asked if she was serious about wanting to attend the inauguration. When she said she was serious, Ellison said she could have his two tickets. "I said, 'You've got to be kidding,' and he said, 'I don't want to be there with Kenny.'" Benedict purchased a couple of gowns to go to the balls, including the Indiana Ball. At the hotel where the URW contingent was staying, it was a mandated four-night stay at $250 a night, and Coss told her she had to pay for the night she arrived. That seemed fair enough to her. "After that was all over, we went through the hotel and there was all of the group that was with the Rubber Workers except for me," Benedict said. "They said, 'Kenny's taking us to dinner.' You could always tell when you're not wanted." Not only was she not invited to dinner, she noticed a couple of field representatives who were friends of Coss in the group and she asked when they arrived. She learned that they did not have to pay for their first night's hotel bill. "That ticked me off. I ended up paying for it out of my own pocket."

Benedict had one other sour experience with the URW International. She applied for a position on the URW staff as a field representative. "I applied and they told me there were no openings," Benedict said. "They had hired I don't know how many men." She tried contacting the Equal Employment Opportunity Commission (EEOC) as she was told by another URW field representative that the union had hired some men during this period. "Nothing came of it. They told me I had to get an attorney and I didn't have the money to fight it," she said. "I thought the EEOC was for everybody. I didn't have the money to fight it and I figured, 'What good's it going to do me to fight for this position when they sure didn't want me anyway.' They were just so against women, it was terrible. Men wanted to be in the driver's seat all the time and the women to be at the back of the bus."

THINGS START TO GO BAD

While Coss and the URW appeared on one level to be succeeding, other signs showed an industry and a union on the verge of turmoil. Tire industry overcapacity led to several shutdowns or consolidations. Uniroyal Goodrich closed its Eau Claire, Wisconsin, factory—the home local of Mike Stone—and also consolidated two tire plants in Kitchener, Ontario, into one. General Tire shut down its auto and light truck tire facility in Barrie, Ontario, in 1992, and Goodyear slated its Madisonville, Kentucky, light truck, farm, and industrial tire unit for shutdown. Not only big tire companies were shutting down plants. Teledyne Monarch Rubber Co. in Hartville, Ohio, just a half-hour from Akron, put four hundred URW Local 99 members on the unemployment line when it sold its industrial tire plant and closed its automotive parts operation. Membership figures during Coss's first term showed the effect of these and other plant closings and cutbacks. For fiscal 1990—the year before Coss took office—the URW had 104,721 average-monthly-dues-paying members. That number decreased to 100,629 in fiscal 1991, 92,517 in fiscal 1992, and 91,304 in fiscal 1993 (table 9.1). During the three-year period the URW had a net loss of thirty-two locals, with the charters of thirty-nine locals revoked or declared defunct; just seven locals were chartered or reinstated.

Those job losses, combined with a couple of other unexpectedly hefty

Table 9.1 Average URW Membership, 1984–93

1984: 116,907	**1989:** 104,276
1985: 121,599	**1990:** 104,721
1986: 115,440	**1991:** 100,629
1987: 108,957	**1992:** 92,517
1988: 104,188	**1993:** 91,304

Source: Report of the international officers to the URW 35th Convention, 1993, Las Vegas.

Table 9.2 Finances in Coss Years

GENERAL OPERATING ACCOUNT	STRIKE BENEFIT FUND
Fiscal year ended March 31, 1991 Income: $12,852,975 Expenses: $13,412,246 Loss: $559,271	**Fiscal year ended March 31, 1991** Income: $1,918,392 Expenses: $389,003 Gain: $1,529,389
Fiscal year ended March 31, 1992 Income: $12,114,977 Expenses: $12,838,808 Loss: $723,831	**Fiscal year ended March 31, 1992** Income: $1,921,134 Expenses: $1,540,436 Gain: $380,698
Fiscal year ended March 31, 1993 Income: $12,388,690 Expenses: $13,539,214 Loss: $1,150,524	**Fiscal year ended March 31, 1993** Income: $1,738,098 Expenses: $780,255 Gain: $957,843

NUMBERS OF LOCAL UNIONS

From April 1990 to March 1993 (the end of the union s fiscal year), the URW showed a net loss of 32 local unions, dropping from 406 to 374 locals. During that time, 39 locals became defunct or had their charters revoked, while just 7 locals were chartered or reinstated.

Source: Report of the international officers to the URW 35th Convention, 1993, Las Vegas.

financial outlays, caused URW finances to weaken, with the union showing a $2 million shortfall from 1991 to 1993 (table 9.2). By that time the URW was down to about ninety thousand members, fifty thousand fewer than in 1981. In a spring 1993 effort to ease the URW's financial situation, the union offered retirement incentives to a number of staff members in an effort to cut costs. Eleven employees—including former President Stone, Vice President Johnston, and Industrial Hygienist Louis Beliczky— accepted the early-out package, which included a $25,000 lump-sum payment. The union estimated it could save close to $1 million a year with the incentives.

Prior to the 1993 convention, the URW revealed it was discussing a possible merger with the Oil, Chemical, and Atomic Workers (OCAW) union in a move that reflected the declining membership and power of both. While the membership rolls of the Rubber Workers had dropped by roughly half in the twenty-year period leading up 1993, Denver-based

OCAW's membership had fallen by more than 50 percent, from 185,000 in 1978 to about 90,000 in 1993. Although there was some talk that two unions with falling fortunes could join together to form a slightly larger union of falling fortunes, both sides seemed optimistic the merger could work. Coss and OCAW President Robert E. Wages met each other in 1982 when they served on their respective union's merger committees during an earlier attempt to join the two unions. "Bob and I both know what it takes to effect a merger. We're not running into the same pitfalls we did before," Coss said. "Things are serious. There's no reason it can't happen."

But in the end the merger did not work out, mostly because of the usual hangup: officer structure. Wages was younger than Coss—forty-three years old vs. Coss's fifty-seven at the time—and came across as a more traditional "fire up the troops" labor orator than the URW president. During the URW's 1993 convention, where Wages was a guest speaker, the delegates and URW officers held a rally at a Las Vegas hotel where union workers had been staging a long-term strike. Wages looked right at home with a rousing speech that reached its crescendo with chants of "Vegas is a union town!" Coss, on the other hand, seemed uncomfortable trying to get a rise out of the same gathering, and was not nearly as successful. The OCAW leader was even a smash during his URW convention speech, in which he likened the North America Free Trade Agreement to a hog. "I don't care if you dress it up and put on lipstick, you can't hide the ugly," Wages said.

Coss, Stanley, and Ellison all ran unopposed for re-election in 1993, but one of the biggest receptions of the convention went to former President Stone, who had retired earlier in 1993. "Everyone was so friendly I thought I might run for something," Stone quipped to a standing ovation. While Stone had fallen prey to the URW propensity to treat its leaders poorly, he found that union members also tended to like an officer even more a couple of years after they had thrown him out of office. After losing to Coss, Stone serviced locals in Wisconsin and northern Illinois and the URW's lone local in Minnesota. He said he looked forward to taking life a bit easier in retirement. He found that after getting over the sting of not having the top job, he felt a great deal of relief. He had even given up his habit of eating Rolaids. "I used to think I had to have the Rolaids because of smoking and being overweight. But it wasn't. It was the job."

During his convention speech, Coss presented the results of a survey of URW local presidents in which the officials ranked higher wages as only the sixth of seven choices in terms of workers' priorities. The top three issues were job security, health care, and pensions. In the past, only one issue was likely to be ranked number one: wages. "We're committed to being a different organization," Coss said. "We're a union in transition. We're not the same union we were three years ago." Some of the changes could be traced back to the success the URW had historically as a bargaining power. There were times, he said, when people in the working class passed that status—as well as the union tradition—along to their children and grandchildren. But because the union had been successful, people could afford to send their kids to college, and the children did not have to work in a factory unless they chose to. "That's not bad, we just have to deal with it," he said, adding that to do that meant sticking to the union's most basic tenet: solidarity. "What we have accomplished we have accomplished together," he said. "That has been and always will be one of our strengths. We must be reminded that the URW is not a thing or a place or one person. It's all of us collectively."

Coss also touted the growing popularity of programs of cooperation between rubber industry employers and URW members. "In this administration, we have operated on the precept that when an employer, by action as well as word, treats our members with respect, deals with them honestly, permits them to feel good about themselves and their place of employment, and trusts them, then the employer is entitled to the same kind of respectful and cooperative treatment," Coss wrote in his report to the 1993 convention. "We have found that many companies are quite receptive to this new way of doing things and I feel that great strides have been made in the development of better labor-management relationships in the rubber and plastics industry."

Unfortunately for Coss and the URW, not all tire and rubber companies were quite as enlightened.

COMPANIES PLAY HARDBALL

During 1993 the URW had battles of varying degrees with Bridgestone/Firestone, General Tire, and Michelin's Uniroyal Goodrich unit. But it was not just big tire manufacturers giving the union fits. In February Acme Boot laid off more than two hundred workers as it prepared to close its Clarksville, Tennessee, production facility by mid-year. URW Local 330, representing the plant workers, said the company was moving Clarksville's production to a new facility in Toa-Alta, Puerto Rico, to obtain a tax break for offshore production under Section 936 of the Internal Revenue Service. The provision stated that if a company created a manufacturing subzone in a U.S. possession and shipped the products back to the mainland, it owed no federal taxes on the profits from those products. The Midwest Center for Labor Research estimated Acme Boot would save as much as $26,725 per worker per year in taxes. The firm said it was trying to become more of a marketing company and less of a manufacturing firm by dividing the Clarksville unit's production among the Toa-Alta plant, another Acme Boot facility in El Paso, Texas, and subcontractors in Tennessee and Virginia. The URW countered by calling for an AFL-CIO boycott of Acme Boot products.

Local 330 President Mitchell Tucker said it would have been simple for union workers to save their jobs—all they had to do was cut their wage and benefit package by more than half. When Acme Boot in May 1992 first said it was considering closing the facility to focus on marketing, company officials told Local 330 the decision was not tied to wages and benefits. But when word came that the work was moving to Puerto Rico, Tucker asked for a chance to negotiate. Acme Boot said the local had to move quickly as officials were going to Puerto Rico within two weeks to cement plans for the new facility. After several meetings, the union said it was willing to take more concessions, something the Clarksville workers were used to. "We put together a package to cut $2 an hour off wages and benefits," Tucker said. Before the offer, Local 330 members made $7.95 an hour in wages, with benefits pushing the total to about $13. But Acme Boot officials said they needed more and told the union it planned to pay the Puerto Rican workers $4.40 an hour in wages and a total package of $5.90 an hour, less than half of what the Clarksville workers made. "We knew then it was a losing battle," Tucker said. "We told them they'd have to do what they have to do, because we can't compete with that."

The average worker at the plant was forty-eight years old when the plant shut down, with about 360 of the employees forty or older with an average of twenty-two years of service. Just 25 percent were eligible to draw a pension. After the decision to close the plant came down—it shut down for good in May 1993—the workers went to the media with their story. First it was local television and newspapers, and then national exposure followed, with the workers profiled in a segment looking at IRS Section 936 on ABC's *Prime Time Live* program. Subsequently, Acme Boot withdrew its application for the Section 936 exemption, though it stuck to its decision to relocate manufacturing to Puerto Rico. "Together we'll make an example of Acme Boot," Tucker told the 1993 URW convention. "It's too late to save our jobs, but if we save even one other person's job, it will be worth it."

The 1993 battles with tire makers all centered on company requests for mid-contract changes to bring down costs. In each case, the firm backed its demands with threats of plant closings or extensive layoffs. URW Local 884 at Bridgestone/Firestone's tube plant in Russellville, Arkansas, was the first to feel the squeeze. Company officials approached the local in late 1992 with an idea to invest $14.5 million in the facility to make it a world-class tube factory. In return, they asked for a five-year no-strike clause, seven-day operations with twelve-hour shifts, and the ability to hire temporary workers at lower pay with no benefits for a certain period of time. When workers first balked at the change, Bridgestone/Firestone said the factory might close, and Local 884 members then relented and accepted the changes.

General Tire also asked for contract revisions at its Mayfield, Kentucky, tire facility to try to bring costs in line. When workers turned back the request in December, the company promised to lay off union members and move the unit's passenger tire production elsewhere. While the tack seemed harsh, General Tire's Polovick said the company laid out all the facility's problems—including a deficit of $4 to $5 a tire on some lines—in an open, honest manner. "We worked with them and shared financial data about the plant that was so proprietary a lot of managers haven't seen the information," Polovick said. He also insisted that the possibility of layoffs was conveyed all along, not used as a bargaining ploy. "We said it not because it was the fashionable thing to do, but because Mayfield had a cost disadvantage."

By far the toughest—and most significant—battle of 1993 and early 1994 was with Michelin over whipsawing-style changes the French-owned firm demanded at its three Uniroyal Goodrich unionized U.S. tire plants the year prior to the regularly scheduled master contract talks. Members of URW Local 753 in Opelika, Alabama, were the first to accept contract concessions. Uniroyal Goodrich threatened to close the plant before the union members, in June 1993, approved changes that caved in to such company demands as rotating shifts, new work standards, new job allocations, and alterations in the unit's maintenance organization. Local 753 members originally overwhelmingly rejected Michelin's offer to "salvage the plant," but the company was relentless, said URW Vice President Stanley, who served as the Uniroyal Goodrich coordinator for the union. "They said we still have to make these changes," Stanley said. "This is Michelin's philosophy and this is what we want and this is what we've got to do." The company eventually told the union that if there were no vote, they would close the plant, even issuing a plant-closure notice. "At that time everybody realized the company meant business," he said. "This is for real. This is not just a threat or bluff." Membership voted again and Michelin had the first of its concession agreements in hand.

Next up was Tuscaloosa, Alabama, where Local 351 in August adopted similar "concession-making amendments" when the company threatened at least five hundred to six hundred permanent layoffs. The URW's hierarchy tried to reject the contract concessions, because under the union's constitution, changes that alter master contract language must be approved by the URW International Executive Board and the Policy Committee of representatives from the three Uniroyal Goodrich plants. The intent of the URW rules is to try to maintain solidarity within the ranks by not letting the companies easily go from plant to plant looking for a better deal on concessions. The Executive Board rejected the proposed Opelika agreement while the Policy Committee withheld approval on the Tuscaloosa concessions. Michelin spared no expense in trying to win over community leaders and others who might influence the workers in those towns. They reportedly brought Opelika community leaders to Michelin's North American headquarters in Greenville, South Carolina, and also drove children around town with signs saying, "Save my daddy's job."

As coordinator, Stanley tried to instruct the Tuscaloosa local that the URW International believed the vote was illegal, would not be honored, and should not take place. Under the master contract process and the URW's own sense of solidarity, one local should never take it upon itself to go its own road; the entire Uniroyal Policy Committee should be discussing the situation. That sense of logic, though, fell flat when matched with the prospect of permanently losing six hundred of eighteen hundred jobs at the plant. "It was a terrible situation," Stanley said. "They voted for it overwhelmingly." And just in case the workforce ignored the threats, Stanley said the word was the company had written up six hundred pink slips at Tuscaloosa and supervisors were walking around with the slips in their pockets, saying: "When you go to the union meeting Sunday, come Monday you're going to get a pink slip."

When the URW International did attempt to veto the concessionary agreements, Michelin simply ignored the URW hierarchy, saying that it had legal and binding agreements that were overwhelmingly ratified by employees at both Opelika and Tuscaloosa. "We are proceeding with the implementation of these agreed-upon changes," a Michelin spokesman said. "We're bound by a collective bargaining agreement at both locations and not by the union's constitution and/or internal union procedures." Faced with Michelin's refusal to respect its authority, the URW International reviewed its options and decided it had none. The company, while not following normal channels, technically had gotten a majority of the locals representing a majority of the members to agree to the changes, as would have been required in normal procedures. "At that time, the feeling was we really can't turn it around," Stanley said. "The membership's not going to reverse themselves." And if the URW took the matter to court the judge probably would decline to issue a reversal on a technical procedure when the will of the people had been exercised through votes at both locals. At best the judge likely would have told the URW to file a grievance and take the matter to arbitration, or file a charge with the National Labor Relations Board.

Michelin at the time was regarded as by far the most anti-union company in the tire industry by both union officials and market observers. It operated five United States and three Canadian Michelin plants without a union, having successfully resisted all organizing campaigns. Since buying Uniroyal Goodrich in 1990, the French firm had closed one U.S. unionized factory and consolidated two Ontario union facilities into one. Michelin made no bones about its goal to operate its unionized Uniroyal Goodrich facilities just as it does its non-union plants. "We are calling into question everything the union has built, brick by brick, over the past thirty years— seniority, the written contract, the grievance procedure," Michelin labor attorney Steven Nail was quoted as saying in a *Wall Street Journal* article.

Kenneth Walters, vice president of the Tuscaloosa local at the time, felt that the local could have gotten a better deal had they gotten stronger leadership from Coss and Robert Dillard, Local 351 president before Walters defeated him in the next election. Walters is one of those union leaders who knows that the membership takes its lead from the local president. Walters joined his first union, the United Food and Commercial Workers union, when he was fifteen years old and worked at the local Brunos Food Store. When the union field representative came to sign him up for the union, the store owner said, "You don't need to join." Walters replied, "'You may fire me next month.' I was lucky and fortunate to be in labor since I was fifteen years old." When he hired on at the Tuscaloosa plant, then owned by B. F. Goodrich, Walters was twenty-two and upset that it took the union steward three weeks before signing him up. "I said, 'I've been looking for you for three weeks. Where have you been? I'm going to be your boss, man.' And I was his boss later on as division chairman," said Walters.

When Dillard failed to provide the leadership Walters expected, he got upset. "He [Dillard] was always scared the company was going to move the plant," Walters said. "Every morning he'd wake up and think they were going to move this place. You can't wake up every morning scared to death. You can't do your job." Walters was not naïve enough to think the local could have stopped Michelin from implementing rotating shifts, but he thought they could have gotten a better deal on items such as dealing with outside contractors doing maintenance work. Had Dillard taken a more forceful lead and told the local that if they rejected the agreement they could water down some of the distasteful items, the outcome could have been different. "We could have modified a good bit of that language, but when you don't have the president's support, you aren't going to do that," Walters said. "Whether the guy's a strong president or a weak president, whatever that guy says multiplies by about twenty times with those people."

While the locals in Opelika and Tuscaloosa put up little or no fight, opting to guarantee their jobs rather than jeopardize their livelihood, Local 715 in Fort Wayne, Indiana, put up quite a battle. The company had asked Fort Wayne union members on several occasions during 1993 for the changes, but the local maintained it would not renegotiate prior to the 1994 master contract talks. The local took its case public, buying full-page ads in two area newspapers detailing the union's position. "In my local union there will be no vote," maintained Local 715 President Ray Wiseman. He said that during master contract negotiations in 1991 the company agreed to language affirming that the pact was for three years and that the firm would not ask for givebacks during that time. The URW sought the clause because not long after Michelin bought Uniroyal Goodrich the company asked for mid-contract changes allowing the two Kitchener factories to consolidate into one. "Michelin owned us in 1991," Wiseman said. "They knew what was in the master contract. It's in poor taste and illogical for the company to sit and bargain, and then come back a year later and threaten to close a plant." Local 715 officials even accused Michelin of artificially driving up costs at its Uniroyal Goodrich plants to make them look like money losers so it would have a better case in asking for changes. Coss said these actions were typical of a company planning major changes: First they make the plant look bad (Michelin claimed the factory lost $30 million in 1993), then put in their changes so they look like geniuses in turning it around.

Despite Wiseman's protestations that there would be no vote or concessions in his local, the situation for Local 715 would get far more complicated. Uniroyal Goodrich first issued a "distress notice" to the Fort Wayne tire plant, declaring it would close the facility if the local balked at agreeing to contract changes. The company told the union it "determined that with the current restrictive work rules, the operation of the plant, even at a reduced capacity, is not a viable alternative." That was followed by the official plant closure notice on November 9, meaning that the tire maker could close the factory in six months if Local 715 did not succumb to its wishes. In December the local voted 800 to 731 against putting the Michelin subsidiary's latest offer to members for a vote. U.S. District Court Judge William Lee had ordered the vote, as he wanted a sense of the overall membership's thoughts on the firm's package. Local 715 declared negotiations at an impasse after thirty-six hours of nonstop bargaining ended December 17.

Then things got really interesting. Wiseman tried to work with two local consultants to find potential buyers and develop a plan to purchase the plant from Michelin, a proposal that never went anywhere. Coss then utilized powers granted to him under the URW's constitution to call a February 12, 1994, special session of Local 715. Coss recalled a discussion he had with Wiseman when the URW president went to Fort Wayne for the first rally to protest Michelin's actions. "I said, 'Ray, for now we're going to take tough positions. We are negotiating for the minds of the people, but at some point the people are going to have to make that decision because *they* are the union. I'm not the union and you're not the union,'" Coss said. Wiseman replied that the people were "too intimidated and too scared to make that decision." Prior to Coss's calling the special meeting, a busload of Local 715 members traveled to Akron and were ready to picket the URW International headquarters building because the URW president had not stepped in to take charge of the situation. "I told them to come on in, so they did and we talked," Coss said. "I told them what my position was, that they were the union, and that when the time came we would handle it appropriately. And they thanked us and left. They didn't picket us."

Stanley said the company went as far as cutting a couple of machines loose, as if getting ready to move the equipment to another location. "Now they didn't ship them out, but that just scared everybody," he said. "I got calls in my office in Akron saying, 'Mike, they're getting ready to take out some equipment. They're unbolting it, and we want to vote.' There was call after call after call that started coming into the Akron office." While there was some question at headquarters as to whether this would be a legal vote, it was determined that the people in the plant should have a say, as had workers in Opelika and Tuscaloosa.

Walters, then the vice president from the Tuscaloosa local, agreed with Coss's decision to call for a vote. "I'm a very strong-minded person, but I also believe that at some point the membership has to make a decision," Walters said. "When it gets to the point where you get to a situation like that and you deprive this membership where they can't vote on something of that magnitude, shame on the leadership. I think we need to focus on telling the people what's wrong with the thing instead of arguing with the company on whether we're going to let them vote, because sooner or later, you're going to vote."

The situation would have been different if the membership had given the local committee prior permission to call a strike, but that was the main reason Michelin sought the changes beginning in 1993 rather than waiting until master contract talks in 1994, according to Walters. Had the demands come during normal negotiations, the membership would have given the normal strike authorization and the company might not have been so zealous in its demands. "There's no question that's why they did it in a non-contract year, because they know there's no strike authorization," Walters said. When the company used the fear tactic of threatening closings and layoffs, there was no way a local could negotiate, Walters said.

"But if you're in negotiations where they have a hammer and we have a hammer [a strike], then you're fixing to lose tires down there. That's how Michelin came and got us."

By the time of the special meeting, Coss said he was receiving threats. He took about twenty people with him from Akron; there were at least five federal marshals present and the federal judge had appointed an election master. "I had determined that the people were going to vote," Coss said. "After we made the presentation I told them we weren't recommending it. We told them if they turned it down, the company was committed to shutting the plant down. Everything was in place with the state. The plant was going to go down. If they turned it down we would negotiate the best severance agreement that we could for them."

"We were prepared to go in there and get our heads blown off," said Coss assistant Borelli. "That's how serious it looked. We were threatened that people were going to be there with their guns and everything else." Wiseman and Borelli were cordial with each other, having gotten along during their days on the Uniroyal Policy Committee. Borelli told him, "I'm sorry this has to come about," and Wiseman replied, "I've got to do what I've got to do." Not everyone on Wiseman's side was quite as understanding of Borelli's position. "One guy said, 'I feel sorry for you. You've got to work for that son of a bitch [Coss].' I said, 'I'm pretty damn proud to work for that son of a bitch.'" When it came time to explain the constitutionality of the vote, Borelli said Coss stressed that the URW leadership was not trying to jam the deal down the membership's throat. They just wanted to make sure the local had an election and that the majority ruled democratically, not just the twelve people on the union's executive board.

In the end, Local 715 voted 1,007 to 411 in favor of the new contract, prompting Uniroyal Goodrich to immediately withdraw its plant closure notice. Afterward, Coss said two of the people who had given him the hardest time during the meeting called him privately to thank him for saving their jobs. Another who had given him an insulting award—a trophy showing the back end of a horse—near the conclusion of the special meeting came up to him at a Steelworkers convention later and hugged him and apologized for having presented the trophy.

Stanley said the wide margin made it clear that the right decision had been made. "That told me that they wanted to keep their jobs and they were willing to live with the changes that Michelin had proposed in order to keep their jobs and take care of their families," he said. "It was certainly better to do it that way than to see 1,300 to 1,500 families out there without any income coming in. It was one of those tough decisions you have to make as a leader and that was what we were elected to do." Many phone calls and letters confirmed that feeling, with messages of gratitude for making sure workers would still be able to send their kids to college and make it to a proper retirement. "That made it worth taking the heat as International officers," Stanley said.

While the URW took its lumps in the battle with Michelin, it turned out to be merely preliminary to what the union would face just months later: the War of '94.

THE WAR OF '94
THE UNWINNABLE BATTLE

For Kenneth Coss, the defining battle of his tenure as URW leader was the War of '94, the battle that directly led to the union's merger with the United Steelworkers of America. While the strike involved at one time more than eight thousand strikers against four companies, the main struggle clearly was the work stoppage by forty-two hundred URW members at five Bridgestone/Firestone locations. For the union, it was undeniably an encounter with an unmovable force. The company was looking for what it called "turnaround" negotiations to make up ground it claimed it lost to other tire and rubber product makers during negotiations throughout the prior decade. Bridgestone/Firestone was losing truckloads of cash for its Japanese owner, and its new chief labor negotiator made a proposal containing massive changes. He and his team hoped that a traditional, fighting union like the Rubber Workers would be able to understand the need for the substantial modifications and would approach negotiations in a nontraditional manner. The union, though, saw it as a blatant attempt to take away everything it had worked and struck for over the years. The URW members truly felt backed into a corner by a company that either wanted them to strike or expected them to accept an agreement that was clearly concessionary.

On its own merits, the War of '94 had all the makings of a legendary battle, but what truly made it a riveting story was how quickly the URW and Bridgestone/Firestone had gotten to the point of being mortal enemies. Just three years earlier the union and company were the toast of the labor/management world, even snagging an award from the Federal Mediation and Conciliation Services (FMCS) for their cooperative dealings. To get a true picture of how relations between the Rubber Workers and Bridgestone/Firestone apparently deteriorated so quickly, however, requires a trip back in time to 1983 to LaVergne, Tennessee. Or, as retired

Bridgestone/Firestone negotiator Peter Schofield called it, the Land of Milk and Honey.

BRIDGESTONE FORGES GOOD LABOR RELATIONS

Firestone's radial truck tire plant in LaVergne was just what Japan's Bridgestone was looking for. Firestone had built the plant just outside Nashville in 1973. In an effort to catch up with the edge that foreign tire makers had in radial technology, Firestone built the LaVergne facility in 1973 to manufacture radial truck tires. Schofield said that senior management, in a bit of backward logic, had decided the best way to learn to produce radial tires was to build this state-of-the-art plant; somehow the knowledge would magically follow. Unfortunately the world—and the tire industry—does not work that way. The facility was plagued with quality and labor problems. The URW began trying to organize LaVergne not long after it opened, and the effort continued through most of the decade. After the union was successful there was a big strike, and following the walkout Firestone did not restart much production at the factory. "I remember walking through that plant in 1980 and so much of it was just dark," Schofield said. By this time John J. Nevin was the top executive at Firestone, and he was charged with improving shareholder value at the faltering company and eventually finding a buyer. Nevin shuttered fourteen of the firm's nineteen North American tire plants and decided the company could not spend money trying to make radial truck tires.

That was where Bridgestone stepped in. The Japanese firm, dominant in its home Asian market, had long been searching for a manufacturing presence in the United States. Bridgestone purchased the LaVergne plant in 1983 and spent nearly $70 million on improvements over the next four years. More importantly, Bridgestone worked hard at nurturing a close working relationship with URW Local 1055, which had had terrible dealings with Firestone. When Bridgestone bought LaVergne, nearly 450 of the local's members were on layoff. But by July 1986, all laid-off workers had returned to work. Coss said in 1991 that the lesson learned at LaVergne could be applied to other plants. "That one went from a terrible, miserable relationship where everyone thought it was hopeless to a nationally competitive plant," Coss said. "We were dealing with a company that wanted to have a good relationship between the company and the workers. It was difficult to get that through to the people working there. We were successful in a completely different type of organizing campaign, more or less showing everyone that working together is to the benefit of everyone."

Once Bridgestone bought LaVergne, the curtain was dropped so the outside world could not look in and see much, Schofield said. "By the time Bridgestone bought the rest of Firestone six years later, the vision that both we and the union had was that Bridgestone had taken this place that was a black hole and turned it into a land of milk and honey—that it was just a wonderful place to work, highly productive and efficient."

From this relationship evolved the most unlikely of occurrences. Bridgestone allowed the URW to organize its new truck tire plant in Warren County, Tennessee—located just about an hour or so from LaVergne—without a traditional organizational campaign. The deal initially was forged in the late 1980s between Mike Stone and Nori Takeuchi, though it was not until 1991, when Coss was in office, that the URW officially chartered the local. The URW had not organized a tire factory since 1981, when Bommarito was in office and the union finally won its election at Firestone's Oklahoma City facility after numerous attempts. So a call from Takeuchi asking for a secret session in Cleveland definitely surprised Stone. The Bridgestone official asked that Stone come alone. Stone had no idea what Takeuchi had in mind, but he trusted the executive because the union had good relations with the company. When he arrived at the firm's attorney's office, Stone met with Takeuchi, another Bridgestone official, and an attorney.

"They said they'd heard me make speeches where instead of fighting each other all the time, if we're going to try to get along to get a contract, companies shouldn't battle unions when we're organizing either," said Stone, who had made that point numerous times in speeches and interviews. The URW president hated it when rubber companies acted nice at the negotiating table but when the union tried to organize one of the same firm's non-union facilities, the company put on a different face and spouted about the evils of unionization. When the Bridgestone crew asked if he truly meant those statements and Stone replied affirmatively, Takeuchi laid out the firm's plan. "They told me they were planning on building a new tire plant," Stone said. "They said they would be interested in working out an agreement ahead of time in exchange for recognition as far as the law allowed. In other words, when we got a majority of cards signed, they would just recognize us. No elections, no battling, no nothing."

Stone did not quite know how to respond. No one ever had posed that question to the union leader. "But I said, 'Sure, certainly we're interested in it,'" Stone said, "so we worked out the contract. It wasn't the best contract in the world, but it's a damn sight better than if we'd had to go out there and win an election." Bridgestone even invited Stone to Warren County when the firm started training its first fifty prospects. Then Bridgestone executive Jim McCann gave what Stone called one of the best organizing speeches he had ever heard. "He just said that the Rubber Workers are good folks," Stone said. "He said unions are not all bad, and that they had an agreement that they were going to work with us and we with them and that's what they intended to do."

The deal happened because Bridgestone at the time believed it had a wonderful thing going with the union at LaVergne, according to Schofield. "They thought if they were going to build another plant in Tennessee a few miles away, some people might think it would be hard to imagine Bridgestone could go through a traditional union-avoidance campaign at the new plant and still have this wonderful relationship going on at LaVergne," Schofield said.

Given this cozy relationship between Bridgestone and the URW, the Japanese company's agreement to buy Firestone in the midst of 1988 master contract negotiations between the union and the U.S. tire maker certainly gave Firestone labor relations people pause to think. Perhaps the union and Firestone could seize on this opportunity to forge a whole new way of life. Schofield, for one, had been with Firestone since 1962 and had been through all the strikes of the Bommarito years as well as the boom and bust days of Firestone. "The day I walked in the front door as a trainee in 1962, the first thing I heard was, 'Well, we're going to get rid of this goddamn master contract,'" he said. The company found that the master contract, first signed by Firestone in 1948 to cover twenty-three locations, had become unwieldy and provided leverage to the union. After World War II, Firestone had agreed to a lot of things because it "was the thing to do," Schofield said, and because the company really had not had enough experience with labor relations up to that point. Through the late 1960s, though, Firestone generally was looked upon as one of the fifty best-run companies in the country, running head-to-head with Goodyear for the ranking of top tire company in the United States. But then came radialization, the firm's debacle with the recall of millions of Firestone 500 radial tires—a disaster that nearly ruined the company—and all the plant closings.

By the 1988 master contract talks, before any of the negotiators knew anything of a Bridgestone scenario, Firestone was prepared to take a strike if necessary. Firestone knew it needed to make dramatic changes if it planned to continue in business, and told the URW that if the union agreed to help, the company would offer workers the "fanciest, jazzed up, razzle-dazzle, job-security scheme" that existed in the United States, Schofield said. "In its original conception there were no exceptions whatsoever. It didn't even have a major catastrophe exception," he said. When Bridgestone appeared on the scene to purchase Firestone, however, every employee in the company thought they had plenty of job security. "Bridgestone didn't buy this company and didn't pay everything they paid for it with the intention of putting everybody out of jobs," Schofield said. "So the company's side of the bargaining issue for 1988 went quickly down the drain."

Still, Firestone and URW officials both felt the need to show Bridgestone something. Company executives knew that Bridgestone eventually would have its people run the firm, and anything they could do to impress the new owners might help their careers. And the union was proud of what had been accomplished in LaVergne; if that could be replicated at other Firestone locations, the URW would be in good shape. Schofield said that he and Joe Zagnoli—then the URW Firestone coordinator— brainstormed to come up with ideas to help Firestone and the URW move forward side by side. Zagnoli suggested bringing in the FMCS during 1988 negotiations to help work through the tremendous number of grievances that had accumulated at the Oklahoma City plant. Schofield thought it was a good idea but did not address the systemic problem faced by the company and union. "Maybe what we ought to do is use the Oklahoma City grievance log as a trigger of some sort of starting point to try to get some help in trying to look at the labor/management relationship in general," Schofield offered.

They agreed to contact the FMCS, which had developed a program in the 1970s called Relationships by Objective. That evolved into the URW's and Bridgestone/Firestone's Partnership for Involvement, begun in early 1989. The two sides, with the help of the FMCS, brought together a roster of some of the best brains in the business: for example, a professor from the Harvard program on negotiations, an attorney who had previously worked with FMCS, and a former U.S. deputy secretary of labor. "We put together a team of all those people plus the federal mediation folks to try to start over again with the labor/management relationship at Bridgestone/Firestone," Schofield said. "I never worked on anything so hard in my life, and I don't think Joe [Zagnoli] did either. Both sides took it seriously."

The program took place at four different levels of the company and union simultaneously. There were senior executives meeting with top-echelon URW officers, low-level workers and plant supervisors tackling problems together, and interaction on at least two other levels. "There were tons of hours and tons of dollars spent on this whole thing. We worked and worked. We flew all over the country with the federal mediation people," Schofield said. "I think that we had made a lot of progress. Now could you see it in the cash register? No." Before efforts like this show up in terms of improved productivity for the company or heightened job security for the union, both sides need much patience. "It takes a lot of work and a lot of time," Schofield said. "You're trying to change people's minds."

Then the problems began, two major ones in particular. First, Bridgestone finally began to put its senior executives into some important management slots, especially some manufacturing slots in the divisions where it was critical to continuing the partnership initiative. These spots were where people had learned all the lessons from the FMCS and outside experts, and had spent time riding the circuit to help build grassroots support from both local management and the local unions. Second, Coss defeated Stone as URW president. "I think Kenny learned a lot of what we had done, and I think he tried to use a lot of what we had done in some other situations," Schofield said. "But the fact of the matter from my perspective is that Kenny wasn't going to touch anything that Stone and his boys had had anything to do with, and he just was not interested in pursuing this initiative anymore. It was very difficult for me to arrange meetings between Kenny and his guys and senior executives at Bridgestone. In my opinion, there were some people in the union who would have been very supportive of continuing the initiative, but it wasn't top-driven anymore and it wasn't being top-driven by the company anymore."

Even before 1991 negotiations began, the FMCS pressured Schofield and the URW, trying to ensure that the initiative did not lose steam. It may have been too late by that point. "There was no one left in the union at any important level that knew anything about what we had been trying to do, and I was losing people on the company side who had the passion for trying to make this happen," Schofield said. "The people in government were looking at both sides, saying, 'What the hell is going on here?' They could see that the merry-go-round was slowing down."

Despite these obstacles, the Partnership for Involvement process still packed enough wallop to get the two sides through 1991 master contract negotiations—and to receive an award from the FMCS. Bridgestone/Firestone requested to be the target company so it could go in and show that it could use its newly learned principles of negotiations and reach a settlement without resorting to traditional bargaining. By then Schofield's boss was Sam Torrence, who was from Bridgestone and had lots of compliments for the program. Torrence and Coss had a very close working relationship. "It was Kenny's first negotiations and it was Sam's time to shine in the industry as the vice president of human resources," Schofield said. "And they settled." The agreement was a bit on the expensive side, he said, but the feeling was if the two sides could get the Partnership for Involvement initiatives to reach full strength, the improved productivity would easily offset the increased labor costs.

PROBLEMS START WITH LAVERGNE

Contract negotiations at LaVergne between Local 1055 and Bridgestone/Firestone were slated for 1992, a year after the master contract negotiations. By then, some of the truth about the LaVergne operation started to seep out, according to Schofield. As soon as Nevin sold LaVergne to Bridgestone and word circulated about the great things happening there, everybody from the company and the union wanted to visit LaVergne. "It was like, 'We've got to find a way to get to the Land of Milk and Honey,'" he said. As with many things, a tale spread by word of mouth can take on a life of its own. But scrutinize the fable closely—kick the tires, so to speak—and the story reads like bad fiction. Schofield recalled sending a team in from one of the plants, followed soon after by industrial engineering people. The answer invariably came back the same: "There's not a lot happening in LaVergne."

"LaVergne, as it turned out, was the plant that didn't work," Schofield said. "They may have had great labor/management relations as far as the union was concerned." But Schofield said the union leadership at Local 1055 quickly learned that whenever there was a problem all they had to do was keep taking the issue up the ladder, and eventually they would come to a Bridgestone official who sided with them. Most of the added production was apparently due mainly to all of the money Bridgestone had plowed into the factory, even adding passenger and light truck capability to the truck tire capacity. "I think what happened in the case of LaVergne is that for the money they put into it, they should have gotten far higher levels of productivity out of the plant than they were getting," Schofield said. Bridgestone officials in Tokyo finally realized LaVergne was the antithesis of the Land of Milk and Honey.

It was at this point, in 1992, with Bridgestone/Firestone still losing enormous amounts of money (as much as a million dollars a day or more), that company officials thought it was unfair to ask workers at all the other plants to make radical changes through the Partnership for Involvement without addressing concerns at LaVergne. When Local 1055 staged a seventeen-day strike at the LaVergne plant on May 1, 1992, the local's timing could not have been worse. "Right after the strike started, the company withdrew its last best-and-final offer and then put a new package on the table that was calculated even more than before to bring LaVergne more into the wind, so to speak," Schofield said. When the local returned after barely two weeks off the job, Local 1055 members did so on the company's terms, which included twelve-hour shifts, continuous operations, and a managed health care plan.

Other URW officials remain confounded by the LaVergne strike. Roger Gates, elected president of Local 713 at the firm's Decatur, Illinois, plant in 1992, said it was his understanding the strike was political. "The local president in LaVergne at that time thought he could outdo the master plants by a little bit," Gates said. "So they went on strike, and there weren't any concessionary issues from the company's side at that point in time. The company was offering them the same thing that the master plants got."

Years later Coss still was unsure why there was a strike at LaVergne, but maintained the company had baited the Local 1055 president into taking his workers off the job. "There was no doubt that [the company] wanted a strike," Coss said, adding that Torrence had given him a subtle warning on the phone not to let LaVergne hit the streets. "I told Sam I thought the two of us should go in. Sam said, 'I can't do that.' So he was telling me there was something afoot, because Sam had the authority to do about anything he wanted up to that point." Coss called Local 1055 President Dan Bailey and told him of the seriousness of the situation and not to jump the gun on a strike. Coss, who was leaving for Canada that evening, also asked the URW field representative on the scene to keep him informed of the status of the talks. Coss told the representative to call him before midnight and to persuade the local to stay on the job until Coss had a chance to talk to them. But talks apparently did not go well between Bailey and the plant manager, and Local 1055 left the job as soon as the contract expired at midnight. The URW president called the next day to see if he could help nip the situation in the bud and prevent it from evolving into a serious confrontation. "Then the company withdrew everything," Coss said. "That's all they wanted to do, was have it be a union strike rather than a lockout, and they succeeded. So the rest is history."

During the short-lived strike another event flattened the Partnership for Involvement (PFI) program for good. There was a big PFI meeting scheduled at a hotel near Bridgestone/Firestone headquarters. The FMCS people and all the outside experts were coming to try to help the two sides continue going forward, even though the partnership was in a limping mode at the time. When the group, including the URW representatives, arrived for the powwow, Local 1055 members were already there to picket the meeting. "Of course the rest of the union guys wouldn't cross the picket line to go into the meeting," Schofield said. "So we went back to our office and reported that we couldn't start our meeting."

By then, Bridgestone had brought in Yoichiro Kaizaki as Bridgestone/Firestone chairman, and he was disappointed at the news. Torrence phoned Coss, who had not come down for the PFI session. Torrence told the URW president the matter had reached a critical point and that Coss really should be there. Schofield said that Kaizaki started looking at the program, then said to Torrence: "Sam, my God, you've been working on this, having all our planes flying and you've been doing all this and you've been doing all that. We're hemorrhaging money. Nothing's changed. When's something going to change?" Kaizaki answered his own question: Things were going to change "now."

"And that was the end of it. We never had another [PFI] meeting," Schofield said. "It was the end of the whole enchilada." For all the work he had put into the partnership, the longtime Bridgestone/Firestone negotiator could not disagree that something had to be done. "I knew how much we needed to have a fix, and I knew how long we tried to have a fix, and I knew that we had tried every other tack in the book," he said. But he could not help going to bed at night thinking how much effort he and countless others had put into PFI and how close the two sides had come to accomplishing something truly special. "Unlike any other time in this industry since rubber tires were ever made, there was an initiative between a company and a union with the best outside help you could get in this country to try to take a situation that had been bad for both parties and turn it around and make something new out of it. It really could have been a landmark for others to follow," Schofield said. "I think we really could have done it. I sometimes wonder if I'm dreaming, if the political implications of both the company and the union really could have supported it long term."

KAIZAKI TAKES CHARGE

While this for all intents and purposes was the end of the Partnership for Involvement program, it was not the end of Bridgestone/Firestone's need to turn around its operation. And Kaizaki's plan for that was simple. "He could not believe that there was any other way," Schofield said. "If we can't do it together, we'll have to do it ourselves. He told us, 'You've certainly given this a good try. And the way that you have been trying to do it is exemplary from a Japanese standpoint.'"

From URW members' perspective, the change was drastic and immediate. On June 18, 1992, Local 1055 ratified Bridgestone/Firestone's last and final contract offer. But they constructed their ballot so members could accept the contract but still indicate their displeasure at having such things as twelve-hour shifts jammed down their throats. "Basically, the company sent a clear message that it was taking a union-busting approach," said Local 1055 President Bailey.

Just a week after the LaVergne ratification vote, Bridgestone/Firestone sent another message that angered URW members and gave a clear indication that the cordial relationship of the Partnership for Involvement had ended. On June 25 the firm issued a sudden notification that it had canceled trips to Nashville and Tokyo that were among the main incentives of the PFI suggestion program. Teams at the participating factories had come up with ideas to cut costs in various processes. Those with the best idea from each plant traveled to Nashville to compete, with the winning team traveling to Japan to give their presentations at Bridgestone headquarters. Since all the teams had made their presentations, the URW members did not think it was fair that the company already had the ideas and refused to follow through with the trips. Steven Gensler, at the time president of Local 713 in Decatur, had some prophetic comments on Bridgestone/Firestone's actions. "Big business is taking advantage and making labor knuckle under," he said. "I think a confrontation with some type of resolution will come down the road."

Torrence still was trying to put on a good face about the situation, telling the URW that Bridgestone/Firestone's commitment to the partnership had not changed despite growing evidence to the contrary. Torrence, however, left his vice presidential post later in 1992. At the time he declined to give specific reasons for his resignation, saying it was a personal decision. He said he and Kaizaki "had a discussion as it had to deal with the activities I was responsible for, and I decided to resign."

Years later, when Torrence had moved on to an executive position with Mack Trucks, he decided against discussing his situation with Bridgestone/Firestone. Others, however, had plenty to say. Coss said Torrence had told him a couple of weeks before that he was going to resign, but that it had to be kept very confidential. "He could not morally do what was going to be required of him," Coss said.

Mike Polovick was a friend of Torrence and said that Sam always had believed that companies and unions had to work together. He was a proponent of allowing the URW to organize Warren County and was closely involved in labor relations at LaVergne under Bridgestone. "Within Firestone, you always had the hawks and doves," Polovick said. "You had the guys who said, 'Screw the union,' and ones who said, 'You've got to work with them.' During the Torrence era and during the first round of negotiations and Warren County, the doves' stock was rising." But the LaVergne strike helped change all that. "I think at that point in time clearly the line was drawn and all the doves were shot and the hawks came back and said, 'See, you can never trust the union. You've got to be strong. You've got to fight them and that's the only way this whole thing is going to work,'" Polovick said. "Whether it was voluntary or involuntary—I think it was a combination of both—it was shortly after that Sam left and the plans were laid. Sam's style and approach were completely contrary to where the company wanted to go at that time."

FMCS mediator David Thorley was another fan of Torrence. Thorley had worked with Torrence in the Partnership for Involvement program, and it was the FMCS that had honored Bridgestone/Firestone and the URW for its work in PFI. But when things started to go badly, Torrence called Thorley and told him he was leaving the company. "He told me point blank why," Thorley said. "The company told him they didn't care anything about this employee relationship. The bottom line is they're losing money and they want to start turning things around. Sam said, 'I don't want to work under those conditions,' and left them." The mediator explained that Torrence's father was a United Auto Workers member and that Sam had gotten a college scholarship from the UAW, so he always understood unionism and the need for labor and management to work together. "But I've always said that you can do all the programs you want, but if that company's not making money, those programs aren't going to work," Thorley said.

Schofield said Torrence's departure likely was related to Torrence being the "fair-haired, round-eyed boy" of previous Japanese management. "The first Japanese management on deck with Bridgestone that realized it hadn't achieved what it thought it had achieved in LaVergne was Kaizaki," Schofield said. "And when he turned around to his man who was responsible for all that, he saw Sam standing there. After hearing so much about this Partnership for Involvement and how great it is and what great results it's going to produce, and then it doesn't, he turns around and sees his head man responsible for that. Whether it was [Torrence's] failure or it was my failure or somebody else's, who did he see standing there? Sam Torrence."

During this period, Kaizaki began a top-to-bottom examination of Bridgestone/Firestone, not just in labor relations, but every detail of the company. He broke the company into twenty-one business units, hand-picking whom he wanted to put in charge of each unit, making that person responsible and accountable. To replace Torrence in charge of labor relations, Kaizaki wanted Charles Ramsey, who had been president of Firestone Fibers & Textiles Co. Schofield described Ramsey as a homey, down-to-earth type of a guy. Ramsey's first job had been as a card-carrying United Rubber Workers member at the firm's tube plant in Russellville,

Arkansas. He earned a college degree, going to school at night, and worked his way up through the financial end of the business. Early in the 1980s, Ramsey was controller for North America but wanted to get into manufacturing and was named general manager of the Russellville operation. When Kaizaki split Bridgestone/Firestone into twenty-one units he made Ramsey president of the tube operation and then president of the textile company, based in Gastonia, North Carolina. "Kaizaki liked Chuck and wanted him to head up 1994 negotiations," Schofield said. "He had other men like Chuck running other parts of the company fixing things that needed to be fixed."

Although Torrence's departure upset Coss, the URW president at least initially displayed some optimism about the prospect of dealing with Ramsey. Coss said Ramsey had a history of being innovative, citing an agreement earlier in 1992 between Bridgestone/Firestone and the URW that led to the firm's building a new tire cord plant in Gastonia with URW members transferred to the new location. The URW president also was understandably worried that relations with Bridgestone/Firestone would continue to deteriorate, saying that it appeared the firm cared only about short-term profits and had no concern for long-term repercussions. Ramsey's reply to this fear likely offered Coss little comfort. "The ideal environment in which to handle these challenges is in a spirit of cooperation from both sides, but there is no value in simply having this state of cooperation if the company is not making progress," Ramsey said. "So sometimes action has to be taken which may not be popular but at least can be measured by performance and ensure the future for all of us."

RAMSEY PREPARES FOR 1994

Ramsey came in and began preparations for 1994 master contract negotiations in late 1992 in a way that Schofield had never experienced before. The goal was simple: the firm wanted a "turnaround negotiation," whereby the company decided it needed to take the old agreement apart and put it back together. It wanted to fix the things that it thought needed to be fixed "come hell or high water," Schofield said. Bridgestone/Firestone aimed to take the entire labor contract that had been in various stages of writing dating back to the individual plant contracts in the 1930s and the first master contract and recalibrate it to meet contemporary needs. "There were so many things about the agreement that nobody in their right minds would do anymore, but it was standard practice for us," Schofield said. Ramsey quickly set up a steering committee but purposely left Schofield off it even though he had been so closely involved in the company's labor relations for three decades. "[Ramsey] said to me, 'You know too much and I don't want you there. I want the plant managers and I want the presidents, and I want to find out what they think is right and wrong. And then you'll be my strong man who stands to my right-hand side.' And that's the way it worked," Schofield said. "It was an immaculate relationship because we had had a good relationship for years."

Schofield instead headed up a collective bargaining agreement (CBA) committee—made up of labor relations representatives from each plant—designed to put into contract language what Bridgestone/Firestone determined would be its final issues and proposals. The process started with both the steering and CBA committees establishing their list of issues, along with a third group that focused on pensions and insurance items. Schofield then attended a meeting of Ramsey's steering committee at which the plant managers and business unit presidents explained from their perspective what was needed to make the plants reasonably competitive. Schofield's committee homogenized the separate lists and got rid of duplication. His group then worked on costing out what the changes, if achieved, would mean in cost savings and improved productivity at each location. Some issues were dropped, modified, or combined with other issues.

It is a normal dance for labor and management to make numerous requests for changes when contact negotiations begin. Schofield even remembered items that kept showing up negotiation after negotiation. Once in a while one side or the other even forgot to change the date on the proposal, leaving it intact from bargaining three years earlier. But the 1994 talks were going to be different, there was no doubt about it. "I do know it's undeniable and can clearly be proven that we all know Bridgestone paid a lot of money for Firestone," Schofield said. "We're all familiar with the Ishibashi family [one of the main Bridgestone shareholders and the firm's founding family] kicking in money out of their own cash drawer. If things had continued the way they were going it could have taken down the whole company. That wasn't going to be allowed to happen."

While the labor relations team geared up for master contract talks, the team did not work in a vacuum. "There were many other people with different names who were heading up different parts of the company that had to have as detailed and grandiose plans to fix their parts of the business as did Mr. Ramsey," Schofield said. "There were other issues going on all over the company. Just fixing the labor problem had been tried and failed too many times in the past." Now the company needed transformations in sales, manufacturing, research and development—no area went untouched.

While the URW may have acted surprised by the enormity of the changes Bridgestone/Firestone sought, URW President Coss said he had received word a year earlier that Bridgestone/Firestone tried to recruit other U.S. tire makers into the so-called "War of '94." Besides the two other master contract firms—Goodyear and Michelin's Uniroyal Goodrich plants—the URW negotiated with a number of other tire companies in the several months following the April expiration of master pacts. Historically, these bargaining sessions produced contracts similar to the master agreements with regards to major economic issues. Coss feared not just the top three companies coming after the union, but a number of second-tier firms as well. Coss said a representative from another tire company tipped them off to Bridgestone/Firestone's plans. "We were told they wanted to—and they're the ones who referred to it—to 'declare war in '94,'" Coss said. The tipster also told the URW president, "It sounds like they want to destroy you."

Schofield, though, claimed no such recruiting took place. Tire companies are allowed to meet prior to negotiations under a nonstatutory exemption to the antitrust laws to share information, brainstorm ideas, and divide up research work when possible, he said. "In all my years attending meetings like that I've never seen a case where a company went into a meeting and said, 'This is where we are going and we want you to come with us,'" Schofield said. "I've never seen anything like that." Schofield acknowledged, though, that Ramsey's manner during these inter-company sessions—organized by the Rubber Manufacturers Association (RMA)—prior to the 1994 talks was different from the manner most negotiators were used to. "Chuck Ramsey is a very face-forward kind of a guy," Schofield said. "He doesn't hide the pea from anybody, so he felt that it was important that he tell the other companies the essence of what we were going to try to do. He didn't go over our specific proposals, but in the meetings he told them—so they would hear it from him—the essence of what was going to happen." As for the term "War of '94," Schofield never heard anyone within the company use the term. He did not say somebody did not tell Coss the company used the term, but the first time he saw "War of '94" was in newspaper articles quoting the URW president.

Jim Warren, chief negotiator for Goodyear in 1994, attended these RMA-organized sessions. Most of the talk was general, focused on what issues the negotiators believed would be top priority in upcoming bargaining. None of the participants were too intense about the meetings—except for Ramsey. "He came in there with an attitude different from any Firestone guy we'd seen," Warren said. "He was in control. He was a different cut of a guy than the others. Now I know why. They were building inventory and planning on taking them on. He came in there and he had his shoulder pads on. The rest of us were in there and we weren't even prepared for the game." Warren had met Torrence right before he left Bridgestone/Firestone, and the Goodyear negotiator could tell the difference between Torrence and Ramsey immediately. "When I met Torrence he was talking about all the good things they were doing. Of course, he was heavy into the involvement and I liked that," Warren said. "With Ramsey, you looked and saw how he behaved, and then what he did. He was on a mission, that guy was. He had been given marching orders, and he was a pit bull."

Ramsey's team aimed to have the entire proposal ready for the URW by the end of 1993, and came close. The team—led by Ramsey and backup negotiator Alfred Policy (then plant manager in Des Moines), along with Schofield—met in January 1994 with URW Firestone coordinator John Sellers, who himself was leading his first set of master contract negotiations for the union, and his backup coordinator, Jim Pope. Ramsey went over an extensive presentation the company had developed called "The Compelling Need to Change." The pitch basically pegged the performance of Bridgestone/Firestone's best plants against the other major tire manufacturers' top facilities. All through the presentation, Ramsey answered questions, gave them copies of the presentation, and told Sellers he would be happy to go around the country and meet with any locals who wanted to see the proposal—with or without the International representatives. "Not surprisingly, that was not a happy meeting, not an easy meeting for anybody," Schofield said. "It certainly didn't make the union happy."

Ramsey did travel throughout the country after meeting with Sellers and Pope to visit the various locals. Some places the union representatives attended and some places they did not. But Ramsey's message at each location remained constant: "This is just our idea of how to accomplish what we need to accomplish." That meant that in one way or another all major areas of the agreement were subject to change. That did not mean the company wanted to rape all areas of the agreement, according to Schofield. "But the company was out to bring a 1930s/1940s era collective bargaining agreement into conformity with what an agreement ought to look like today in this kind of manufacturing environment," he said. Bridgestone/Firestone needed these massive changes for one reason, Schofield said. While Firestone had gone through all the plant closings and restructurings of the 1970s and early 1980s, other U.S. tire companies had made incremental changes in their labor contracts and left Firestone behind.

Just how did Bridgestone/Firestone expect the URW to react? "I think in my opinion the only realistic impression was that this would be overwhelming," Schofield said. "The local parties believed the company had never gone to the table in the past without a bunch of demands and proposals." So what was different? he said the union wondered. It was as if the URW responded: "You've got more. We'll just say 'No' louder and eventually you'll pick them up and we'll go home and our labor contract will march into the future." But this time was different. "I truly do not know of any other way that we could have gone through this, assuming that the owners of the business got what they decided they had to have," Schofield said.

It was clear how the URW negotiators felt about the Bridgestone/Firestone proposal. "The comment from our side was: 'You can't eat an elephant all at once,'" said Local 713's Gates. "If you're going to eat an elephant, you're going to have to do it a bite at a time." From the URW's perspective, they had seen concessionary proposals in the past from Firestone. That was nothing new. In the past, the firm often put concessionary items on the table only to withdraw them later. What especially puzzled the Rubber Workers was the 180-degree turn Bridgestone/Firestone had made in attitude from just three years earlier. It was clear to the union that the Bridgestone/Firestone plan included the wish list of every plant manager running a master contract factory. Gates said it appeared the firm went through the master contract and all the local supplemental agreements from the factories covered under the master pact and cherry-picked what they liked and either rewrote or changed what they did not. "They tried to combine all the contracts into one master agreement, and they rewrote the whole book from front cover to back cover and that was their proposal: just this book," he said.

Sellers, as first-time coordinator in negotiations of this magnitude for the URW, obviously came upon more than he had bargained for. "One of the things that I say tongue-in-cheek is that I heard they wanted a coordinator for Bridgestone/Firestone and I begged and pleaded with Kenny [Coss], but he gave me the damn job anyway," Sellers said. "And that, unfortunately, is pretty accurate." He knew even before negotiations started that the negotiations would not end in a peaceful settlement. "From what we were hearing from the locals, what we were hearing from the rest of the industry, and what we were hearing from the company itself, not too long after I became coordinator it was clear that the company was just positioning itself to propose radical changes." Bridgestone/Firestone also entered unprecedented territory by making the comprehensive proposal as early as it did. "Normally we sit down at the table and exchange proposals. That did not happen," Sellers said, noting that the terms Bridgestone/Firestone ultimately implemented barely differed from this original proposal.

Ramsey said it was not as if Bridgestone/Firestone were asking its employees to work at a poverty wage. Before negotiations he said its URW members at the master contract plants averaged $62,000 a year in wages and benefits, and it estimated that would rise to $65,000 a year. While asking for cutbacks in a number of areas, workers would be paid eight hours of overtime pay every other week under the twelve-hour schedules and would be paid for up to two weeks in lieu of vacation, meaning they would get fifty-four weeks worth of pay. "There's any number of people in this country more than happy to take that kind of job," Ramsey said. "That's among the highest in the country." Throughout the process, Ramsey and Bridgestone/Firestone continually preached that the firm had to make up a competitive deficit of as much as $5 a tire on certain lines, and they expected the union to help make up a substantial portion of that in the 1994 negotiations. "We're not blaming the union. It's not necessarily anyone's fault," Ramsey said at the time. "The fact is that's where we are. To point blame will not change anything. How we move forward to change the system and attempt to improve is what's important. We've made it clear from the start what it would take to get an agreement. The union must deal with the company's need to change."

When actual negotiations commenced in March nothing much happened, according to Schofield. He said the information had been given to the union in January and the Bridgestone/Firestone team had toured the country giving presentations, yet when they arrived for bargaining some union people appeared unaware of what the company was proposing. Much of the first month was therefore spent again going through the proposal, the slide presentations, the contract language, the cost justification. Item by item through the entire contract. "And then the union really didn't give us anything," Schofield said. "I think we all hoped and really expected that this was enough of a different way of doing things that the union would respond differently than it ever had before, that they would say: 'You guys seem to be serious. How shall we proceed or what do you want to do?' But they came right back about three weeks later with the same proposals that we had seen over the past ten years. It was like this had never happened. It was like all this work had never really happened."

Local 713's Gates had a different take on what happened during negotiations. He blamed the inexperience of Ramsey as a negotiator, saying he did not know how to work a deal or build momentum from any conversation. Whenever Sellers would ask about a specific item, Ramsey invariably came back saying he did not need it all, but never agreed to move on anything. "You never knew how to read the guy," Gates said. "He was sending mixed signals. If there's any issue you'd want to get into details and discuss, he didn't know how to keep the thing flowing and get to resolution on any individual item. The fact is I don't think we resolved anything."

Sellers said he could never get down to Bridgestone/Firestone's short list, or the issues it most cared about, because there was no short list. "It was all of that," Sellers said. "Even though Chuck Ramsey many times during negotiations said, 'No, we don't have to have all of it.' But when you would go item by item, there wasn't anything that he wanted to let go of." The firm's stated reason for the changes was that it was still losing money and its costs were higher than the rest of the industry. "Their never-ending mantra for the compelling need for systemic change. That meant, 'We want it all,'" Sellers said. "There just was never any way to get any dialogue going. I have never been in a negotiations where you couldn't at some point sit down and say, 'Look, if we do this, this, and this, can you do this, this, and this.' That never happened."

About the only thing the two sides agreed to in the initial round of negotiations was on May 16 to recess negotiations until Goodyear, selected as the target company for the 1994 negotiations, could get a contract ratified.

TAKING A BREAK FOR GOODYEAR NEGOTIATIONS

As Bridgestone/Firestone and the URW took a break from talks to allow the Goodyear scenario to play out, the URW and Goodyear had an extremely difficult time getting a contract ratified. The original tentative agreement came easily enough, as the April 25 tentative pact maintained COLA; raised the pension multiplier from $30 to $37 per month per year of service; consolidated master contract workers into one health care plan with some deductibles to be paid by URW members but allowing for better 401(k) savings benefits; brought workers a $500 signing bonus; and called for a new performance-based bonus system tied to company profitability.

One thing the contract did not have, though, was a general wage increase. While the COLA had raised workers' wages about $9 an hour since the URW first won the benefit in 1976, the union members saw that as just keeping them even with inflation. Only a general wage increase above and beyond the COLA truly improved their purchasing power, they felt. And the southern coalition of Goodyear URW locals clearly believed Goodyear's financial situation was improved in 1994 and workers deserved to share in the increased prosperity. In addition, workers were not happy about having to pay health care deductibles because they were used to traditional "first dollar coverage." The pact also included a provision that could have some future retirees paying a portion of health care premiums. Consequently, five of the nine Goodyear locals rejected the pact, led by the southern tire plants in Gadsden, Alabama; Union City, Tennessee; and Danville, Virginia.

While the Goodyear ratification process continued, URW members at the three Uniroyal Goodrich Tire Co. master contract plants that already had given concessions in the prior year ratified their new master agreement. The pact was similar to the Goodyear agreement with some differences, including freezing COLA raises for a year and using some of the COLA money to help pay for the pension increases. Importantly for workers, though, the contract guaranteed a three-year moratorium on plant shutdowns, and in an attached letter of understanding, Uniroyal Goodrich promised to invest a minimum amount of money each year in the three plants.

And although the Uniroyal Goodrich ratification was completed, Goodyear locals rejected its tentative agreement for a second time despite a letter of endorsement from URW President Coss and Secretary/Treasurer Glenn Ellison. Vice President Mike Stanley declined to sign the endorsement letter. His home local in Union City, along with Danville and Gadsden, again rejected the second tentative agreement. The three locals combined represented just more than half of the 12,200 URW members covered by the master contract, meaning that together they could block any agreement. The latest proposal made several improvements, allowing workers to choose fully paid health care coverage and granting full health benefits to retirees with thirty years of service. But again, there was no general wage increase. There was even a four-hour strike at five of the locals just before the second agreement was reached.

After the second rejection, Goodyear took its case to the people, with Chairman and CEO Stanley Gault and Vice President of Human Resources Mike Burns publishing a question-and-answer session about the negotiations in the May 31, 1994, edition of the firm's *Akron Daily Digest*. Burns said the second tentative agreement would increase wages by $1.75 an hour with COLA alone. "Today, total compensation for master contract associates, which includes earnings and benefits, averages more than $67,000 a year," Burns said. "When the contract expires in 1997, that will have increased by more than $10,000. Paycheck earnings now average nearly $45,000. By 1997, that will have risen to nearly $49,000." He added that the higher pensions represented more than a 15 percent increase in cost to Goodyear.

In the end, it was workers at Local 878 Union City who ended the stalemate, as they changed their vote on June 23. Local 831 in Danville also gave approval in the end, with only Local 12 in Gadsden standing by its original vote. The locals apparently were convinced during a June 16 meeting that the company would go no higher.

One reason the situation dragged on so long was that Coss lacked the power or the moxie to settle, according to Thorley, the federal mediator during the contract negotiations. "Kenny couldn't deliver as a president," Thorley said. "I always said a president had to be respected enough that he could sell what he said he'd deliver. Kenny couldn't do that. He wasn't willing to put himself on the line to sell a package. I don't know why. I just think it was his makeup. I hate to say this but it was almost like he was insecure." Thorley said by the end of the Goodyear talks in 1994, the Goodyear local union leaders did not even want Coss there. The mediator said the difference between Coss and Stone was that when Stone told the company it was good enough for him, he went back and fought like a dog to get it passed. "Kenny would go back and if anyone spoke in opposition, he was done," Thorley said. "He would just go into a shell and agree with them. And that hurt him with the companies. The companies didn't respect him. They lost a lot of confidence in him."

Goodyear chief negotiator Warren did give Coss and Ron Hoover, the union's Goodyear coordinator for the negotiations, a lot of credit for preventing a strike at Goodyear in 1994. He said Hoover had trouble getting the southern coalition of Goodyear locals together. "They're [the southern coalition] just so damn jealous of each other, they're afraid one is going to get something they're not going to get," Warren said. Warren credited Don Northcraft, president of the Topeka local, for bringing the union together in 1994. "I think he could see the infighting in the union was hurting the process," the Goodyear negotiator said. "He was smart enough and far enough from the forest that the trees weren't getting in the way. He did as much to pull that union group together as probably anyone in that group."

As for the settlement, Warren said the Goodyear locals got all they could have in 1994. "We really didn't have anything more to give the union," he said. "It was all out there. That was one where they didn't leave with anything on the table. If they were going to strike, they'd have had to take a tent. We didn't have any more."

THE BRIDGESTONE/FIRESTONE STRIKE BEGINS

When the URW reached a master contract with one tire maker, it naturally expected the other firms in the master process to follow suit. That generally was what happened, with small differences here and there. Master bargaining was a process that had started in the 1940s and was viewed as beneficial from many angles. It helped keep industry participants on a level playing field with regard to labor costs. It helped streamline negotiations, enabling one set of negotiations to settle issues across many plants within one firm and also across a number of companies competing in the same industry. On the negative side, master contracts were seen by detractors as an archaic process that demanded a "one size fits all" solution be adopted in a world where individual concerns needed to be addressed. The process also tended to drive up wages and benefits at non-tire operations included in master contracts of major tire firms far beyond what other manufacturers in these non-tire industries were paying.

Bridgestone/Firestone had stressed many times during the negotiations that it would only accept a contract that met its needs. These were the negotiations the firm had been waiting for since before Schofield joined Firestone in 1962: the chance to break the pattern. So when Goodyear's contract finally got settled, Bridgestone/Firestone surprised no one when it refused to buckle under and follow the pattern. Goodyear's settlement was acceptable to the Nashville-based firm in some ways but not in others. "Goodyear had incrementally been improving their contract throughout a twenty-year period while we weren't doing that," Schofield said. "Goodyear's issues were not our issues."

There were ten main areas of contention between the URW and Bridgestone/Firestone that included reduced health care coverage with co-pays and family premiums of $68 a month; a provision to allow the company to pay workers for one or two weeks of vacation a year in lieu of time off; holidays at a reduced pay rate; continuous operations with twelve-hour shifts, with overtime for hours past forty each week, but not past eight each day; discontinued supplemental unemployment benefits; COLA payments tied to increases in productivity; no supplemental agreements at the local union level; wage reduction of $5 an hour for warehouse classifications; lower wages for new hires to be made up over a three-year period; and changes in the incentive pay system.

Given the differences, it came as no surprise when the URW canceled the day-to-day extension of the prior contract that the two sides had been operating under and set a strike date. Many industry observers believed Bridgestone/Firestone in reality had invited the walkout because of its inflexible stance. "No, we did not want them to strike," Schofield said, "but from a practical standpoint I don't think any reasonable man could have expected them not to strike. If there ever was a reason for a strike, this was it."

On July 12, 1994, more than forty-two hundred workers at five Bridgestone/Firestone locations began a strike that would change forever the course of URW history. For years afterward, the debate raged on whether it was a strike that should have been called. Or was this a time for a strong URW leader to step in and tell a rank and file that was primed to strike point-blank that this was not the fight to pick? A leader to tell them this was a time to stay on the job, fight the fight from within, and not be goaded into a walkout that a union the size of the URW no longer could sustain, let alone think of winning. Did they need a leader to impress his will upon the local union leaders—no matter the URW history of autonomy and bottom-up ruling—and make them keep their people in when every ounce of their souls told them they should strike?

Roger Gates, from the Decatur local, said it actually was quite an accomplishment to keep the union's Bridgestone/Firestone Policy Committee from striking before July. "Given the structure of the plants and the history of what we'd been through before and the strikes, we had our people where they thought that was the only answer at that point in time," he said. "Some of the vocal ones in the plant had wondered why we hadn't hit the bricks before. So it wasn't a matter of trying to get the people out at that point, it was a matter of trying to hold them in."

Gates was not among those anxious to strike. The Decatur plant, in fact, had been through some tough times in recent years. In early 1991, Bridgestone/Firestone laid off about five hundred workers and knocked the plant down to two shifts. The workers were told to consider the layoff permanent, so many took what little severance they had coming because they never expected to come back to work. By late 1993 the operations employed roughly eight hundred, down from about fifteen hundred just three years earlier. It was the swing plant and appeared to have no future at that point. But then Bridgestone/Firestone starting recalling workers in Decatur. They recalled the two hundred people still on recall (those who had not earlier taken the severance pay) and began hiring additional people off the street, boosting employment back up to about 1,250 at the time of the strike. So Gates was not especially keen on taking his workers out just as their fortunes appeared to be rising, but several members of the union's negotiating committee thought if the union struck the whole dispute would settle quickly. "They felt that the company would come around, and I'm sure there were people in the plant who thought the same thing," Gates said. "That was what they thought was going to make the company take us seriously. Up to that point in time, what had we done to make them move at all?"

Despite his misgivings about the strike, Gates also thought not much would have been accomplished by staying on the job. "If we had stayed in and tried to do an in-plant thing, we'd probably have just gotten a bunch of people fired. There just weren't any good answers at that point in time." Gates also was not among those who thought the strike would be quick and painless. "I felt if we did go out we were going to spend all the time we wanted on the street. Having said that, I didn't think it would take as long as it did either. My wife had gone to a fortune teller. She told her there would be an agreement before Christmas. She just forgot to tell her it would be the Christmas of 1996."

The city of Decatur itself was hit particularly hard during 1994, as the Midwestern city became known as "The War Zone." Joining URW Local 713 on the streets were the United Auto Workers striking at Caterpillar, and the Paperworkers union at A. E. Staley's. "It's a problem for the community, because the community has a hard time helping three locals out at once, so it makes it less resources to draw from," said Gates. "But the three [locals] worked on a lot of things together. We put together some of the biggest rallies in the county."

Sellers was convinced Bridgestone/Firestone wanted a strike and was prepared for it. Besides the normal inventory buildup prior to contract negotiations, the firm's parent company had pledged at least three million tires for the effort, and the company had hired security and law firms the union claimed were well known for "union-busting" measures. "Bridgestone/Firestone was not prepared to compromise on its position," he said. "And they will no doubt tell you the same thing about us, but those weren't our proposals." The URW, according to Sellers, pretty much had proposed keeping the status quo. The union wanted the Goodyear pattern on economics, and it proposed common expiration dates for the LaVergne and Bloomington, Illinois, plants so those tire facilities in effect would be included in future master contract talks. That was pretty much it.

Like Gates, Sellers saw little chance to keep the Bridgestone/Firestone locals from striking. "Early on I tried to get our guys to do what I would call offensive bargaining, and look at alternatives other than striking," Sellers said. "Really the consensus was we wouldn't be able to condition the membership to that approach. The membership just would not understand what we were trying to do. The membership was geared to strike." It was not long, though, before he realized the URW as an institution lacked

The streets of Decatur, Ill., are a sea of red as 3,300 participate in a solidarity march on Labor Day in 1994. The city was nicknamed the "War Zone" that year because large locals from three unions—including URW Local 713 at the Bridgestone/Firestone tire plant—were on strike simultaneously. *(USWA/URW photo files)*

the size and financial resources to sustain a fight at that level. Still, the URW retained hope, according to Sellers. "I don't think we ever felt that it wasn't winnable," he said. "There was a debate amongst ourselves about what was the proper strategy. Were we better off to make an unconditional offer and get more of our people back in the plants and continue to try to negotiate, or continue to hold the strike? And consensus for quite some time was to continue to try to hold the strike."

Coss said Bridgestone/Firestone did a good job in whipping up the emotions of the people to the point where they would want to strike. At one negotiating session Coss sat in on, he said he asked Ramsey to pick out six items that were especially important to the company—just not everything that affects the most important aspects in the workers' life, such as seniority, wages, and benefits. As URW president, Coss had another role in master contract negotiations, in trying to keep the playing field as level as possible in the rubber industry with regard to labor issues. He knew if one firm was successful in gaining changes, all the other tire companies would want exactly the same thing. But Bridgestone/Firestone would not whittle down its demand. The firm wanted everything. So Coss said, "Then what you're telling me is you want a strike." The URW president claimed Ramsey replied that the "people have to hurt very badly before they'll be willing to do what we want."

Right after this session, Coss said he met with the URW's Bridgestone/Firestone Policy Committee and told them it would be better if they stayed on the job because he had no doubt the company would replace them. The firm already had shown it was prepared to follow that path in LaVergne. While it appeared that the group might opt against striking, as soon as some of the local presidents left and went back to their home locals, they were hell-bent on striking again, according to Coss. Despite some detractors saying he should have been a stronger leader and not allowed the strike to happen, the URW president said that was not his role. "It's up to [the committee] to vote," Coss said. "We didn't direct them to do anything. All we were doing was acting as advisers." The constitution in extreme cases allowed the president to go directly to the local membership, as Coss had done earlier in 1994 at Fort Wayne. But this situation was different because the membership of each local already had voted all of its authority to the Policy Committee, including the ability to call a strike. So Coss said he never considered going directly to the rank and file to try to get them to rescind strike authorization. "You can't explain strategy like that to a bunch of angry people," he said.

Dan Borelli, Coss's assistant, said he thought Sellers lost the committee early on. "I think the guidance to keep them going to hold out, to get something for them to pattern or come close to the pattern, would have been a wiser decision," Borelli said. "However, you had a couple of pretty tough hombres out there who thought they could take on the whole world, and they were able to convince some of the followers that we could take them on and beat them." Borelli also believed that Bridgestone/Firestone had something to prove to the rest of the industry, especially if it were true that another tire company—in all likelihood Goodyear—had tipped off Coss and the URW. "I think that Bridgestone wanted to show Goodyear they should have listened to them," Borelli said. "I don't think you can underestimate the pride of the Japanese culture. Being prideful, they were hell-bent to show the other companies and to show us that they could whip us and for all intents and purposes they did whip the Rubber Workers."

Goodyear negotiator Warren was surprised that Bridgestone/Firestone held out as long as it did. "I was one who was wrong on that one, because I kept saying, 'They'll fold,' but they didn't," Warren said. "I got some better understanding afterward why. They built tires and shipped them over here from Japan. And they built up an inventory. They anticipated this." The Goodyear negotiator said his management asked if Bridgestone/Firestone could hold its position, and Warren kept telling them no. Then the Goodyear sales staff would report that Bridgestone/Firestone had guaranteed General Motors that it would meet its original equipment obligations, and Goodyear could not figure out how. "Then we found out they had rented warehouses up in Minnesota and Wisconsin and had filled these warehouses starting way before 1994, shipping the tires over," Warren said. "At that time Japan was having a terrible economic crisis, but those Bridgestone plants over there were going balls to the walls and sending the tires over here. That was well orchestrated and well planned. It surprised us."

One man who does not buy that a strike was inevitable was Continental General's Polovick, who also was a former Firestone negotiator. "I still say the strike at Bridgestone/Firestone would never have occurred had Kenny Coss demonstrated the kind of leadership that [Peter] Bommarito was capable of," Polovick said. "Although the URW prides themselves on their autonomy and democracy, in a negotiation process, at the end of the day, you have got to have the guy who can cut the deal, and Kenny couldn't do that." Polovick also dismissed Coss's argument that it was the local union presidents who refused to play ball, and thought that the URW president copped out with his "they're the union" rhetoric. "You're not the International union president just to advise people. You're '*the man*,'" Polovick said. "The funny thing about Coss was that he did demonstrate this when he stepped in at Fort Wayne when Ray Wiseman refused to allow the employees to vote. Coss came in and conducted an election. Now that to me was leadership."

Polovick, though, also said he thought Bridgestone/Firestone definitely wanted the strike because the firm no longer had the patience to make changes the old-fashioned way—by getting concessions at the local level. "Companies had options to make the kind of changes that they needed and not do it at that master level," Polovick said. "And that's where I think Bridgestone/Firestone was particularly greedy in the [1994] round of bargaining. They said, 'We're going to do it all. We're going to fix it at the masters. We're not going to screw around at the local level.'" The Rubber Workers historically had shown it would allow companies to make changes if the firms could convince the local plants to do it. But URW officials felt it was inappropriate for the union as an entity to make the givebacks. "It was each local's responsibility to decide its own destiny," Polovick said. "If you look at the URW three to five years prior to that time, there was far more recognition of the companies' needs than there was the entire history of the URW before that."

So either Bridgestone/Firestone had lost its patience for that type of approach, or they got word from the parent company that they were tired of hearing the excuse that much of the firm's problem was because of the union contract, Polovick said. They were told this was the time to fix it, but once it was done the parent did not want to hear the "labor excuse" again. Many of the demands were constructed to get a rise out of the union. "When you look at some of the demands they had on the table, they were unnecessary and in many cases they were inflammatory," Polovick said. "They wanted to do away with paid union time. That might save you a few dollars but in the scheme of things it's not [saving you anything]. Really that's an affront to the union. That's waving a red flag in front of a bull."

From Polovick's perspective, the URW did not make a bunch of outrageous demands, but that did not leave the union faultless for the whole situation either. "Bridgestone had made noise all along," Polovick said. "They had not surprised the International. They had in fact met with the International well ahead of negotiations. They'd met with employees and gone to them directly and told them the things that were important and what they had to do." Had Sellers as coordinator stepped forward and agreed early on to move on such major issues as operating the tire plants on a four-crew schedule and easing health care costs, the union would have made it difficult for Bridgestone/Firestone not to come to some sort of agreement. "I won't say that it would have been really easy for the Rubber Workers," Polovick said. "Their problem is they wouldn't take charge. They wouldn't take control of the negotiations."

Some within the URW agreed that Coss could have kept the workers in, if he truly had wanted to. "I know we have autonomy and everything, but there comes a time when the president tells them, 'You aren't going out,'" said Gary Diceglio of Local 2 in Akron. "I think he has that right. I think he has that power. Would they have listened to him? I don't know. Would they have listened to Pete Bommarito or Mike Stone? Yeah, I believe they would have. Kenny didn't command the same aura about him that the others had, especially Pete. Right, wrong, or indifferent, that's what a person has to do on that level. The president has to take the blame or the credit, and I don't think Kenny was willing to do that." Curt Brown, URW public relations director, said the union had plenty of warning to know that the strike should not be called, and that it was Coss and Sellers who should have stopped it. "You don't go on strike when the company wants you to go on strike. You stay in the plant no matter what," Brown said. He also thought Coss chose the easy way out by passing the buck to the Policy Committee for wanting to call the strike. "Someone's got to say, 'Dammit, if you do this you're destroying yourself,'" Brown said. "As it happened, it destroyed the entire union."

WAR OF '94 ELSEWHERE

Although the main battle during the War of '94 clearly was with Bridgestone/Firestone, the URW also struck three other foreign-owned tire makers that summer, with the longest-running walkout against Pirelli Armstrong. Though it was doubtful these other firms—two Japanese-owned and one Italian-owned—had actually joined with Bridgestone/ Firestone in a true "War of '94," many of the proposals were similar enough that at the least the firms were taking advantage of the URW's weakness at the time.

The first strike came June 21 when fifteen hundred members of Local 915 walked off their job at the Dunlop Tire plant in Huntsville, Alabama. Dunlop, owned by Japan's Sumitomo Rubber Industries, was asking for more concessions than Local 915 said it was willing to give. The company said the main issues concerned cost reductions and productivity gains needed to return the unit to profitability. Next, about sixteen hundred URW members at three Pirelli Armstrong tire plants struck on July 15. Only the plants in Nashville, Tennessee, and Hanford, California, were off the job long term because, just before the strike, Italian-owned Pirelli announced plans to sell the Des Moines, Iowa, plant and get out of the farm tire business. Local 164 in Des Moines voted September 1 to end the strike there and go back to work under the terms of the previous contract as the plant was purchased by Titan Tire Corp. Local 1023 at the Japanese-owned Yokohama Tire Corp. factory in Salem, Virginia, was the last tire plant to strike in 1994, leaving their jobs July 24. At that point, the URW had a total of eighty-two hundred union members picketing ten plants that normally would produce about 170,000 tires a day, or 19.5 percent of total U.S. production.

The Dunlop and Yokohama strikes settled relatively quickly, with the Dunlop local approving a new contract September 23, ending its strike after ninety-five days, while the Yokohama local approved a new contract October 5 after eleven weeks of picketing. But the Pirelli Armstrong strike action in Nashville and Hanford continued much longer, more closely mirroring the issues of Bridgestone/Firestone. In late 1993, company executives asked for contract alterations the workers considered concessionary. The firm wanted changes in such things as health benefits and job classifications in return for a three-year guarantee on jobs. When Pirelli Armstrong CEO Paul Calvi met with the Local 670 Executive Board in Nashville, he explained what he wanted and that he would have a meeting with the members and that there would be a vote on the proposal, said Local 670 President Stanley Johnson. "I told him, without question, we understood the severity of the situation," Johnson said. "We were willing to consider reasonable concerns that they had, but that the union was the representative party, and that if any votes were taken, they would be taken by the union and that no vote at his meeting would occur."

The membership was unimpressed with Calvi's presentation and candidly told him so. Johnson said they told him: "Look, you're asking for unreasonable things. We are certainly willing to be competitive with the industry and want to be competitive, and we want to help the company make money. But what we don't want is for you to come in here and tell us what you are going to do." At that point Calvi basically told the members that they could either make the changes then, or the company would be back in 1994 negotiations to force them to. "Much like every other major purchase by foreign-owned tire makers, Pirelli probably overpaid for the facilities and didn't really know or understand what they were buying when they bought it [in 1988]," Johnson said. "Pirelli was a high-end, high-performance tire maker that in a rush to get into the American market, bought a manufacturer of primarily replacement tires [after it lost out to Bridgestone in buying Firestone]."

It was much the same out in Hanford, said Sonny Milton, president of Local 703 there until he retired in 1998. "When Calvi got up on this podium and we were right up there by him, he was telling the plant what he had to have," Milton said. "When he got through, I told him, 'I think you're dreaming, man. There's no way on the medical you'll get what you're talking about. This is not the other countries. This is the United States,'" Milton said. "They drove us out [on strike]."

Calvi also did not understand the U.S. labor market, according to Johnson. He heard that Calvi had told one of his human relations vice presidents that he had taken on the union in Spain and won after a six-week strike. The vice president reportedly responded: "Six weeks won't even start it here. Six months probably won't handle it here. You don't understand the people you're dealing with." Johnson said the point was that the URW was a reasonable union, it was willing to negotiate, but the members would not be dictated to.

As the strike unfolded many of the proposals of Pirelli were similar to those of Bridgestone/Firestone, but Pirelli went farther by moving to terminate health benefits for retirees. The Italian-owned company even filed suit just prior to the expiration of the master contract to prevent the URW from interfering in the termination of the retiree benefits. Pirelli also started advertising for replacement workers seven days prior to the contract expiration. The retiree issue hit very close to home for Johnson, whose father was one of the Local 670 retirees who would be affected. The local was ready and willing to strike, having earlier given strike authorization. Still, calling a strike is the toughest decision a local president has to make, and Johnson did not take it lightly. "I think everyone recognized that the strike had to occur," Johnson said.

In early September, the company faxed a proposal to Ellison, the URW secretary/treasurer who was the union's coordinator for the Pirelli bargaining. It had more concessionary proposals than had been offered at the table, and said that future retirees would not be entitled to medical benefits. Pirelli told the union it was going to implement those terms, although the URW had no legitimate chance to bargain on the offer. Although the union members did not know it at the time, it was this proposal that would be the key element of an NLRB charge that later would lead to the strike's resolution.

On September 9, the company began hiring replacement workers. "Before that the company, through their advertising, began to interview scabs," Johnson said. "We found out about those interviews taking place. We found out where they were taking place. They started out at a hotel. We went to the hotel and provided informational picketing. We let the scabs know that we were aware of the situation, and to inform them that we would appreciate them not agreeing to go to work there given the circumstances." Johnson placed "scabs"—as unions refer to replacement workers—into two categories. One group is individuals who do not care about other individuals and will steal their livelihood for their own betterment. "They are the lowlife of the population," Johnson said. The other group are those who are just ignorant and do not understand the relationship between unions and companies, or the importance of a labor contract. "They're blinded by the offer of the company to provide jobs and wages."

By the time Local 670 members found out about the next location for interviews, the company had hired a private security force similar to the one hired by Bridgestone/Firestone. The same force then was hired to regularly patrol the picket lines at the Pirelli Armstrong facility. There were some allegations of violence connected to the Nashville strike. On October 12, four picketers were charged with reckless endangerment when a group of about three hundred picketers began throwing rocks at vehicles. About fifteen cars were damaged and more than seventy-five policemen were

Strikers from Local 670 at the Pirelli Armstrong Tire Corp. plant in Nashville, Tennessee, gather around a truck making deliveries to the plant during the "War of '94" (Rubber & Plastics News *photo. Copyright Crain Communications Inc.*)

called to the scene. In more serious instances, the home of a former Vanderbilt University football star who was working as a replacement worker was damaged when a device exploded outside the front door of his home in October. A second strikebreaker discovered a bomb outside his home in late October and in early November another replacement said her car was set on fire.

Throughout the strike Johnson denied the union had anything to do with the incidents, and said to his knowledge no individual union member was convicted of doing harm. He added that the security force hired by the company in some instances attempted to create situations to make strikers look as though they were violent. The local videotaped incoming cars to try to get an idea of how much turnover was occurring, he said, not to get license plates numbers to find where the replacements lived. Johnson said the local also was careful about who was allowed on the picket line. Anytime there was someone they did not recognize they asked for identification to ensure the company had not sent someone there to start an incident and make the strikers look bad.

Local 670 stayed remarkably united, having only one individual cross the picket line during the eight-month strike, and that person quit when the strike was settled. On a typical gate change the local had 50 to 150 strikers at the gates, with people like Jim Vantrese holding down the fort. On a November day four months into the strike, Vantrese stood alone, protecting an obscure entrance. He carried a sign that said, "You are temporary. We are URW." Vantrese was one of the lucky ones as he was able to make ends meet working a number of odd jobs such as repairing go-carts and painting. His children were grown and his house almost paid for, so he was able to keep his bills low. Vantrese admitted to having feelings of sympathy once in a while for the replacement workers going in—seeing the abuse they took and knowing how the company would treat them. But the feeling went away quickly. "Anybody who takes a man's job when he's out here trying to hold his own is lowdown and I hate them," he said.

Rallies attracted more than three thousand supporters on numerous occasions. Besides support from other Rubber Workers locals, help came from several other unions as well. "We went out and talked with local unions about our situation and what was at stake not only for us but for the entire labor movement," Johnson said. "These unions responded not only with people at the picket line almost on a daily basis, but they responded with food and monetary donations. It was a tremendous outpouring."

Hanford was not quite as unified, with fifty to seventy-five people crossing the picket line, mostly out of the skilled trades, according to Milton. "That bothered us quite a bit, but the ones who went back in were mostly newer people," he said. "I don't think we had but one guy with longtime service go back. That hurt us, but it hurt the company too because the people they had in there didn't know what to do on the machines."

BRIDGESTONE/FIRESTONE HIRES PERMANENT REPLACEMENTS

As the strike against Bridgestone/Firestone and Pirelli Armstrong dragged into December, the strikes became the longest at the time in tire industry history, begging comparisons to the URW's historic walkout in 1976. Other than length, though, the strikes bore little resemblance. In

1976, the strike had started with sixty thousand URW members and rose to as many as seventy thousand. The original action affected forty-seven plants in twenty-one states and shut off a majority of the tire capacity in North America. In 1994, about eighty-two hundred workers were the most on the street, a number down to five thousand by December. At one time in 1994, pickets were at eight tire and two non-tire units, with the five tire plants still out in December accounting for just 11 percent of North American capacity. In addition, Bridgestone/Firestone still had seven North American tire plants operating that either were non-union or were not covered under the master contract bargaining. So, while in 1976 the URW had effectively shut down an industry, the same union—about half the size it was in 1976—could not even shut down a single company eighteen years later.

There was one other major difference from 1976: the company's use of replacement workers. Between strikebreakers and crossovers, the company was able to produce as much as 50 to 75 percent or more of normal capacity at most of the plants. There was sporadic violence throughout the Bridgestone/Firestone strike, but nothing of a wide-reaching scope. A striking worker in Des Moines was arrested and charged with the bombing of a replacement worker's home. In Noblesville, Indiana, the local president was arrested in late November 1994 on charges of criminal mischief and criminal recklessness. Police alleged he shattered the windshield of a car driven by a salaried worker from the plant. Just before Christmas, Bridgestone/Firestone fired thirty striking workers for incidents connected to the strike, though the company later was slapped with an NLRB charge because of the attempted firings.

Bridgestone/Firestone implemented the terms of its last and final offer in August, about a month into the strike, and began looking around for temporary replacements to produce as many tires as it could. The company had not seen a strike last longer than the industrywide walkout of 1976, so many in the firm believed that around the middle of September the two sides would start talking again with the help of federal mediators and some real progress would be made. The lines of communication were open, but there was little communicating going on. So when the strike stretched into early December, surpassing the length of the 1976 work stoppage, Bridgestone/Firestone officials started wondering, "What if they don't come back?"

That was when the company seriously considered the matter of permanent replacements. "This was another tricky area if you're going to do it and get away with it," Schofield said, "and this was the largest one in the history of the country." It also was a sticky logistical matter for Bridgestone/Firestone, which had several groups of employees to deal with. There were the strikers, the union members who had crossed the picket line, and the temporary replacements. It was determined the first order of business was to offer permanent positions to the temporaries, who had been promised from the start they would never be put in the position of being asked to go permanent. "They were told they could either take the permanent position or stay a temporary worker," Schofield said. "But if you stayed as a temporary replacement and we received an unconditional offer to return to work, then you're out."

Bridgestone/Firestone ran ads for the jobs the last two weeks of December and took some prospects through the pre-interview process. When the strikers had not returned by the beginning of January, Bridgestone/Firestone pulled the plug. They were going to hire permanent replacements. "It was a terrible decision to have to make," Schofield said. "I didn't have to make it. It was Chuck Ramsey's decision. Everybody knew it was a terrible thing."

Nobody knew that any better than the group of strikers, who faced the prospect of actually losing their jobs. They had to watch people go into work each day and take the livelihood they had counted on for decades. At best, they considered these people scabs. At worst, they were traitors from their own union who had crossed the picket line after standing as URW brothers or sisters all these years. Having Bridgestone/Firestone declare that replacements now would be considered permanent put more pressure on the URW, both at the International and local level. While the problems of crossovers had hurt to a varying degree—more at some locations, such as Oklahoma City, and less at others, including Noblesville—many more URW members began crossing the picket line after the company's announcement. Akron's Local 7 returned to work unconditionally shortly after the Bridgestone/Firestone January 4, 1995, bombshell. Though Local 7 members incurred the wrath of their URW brethren for having broken ranks, the local's falling was more symbolic than anything else. Because Bridgestone/Firestone had long since ceased making main-line tires in Akron, Local 7's membership had dwindled to a couple of hundred and had no practical effect on the War of '94.

Sellers also maintained—though Schofield denied the charge—that Bridgestone/Firestone strategically chose that time to announce it was hiring permanent replacements because it knew the URW was putting together a counterproposal. "We had federal mediation in here and in the middle of all that they notified us," Sellers said. "We first heard it through the news media or through people from the locals who had heard it on the news that they were going to be permanently replaced. The company knew how disruptive that would be. Now suddenly you've got a group of local union presidents who have to spend time on the telephone back to their locals dealing with that problem of permanent replacements. It was just clear [the company] was not interested in doing an agreement. At that point they were just bent on breaking us."

While many have suggested that URW President Coss should have shown stronger leadership by stopping the strike from happening, Local 713 President Gates said it was at this juncture Coss needed to step forward and unconditionally call the strike off but did not. "I think the International should have made the call there instead of trying to sway people to do it," Gates said. "They didn't make the call. I guess that's the one thing I feel bad about, because I think the International should have stepped in. Everybody was saying it was the thing to do but nobody was willing to pull the trigger."

At Decatur a total of 325 of 1,250 original strikers crossed the picket line, but only 73 of those did so before Bridgestone/Firestone made the permanent replacement decision. And it created a terrible situation for both the local union leaders and individual rank-and-file members. "There were some good people put in some bad positions to make decisions that they shouldn't have ever had to make," Gates said. "You've got people out there with thirty years of service permanently replaced. They don't know if they're going to have their benefits or their retirement. It's a damn tough decision and they shouldn't have had to do that. There were fathers that stayed out and sons that crossed. Brothers that stayed out and brothers that went in. There are families that still don't speak to each other." It was almost more than a first-term president like Gates should have had to observe, seeing the solidarity of a local in one of the most symbolic union cities in the country ripped apart. "It tears you up because the local and the union are only as strong as the people, and every time someone crossed the line it made you that much weaker," he said.

The URW as a whole was not making a great show of solidarity either.

That January, a special convention was convened to try to raise dues to build up the strike fund and provide some assistance for Rubber Workers still off the job. When the strike started the URW boasted a strike fund of more than $12 million. That sounds like a lot of money, but with any-where from four thousand to eighty-two hundred members on strike, drawing weekly benefits of $100, the URW was paying out between $400,000 and $820,000 each week. Even after borrowing money from the AFL-CIO, the strike fund was depleted quickly. At the special convention in Las Vegas, delegates argued long and hard before adopting a watered-down temporary measure designed to repay what had been borrowed, but did not generate any new assistance for those still on strike. The action was not surprising, given that the Rubber Workers had a long history of vehemently opposing most requests for dues increases. At the 1990 con-vention, when strike benefits were increased from $35 to $100 a week, the delegates adopted no corresponding measure to put more money in the strike fund.

While not totally unexpected, the delegates' seeming lack of compas-sion at the January 1995 special convention did not sit well with people like Local 713's Gates. "It was disheartening to go to that convention and hear your fellow union brothers talking against a raise in dues because they were worried about their personal politics back home when we had mem-bers who were losing homes and not being able to make car payments," he said. "And here are these people who are working and can't afford a few dollars a month when we're losing thousands of dollars a month. Honest-ly, it pisses you off, and some of them were close to us at the time." Gates also countered the argument that strikers made do in 1976 with just a cou-ple of weeks of strike benefits. "There's a lot of difference now," Gates said. "For one thing, the 1976 strike was four months. And the cost of living was a lot cheaper in 1976. People hadn't been permanently replaced in 1976. Their jobs never were threatened in 1976."

Others disappointed by the lack of definitive action at the special con-vention included Coss and Local 670 President Johnson. Coss recalled still being at the podium as the session was ending and voicing his displeasure at the group. "At the end of that meeting I said—and I was very upset or I probably wouldn't have said it—that I never thought I would be ashamed to be a Rubber Worker." Coss especially was upset because it was the big, well-off locals that opposed paying an extra few dollars a month to help out union brothers and sisters who had been through so much. "I was upset at the membership because they wouldn't do what was right," Coss said.

Local 670's Johnson at the time thought the URW could still win the strike, but the union needed to be aggressive and show solidarity. He described the measure that finally passed the special convention as a "Band-Aid." "Dues is always a tough question, and sometimes if you're not in the fight, it's hard to see the necessity to carry it on," Johnson said. "The issue was convincing them that it was a strike for all. The statement I made on the record was, 'Either you're union or you're not, and if you're not, get up and get out.'"

GOOD NEWS FOR PIRELLI LOCALS

In March 1995, the Pirelli locals at Nashville and Hanford got the news they had been hoping for. Because Pirelli had implemented terms different from those the union had had the opportunity to bargain on—even though the terms were apparently even worse than what had been offered —the NLRB ruled that Pirelli had engaged in an unfair labor practice. When the URW then made an unconditional offer to return to their jobs under those conditions the company was obliged to take the workers back or begin facing a major back-pay liability. After the ruling came down, Pirelli asked for an adjournment to negotiations so they could take time to respond. "Within a week to ten days we were back in the plant," Johnson said.

Federal mediator Thorley, who had mediated the Goodyear pact back when 1994 negotiations had first begun, was working on the Pirelli Armstrong talks at this point. "Pirelli Armstrong might have ended up winning it if they hadn't committed the unfair labor practice," Thorley said. "But that was a plum. I'll give [URW General Counsel] Chuck Armstrong a lot of credit. When they proved it was an unfair labor practice action, that defeated Pirelli Armstrong. They were done." Pirelli Armstrong had bad management, in Thorley's opinion, as the mediator noted that the firm had made a blatant error. "They brought in a new attorney when we started meeting again. He said, 'You probably read about Custer's last stand. That is where we're at.'" While Pirelli obviously was at a disadvantage in negotiating a final contract, Thorley convinced the union they should not try to bleed the company too much. "I told them, 'You won the thing.

Don't bury them, because it could come back to haunt you. There were some things you agreed to that they probably need to turn it around. Let them have it.' And they did."

Going back unconditionally certainly was a mixed bag, and there was the added pressure of the scabs who were still working in the plant, Johnson said. At first 380 of the original 500 strikers returned in Nashville—the other 120 eventually got their jobs back—but about 600 strikebreakers working. Pirelli had made room for extra workers by implementing a seven-day operation instead of the five-day schedule from before. "The first shift back we were not allowed into the parking lot," Johnson said. "They held us out and then let us come in all together, which actually worked to our benefit. It created the sense of solidarity that we were going to do anyway in the parking lot." Working side by side with the replacement workers created a tense working environment, but Johnson said to his knowledge no one was terminated because of action taken toward scabs despite a prevalence of allegations. "There were strong emotions," he said. "These were the same people in some cases who we'd seen cross the picket line for months, waving dollar bills and flipping birds—everything you can imagine, even showing weapons. I personally saw many, many weapons lying in the seats."

The Pirelli Armstrong contract finally was settled about six weeks after the unconditional offer to return, and by September every scab was out of the facility, according to Johnson. He said the strikebreakers were laid off during a business downturn, and since they were all under probation at the time of layoff they had no recall rights. "That was one of the greatest days when the layoffs were announced and the scabs were running to the newspapers and the newspapers were publishing stories about 'Pirelli replacements fear for their jobs.' I got to have this quote in there that said, 'Well today now the shoe is on the other foot. Now they know how we felt,'" Johnson said.

The Local 670 president said that while it was a poor situation, the workers knew they had to do what was needed to make the operation a success. "We understood that that was our plant and it was our livelihood, and if our livelihood was to continue we had to make that plant productive," Johnson said. "We took control and that plant was running at an efficiency far beyond what it had done pre-strike."

CALLING OFF BRIDGESTONE/FIRESTONE STRIKE

During this whole process, the URW kept holding out hope that the NLRB—as it had in the Pirelli walkout—would uphold the strongest of the union's charges against Bridgestone/Firestone and declare the company had not bargained in good faith. If the NLRB declared the walkout an unfair labor practices strike, all bets would have been off and the union placed in a much better bargaining position.

In a negotiation such as this, with Bridgestone/Firestone seeking "turnaround changes," having expert legal counsel was mandatory, according to Schofield. "You've got to have your ducks lined up, so that by the time you're ready to go, you know what you have to do and hopefully you can do it and hopefully you can do it well enough so nobody can get you rapped with an unfair labor practice charge, because that's the part you fear the most," he said. Bargaining in good faith is a basic requirement, because if the NLRB determines a company has not done that, the unfair labor practice charge can put the firm back to ground zero. "That was a particularly touchy subject with us because the union wasn't bargaining with us," Schofield said. "We bargained with ourselves from March until July when the union finally struck. We would fall back on our positions, we would change our positions. We had to be able to demonstrate to the NLRB that we had not gone in, put a set of proposals on the table, and failed to move from our initial position. But if the other side isn't bargaining with you, then in order to make that demonstration you've got to kind of bargain with yourself. You need to change your positions, back off your positions, move here, move there, to be able to show that you have always been willing to make changes to your positions."

Ramsey also emphasized to the union over and over again that this was what the company needed to accomplish, all laid out in dollars and cents. Then he explained the company's ideas on how to get to that financial goal. In fact, if the union gave Bridgestone/Firestone everything it asked for the company actually would have exceeded the final goal because the firm knew it had to have items in its proposals it could throw away along the road. "And Ramsey would say to the union: 'But this is just one group of people's ideas as to how to accomplish our objective. Give us yours.' But they didn't," according to Schofield.

The respective legal counsels also had to make a lot of judgment calls along the way, given the fluid nature of labor laws and the possibility of the case taking as long as a decade to decide. As the years go by, the administration in Washington can change and new people get named to the NLRB and related agencies. There can be different faces interpreting the law on the Supreme Court. Most times long-running cases are settled by the parties, so no one knows for sure what the outcome would have been, and there was therefore no case law for the attorney to look up in a book to get easy answers to questions. "So the person who is going to call the legal shots has to wake up today and look at the briefs he was given last night, and he's got to read those things and as things are happening today make his guess what should the company or what should the union do," Schofield said. "We were fortunate in those situations that we had good legal advice."

Word came that the NLRB apparently agreed Bridgestone/Firestone met the requirements of lawful bargaining, because the labor board decided against upholding unfair labor accusations against the company, despite the fact that government attorneys had previously told the firm's counsel that "we think we can nail your ass," according to Schofield.

The NLRB ruling increased the pressure for the URW to end its strike. By then it was May 1995 and the one-year anniversary of the strike was about two months away (table 10.1). With permanent replacements and cross-overs staffing the facilities, the union feared those workers would petition the NLRB to decertify the URW as bargaining agent at the plants. Such action is allowed when a local has been without a contract for a year. Workers on strike would get no vote in such elections, so the decision would lie in the hands of strikebreakers and crossovers. But if the union offered to return to work unconditionally, those URW members would get to vote in a decertification election, even if they had not yet been called back to work.

Again Gates waited for the URW International to call off the strike. He was not the only one who wondered why the URW had not called the strike off. He had been to Washington, D.C., a number of times since the walkout began. He and others had met with Secretary of Labor Robert Reich and a number of senators and representatives. "Every time I would talk to any of these individuals, their first question was, 'Have you made an offer to return to work?'" Gates said. "The next question would be, 'Why not?'" These outsiders reasoned that the URW members needed to protect

Table 10.1 War of 94 Status

DES MOINES, IOWA	NOBLESVILLE, IND.
1,355 originally on strike	322 originally on strike
865 still on strike	269 still on strike
346 crossed picket line	29 crossed picket line
144 retired	24 retired
DECATUR, ILL.	**AKRON, OHIO**
1,206 originally on strike	153 originally on strike
685 offered to return to work	135 offered to return to work
315 crossed picket line	112 had been called back
206 retired	16 retired
OKLAHOMA CITY, OKLA.	**TOTAL FOR ALL 5 LOCATIONS**
1,005 originally on strike	4,041 originally on strike
441 still on strike	1,575 still on strike
551 crossed picket line	1,241 crossed picket line
13 retired	403 retired
	820 offered unconditionally to return to work
	112 called back

Source: *Des Moines [Iowa] Register.*

their jobs—that it was obvious they could not win the strike from the out-side. They needed to get back in the plant and try to get control. "It was the same way when we met with the attorneys from the USWA before the merger ever took place," Gates said. "There was a lot of intelligent people wondering why we hadn't gone back to work."

By this point in the strike, the URW's solidarity was greatly weakened. Of the original 4,200 strikers, 1,241 had crossed the picket line, another 405 had retired, and about 120 at Akron Local 7 already had surrendered. Gates's position was that it was time to go back. Others agreed but were not ready to take action. He told them he had a membership meeting coming up and he would ask them to decide whether or not to call off the strike. "It was one of the hardest things I've ever had to go through," Gates said. "The fact that we weren't going back together. We had to stop the bleeding, and the bleeding was our people crossing the picket line and we had to put a stop to it." To do that meant abandoning the strike and offering to return to work, an action Local 713 took by a 2 to 1 majority on May 7, 1995. By doing that, the local ensured that the only way workers could now go back was by seniority and by job openings. "It put an end to people running across the picket line," Gates said. "I don't regret it whatsoever. I think it was the thing to do. I just think there was a better way of doing it."

Gates and his officers had to be very open with their members about what to expect. An unconditional return meant just that. There were no conditions. They would be working under the conditions of employment that Bridgestone/Firestone had implemented the previous August. "We really didn't have any trouble once we went back in there," he said. "We had very few discharges from our own group of people. I think part of that was we told them to watch their 'p's and q's' when they went back in, and being open with them that there wasn't an arbitration procedure. There wasn't any protection for them while we didn't have a contract."

Just four days later, on May 11, the URW International Executive Board voted to approve a merger with the United Steelworkers of America union. Another ten days after that, the remaining three striking URW locals unceremoniously ended their strike through a letter to Bridgestone/Firestone offering unconditionally to return all their members to work. The URW hierarchy tried to say the offer was not a surrender—calling it a "change in strategy"—meant to keep the locals from being decertified. "We felt that all of the strikebreakers would probably support the company's positions," said URW Vice President Stanley. "And if the others had crossed the picket line, they would certainly support the company's position if asked to do so. In order to give our people who were on strike the opportunity to vote and keep the union in, the URW made the unconditional offer to return."

As the URW waved the white flag it was a clear sign that the union realized the inevitable. It could no longer win a fight of that magnitude. The Rubber Workers needed a savior, and they hoped and prayed that savior was the United Steelworkers of America. If that were the case, then maybe—just maybe—Bridgestone/Firestone had not yet heard the last from its unionized workforce.

CHAPTER 11

"OFFICIALLY, WE ARE NOW STEELWORKERS"

Delegates to the special URW convention in 1995 had a mission much different from that of their URW ancestors who met in September 1935 at the Portage Hotel in Akron, Ohio. They had to decide whether to merge with the United Steelworkers of America, a larger union where the URW likely would lose its history and tradition, or whether they could remain a small, struggling independent union and face what Coss called "the possible disintegration of the URW as we know it."

The 1935 gathering of rubber workers assembled in the heart of the rubber industry. Most of the major tire companies had set up shop in Akron, a city where the smell of rubber was omnipresent, where tens of thousands of men and women labored at tire and rubber product factories that made Akron the self-proclaimed and indisputable "Rubber Capital of the World." The delegates wanted to stand up for themselves—defying even the wishes of the American Federation of Labor—to form an international union where workers could band together and get their fair share from employers; not just better wages, but also better benefits, working conditions, and job security.

Sixty years later the United Rubber Workers—the union born at that Portage Hotel convention all those decades earlier—found themselves at the David L. Lawrence Convention Center in Pittsburgh, a city synonymous with steel. It was the home turf of the United Steelworkers of America (USWA), the union seeking to take the URW under its wing. While termed a merger, in all practical terms this union of unions was a takeover. The resulting organization would bear the Steelworkers name, with the URW becoming the Rubber/Plastics Industry Conference of the USWA—R/PIC for short. Not exactly a name for the Rubber Workers to hang their hats on.

The URW delegates to the special convention of 1995 were not asked to create or build something. They were asked to end something that had been alive for nearly six decades. Their decision was a challenging one. If they chose a merger, the delegates would in fact make the URW a mere footnote in labor history. The union would forever be known as "A Mighty Fine Union," as it liked to call itself over the years, one that was democratic to a fault and never afraid to stand and fight the large tire and rubber companies. But it also would be known as a union that in the end needed a savior, as an organization in retreat, lacking the size and resources to go it alone. The URW would be just another in a growing line of too-small unions that ultimately folded or joined forces with other unions in order to have the critical mass necessary to battle companies that kept getting bigger in an era of global consolidation.

The delegates had to look beyond tradition and history. While most URW members probably would have preferred that the URW survive— and thrive—as a stand-alone entity, they had to face reality. URW membership had fallen from a healthy 194,000 members in 1974 to less than 100,000 by the time of the merger convention. The 1994 strike busted the URW's strike fund in a matter of weeks. The union lacked the strength and resources to bring one company to a standstill, let alone the entire industry.

So the pragmatic delegates supporting the merger with the Steelworkers knew that while history was nice, the URW needed to be part of a union with the money, size, and resources necessary not only to provide basic services to members, but also to take on companies when needed. They knew they must not base their decision on the events of the past, but act for the benefit of the next generation of hourly workers in the tire and rubber industry. And the Steelworkers union was the most palatable choice to come before the URW.

The journey to the URW special convention was both agonizingly long and jarringly quick. The URW had talked merger on and off for twenty-five years, sometimes seriously and sometimes not. On this occasion the timing was right. The bitter fight against Bridgestone/Firestone and the other tire makers cost the URW roughly $20 million in strike benefits and other expenses, according to Coss. So the union's coffers were drained and in need of a cash infusion. It had been apparent for years to URW officials that there was no place in labor for small unions. "I thought we should merge for a number of years," said former URW President Mike Stone. "Smaller unions can't survive anymore. You spend all your time servicing locals and you can't take on fights like the one against Bridgestone/Firestone."

Enter the United Steelworkers of America. The Pittsburgh-based union had membership of nearly six hundred thousand, boasted a strike fund of $166 million, and prided itself on taking the fight to international companies. When Coss attended the February 1995 meeting of the industrial unions of the AFL-CIO, he sensed a different reception than in the past. At these meetings, leaders of other unions would be supportive and sympathetic toward the URW's plight in its still-raging battle with Bridgestone/Firestone, which by that time had begun hiring permanent replacements. A number of these other industrial unions donated money to support some of the striking URW locals, but their approach to Coss definitely had changed. Prior to the War of '94, the URW was a sought-after merger partner. "Before this, of course, we were the plum," Coss said. "Everybody wanted us because we were a good, solid group. We had as good a wages and benefits as anybody in industry overall; we were well organized and were a good industrial group where most of the benefits were supplied by the employer." But now the big rush of union leaders wanting to test the waters of merger ceased.

The lone exception was USWA President George Becker, who came forward and sought out Coss at the meetings. He singled out the URW president and told Coss all his union would do to help out the Rubber Workers in its fight with Bridgestone/Firestone, and all of this without once mentioning merger. So Coss took it upon himself, without informing anyone else in the URW, to approach Becker. "I went over and I sat down and said, 'George, now I haven't discussed this with anybody else, but I'd like to know what your feelings are if we at least looked at a merger,'" Coss said. "He was so happy. He's pretty laid back but he was just so enthusiastic."

Becker brought Coss in for talks shortly thereafter, and Coss then took the matter to the URW Executive Board. Coss cautioned board members that if they wanted to go forward with discussions, they had better be serious about it. There was to be no more teasing and then pulling out—as had happened with previous merger negotiations—because at this juncture the URW no longer could control its own destiny. By this point in Coss's tenure, the URW already had discussed potential mergers with no fewer than three unions. This time Coss knew his union could not afford to waste time. "No union of a hundred thousand has the numbers and resources to be totally effective in the world today," he said. So Coss told the URW Executive Board this set of merger negotiations had to be different; there had to be a certain sense of urgency.

The Executive Board took Coss's urging to heart on March 16, 1995, unanimously passing a strongly worded motion to pursue the merger. The motion said to "put out an extensive effort to looking into the merger with the United Steelworkers of America. . . . Hold meetings that are necessary and do not put off." URW Vice President Mike Stanley, as merger committee chairman, was the URW's point man in working out the details with the USWA. "The charge was to sit down and work out the best arrangement and document for a good merger," Stanley said. He saw many benefits to joining with the Steelworkers outside of the USWA's $166 million strike fund. "The Steelworkers have a lot of strong, good experience with corporate campaigns and strikes carried across the ocean," Stanley said.

Coss admitted later he had ulterior motives for naming Stanley to chair the committee. By that time friction between the top two URW officers had become almost unbearable. Stanley, in fact, already had privately decided not to run with Coss again when the URW chose its officers in 1996. "I figured he'd have to more or less operate openly on [the merger] because Mike was pretty well known for leaving his options open both ways on things," Coss said. "I figured the best thing to do was have him directly involved. Then he's either going to have to be for it or against it." Of course, taking that argument the other way, some URW insiders said it left Coss an out: If the merger failed—as the other potential mergers had—then he would have Stanley, as merger committee chairman, to blame as a ready scapegoat.

The Steelworkers did have a lot to offer besides the strike fund, although it was the available cash that grabbed the attention of the Bridgestone/Firestone workers who had been on strike and had seen their employer give most of their jobs to strikebreakers. The USWA proposal set up the Rubber/Plastics Industry Conference, with officials elected directly from the conference; allowed the URW locals to keep bylaws and dues in effect for five years; and assured URW staff members that they could keep their jobs in their present location for five years.

Coss wanted to make sure that what derailed other potential mergers did not happen again. Over the years, the URW got at least to the discussion stage on mergers with eight or nine different unions, but never could nail down a deal. The talks normally bogged down on one issue: officer structure. Union officers who were in control wanted to stay that way. So at first the Rubber Workers generally limited negotiations to smaller unions with the clear intent that the URW be the controlling organization. "But for the same reasons the URW never talked with larger unions, these [discussions with smaller unions] didn't work out," Coss said. The URW had such talks with the similar-sized Oil, Chemical, and Atomic Workers union in the mid-1970s and again in 1993, and with the smaller International Chemical Workers Union. Other unions considered from time to time included the International Union of Electronic Workers (in the early '80s and again right before talking to the USWA) and the United Auto Workers (also in the early '80s). The Auto Workers talks failed because URW members feared they would completely lose their identity in the massive UAW, an argument that also surfaced in the Steelworkers talks.

But as discussions between the URW and Steelworkers moved first from the USWA helping out in the fight against multinational Bridgestone/Firestone to serious merger negotiations, Coss liked what he saw more and more. "Once we began to strategize, we found [the USWA] really is the premier labor organization in North America. The Auto Workers are bigger, but the Steelworkers are more active in the area of organizing. They do it very intelligently. They don't use the old style of going in and calling names."

Coss also said there was a similarity in the two unions' approaches to the globalization of industry. The tire market, in fact, was a perfect example of what U.S.-based labor organizations had to deal with in the 1990s. By 1995 all the top U.S. tire manufacturers except for Goodyear and Cooper Tire had been purchased by foreign companies. The Rubber Workers union increasingly had to negotiate with management whose first priority was to overseas shareholders and employees. The USWA, likewise, had gone through some difficult times. Its membership had dwindled from 1.2 million in 1972 to 570,000 in January 1995. The Steelworkers, however, diversified in an attempt to maintain a high level of members as its core base of actual "steel" workers withered. In 1994, the USWA published a breakdown of membership titled "We Are Everybody's Union," trying to show how the union had branched out. The statistics showed that 44 percent of its members still worked in either primary metal industries or fabricated metal products, with another 7 percent in metal mining. But a variety of industries accounted for the balance of membership. No fewer than nine non-steel industries accounted for anywhere from 2 to 9 percent. The USWA also had bolstered itself with seven previous mergers in its history.

"Anyone who has any outlook on labor knows the labor movement has to consolidate and expand," Coss said. "All factors lead to we have to get bigger."

Labor analysts for the most part gave a "thumbs up" to this marriage of unions, although they acknowledged a number of negative events led to the merger. Some called it a "marriage of convenience" as both unions had taken incredible blows the prior two decades because of industry restructuring and increased international competition. "Basically, the URW is now a union with no options. A merger will provide strength for the URW because the Steelworkers are a very sophisticated union which has bargained with various-size companies in the past," said Greg Tarpinian, executive director of the nonprofit union consulting firm Labor Research Association of Ohio.

It was clear the URW would lose its identity and sense of history, leading to much of the opposition to the merger from URW members. The two unions also realized that gaining URW members' approval on the pact was no sure thing. Other areas of concern included higher monthly dues and a dispute over the URW's three elected officers being guaranteed higher-paying jobs within the USWA. The three officers also originally were to have those jobs guaranteed until 1997, a year longer than if they faced re-election under an independent Rubber Workers union. These issues, along with several others, were key subjects at the convention. That sparked the URW and the USWA to put on a big public relations push leading up to the convention, with the USWA treating it like an organizing campaign—perhaps the biggest in its history.

The USWA's Executive Board approved the merger, but the URW's constitution demanded convention action. A May 25, 1995, URW news release, however, foreshadowed some trouble ahead. The release noted the unanimous support of the URW's 70-member International staff and the "overwhelming"—but not unanimous—support of the URW Executive Board. "Everyone was together until after it was put together," Coss said. "Then there was some very blatant politics played on the executive board." Three board members still refused to approve the deal, and one suggested the URW shop the USWA's offer around to other unions to see if the Rubber Workers could get a better deal. "That's not honorable," Coss said.

Coss also recalled executive board member Stanley Johnson, president of Local 670 at the Pirelli Armstrong plant in Nashville, as being "violently against the merger" at board meetings. The URW president even claimed he was informed that Johnson told another URW official to make sure they had "every policeman in Pittsburgh [at the merger convention] because I'll do everything I can to create a riot before I see us join them." Coss also said Johnson swore he would do everything he could to disrupt the convention to keep the merger from passing, and that he and Kenneth Walters, another executive board member opposing the merger, kept trying to throw roadblocks in the way of the merger. "They were going to play devil's advocate with whatever it was concerned with the merger," Coss said. "Actually it played a real useful purpose in some cases because it had the Steelworkers put some things in writing that they might not have otherwise."

Johnson strongly denied Coss's allegation that he threatened to cause a riot and the Pittsburgh police force would be needed en masse. "I have absolutely no earthly idea where that came from and I have absolutely no recollection of making that statement," Johnson said. "Ken Coss and I had some confrontational discussions individually. At worst, anything I would have said to anyone would have been that we are a strong and vibrant union, and we are certainly going to have a fair and open debate. No way, shape, form, or fashion would I have ever made such a statement, and if anyone said that I did, I would challenge them to produce it. That would be a ludicrous statement to make."

Johnson, of course, did not deny emerging as one of the main leaders of the merger opposition. The executive board member, however, said he was not necessarily against the idea of merger from the beginning. He did understand the gravity of the situation, but had an inherent pride in the Rubber Workers union. His Pirelli Armstrong local in Nashville also had been involved in the War of '94, but by this time was back on the job. "I was proud of being a Rubber Worker," Johnson said. "We had a history that I think warranted that pride, and I think our local union had a history that warranted that pride." He also wanted the URW to explore other options, saying that the merger was on too much of a fast track and being pushed down members' throats too quickly. "I thought if you believed enough and you were committed enough and that if you would provide strong leadership, that you could make things change. I was proud of what we were and I was proud of what I was." But despite his stance, he said he never said anything negative or detrimental toward the USWA. "I saw the Steelworkers as a vibrant, fighting union. I just saw my union at the time as the same."

So if either union had figured gaining the needed votes for a merger would be easy, the division of the URW Executive Board put any thoughts of complacency to rest. At the news conference revealing merger plans, the two unions stressed how helpful the USWA would be in the still-unsettled fight with Bridgestone/Firestone. "If [the URW] is still in this situation in June when the merger happens, then goddamn it, we're in that fight together," said USWA President Becker at the news conference. "That's just the way I feel about it, strike fund and all. We love to fight, we love to struggle. When [the URW has] a fight, we have a fight." The URW also took the unusual step of agreeing to pay for hotel accommodations for up to five delegates from each of the union's 360 locals, an expensive move the union had not made in more than twenty years. The reasoning for the financial outlay was simple: The smaller locals overwhelmingly favored this merger because they would not see the same dues increase as the larger locals, and URW officials wanted to make sure they attended the convention because it was clear that every vote indeed would count.

It was easy to find opposition to the merger. "[URW officers] are taking care of themselves, and the rank and file are going to have to pay for it with higher dues," said an officer at a large tire local. "There should be URW people in leadership roles. Just not Ken Coss, Mike Stanley, and Glenn Ellison. They're part of the reason we're having the problems we are." Other rank-and-file members said the URW should have considered other options, including another look at the United Auto Workers. But the UAW was even larger than the Steelworkers—leading to even more of an identity crisis—and had virtually no Canadian presence, a fact the twelve thousand URW members in Canada found intolerable. Still others complained about the relative speed with which the merger was put together—from approval by the unions' executive boards to a special convention vote in about seven weeks. To that last argument Coss countered that there had been adequate time to send out materials and hold informational meetings all over the United States and also in Canada. "When people said, 'What's the rush?' I said, 'Oh my gosh, we've talked about this since the 1970s constantly.'"

Sonny Milton, from Local 703 in Hanford, strongly disagreed. His local was in northern California, and he said URW officials called him the night before a meeting was scheduled in Los Angeles and asked him to attend that session. But Milton had an arbitration scheduled and there was no way he could make the long drive on such short notice. "I knew they were going all across the country. They didn't get to this country, and we were the largest local they had in this part of the country, and that tees me off." Milton also said he had a week or less to go over the book on the proposed merger document—not nearly enough time to give it proper study. So Milton responded in the best way he knew, by casting his local's five votes against the merger. "I voted 'No merger' and I made that plain to them. I would have supported a merger had they all met in the way that they should have and let us all know and have our input into it."

URW members from Bridgestone/Firestone locals emerged as the strongest advocates for the merger. They had the most to gain, as many of their members had lost nearly everything from the War of '94. "We just don't have a choice," said Leroy Shover, a machine operator and member of Local 138 at the Bridgestone/Firestone rubber product plant in Noblesville, Indiana. "You look at a company like Bridgestone/Firestone and you just see their deep pockets. There's no way we could compete with that. . . . It's been really tough. I just want to finish it up and retire. And it looks like we need the Steelworkers for me to be able to do that."

As the special convention drew near, all indications pointed to an extremely close vote. The URW—whichever way the vote went—would continue its history of being nothing if not democratic to a fault. "The URW is a tough bargaining union," Becker said before the convention. "We're an organizing union. I think it's a good match. I know if it were a 50 percent majority, it would go. We're really struggling with the two-thirds."

And it was that question of whether the merger actually needed a two-thirds vote that proved to be *the* question of the convention.

STARTING THE DEBATE EARLY

When the URW and USWA held informational meetings across the United States and Canada trying to sell the merger, one constant in their message was that the marriage would need a two-thirds vote of convention delegates. That clearly was what most of the delegates believed the URW constitution required. But when delegates began arriving on Thursday, June 29, preparing for the convention to start the next day, they received a shocker in their packet of informational material. On the top of the packet was a memorandum from URW President Coss to all delegates, the thrust of which was simple: the convention's Rules Committee and top officers of the URW had decided the merger needed just a simple majority. A vote of 50 percent plus one could end the nearly sixty-year history of the Akron-based Rubber Workers union.

Coss played both sides of the fence in his memo. The argument for two-thirds, he said, was it took that percentage to amend the union's constitution, and a merger was viewed as the same as an amendment to the constitution. "That argument has some appeal and, in fact, when I first considered the issue I indicated to a number of people that that seemed to make sense," he wrote. But in the weeks leading up to the convention, Coss said a number of local union officials argued that the provision dealing with amendments did not apply; that a merger was treated separately under the constitution. Coss said he studied the issue closely, gathering opinions from legal counsel and parliamentarians, and determined the constitution did not specifically require a two-thirds vote to approve a merger. The URW president then said the constitution authorized him to decide "all questions of law, disputes, or questions in controversy."

"Acting under that language, I have reached the conclusion that the only fair interpretation is that majority rules," Coss wrote in the memo. "It seems to me that in the absence of definitive language in the constitution to the contrary, majority rule is a bedrock principle in our society and in our union and it should govern." Ever the politician, however, Coss left himself an out by saying his interpretation was subject to reversal by the union's Executive Board and also by the convention, which always was the ultimate governing body of the Rubber Workers union. Coss received pressure from both sides on the issue. While most delegates strongly believed in the two-thirds, USWA officials wanted Coss to issue a strong interpretation in favor of a simple majority vote and let the convention delegates override that decision if need be. "It was so touchy, I wanted the delegates to decide," Coss said. So he left the issues up to debate by the delegates—and debate the issue they did.

The delegates, in fact, did not wait for the convention to start before venting their anger at being blindsided just hours before convening the merger session. The man who felt the brunt of their venom was URW Vice President Stanley, who really took the matter to heart. As merger committee chairman, the URW's number two officer had traveled extensively to locals and district meetings trying to convince the membership the URW needed this merger.

Vice President Mike Stanley's speech announcing he was "flipping" sides to support a vote of two-thirds rather than a simple majority to approve the merger was one of the most dramatic moments of a convention filled with drama. (Rubber & Plastics News *photo. Copyright Crain Communications Inc.*)

The Thursday evening before the convention, Stanley was the only one of the URW's three top officers seen out talking to the rank and file. It proved to be a very late night for the vice president. He was cornered by merger opponents—many from Local 12 in Gadsden—outside the gift shop of the hotel where most of the delegates were staying. The angry—but by no means out of hand—group of one hundred-plus URW members wanted some answers for the sudden change. After all, the URW and USWA dog-and-pony show visiting all the districts had repeatedly said it took two-thirds to pass. The delegates in that lobby felt the Rules Committee, and also primarily the top three URW officers, were trying to skate the merger through on a technicality; that they knew a 50 percent majority was certain but that a two-thirds standard was up in the air.

Stanley took his browbeating like a man. He stood in the hotel lobby until nearly three in the morning, with the convention slated to begin about 9:00 A.M. Stanley told the lobby crowd that yes, everyone had been told it was two-thirds. Then the URW staff researched the constitution after hearing complaints from some local presidents and found this issue was not expressly covered by the constitution. So a 50-percent-plus-one majority could indeed bring about the dissolution of the URW. Stanley knew that regardless of the substance of the argument, those cornering him in the hotel lobby simply were opposed to the merger. He knew it would have been easy to walk through the crowd, keep his mouth shut, get on the elevator, and go upstairs to his room, escaping the ordeal. But he thought that as vice president that was not the right thing to do. "I felt whether they supported me or didn't support me, I was their vice president and they had a right to question me and I had the obligation to respond. The right way to respond to them was to stand there and to try to talk through it."

The URW vice president and the opposition stood their ground, and it clearly appeared to be an argument in which neither side would change their minds. Stanley, however, proved this assumption wrong during the convention's first day. As he stood there debating the point into the morning, he started to rethink his position. "They were right. There's no denying that that's what had been previously reported out," Stanley said. What Stanley also heard was that many locals objected to the procedure, that they would vote for the merger at two-thirds but would vote it down on principle at a simple majority. So he called Coss and Ellison and told them he planned to address the convention at the earliest opportunity and say he now supported the principle of two-thirds. "I don't think Kenny really liked it," Stanley said. "I think Kenny felt that the merger would pass by 50 percent but would not pass by two-thirds. I told Kenny, 'I don't believe that. I think if we get up and present this thing to the membership in the right way and let them have the opportunity to debate this, I am convinced that this thing will pass by two-thirds.'"

When Coss received the early morning phone call from his vice president, Coss was not surprised. "I just thought, 'Well, that's Mike.' That's what we always said, 'That's Mike.'" But that did not mean Coss was happy about it. Stanley attended all the board and committee meetings when the decision to go with a simple majority was made and never once voiced an objection until the day the issue was to arrive on the convention floor. "And then he calls me at five o'clock in the morning and said he thought it was only right that he told me he was going to speak against it." Coss also had another reason to be hot—a more practical one. In his heart of hearts, the URW president did not think they had that many votes. "There was nobody, including myself, who ever thought we'd get it. We thought it wouldn't go through at two-thirds."

As dawn broke on the convention's first day, Stanley's plan to switch his views on this issue started a buzz around the convention center. Craig Hemsley, a URW staff member and strong merger supporter, was caught off guard when Stanley informed him of his decision. "I said, 'Mike, you're committing political suicide.' He said, 'I've got to do what I think is right.' I said, 'Mike, they're going to cut you apart.'"

The delegates began debate on the issue soon after the convention opened, with everyone having strong opinions one way or the other. "They're changing the rules we've always used, and they're going to get this through the back door," said Don Workman, vice president of URW Local 665 at the Continental General Tire factory in Mayfield, Kentucky. John Nash, president of the URW local at the Kelly-Springfield Tire Co. in Tyler, Texas, said the principle transcended the merger itself. "It's always been two-thirds. Regardless of how you feel about the merger, it's always been two-thirds. Let's not be divided by this procedural issue. Let's look at the merits of the merger."

Other delegates disagreed, saying democracy should be 50 percent plus one. And members from Bridgestone/Firestone locals had more pressing motives for why the merger needed to go through, no matter what the percentage. "You're asking for a one-third minority to rule the convention," said one delegate from Local 310, which staffed the Bridgestone/Firestone factory in Des Moines, Iowa. "You have a job. We don't. We're out there struggling. We lost brothers due to this strike."

Stanley's address was by far the most interesting of the debate. He said he still believed the union's constitution was silent on the matter, but looked on it as a matter of fairness because of what he as merger committee chairman had told the rank and file all along. Many of Stanley's critics were not surprised by the vice president's switch. Privately, some inside the URW dubbed him "Flipper," for it was not the first time he had "flipped" sides.

Whether Stanley's change was political opportunism—as his opponents suggested—or simply the right thing to do, Stanley delivered a forceful, seemingly heartfelt address that he felt played a key role in getting the merger to pass. He dismissed the nicknames that were attached to him after he "flipped" on the issue. "I kind of laugh about that stuff. I know some felt like I was an opportunist," he said. "All I can say is, in my own mind, in my own heart, I feel like I did the right thing for the entire convention." Had the merger slid by on a simple majority, the union's solidarity would have suffered in the long run. If Stanley had to make a personal sacrifice, then so be it, he said. "If me doing what I did takes out all that argument and all they criticize is one person, then it's well worth it. The goal was to make the movement go forward and make the labor movement stronger."

The URW delegates, who also took their parliamentary procedure seriously, never technically settled the constitutional question, but they did the next best thing: They simply changed the rules of the convention, stating that two-thirds was the percentage needed for passage. By doing so they told the union's top three officers they disliked what they viewed as loophole politics. Whether they were for or against the merger, delegates believed strongly that the constitution called for a two-thirds vote. If they could not pass this difficult standard, then they would remain the United Rubber Workers. They knew it would be difficult to gain a two-thirds margin, but they never felt that merging the URW into a larger union should be easy. Many delegates said that had the measure to allow a simple majority to rule been adopted, the merger might well have been defeated. If the URW delegates believed its officers were trying to shove the deal down their throats, they would show their displeasure in the union's democratic tradition—with their votes.

POLITICS RULE THE DAY

The special convention itself was nothing if not political—both in floor debate and, more commonly, in activities that took place outside the actual convention. From the lobby abduction of Vice President Stanley, to fliers and trade booths, to outright accusations that the URW officers were looking out only for themselves, some of the side issues took on a life of their own.

Merger opponents donned T-shirts portraying the USWA logo inside a big red circle with a slash through it. One flier played the financial angle, calculating how a union member earning $15 an hour, working a forty-hour week plus eight hours overtime, would pay $40.56 in monthly dues to the USWA, compared with $29.61 to the URW, a 36 percent increase.

Supporters of the merger joined the fray as well. The informational

This delegate was one of many who wore shirts urging a vote against the merger. (Rubber & Plastics News *photo. Copyright Crain Communications Inc.*)

package given to delegates included a sheet detailing all the "Reasons to Merge." The USWA also offered tours of its headquarters; set up informational booths promoting such union services as its organizing, civil rights, and pension benefits; hosted a cocktail party on June 30; and hired labor folk singer Anne Feeney to entertain during breaks in convention activity. Feeney was the only person arrested during a march of eight thousand in Decatur, Illinois, during the War of '94. She made her own personal statement by lying down in the middle of an intersection, snarling traffic. When police approached her, dozens of Decatur motorists left their vehicles and screamed at police to leave her alone, but officers made the arrest anyway.

Opening remarks by most of the particulars were standard, predictable fare. USWA President Becker—then sixty-six years old and a longtime unionist, but president of his organization only about twenty months—played well with the delegates. "The sheer emotion of all of this brings me to tears," he said. "We fight the same type of employers. We're in a war, brothers and sisters." Becker also urged the URW members to be nosy and critical.

Stanley told delegates how tire and rubber companies are doing their best to destroy the URW in the United States and Canada. "They do not want to share with you, the people in the plant," he said. The URW vice president also said he knew the democratic membership would hotly debate the merger, and make the right decision in the end. "I believe in this membership. I believe in this merger. Success is not a journey or destination that comes easy."

URW President Coss related how Becker offered help with the Bridgestone/Firestone battle, telling him the USWA would consider it their fight. "It is a well-known reality if you cross [the Steelworkers], they will get you as long as it takes." That was one of frequent references made during the convention to the USWA's well-publicized struggle with multinational Ravenswood Aluminum Corp. and its CEO Marc Rich. The story became fable-like in proportion. Mention "Ravenswood" to anyone, and there was a knowing look of recognition, often accompanied by an, "Oh yes, you're right." The inference was clear: While the URW stood up to Japanese-owned Bridgestone/Firestone and lost, the Steelworkers had the money, power, and resolve to knock out its foreign-owned foe.

Ravenswood in November 1990 had locked out eighteen hundred USWA members in Ravenswood, West Virginia. The company demanded concessions, the USWA balked, and Ravenswood hired replacement workers and a "massive goon squad" to protect them. The Steelworkers launched a domestic and international pressure and public relations campaign to expose the firm's union-busting tactics. The USWA demonstrated at the Indianapolis 500 and the Kentucky Derby, and international demonstrations took place in Great Britain, the Netherlands, and Switzerland. The local union built a strike headquarters named "Fort Unity" and organized solidarity rallies that drew as many as seven thousand supporters. The USWA filed complaints with the NLRB, the Environmental Protection Agency, the Equal Employment Opportunity Commission, and

USWA President George Becker, very popular with the delegates, addresses the convention. (Rubber & Plastics News *photo. Copyright Crain Communications Inc.*)

the Occupational Safety and Health Administration. After twenty months and a congressional investigation into Ravenswood's safety record, the union said Rich and the company gave up. "Strikers, their families, and supporters marched back to work, having won an unprecedented victory and a tremendous contract," went a recap of the story given to all URW delegates.

Stanley also glowingly discussed the victory in his opening address, and told how impressed he had been. "I asked George Becker, 'How could you afford to do it?' George said, 'How can you afford not to? You can't put a price tag on your membership.'" Many of the delegates could see Stanley picture in his mind the URW—bolstered by the USWA—achieving just such a victory with Bridgestone/Firestone.

Some of the political issues were handled fairly easily. The Steelworkers agreed to allow URW locals five years to phase in USWA bylaws and higher dues structures, instead of the three years in the original agreement. Delegates also decided, following *Roberts Rules of Order,* to vote by secret ballot instead of by voice vote, an issue many delegates considered key. Supporters of the voice vote—mainly merger opponents—wanted delegates held accountable. They knew some would voice opposition to the merger, but vote for it once inside the voting booth. Those pushing for a secret ballot said the private booth was the great determinant. "The secret ballot allows people to vote their conscience and not just the party line," said Local 677 President John Cunningham. "You vote not according to someone standing before you, but by your own resolve."

What made the issue so vital was that a number of locals, including Goodyear Locals 2 and 12, had mandated that delegates vote against the merger. "Our membership took action," Local 2's Doug Werstler said. "If you wanted to vote for the merger you couldn't because our membership took unanimous action to vote against the merger." He was angered when a Local 2 member who attended the convention but was not a delegate tried to talk the Akron contingent into supporting the merger. "We felt that, 'Who are you to come in and tell us [what to do] when our brothers and sisters paid our way here. You pay dues to that local and they told us what action they wanted us to take.'"

Some delegates facing local mandates confessed later to questioning the validity of such decrees, and also to having second thoughts on their vote itself. Local 12's Mickey Williams did not feel it was proper for the membership to take such action. Nobody opposed the action during local meetings; they just thought it was the thing to do, Williams said. But he thought delegates should be sent in with an open mind. "Membership should elect the responsible people and elect them for their wisdom and their perseverance to do personally what they feel is the right thing for the local union," he said. Williams did vote against the merger, but not without some thoughts to the contrary. "I had some reservations about voting against it because of the financial condition of the URW and also the War of '94. It was looking bad for us, I thought. But at the same time I thought that there were ways we probably could overcome our problems. I'm not sure we were ready to address them."

Local 2's Gary Diceglio said there was no way he was going to change his mind once he got to the convention, but he did come close. "I really thought about it after looking at the Steelworkers and seeing what was going on. But I couldn't do it because I told everybody I'd vote no. [Vice President] Dick Davis from the Steelworkers almost had me convinced that we needed to go with them." Diceglio also believed the USWA was able to change enough votes to make the difference. "I still argue to this day that some of the people from Local 2 voted for it. I couldn't tell you who, but they all say they didn't. I know I didn't. I showed my ballot to somebody just so they wouldn't accuse me of it."

Coss also maintained that a number of delegates voted for the merger in the privacy of a voting booth after publicly voicing the opposite view. "I was told that by several," Coss said. "They came up to me and said it would be political suicide for them in their local, but they knew for the survival of the organization we had to do something. One reason I know this is I had so many people call me and come up to me and say, 'Whatever you do, don't permit a roll call vote.'"

Another more time-consuming debate brought the ethics and motives of the URW's top three officers into question. Merger opponents saw that their dues would climb, while Coss's annual salary would jump from $82,300 to $99,000, and Stanley's from $78,000 to $89,000 a year. They also disliked that the officers had these jobs guaranteed through 1997, while they would have faced re-election in 1996 if the URW remained independent. The delegates felt the officers would serve a year longer than the period for which they had been rightfully elected. A change in the merger agreement moved the officers' election back to 1996—what they were elected for—but there was a feeling among many delegates that this was not enough. The word around the convention center early Saturday was that Coss would offer to quit if that allowed the merger to go forward.

Following the tours of the USWA headquarters and then lunch, Coss—in one of the many dramatic turns of the convention—took the podium and told delegates he would move to put his office up for election as soon as feasible following the merger. "If that is your desire, it will be part of the merger agreement," Coss said, stressing that his personal welfare was not what led to the merger. "I made two promises when I was first appointed secretary/treasurer of the URW. First, I said I'd never lie to you. And second, I said I will stay no longer than what I'm wanted."

Many saw it as one of the convention's turning points. "I think the people saw what Kenny's position was on the merger and he demonstrated some strength there, that he was ready to give everything up for the merger," said Kenneth Finley, at the time an assistant to Stanley. "I think that had an impact on the delegates."

Delegates overwhelmingly declined the motion, saying that the business of the convention was to decide a merger, not vote on a president.

BRINGING IN LABOR'S BIG GUN

Although the merger was the topic of discussion, the most anticipated speaker of the convention clearly was United Mine Workers President Richard Trumka. One of the most fiery and energetic present-day speakers in the labor movement, Trumka ignited the convention. At the time, he was the vice president on a reform ticket to overturn the status-quo leadership of the AFL-CIO, a post he went on to win later in 1995. Trumka was regarded as one of the new breed of labor leaders. Well educated and professional in appearance, the Mine Workers president still could fire up the rank and file, lead an industrywide strike, and conjure up memories of labor's glory days.

Trumka did not disappoint in his sermon-like address to the URW delegates. He told the convention that years from now, 1995 will not be remembered for the O. J. Simpson case. "They'll think of it as the year the labor movement started to grow again, as the year labor started to fight back again," he said. "It will be the year labor started to organize and mobilize and kick some living ass again." He said unions in general, and the URW in particular, had to quit talking about the past and start fighting for the future. Whether it was battling a Japan-based giant like Bridgestone or a homegrown union buster in the United States, labor now was operating in a climate where 40,000 corporations controlled 210,000 worldwide subsidiaries, and the top 1,000 multinationals had assets of $28 trillion.

Trumka said given that situation, the old bargaining tack did not work anymore. Bridgestone, for example, operated in seventeen countries. Unions must fight globally, having the resources to strike effectively.

Unions cannot win on the picket line any more, but they could lose a lot on the picket line. When all the speeches and debate were done, Trumka reminded delegates, the merger was their decision and no one else's. "Don't make the decision just for yourselves, not even just for your members," Trumka urged. "You're making this decision for the next generation of workers in this country. Make this decision for your children and my children."

Very few unions could go it alone, the Mine Workers president said. The URW and other unions had lost members. They must find out why and revamp strategies to grow again. "For many, the only way is to merge and effectively combine resources and have the critical mass that's needed. For you, I believe in my heart that the USWA is the perfect match for you."

Throughout, Trumka had the delegates captivated, save for a small group of merger opponents who sat quietly and respectfully. When Trumka said the vote was not just about getting a stronger voice in politics, and not even just about gaining access to the Steelworkers' $166 million strike fund, delegates agreed. When he screamed that the merger was about having hundreds of thousands of workers behind you instead of just tens of thousands, they cheered. And when he told them the issue was about protecting the URW's long, proud history, dating back to the sitdown strikes earlier in the century, they stood and believed. "The URW stood tall for your members," Trumka said. "Remember, you don't give up that history. You are perpetuating that history." Building the crowd to a frenzy, he reminded them of what was at stake. "Make sure it's a strong union the next day and the day after that. You're not just Rubber Workers. What we are is union. What we are is family. What we are is brothers and sisters."

At that moment, there were few in the convention who disagreed—and that was just what the URW and USWA hierarchy counted on.

NOT SO MUCH SOLIDARITY

"Solidarity Forever" is the anthem for all of labor. Set to the tune of the "Battle Hymn of the Republic," the song shows how the combined strength of all union brothers and sisters is much more than the individual strength of each individual worker can ever hope to be. The chorus ends with the line, "For the union keeps us strong," indicating that whatever a member might be going through, he can lean on his union brethren for direction and guidance. But during the special convention there was little solidarity in evidence. The division within the URW was apparent. You were either for the merger or you were against it.

Those in favor were Bridgestone/Firestone locals, which had lost the most in the War of '94; Canadian locals, which were impressed by the USWA's strong presence in Canada; and small locals, which felt neglected by the URW. This faction believed that the Rubber Workers union did not have sufficient resources to provide proper service or enough numbers behind it to stand up to companies. They felt the URW could not remain a viable union as its membership dwindled.

Those opposed to the merger included most of the locals in the Goodyear chain, including those at subsidiary Kelly-Springfield Tire Co.; most of the large tire locals; and many of the members located in right-to-work states. Goodyear locals felt they had enough strength among themselves to stand up to their company. The big locals were not looking forward to the higher dues structures. And those in right-to-work states feared an exodus of members when dues became more than the rank and file deemed union membership to be worth. Merger opponents also feared a loss of identity in the much larger Steelworkers union, contended the marriage had been arranged too quickly, and continued to pound home the theme of the top officers taking care of themselves.

Debate took place everywhere that weekend: on the convention floor, in the corridors and hotel lobbies, in restaurants and lounges. Everyone thought the logic of his or her argument should prevail. "It's just that ninety thousand members don't have the political or economic clout to take on multinationals," said Floyd Sayre of URW Local 644 at the Shell Chemical Co. plant in Mount Pleasant, West Virginia. "The Steelworkers have that clout." Sayre also was impressed by the mystique of the Ravenswood battle. "Only eleven people crossed the picket line. Why? Because they were financially taken care of by the Steelworkers. I'd rather be an active Steelworker than a former great Rubber Worker."

For the Canadian contingent and the small locals, the merger convention offered a rare opportunity to take center stage. With the outcome of the vote expected to be close—especially with the two-thirds rule in effect—every vote indeed counted. The clout carried by the twelve thousand Canadian URW members, bringing more than one hundred crucial votes, and the small locals, even those with just one vote each, could not be overlooked.

A banner at the special merger convention in 1995 stands in favor of merging with the United Steelworkers of America. (Rubber & Plastics News *photo. Copyright Crain Communications Inc.*)

Local 677's Cunningham, from Kitchener, Ontario, remembered that it had not always been that way for Canadians in the URW. He recalled a meeting at which URW officials once said, "Everyone, it's time for the Pledge of Allegiance. And you Canadians, do whatever it is you do." At one time, the Canadian contingent were looked upon as socialists, but then people started listening to what was going on in the country in the areas of health care and civil rights. "All of a sudden, we're not fools or subversives," Cunningham said. "Almost to a person, the Canadians garnered great respect." That respect was vitally important, he said. "I always asked the question, 'Was the URW a national union that happened to operate internationally, or was it truly an international union?' It used to be the former, but toward the end, it made great strides."

Even before the convention, the Canadian district was developing a plan should the merger fail, according to Cunningham. The locals up north had suffered greatly in the previous five years. Michelin-owned Uniroyal Goodrich had consolidated two tire plants into one, and General Tire closed its Barrie, Ontario, tire factory. One option was to join the USWA as a district on its own. "The USWA has well-trained people and they serve small locals on a scale never seen before," Cunningham said. The USWA already had more than 150,000 members in Canada, 100,000 in Ontario alone, he said. Canadian URW members were not interested in joining the United Auto Workers—as many URW members had pushed to do—because the Auto Workers had virtually no Canadian membership because of an agreement with the Canadian Auto Workers union. "People would say, 'Hey, we hear you're going to leave us,'" Cunningham said. "We would say, 'No, it's not that we're going to leave you, it's that we think you're leaving us.'"

The Canadians brought a busload of delegates to Pittsburgh, all geared toward making the merger a reality. "I always felt if there were any chance of the Rubber Workers surviving and going ahead, I would have voted the other way, but I didn't see it," said John Fuhrman, then president of URW Local 67 in Kitchener. He also got a kick out of a bit of convention maneuvering by fellow Canadian James Webber, then president of Local 73. During the convention's second day, Webber quietly snuck through a motion that the convention—originally scheduled for three days—would stay in session until the vote on the merger was completed. "The reason [for the motion] was that the 'no forces' were out trying to stop the process and I didn't want to give them another night to work on it," Webber said. As the day grew long, some delegates wanted to adjourn, but found the question already had been addressed. "I knew what Jimmy did," Fuhrman said. "I was snickering in my chair. Jimmy knew exactly what he was doing. But nobody picked it up at the time, and then they got caught with it."

The relatively soft voice of the small locals also boomed much louder at the convention, and most supported the merger. The merger was about clout, not identity, to Kevin Fencil, president of one-hundred-member Local 116 at Castle Rubber Co. in East Butler, Pennsylvania. "It doesn't matter what union we're in, as long as we're in a union," he said. "I think it's the most positive thing in a while." His local had a good URW representative, but the representative was spread too thin, having to service twenty-eight locals. Fencil said the URW had assigned five different representatives to his local since he joined the union. "The first one served ten locals, the second fourteen. Now it's up to twenty-eight."

Bridgestone/Firestone delegates made sure their plight was never far from the forefront. With many of their workers still not back on the job—watching strikebreakers taking home their paychecks—they had a hard time seeing the other side of the argument. "It was heart-wrenching to be there and to hear people talk against it," said Local 713's Roger Gates. "From where I was coming from, it was our salvation. It was the lifeline and we were out there drowning." Gates also thought some merger opponents were more concerned with their own political future, hoping someday to be a URW officer. "Who the hell wants to be president of an international union that doesn't have any clout?" Gates wondered.

While merger supporters seemed low key, opponents of the marriage made their points vocally—and visually. They wore anti-merger shirts and buttons, passed out fliers, and did whatever they could to sway votes. The opponents were not going to leave the convention wondering whether or not they tried their best to quash the merger. "It's not that I'm anti-United Steelworkers, it's just that I'm anti-merger," said Doug Werstler of Local 2. "I feel we should be in control of our own destiny." One local first heard about the merger on the radio, which greatly angered the membership, said Andy Burney, a delegate from Local 959 at the Kelly-Springfield plant in Fayettesville, North Carolina. Then no top URW officials returned calls seeking more information from the local, located in a right-to-work state where union membership is voluntary. "Our members told us, 'You get a merger and we're getting out.'"

Local 12's Larry Thrasher did not oppose the merger long term; he just disagreed with the Steelworkers' philosophy. "My take on it was, I believed so strongly in employee involvement, and here they come a bunch of junkyard dogs that want to kick the hell out of some big company's ass," he said. "That was their rally call and it wasn't something I really believed in."

THE FLOOR DEBATE

After a day and a half of preliminaries, the delegates were ready to get down to business. They had been lobbied by the USWA. They had listened to speakers and singers. They had toured the Steelworkers headquarters building in downtown Pittsburgh and been wined and dined at cocktail parties. And they had argued the points both on and off the convention floor. All that remained was a presentation on the nuts and bolts of the merger agreement; a debate of the pros and cons of this union of unions; and the vote.

Going over the fine points of the merger agreement itself took roughly two hours. One report that particularly caught the ears of the delegates came from Leo Gerard, USWA secretary/treasurer. He explained the union's finances, enormous compared to the URW's. Assets were kept in three areas: The general fund had $64 million, the operating fund $15.6 million, and the all-important strike fund had $166.4 million at the time. Monthly revenues totaled $19.8 million, with 44 percent, or $8.6 million, returned to local unions. Gerard also described how the USWA prided itself on providing top-notch services, including a legal department, economists, hygienists, and professionals in pensions and benefits. The Steelworkers had four hundred field representatives and forty full-time organizers on staff. "You don't win wars with generals. You win wars with soldiers," he said.

The session also provided delegates with a glimpse of what could be their new leadership. The USWA officials came across as aggressive, showing the traits of a fighting union, which clearly impressed the URW members. "This is not about keeping money in the bank; it's about keeping powder in the guns," Gerard said. "We're firing off the first shot in the rebirth of the North American labor movement. We want no more PATCOS [Air Traffic Controllers], no more union busters, no more destruction of jobs and families, no more destruction of our hopes and dreams and aspirations."

This part of the convention also brought one of the most dramatic moments in a weekend filled with drama: the URW Executive Board's minority report, presented by Stanley Johnson. In an impassioned plea, he said URW members should not look for someone else to bail them out. "There is no knight out there," he charged. "We're only as tough as we perceive ourselves to be. If you want to be saved, you're going to have to save yourselves." He said the URW had busted its strike fund before and recovered, and stressed that the union's founding fathers had faced far tougher times than these. "I for one am not willing to give up what those before me fought for. I am proud to be a Rubber Worker." He said the URW should pursue other options, or even increase URW dues to the point where proper services could be provided. Johnson called the proposed Rubber/Plastics Industry Conference a glorified policy committee. "If we lack the same determination as our founding fathers, then shame on us," he said. "We're not near as tough as them. They laid down their lives for us. They laid down their sweat and blood."

Given his executive board position, Johnson naturally had become one of the leading forces guiding the merger opponents. But even he came under fire from some in his own camp. Thrasher said Johnson tried to call off the fight, and even claimed that Johnson—who did join the USWA staff sometime after the merger—already had been promised a job by the Steelworkers during the convention if he called off the fight. "I won't ever forget it," Thrasher said. "The day before the vote he walked into our caucus. Now we'd already counted votes and we had it won. We knew we could beat them. And he walks in and says, 'Guys, they've got us beat. I think we need to just back off of this thing and let it happen.' He even tried to get our caucus to quit meeting. He went from being the leader of our caucus to telling us to forget about it."

Local 12's Mickey Williams backed up Thrasher's version of events. "He absolutely said that," Williams said. He added that it was important to remember that while merger opponents prevailed in the debate over majority versus two-thirds, their group undoubtedly was in the minority. "We were just hoping to get enough of that minority to stop it from happening. So Stan was feeling that pressure of this great large group of people who wanted this to happen." Williams said caucus members had all kinds of reactions. Some just walked away in frustration, others thought Johnson had cut a deal with the Steelworkers, and still others wanted to continue the fight. "We thought we were going to win the thing," Williams said. "I don't know what happened with Stan. He did a very good job speaking at the convention on behalf of the folks who did not support the merger."

Johnson and his supporters, however, vehemently deny the claims of Thrasher and Williams, and said that the leader of the great minority never stopped working to defeat the merger. "If I didn't believe that we wouldn't have had them, I wouldn't have kept working," Johnson said. "This thing was worked until the last vote was counted. There were people talking with people when they were in line to vote." And the allegation that he had already been offered a USWA job was ridiculous, he said. "Common sense would tell anyone if Stan cut a deal with the Steelworkers prior to the convention, then why in the hell would he be standing on the podium fighting to get a 'No' vote?" Johnson said. His supporters concurred. "I never heard that, not from old Stan Johnson," said fellow executive board member Kenneth Walters. "I'm going to tell you when Stan Johnson gave up. Stan Johnson gave up when they read the vote out and they had that big yelling party. I knew where Stan Johnson was at all times. He worked as hard as he could."

During the actual floor debate, arguments made earlier in the weekend and in the time leading up to the convention were reiterated. "I couldn't care less what you call me, as long as I'm fighting for people in the plants," said Ray Wiseman, president of Local 715 at the Uniroyal Goodrich plant in Fort Wayne. "We're down to ninety thousand members now. If we don't merge we're going to be seventy thousand and then fifty thousand and then we're going to be gone." Wiseman was one of the few large tire local presidents outside of Bridgestone/Firestone who voiced support for the merger. Tony Carr, from Local 998 at Bridgestone/Firestone's Oklahoma City plant, thanked all who had helped during the strike. "You've been union brothers through and through," he said. "The world is watching what we do. What does it tell the world if we leave without a merger?"

The floor debate started at 6:25 P.M. on Saturday, July 1, and lasted barely half an hour. Delegates nearly halted debate after five minutes, apparently figuring the time for talk was past. The Rubber Workers were discussing the most important issue in the union's history, and delegates had spent more time at the 1990 convention debating whether to rip out non-union-made paneling at URW headquarters.

Clearly, the only thing left to do was vote.

"IT'S STEELWORKER TIME"

The drama that was this convention climaxed at roughly 11:30 P.M., about three hours after the balloting process began. Local 959 President Ken Nettles, chairman of the convention's Tellers Committee, stepped to the podium to announce the results. With just three votes to spare, the merger proposed just a few months earlier had been approved by a 617 to 304 margin. "Officially, we are now Steelworkers," Nettles said.

As the celebration erupted, it was clear that not one thing had cinched the deal and ensured the narrow victory. Instead, it was a dozen actions

George Becker speaks as Mike Stanley roars his approval after the delegates approved the merger by a razor-thin margin. (Rubber & Plastics News *photo. Copyright Crain Communications Inc.*)

that taken separately seemed insignificant, but when taken together added up to a merger between the URW and the USWA. There was the Canadian contingent finally getting the chance to force its will on its larger American brethren. And the tiny locals making certain that even their one or two votes spoke volumes. Or it was Local 7 President David Yurick, also an executive board member, coming to the convention late after his father's funeral just to make sure that he was able to cast his ballot in favor of merger.

Then there was the near disaster regarding a box of thirty carry-in votes from locals not able to attend. Coss said virtually all the carry-in votes—found in a closet by the URW president after overhearing a staff member discussing the box—were from merger supporters, and they almost did not get distributed to the proper delegates in time. There was field representative Hemsley delivering fifty of a possible fifty-two votes from locals he serviced. And that was not even considering the private polling booths, which undoubtedly played a silent but vital role in putting the merger over the top. "The merger was done in true Rubber Workers fashion," said John Sellers, a merger supporter. "There was a lot of maneuvering going on. The proponents and the opponents went at one another hammer and tongs and tried to get the votes to win the day. You could find those three votes in a hundred different places."

None of that mattered anymore. It was time to celebrate—and to start the healing process. URW President Coss introduced the URW clan to their new leader. "Ladies and gentleman, brothers and sisters, with a great deal of pleasure I present to you, your new president, George Becker," he said amid chants of "Union, union, union."

"This is the most beautiful sight in the world," Becker said, gazing into the crowd of cheering, screaming Steelworkers. The USWA leader no longer was nattily attired in a suit and tie. In its place was a "Junkyard Dog" T-shirt given to him at a URW district meeting in Philadelphia. "You gave me this T-shirt and told me to wear it the night we won. They call me a junkyard dog. Well, I'm your junkyard dog."

That was when the strange phenomenon that is union politics took over. Stanley Johnson asked to be recognized. The same Stanley Johnson who earlier that day in his capacity of executive board member had urged delegates to vote down the merger. "This has been a highly charged, emotional event, brothers and sisters," he said. "I want you to know that we support the action that was taken, and I would like to make a motion that this convention make this vote unanimous, and that we go forward together as brothers and sisters of the United Steelworkers of America." Becker called for a voice vote on the motion, and delegates roared their approval. Becker then asked, "What time is it?" The reply: "Steelworker time." And then the delegates joined arms to sing an emotional rendition of "Solidarity Forever," but this time as members of the United Steelworkers of America.

Immediately, with emotions still running high, both the officers and the rank and file started looking forward. "It took a lot of courage for them to do it," Becker said. "And a two-to-one vote is almost an impossible thing. It took a lot of sacrifice for them to do this, and by God we're not going to let them down." Attention also turned almost immediately to turning up the heat on Bridgestone/Firestone. They wanted to repeat the magic of Ravenswood. "We'll let them know this is our fight," Becker said. "We'll carry it straight to Japan. The struggle for Bridgestone/Firestone is just starting."

Local 998's Tony Carr said the Steelworkers would bring a new energy to the battle. "They went out for the destruction of the Rubber Workers," he said immediately after the vote. "Now, instead of a hundred thousand members, now they wake up and with all of this effort, they've got a seven-hundred-thousand-member union." Local 310 President Bernie Sinclair from Bridgestone/Firestone's Des Moines, Iowa, plant said a few hundred people at his facility remained out of work. "But at the end of our plant there's a sign that says, 'Hey Firestone, it ain't over yet.' And it ain't over yet."

Other companies with an adversarial relationship toward the URW had also better rethink their position, Vice President Stanley said. "With strength in numbers and the history of the Rubber Workers, and the history of the Steelworkers, we'll be able to have success in collective bargaining. If that doesn't work, plain and simple, we fight. I've always said, if you're going to be a bear, be a grizzly."

After Johnson moved to make the merger unanimous, other merger opponents stepped forward to give their blessing as well. Local 2 President Frank Buzaki asked for the right to take the URW podium seal back to his local in Akron, in the city where it belonged. "Our local fought very hard against becoming United Steelworkers," he said. "We're going to be like Harry Truman and say 'You've got to prove it.' We are going to be a proud Steelworkers union, but we will hold the Steelworkers International accountable for what they said they'd do."

Danny Bruce, from General Tire Local 665 in Mayfield, Kentucky, said he had opposed the merger, but that he now was completely behind the USWA. "It's going to be hard to say that we're not Rubber Workers after thirty-four years, but I will support the merger." Sam Odom, president of Goodyear Local 878 and uncle of URW Vice President Stanley, said that although his delegation of twenty-six members fought hard against the merger, by having a two-thirds vote it was done right. "It was done by our constitution, and we will be one of the best Steelworkers locals."

But that was how the United Rubber Workers had always operated. They loved their democracy and they never backed down from a fight (even if it was internal), but when they left the convention that night, they departed united as Steelworkers. "We fought a good fight," Local 2's Doug Werstler said. "Our people were against it. Now we're Steelworkers and we'll fight just as hard to be Steelworkers. Everyone came together at the end. The one good thing about the union is when it's over, it's over." Even Larry Thrasher, one of the hardest-working merger opponents, had no problem putting the fight behind him and looking ahead. "If I'm beat I'm beat," he said. "They didn't do anything that we didn't do. They just had more money to do it with."

For the United Rubber Workers union, its time as an independent union truly was over. Dan Borelli, who survived the frantic moments as the final count was in doubt, was contemplative in victory. "I guess when it was over and myself and other people were cheering, I was saddened. I knew we had to do it, and I worked hard to see it get done. The merger was the best thing, but it was still a sad occasion to see the Rubber Workers not be the Rubber Workers anymore."

EPILOGUE

THE USWA TAKES OVER
— QUICKLY

Under terms of the United Rubber Workers' merger with the United Steel-workers of America, things were supposed to change slowly. But it did not take long to realize that when such a major upheaval takes place, it will never be business as usual. That is especially true when a group of officers who are used to being in charge suddenly has to answer to someone else. Even though URW President Coss, Vice President Stanley, and Secretary/Treasurer Ellison all had actively pushed for the merger, human nature dictates that leaders at that level do not take well to subordinate roles.

The newly anointed Steelworkers had not even left the merger convention in Pittsburgh when controversy started. Dennis Bingham, president of Local 87 and one of the three members of the URW's International Executive Board to oppose the merger, threatened to pull his local out of the USWA. Bingham even said he had a letter from his local authorizing this action. Coss said he told him, "For one thing, we're Steelworkers now. We couldn't even deal with it if we wanted to. For the other thing, it's improper. You're a part of this organization, and everybody can't just decide who they want to go with. It's majority rules."

Bingham and Local 87 were far from finished, however. In August, they officially tried to pull Local 87 out of the Steelworkers union and join the International Union of Electronic Workers, which like Local 87 represented a number of General Motors employees in and around Dayton, Ohio. Bingham went as far as changing the locks at his union hall as the USWA tried to take control of the local and force Bingham from office. When push came to shove, however, the AFL-CIO vetoed the secession from one of its affiliate unions to another. Local 87 members, though, did show that they would not be pushed around either, later re-electing Bingham to the presidency of the local.

One of the first visible fissures after leaving Pittsburgh came between Coss and Stanley, which really was an extension of the problems the two top leaders had had prior to the convention and then during the merger session itself. There was a wildcat strike at the Uniroyal Goodrich local in Opelika, and Stanley went as coordinator of the Uniroyal Goodrich locals. The two argued because Coss said Stanley had not followed the legal requirement of telling the workers they had to go back to work or else the USWA could be found liable for the company's lost production. When Coss called George Becker and the USWA president refused to let him handle the situation as he saw fit, Coss saw it as a clear indication that things definitely were not the same and that the transition would not be nearly as gradual as expected. "The first week, they rearranged locals, and things that were supposed to take five years were done," Coss said. He also felt that Becker was not comfortable with some of the programs of cooperation the URW had developed with several of the tire companies. About this time, the final URW president found out he was suffering from prostate cancer, a battle that would take a good deal of his time and effort to fight. So when he was talking with Becker at a meeting a short time later and Becker asked him why he just did not go ahead and retire, Coss replied, "Normally I'm not influenced that way, but I've got a health problem and so forth, so I will go ahead and retire." The two worked out the conditions of his retirement. "It wasn't what I had bargained for, having to deal with the internal stuff," Coss said. "I thought that I would serve a real purpose in some of the programs that we initiated. It turned out they weren't too interested in continuing a lot of those anyway." So, with the uncertainty surrounding his health, Coss—who did beat his health problem—thought the best thing to do was go ahead and retire and turn the Rubber/Plastics Industry Conference over to someone who would be more compatible with the USWA.

POSTSCRIPT ON COSS

How Ken Coss is viewed as the final URW president undoubtedly will be colored by the War of '94. When a walkout such as that blows up in a labor leader's face, his opponents often choose to use revisionist history when looking at the rest of that person's record. Coss, for example, did lead a respectable first round of negotiations and saw pensions for master contract workers rise from $23.50 to $37 per month per year of service during his two sets of master bargaining, a 57 percent increase. He also made some strides in terms of educational programs and showed strong leadership during the dispute in Fort Wayne, ensuring that the local's members had a say in their future—or lack of it. Supporters said Coss may have demonstrated his finest leadership in pushing for the best merger the URW could hope for given the dire straits the union was in at the time. They said there would have been no merger with the USWA if Coss had not pushed for it.

But detractors look past these achievements, choosing instead to see a president who never lived up to the promise of what may have been a perfect campaign in 1990. They see Coss as the leader who in the end took the URW into a fight it could not win, taking the union to its ultimate demise. Those holding Coss in a negative light were especially passionate in their opinions of the final president of the United Rubber Workers. One common theme was that Coss was a great politician, but in over his head as president of an international labor union. "I think Kenny believed that you could work through most things and partnership cooperation was the way to do business," said one URW member who asked not to be identified. "I think once the companies drew the line in the sand he didn't know how to react to that. I don't think he had an aggressive nature or an aggressive tendency. And I think he and [Vice President Mike] Stanley were just both in over their heads. I think they had good intentions and good hearts. I don't think either one of them would ever do anything to intentionally try to injure either the organization or any individuals within it. I think they were just in deeper water than they could handle."

Tom Jenkins was one of those who blamed Coss for the ruin of the URW. Jenkins said the two of them had been friends for years and that Jenkins, a longtime URW staff member, supported Coss's bid for secretary/treasurer. But the two had a falling out before Coss's election for president, and Jenkins said he was the first person at the Akron headquarters to be reassigned to the field after Coss won the top position. "He's one of the few people in this world that I absolutely hate for what he did," Jenkins said. "It's my opinion that he was the lead person in the demise of the United Rubber Workers, and I'd tell him that right to his face. There is a bitterness there in my heart for that guy."

A former staff member said Coss did not give the proper direction to the URW as leader. "My opinion was he didn't lead. He was just there," said the staff member, speaking anonymously. "Kenny didn't do well when it came to taking any kind of advice. Kenny would try to find someone to blame rather than taking responsibility himself, which is not a good attribute when you're the top guy. You've got to have an ego for that kind of a job. Pete [Bommarito] certainly did. Pete had one of the biggest egos in the world, but you knew he was going to be behind you if you needed him. Mike [Stone] had an ego but his was probably more in check. But Kenny just let it go to his head."

Larry Thrasher of Local 12 said that Coss was a friend of his, but also thought he was in over his head as president. "He was probably the best secretary/treasurer the Rubber Workers ever had—a very intelligent man," Thrasher said. "That shows that getting in there is not necessarily the hard part. Once you're in, you're catching it from both ends. First, you're catching it from the people who voted against you. Secondly, if you don't perform well, you're catching it from the people who supported you. There's nothing more horrible than catching it from people who supported you."

Continental General negotiator Mike Polovick viewed Coss as a true enigma. "He had excellent ideas about what could and should be in terms of how labor and management could relate to each other," Polovick said. "I think it's unfortunate that Bridgestone/Firestone chose to take advantage of Coss in terms of the strike, because Kenny Coss should have been the union leader who could have brought about a significant change in labor relations on a positive note in the industry. Unfortunately, he's viewed as the guy who took it to its lowest point." Coss may in fact have been too far out in front of the organization while there were still URW members who wanted to retain the status quo of being an adversarial organization. "Where Coss had a vision of the future was that there could be a true partnership with the companies, where we could improve productivity and the employee would benefit in terms of improved wages and benefits," Polovick said. "But the dinosaurs couldn't see that, and I think they viewed Coss as weak and willing to give up too much."

Some say one of the main problems was that Coss and his two officers, Stanley and Ellison, did not see eye to eye on many issues, especially in the second term. Annalee Benedict was on the union's International Executive Board while Coss was president so she got an up-close view of his performance as president. "I did support Ken Coss and I've been sorry ever since," Benedict said. "He just led us down the path of destruction." She said there were times that Coss and Ellison would argue with each other during board meetings, and that Coss seemed to do a lot of dealings behind closed doors. "His head just outgrew his body and he just couldn't be reached for a while," she said.

Kenneth Walters was on the International Executive Board during Coss's second term, and saw a definite difference in the URW president's performance. "Kenny Coss did a pretty good job the first three years," Walters said. "Those last three years he just did not really have that fire in his belly." And of course the internal politics—something the URW was famous for throughout its history—did not help. Instead of bickering about such trivial matters, Walters said the officers should have been concentrating on what the companies were doing.

Ellison said later that he and Stanley had discussed the situation and would not have run with Coss again in 1996 if the URW was still in existence. The union's final secretary/treasurer even said he wished he had never run with Coss in the first place. "That's a phase of my life if I had it to do over again, I would not have done, even though I never would have been an officer," Ellison said. "This may sound crazy, but I never felt exactly right about going against Mike [Stone]. Mike had always been a gentleman. I thought he did a good job."

Stanley confirmed that he and Ellison had discussed not running again with Coss. "When we got elected in 1990, I think Kenny's ideas about education for our local leaders and the membership and education for our staff and all of us, and how to move against the companies on a nonconcessionary basis, that was the right way to go," Stanley said. "I think he had the right vision at that time to carry us forward." But Stanley believed that Coss lost his focus on the real direction to lead the URW. He thought the URW president had good ideas but was not sure exactly how to implement them, and that the union's organizing efforts were faltering. "There were some very strong differences of opinion on how we should lead our union. We needed to be more active first of all in organizing the nonunion tire plants and to go to some areas that had common ground to our industry." Despite these differences, Stanley and Coss still were able to work effectively toward the merger, the vice president said. "Even then, I was still willing to give it a chance, even though things had not worked out quite the way I hoped they would," Stanley said. "We worked fairly closely with each other right up until the merger convention. It was kind of like old times, like we could really just sit down and talk and do the things we needed to do."

Coss said it was unfortunate that his administration followed in the footsteps of so many other past URW officers who did not get along. He was not sure what caused the trouble between himself, Stanley, and Ellison, but said at one point the other two officers tried to undermine his educational program with the executive board. "I think Mike's idea was to get in there and work himself into being the president at some point, and he might have done it if he'd have been a patient guy. But he got into too many scrapes," Coss said. "I don't know what I ever did, but I did have a problem with Glenn. Honest to goodness, to this day I don't know why. All that political stuff. It's no sense trying to make any kinds of heads or tails out of that stuff, because there's no rhyme or reason to it."

Not everyone, however, forgot about Coss's accomplishments. Roger Gates from the Decatur local said Coss definitely did the right thing in pushing for the merger. "There wasn't any doubt there wasn't a merger with the Steelworkers without him promoting it," Gates said. "He bellied up to the bar, so to speak, and helped make that come about." As for the Bridgestone/Firestone strike debacle, Gates said that not all the fault can be placed on Coss. "I don't think anybody could have changed what happened with us and Bridgestone/Firestone. I don't think Jesus Christ could have stopped it at that point in time. That may sound terrible to use his name, but it would have been hard for anybody to make it turn out differently."

John Sellers also said Coss should be remembered not for his failings but for his leadership through the period of the merger. "Kenny pursued merger. It was the right thing to do. I think today that sentiment is shared by far more than the two-thirds it took to pass it," Sellers said. "It's easy for everyone to second-guess. I don't think it really would have mattered who was at the helm during that period of time. I think the same things would have happened. Bridgestone/Firestone was going to take us on. The others were encouraged by that and followed suit. There definitely would not have been a merger without Kenny."

Coss always received much support from the URW's Canadian contingent, and that did not change. James Webber, the former president from the Epton Industries local in Kitchener, Ontario, said that criticizing Coss after the fact was nothing but Monday-morning quarterbacking. Without Coss pushing for the merger, he said, Bridgestone/Firestone now would be operating union free. "Whether people agree or disagree with Kenny is one thing, but let's look at the facts," Webber said. "And the facts were that in my opinion Bridgestone/Firestone basically made the Rubber Workers strong again by forcing events that led to the merger."

Coss's longtime friend and ally Dan Borelli said if Coss had any major faults it was that he was too trusting—both of fellow URW members and of the companies he dealt with. "Being the right-hand man I should say everything he did was perfect, and I can't," Borelli said. "He made some mistakes in some of the staff assignments we did. I think we did a couple of great organizing campaigns, and we did it by trusting some of the Mike Stone people, like John Sellers and Ron Hoover." Coss also made strides with the education programs he started, and those will continue to pay dividends for the Steelworkers union.

Jim Warren, the Goodyear chief negotiator in 1994 negotiations, said Coss would have prospered if given the proper support. "I thought Kenny Coss was maybe too nice a man for the job he had," Warren said. "He was bright enough. I thought he had some excellent ideas. If the URW had not gone broke and Kenny could have gotten some support instead of Ellison and Stanley fighting him all the way and making every minute of his day so miserable, I think Kenny could have done an awful lot for the Rubber Workers and the companies that they represented." But because of what happened in 1994, "Kenny went out as almost a loser when he really wasn't. I don't think anyone could have pulled that out without the help. I don't think any one man's good enough to do that."

JOHN SELLERS: THE NEW LEADER

Before Coss announced in January 1996 that he would not run for re-election later that year as USWA executive vice president to oversee R/PIC—and in fact would retire—two candidates already had emerged: former Vice President Mike Stanley and Stanley Johnson, the International Executive Board member who had so opposed the merger.

Mike Stanley, by this point, had vacated the administrative vice president position in R/PIC and was appointed as a special assistant to Becker. In that post, he helped put together the USWA's Rapid Response political awareness program. But he still aspired to take Coss's role. Then Coss retired, and Becker appointed John Sellers to fill the executive vice president post until an interim election that fall. With the appointment of Sellers, Stanley was smart enough to see the handwriting on the wall. "It's basically one of these things that you kind of understand," Stanley said. "Being a vice president I know that the president has to have the authority to appoint people who he feels should be in place. It's pretty well understood. I've got enough respect for George Becker to trust his judgment on that." Johnson too did not follow through with his candidacy and ended up with a high-ranking Steelworkers staff job—a fact that did not please many merger supporters, who thought such jobs should go to loyalists who helped bring the marriage of unions together.

With the two main candidates out of the way, that left Sellers a clear path to be the new leader of the Rubber Workers as a unit of the USWA and to an unopposed victory in September 1997 to a four-year term as the R/PIC leader. With Sellers, the Rubber Workers would have as their torchbearer a leader whose soft-spoken demeanor did little to tip off his inner intensity—or his background as a militant labor leader at Local 639 at the Voit sporting goods plant in California. Within two years of going to work at Voit in 1966, Sellers became involved in the URW local. His first elected office was as an executive board member. He was then elected vice president and took over the top Local 639 spot when the president resigned.

When Sellers first got his job at Voit, he had no intention of staying at the factory long term, let alone choosing a career as a labor leader. It was just something that evolved slowly. "I viewed that job as a stopgap. I got involved in the union probably for many of the same reasons other people do. I didn't like the way things were in my plant. Maybe dignity is an overused word, but to me it was really an issue of dignity. I just didn't think that people were treated the way that they should be treated. Probably for that reason more than any other I got involved." At the plant, there were lead people who were not foremen yet acted as if they were. They directed the workforce without any tact or conscience, Sellers said. "I couldn't believe this was a culture that was ingrained in our plant. As I began to read the collective bargaining agreement and talk to people about it, I came to the conclusion that, 'Dammit, they can't do that but we're letting it happen.'"

Employees worked an incredible number of hours because of mandatory overtime. It was normal to get a call in the middle of the night to come to work—and you had better answer the call. Health and safety also were a concern. Workers were ordered to do things that obviously were dangerous, and Local 639 officers were doing nothing to stop it. "We went

John Sellers, very hands-on as the USWA executive vice president in charge of the union's Rubber/Plastics Industry Conference, addresses a rally at a Sam's Club. The union was demonstrating because the store sold tires made by Continental General Tire Inc., a company the union was on strike against at the time. (Rubber & Plastics News *photo. Copyright Crain Communications Inc.*)

through quite an evolution as a local union," Sellers said. "A lot of us who others called 'young Turks' got involved at the same time and we made some changes. It wasn't always pretty, but in the end it changed for the better. It really wasn't a case of changing that much contractual language. It was more enforcing what we had. It was a huge culture change for us and for management and it certainly wasn't painless."

The pain came in the form of a nasty strike in 1974, where Sellers himself was "permanently replaced." Although it was not fashionable at the time, the Voit plant was in Orange County, a very conservative area. On the first day of the strike the company already had an injunction limiting the number of pickets, even though the local had yet to appear in court. Local 639 had struck before, but nothing like this. Previous work stoppages had lasted just a couple of weeks or so, not six months like the 1974 strike. Sellers said the issues were quite similar to those brought forth by Bridgestone/Firestone in the War of '94. Voit came in with a sea change of proposals covering work rules, reduction in benefits, and lower rate of pay for down time. "It was a takeaway proposal," Sellers said. "There was just absolutely no movement in negotiations. They were just geared up to take us on."

Local 639 did not back down. When his predecessor went on sick leave because of stress, Sellers suddenly was in charge of the local. "We were probably in contempt of court countless times," he said, "because we were just not going to limit the pickets. And they permanently replaced us. They scabbed the plant, although not successfully." Sellers said Voit probably was able to hire about three hundred people—normal staffing was about one thousand—and only a handful of union members crossed the line. Sellers himself was sued by the company for $500,000 for allegedly "doing grievous harm to their business," though the company never collected anything from him.

While Sellers never had to pay up on the lawsuit, he readily admitted to being a militant leader as president of Local 639—even butting heads against URW representatives sent to help settle the strike. "I didn't want to take a surrender agreement, and at that point in time, before it was over we had people from the district level and from Akron who had been sent out there to resolve the strike," he said. "By then the company would not meet with me or the local union committee. There were a number of times that we were told by the International that [Voit] said, 'Here's the deal. It's not going to get any better than that.' We'd take it to a membership meeting and I would speak against it, and we would shoot it down. We ultimately got a contract. The similarities between what happened with Bridgestone/Firestone and what happened there were striking. It was a contract where we gave up some things, but certainly not as bad as what they had on the table when it started. So we went back to work. As part of the agreement, we got everyone back."

Just to show that he was able to work with the company, Sellers and Local 639 spent the next two and a half years rebuilding the relationship with Voit. During the next contract, the two sides conducted peaceful negotiations that resulted in an agreement two weeks ahead of the deadline. Despite his reputation as a militant, Sellers said he never was a table pounder during contract talks. "I've always tried to be rational at the table rather than yelling or screaming. On occasion I think it's good to show a little anger. But if you do it all the time, I think everyone just assumes you're a madman they're never going to be able to talk any sense to."

At some point, Sellers became a career labor leader. "Somewhere along the line I decided, 'This is what I do.'" It was in Sellers's second elected term that URW President Peter Bommarito appointed him to the URW staff. Bommarito had first approached Sellers in 1976 but Sellers declined. Sellers had three teenagers at that point and did not want a job that required extensive travel. "I hadn't thought about it previous to that, but we had a conversation at that point in time," Sellers said. "It went kind of like, 'Sellers, I hear good things about you.' I also was about $100 ahead of him in a pinochle game. Maybe he just wanted to give me something else to think about." Bommarito asked him to send a letter and resume so he'd have it on file and that someday he would still like to put Sellers on staff. "I think he called me probably six months before the 1978 convention, and he said, 'You ready?' and I said, 'Yeah.'"

Sellers was on the URW staff for just about eighteen months when he was laid off, strictly by seniority, as is the union way. He elected not to go back to the Voit plant, instead staying on leave of absence. He went to work for a law firm that specialized in workers' compensation applications. Sellers did not return to the factory for a number of reasons, the biggest of which was that it would have been disruptive. His successor as Local 639 president was doing a good job, Sellers had moved on, and he did not want to take that step back. "It would have been tough to not be involved," he said. Sellers got back on the URW staff in the spring of 1981, while Bommarito was still president. During the 1980s he serviced locals and worked at organizing. He also was appointed by Stone as assistant director of District 3 in California. He supported Stone in the 1990 campaign when Coss unseated Stone. Although Sellers had opposed Coss, the new URW president brought Sellers to URW headquarters in Akron in 1992, first as political education director and then as organizing director.

He and Coss did talk about Sellers succeeding him shortly before Coss stepped down. "Before that I decided that if Kenny did retire, looking out there at who I knew would run, that I was going to run. I was organizational director at the time and, frankly, I wasn't going to see it get handed to Mike Stanley." Becker called to tell him that Coss was retiring March 1, 1996, and that Sellers would be appointed to the post. Sellers thanked him, they agreed upon a date Sellers would go to Pittsburgh for the announcement, and that was pretty much it. And what did Becker see in Sellers? "I think a willingness to get my hands dirty," Sellers said. "If you know me, you know I don't do the job from afar. I don't mind getting involved in negotiations at any level—not just the high-profile stuff in the tire industry." And more then anything else, Sellers said, he has a willingness to do the job and get involved in the actual fights.

For the first four years on the job, Sellers received mostly positive reviews. "I think John has done a marvelous job," said Johnson, one of the two who originally planned to run for Coss's job. "I think John has taken on a very tough assignment to balance the transition, and I think he's done a fabulous job at helping that transition be extremely successful."

Others were equally complimentary about Sellers's leadership ability. "He's a workaholic," said Mickey Williams of Local 12. "He's done a very good job with pattern bargaining in the rubber industry. We're going to look back on John as the anchor that kept us here. If we hadn't had the resources we couldn't have done it. But I think also if we hadn't had a person like Sellers we could have washed up in a sea somewhere, just kind of going back and forth with the waves." Thrasher, Williams's vice president at Local 12, also has been a longtime friend and supporter of Sellers. Thrasher first met Sellers at a convention and immediately liked him because of Sellers's character. "John is as qualified a person as we've had up in the rubber industry," Thrasher said. "John's got some real concern for the people he represents, and to me that goes a long way."

Craig Hemsley described Sellers as intelligent, with a personality like Stone's. He said Sellers was educated and a good organizer, service representative, and organizational director for the URW. "I think he fit in real well," Hemsley said. "I think he's exactly what Pittsburgh looked for. I know they're satisfied. John's word is good. You can trust John Sellers. John's his own man." Dan Borelli, who also worked as Sellers's assistant, said his boss had kept very busy. "He travels an awful lot," Borelli said. "I think the hardest part is once you get caught into the new culture, you either dive into it or you hang out. People find fault with John diving into it and moving to Pittsburgh. John feels he had to go there to do a good job for the Rubber Workers. I disagree with that."

Sellers was not without his critics. Some Rubber Workers point to the fact that Sellers did not come from a tire plant so he could have trouble representing those workers. Others said Sellers was doing his first job as URW coordinator during the War of '94 debacle. One rubber industry executive called Sellers an extremely nice man but not the strongest of leaders. "You can't help but like John Sellers because he gives so much of himself," the executive said. "Does that make him an effective leader? No. Does it get him re-elected? Yes. Do people have a warm feeling in their heart for him? Yes. Would he be the first one they call to solve a tough problem? I don't think so."

GRADING THE MERGER

Borelli said it was clear that the merger had neither been as good as it could have been, nor as bad as opponents thought it would be. There were problems with interpretation of the merger document, and the transition was much quicker than anticipated—with no identity left in Akron, where the URW was born, by 2001. But the biggest disappointment has been the lack of organizing success, according to Borelli. "We were told prior to the merger, 'We have a petition every single day of the week. We have an election five days a week, and we win five of them.' I haven't seen that. I haven't seen an election or petition every day. And I know it didn't shut off right after the merger."

Roger Gates said the USWA has been even better than he expected. "They've been great. When I was for the Steelworkers, I recognized that it was a honeymoon. I didn't go into it blind. Like I said, it was a lifeline. Whether it would have been the Steelworkers or the Auto Workers at that time, I would have been grabbing for that lifeline." But after seeing the way the USWA operated, he liked it even more. "I think they're head and shoulders above every union that I know anything about. They're active politically. George Becker and his group, they get things started and they get things done. They push issues and they're not afraid to do battle."

After attending a USWA convention, it was obvious there was less chance of speaking against an issue, according to Patrick Warlow, from Local 88 in Kitchener. Important issues, including a dues increase, were presented to delegates for the first time right at the convention—then a vote would soon follow. With the URW, there would be advance notice on most of the amendments and resolutions being presented, so the local leaders and delegates had a chance to tell members about them beforehand, and then get some idea for members' feelings on them. "I wasn't able to tell our people about the dues increase," Warlow said. "And whereas the Rubber Workers would have a pro and a con microphone, the Steelworkers had one mike and it seemed like it was lined up with all pro people. Then they would vote to end debate. You never had a chance to oppose anything."

Speaking for the opposition, Williams was one merger opponent who changed his tune after seeing the USWA in action. The Steelworkers have backed up what they promised and fought some gigantic battles in the rubber industry that Williams knows the URW could not have maintained. "We couldn't have survived without them," he said. "I've got some mixed emotions about the Steelworkers, but it's mostly emotions. It's not fact. Those guys have done what they said they'd do."

STAN JOHNSON RESURFACES WITH USWA

Stan Johnson had a complete change of heart after the merger, and landed a job with the USWA that upset many merger supporters. "In retrospect, we did the right thing," he said. "And I know that's something that sometimes will not be perceived as a legitimate comment simply because of where I landed personally. But regardless of where I landed personally, I think if you will talk to many of the local leaders out there, especially those local leaders who were opposed to the merger, that the Steelworkers brought us what we were struggling to keep. They brought that fighting mentality, that aggressive nature, the willingness to put it on the line. So a lot of what came from the merger was what we perceived we were fighting

Former URW members know the USWA has the might to support them in their battles. Here, workers picket at Goodyear in Akron when the company announced it was sending Akron jobs to Mexico. (Rubber & Plastics News *photo. Copyright Crain Communications Inc.*)

to keep. And we were so proud of who we were and what we were and how we did it, that we didn't see it."

Although Johnson's appointment to the USWA staff was not universally welcomed, Johnson and other merger opponents viewed it as a good sign that the USWA did not necessarily brand all opponents as troublemakers and place them in an eternal doghouse. They said that Becker saw qualities in Johnson and others that would be assets to the USWA and was not afraid to take criticism in hiring the right person.

Johnson himself seemed as surprised at his eventual hiring as many of the merger opponents who were angered at his recruitment. After the merger convention, Johnson went back to Nashville with no expectations. If anything, he figured that he might suffer for being the perceived leader of the opposition. When R/PIC held a presidents' meeting, Johnson floated the idea of running for Coss's position. "Clearly that would not have been an agenda that George Becker or anyone else would have probably preferred," Johnson said. Subsequent to that, USWA Vice President Dick Davis mentioned to Johnson that they would like to have him on the Steelworkers staff. Johnson just kind of passed it off without paying much attention to the suggestions—or the possibility. Then one day Johnson got a call from Davis. Becker was going to be in Nashville for a meeting of the Bridgestone/Firestone World Labor Conference, and while he was there the USWA president wanted to meet with Johnson. Becker said he wanted Johnson to come on staff. "I'll tell you, I was pretty shocked at the whole thing," Johnson said. "I considered myself a strong local union president, strongly backed and strongly positioned—and I wasn't too keen on giving that up."

Becker, though, kept telling Johnson how he wanted him to come to Pittsburgh, and what the job would entail. "I said, 'George,'—and this is the thing that locked me to the point that I was willing to connect—'do you have any idea of the political crap I'll take if I take a staff job for the Steelworkers?' And he looked me dead across the table and I'll never forget it. He said, 'Stan, do you have any idea of the crap I'll take for putting you on?' Immediately, I connected with him. I think we formed a respect for each other. Certainly, I formed a respect for him beyond what I'd had before."

Johnson went to work in April 1996, less than a year after the merger, as one of the national coordinators for the USWA's Rapid Response political action program. A year later he took on the duties of the dislocated workers program and then a year after that he became an assistant to Becker. In 1999 Johnson was reassigned to Birmingham, Alabama, an area closer to home.

Local 67's John Fuhrman said he did not have much respect for Johnson, nor think he deserved the USWA job he got. "Every time after an election vote with officers [including board members], the first thing you say is, 'There are things that go on in this room that are not to be repeated.' And if you don't agree with any decision, you state it up front," said Fuhrman, himself a former URW International Executive Board member. "If you don't have enough guts to tell us that you're against something and you're going to speak against it at the meeting, keep your mouth shut, and he didn't do that." It irked Fuhrman that someone like Johnson would get a staff job whereas someone like Jim Webber, who helped deliver the Canadian vote, was overlooked and had to take a job with another union after Webber's home plant shut down.

But it was to the Steelworkers' credit that they did not blackball opponents of the merger, said Local 2's Werstler, himself opposed to the merger. "We've been Steelworkers all the way since the vote," he said. "If we had to merge we've done real well with the Steelworkers. We get respect from the International people that I didn't think we would, especially as autonomous as Local 2 was. They see our passion and understanding."

Unfortunately for Johnson's Local 670 union brothers, their story did not have such a happy ending. In early 1996, Pirelli announced it planned to invest heavily in the Hanford facility and put the Nashville operation up for sale. When a couple of potential sales fell through in late 1996, Pirelli shut down the operation, but paid the workers through March 1997. The local's contract had a clause calling for either a six-month notification of closing or payment in lieu of the notice, so the tire maker chose to close it and pay off the workers. "There were a lot of emotions when it did shut down," Johnson said. "These were marvelous, marvelous people, who stood for something they believed in [during the War of '94]. In many, many cases they actually stood up for the rights of others instead of the rights of themselves. Some of these people—young people with young families and tremendous responsibility—stood with amazing solidarity for eight months with one person crossing the picket line. People like that shouldn't suffer. People like that shouldn't lose. It shouldn't happen that way. It was the most amazing group of individuals that I have ever been around or probably will ever have the opportunity to be around. The commitment was unbelievable."

While Hanford got the investment in 1996, it too was closed five years later when Pirelli deemed the operation not cost-efficient enough.

MAKING A DEAL WITH BRIDGESTONE/FIRESTONE

After the merger, the Steelworkers wasted no time in turning up the heat on Bridgestone/Firestone, the URW's number one enemy and the company that helped put the Rubber Workers into a must-merge position. The USWA tried to put the pressure on in a way the URW could not have afforded, taking the battle all over the world, including to parent company Bridgestone's headquarters in Tokyo. The Steelworkers dubbed the cam-

paign "Black Flag Firestone," in reference to the racing term whereby a rac-
er is told to leave a race for committing an egregious offense. The union
picked the "Black Flag" terminology because Bridgestone/Firestone had
re-entered Indy car racing after a more than twenty-year absence in an
effort to boost its Firestone brand. Despite the major financial effort put
into the USWA's corporate campaign, Bridgestone/Firestone continually
claimed that "Black Flag Firestone" was having no effect on its business.
Taking a look at the bottom line, the company seemed to be telling the
truth. Throughout the second half of the 1990s, Bridgestone/Firestone saw
its sales and profits soar. The Bridgestone subsidiary had lost hundreds of
millions of dollars since the Japanese company purchased Firestone in
1988 through the mid-1990s, when it posted its first modest profit. Even as
Bridgestone/Firestone faced the War of '94 and the USWA's corporate
campaign, the company gained market share each year, and by the end of
the decade even talked about unseating Goodyear as the top tire maker in
the United States.

A number of industry observers, seeing the situation, figured the game
was over. Bridgestone/Firestone had no reason to negotiate. It was operating its master contract tire plants with no contract in place, utilizing a
blend of permanent replacements and union workers. There even were
some discussions that the company would push to have the USWA decertified as the bargaining agent in some of the factories, but that became less
of a possibility when the URW ended the strike with its unconditional
return. Then something strange happened. Word leaked out in late 1996
that Bridgestone/Firestone and USWA officials at the top level had been
involved in secret discussions that were leading to a tentative agreement.
When the world seemed to stop watching, the two top warriors of
labor/management battles put away their gloves. In a war that had lasted
more than two years with many flash points, the ending was both unexpected and anticlimactic.

The final historic agreement forged in November 1996 and ratified by
the locals was in itself a making of classic compromise—the type of give-
and-take that could have stopped the record-breaking strike from occurring in the first place if both parties had dealt in good faith from the
beginning. From the company's standpoint, if the continued pressure
from the Steelworkers truly had no effect to the bottom line, it was at the
very least a nuisance. Signing a contract meant no more protests at the

Indianapolis 500; it meant not having the USWA drum up ways to have the conflict brought back to public and media attention; and it meant more than three years of relative peace in its factories as its financial standing soared. For the USWA, having a negotiated contract in place was much better than working under company-imposed terms after making an unconditional surrender. The agreement also meant no talks of decertification and gave the union time to regroup and re-establish some semblance of a relationship with a company that for all intents and purposes had beaten the union.

Dan Nelson, professor emeritus of history at the University of Akron, did a case study for one of his books on the Bridgestone/Firestone situation. He was going to focus on the struggle between the United Auto Workers and Caterpillar as a vignette to illustrate how unions got into trouble in the 1990s. "But then I found this incident more interesting in a way because it seemed to suggest that there was life, like heat in the ashes, even when a union had seemingly collapsed, almost vanquished, and yet they seemed to come out of it in pretty good shape," Nelson said.

Becker himself said the USWA had to mobilize the labor movement throughout the United States and eventually throughout the world to be able to reach the Bridgestone/Firestone settlement. "We were dealing with a company that after the merger felt that the thing was over, that the strike was terminated, that everything was done by the union," Becker said. "Local unions couldn't represent people in the plants. They weren't permitted even to get inside and represent people. And I mean it was in such disarray that we had to settle it. The labor movement had to settle it, not just the Steelworkers."

Roger Gates in Decatur was one who made no apologies for the December 1996 settlement. "It was deemed a victory when we got one and I still think it was a great victory," he said in early 2000. "Some people still think it was a shallow victory." But the Bridgestone/Firestone locals won improvements in health care premiums, cost-of-living increases, and holiday pay, along with a general wage increase. "There were a lot of items that we did recover."

Gates and the other local presidents also had to deal with another pressing problem after giving up the strike: dealing with three distinctive sets of workers. Most of the Bridgestone/Firestone factories ended up with strikers who stayed out until the work stoppage was abandoned; union members who had crossed the picket line; and replacement workers, known as "scabs" in union lingo. When the agreement was reached in November 1996, the five tire plants that had gone on strike were staffed with two thousand recalled strikers, thirteen hundred union crossovers, and eighteen hundred permanent replacements. "Our members had the most animosity toward those who crossed the line, and the replacements next," Gates said. "They didn't have the same resentment toward the replacements that they did against our own crossovers. It's just a different level of resentment. They were supposed to be their brothers, and our members felt betrayed." Although there was much anger, it was almost comical at other times, according to Gates. "There were several who made [solidarity] speeches before they went back in. It got to be a concern when a guy stood up at a membership and said how strong we have to be. We'd say, 'We've got to keep an eye on that guy because he's going to cross the picket line.'"

Some of the crossers actually sent in checks to pay union dues as "core members," a changed status in which the employee no longer is considered an active union member but still must pay dues in a closed shop. Gates said the members each had their own reasons for crossing—reasons the individual may have seen as legitimate. "There were guys who would come into the hall and cry about how they were about ready to cross. We had three who went in and came back out and stayed with us. They would physically cry and talk about it. Some of them would tell about the health problems of the family and how they had no choice," Gates said. "I had sympathy for some of them. There were a lot of them who were friends. There were a lot of them I ran around with and talked to. I knew their wives, knew their kids, and some I had socialized with. Still, we don't speak today."

At the Decatur local, the active members fined each and every crosser. They had monthly trials and fined each crosser $100 a day, 325 crossers in all. And the fine did not necessarily end when the strike ended—the local figured out when the crosser actually would have returned under seniority rights. Of those fined, however, only one individual paid the fine, about $4,500. "I told the guy up front that I don't think there's any way I'm going to be able to collect it from you," Gates said. "I don't want you to think we're misleading you. And I'll tell you I don't know if the guys will accept you even if you do go ahead and pay the fine. He felt like he wanted to do it."

Some of the replacement workers actually became active members of the local, taking the oath of membership and participating in membership meetings. "We actually had one run for trustee," Gates said. "He didn't win, but he beat a couple other guys. Him and a couple others have served as elected department stewards." As the years passed, Gates said it no longer grated on him to issue the oath of membership to scabs because he knew that to go forward the new, factional union had to work together.

Unfortunately for the Decatur local, its fortunes changed for the worse in 2000–2001. Bridgestone/Firestone was faced with a massive tire recall related to tread separation problems for tires used mainly on the Ford Explorer. The Decatur plant was singled out as a source for a disproportionate percentage of the failed tires. As Bridgestone/Firestone's sales fell over the next year, and Ford implemented an even larger recall of Firestone tires, the tire maker in June 2001 issued a six-month closure notice for Decatur. The factory produced its last tire in December 2001.

Other locals dealt with the problem of scabs in less severe ways. At Des Moines, members originally ruled that those who crossed over could not vote for a year while new hires—replacement workers—would have full membership privileges. But when Bob Bianchi returned as president in 1998—he had served as the local's leader earlier before being defeated in 1992—he rescinded the one-year waiting period. "You can't keep division among your own ranks and be a survivor. You have to have peace," Bianchi said. Because Iowa is a right-to-work state where workers are not required to join the union, Bianchi also had an uphill battle to get replacement workers and crossers to join the local. As of early 2000, he said about half the strikebreakers had joined up and all but two or three of the crossers. "When we first went back the animosity was very strong," he said. "There was no fighting, just a lot of ratting on. It's gotten better, though it's far from being perfect like it used to be."

NEW BATTLES

The Steelworkers did not have to look too far to find other battle partners willing to go to war in confrontations nearly as nasty as the one with Bridgestone/Firestone. Workers at Continental General Tire Local 850 in Charlotte, North Carolina, started a strike in September 1998 that lasted just short of a year and saw the company hire replacements. And locals at two Titan Tire International facilities—one in Des Moines, Iowa, and one in Natchez, Mississippi—became embroiled in a battle with the company that started in 1998 and was not settled until late 2001. With Continental General, the foe was another foreign-owned tire maker, while at Titan the union faced Maurice "Morry" Taylor, a one-time Republican presidential candidate who liked to call himself "The Grizz" and had little use for labor unions.

In the case of the Charlotte strike, Polovick, Continental General's chief negotiator, contended that the USWA wanted the walkout to prove a point to Bridgestone/Firestone. "All through negotiations we tried to put our issues on the table, and the union said, 'We're not interested in that,' and, 'We want what we want because we want it and that's it,'" Polovick said. The USWA, he contended, played its silly game of making massive information requests, trying to get potential unfair labor practice charges set up even before the contract expired. "And just as I think Bridgestone/Firestone wanted a strike in 1994, I think the Steelworkers wanted a strike with us," he said. "Quite frankly I think they were setting the stage. They wanted to make sure that when it came time to negotiate with Bridgestone/Firestone the next time around they wanted to demonstrate that this was a completely different group that they were bargaining with."

The Steelworkers did not play much of a role in the 1995 round of contract talks that took place just a couple of months after the USWA and URW merged. But in 1998 nothing could take place without a USWA International representative there, Polovick said, and that made a huge difference. "Had the International not been involved in 1998, there would have NEVER, NEVER, NEVER been a one-year strike. We would have had a settlement." He made this claim because the company and Local 850 officials, led by longtime Local President Earl Propst, had worked together and developed a rapport that enabled them to reach agreements in the past. "One time I was talking to Earl out in the parking lot and a USWA guy came out there to make sure nothing was going on," Polovick said. "Steelworkers International reps went out of their way to subvert the relationship that had existed."

The message the USWA sent was that it wanted everyone to be part of the pattern bargaining process that had long been practiced in the tire industry until tested by Bridgestone/Firestone in 1994. The Steelworkers also took the offensive in terms of bargaining more than the Rubber Workers ever had. The USWA was active well in advance of negotiations, getting the local to have parades, bringing the union members together, and telling them not to trust the company. "They were just poisoning the relationship and priming the pump for a strike," Polovick said. Then there was the constant effort aimed at getting Continental General to commit unfair labor practices. "I've been in this business since 1976 and I have never seen a situation where everything they did until the last couple days of negotiations was focused more on getting the company to commit an unfair labor practice than on trying to reach a settlement," Polovick said.

Sellers did concede the union had a big agenda at the Continental strike in Charlotte. It wanted to expand the agreement to include Continental's other two U.S. tire factories and create something akin to a pattern agreement. "Before the strike started, the last couple of days I still felt like we could get an agreement," he said. "We were down to the short list. Neither side was willing to stick their toe in the water over the continuous operations issue." The R/PIC leader said the local had indicated all along they would consent to continuous operations if all the other things in the agreement fell in place. "Mike [Polovick] kept saying, 'We've got to have that.' Mike still had things on his list of 'gotta haves' that we didn't think were real. I and Earl Propst kept saying, 'If you do this, this, and this, we'll get our guys to move to here.' It just didn't happen."

When the strike started, both sides firmed up quickly on their positions and Continental General hired a high-profile security firm and put up a fence at the property. The union claimed that Continental General gave them no actual comprehensive economic proposal until October 11, three weeks after the strike started. The firm's December 9 settlement offer actually asked for more givebacks and concessions, Sellers claimed. "The next time we sat down, it was just a different atmosphere," he said. "What we began to see from Conti was more like what we'd seen from Bridgestone/Firestone in 1994."

The Steelworkers were faced with a far different challenge in mounting a corporate campaign against German-owned Continental General than they had faced against Bridgestone/Firestone. Whereas Bridgestone/Firestone had a nationwide chain of tire and auto service center stores that could be a focus of the U.S. campaign, Conti General had no such stores. The union—under the pledge it would last "One More Day"—attended shareholder meetings of parent Continental A.G. in Germany, paid analysts to do work-ups on the company's financial state, advertised on billboards and radio, disrupted a tire industry conference where a Continental General official was supposed to speak, and had informational picketing at tire dealers and Ford dealers that used Continental General tires.

Continental General was determined not to lose business because of the strike. At first it had inventory in place, then decided to hire temporary workers because it did not want the union to think the firm would do nothing and then just give in to the strikers' demands, Polovick said. But it came to the point where there just was too much attrition among temporary workers, so the tire company made the decision to hire permanent replacements. Polovick, though, said the move was done as a business decision rather than a threat to the unionists. "We're just telling people we're putting our cards up on the table right up front," he said. "I think what you do in any kind of bargaining, you put the cards on the table face up. Let the people make their decision based on all the information. I don't view that as a threat. I view that as saying clearly, 'Here are my intentions.'" Polovick was critical of the way Bridgestone/Firestone proceeded when that firm hired strikebreakers during the War of '94. That was why Continental General first privately advised the union when it was going to hire temporaries, then let time pass so the union could make a decision on its strategy. The firm followed the same process when it looked to hire permanent strikebreakers. "Everything we did, we did it with the purpose of making sure they understood what our intentions were so they could hopefully decide to get back to the bargaining table and bargain seriously so we could come to a settlement."

It was a cumulative effect of the strike and the corporate campaign, John Sellers said, that brought that strike to a settlement just a day before the first anniversary of the walkout. There was the corporate campaign and a change in leadership at the corporate level in Germany, along with a reaching out at the top from Becker and Stephan Kessel, the new Continental president and CEO. "From that meeting between the two of them, we developed a process and really had some productive meetings," Sellers said. Not only did the two sides settle the Charlotte strike, they also agreed on new contracts at the two other Continental tire plants in the United States, in Mayfield, Kentucky, and Bryan, Ohio. The agreement brought Charlotte workers their first general wage increase at Charlotte since 1989; full restoration of COLA; increases in pensions; and other gains for the union. The Local 850 contract was to last until April 30, 2006, which would put the Charlotte workers in line with the historic tire industry cycle. The

Mayfield and Bryan pacts lasted until later in 2006, still not too far behind the Charlotte expiration.

Sellers said dealing with Titan and Morry Taylor was a different proposition. "Morry doesn't do things because other people want him to do them," Sellers said. "He doesn't want to do what someone else wants him to do." There were a couple of times when Taylor's key people were handling negotiations that Sellers thought the two sides were getting close, but then the talks would fall apart. "There just doesn't seem to have been any desire on Morry's part to want to settle," Sellers said. "There's not a process where you can actually get proposals and counter-proposals, and then go back and forth. If Morry stays out, it moves closer together. If Morry gets in, it moves away."

THE FUTURE OF LABOR

While there always is a tendency to want to look back and admire what has past, it is vital for all of organized labor, including the former Rubber Workers in the USWA, to look forward. From a numbers standpoint, the future for labor looks bleak. The percentage of workers belonging to unions has been on a downward trend since soon after World War II. In the 1950s, unions represented 35 percent of the nation's workforce, but by 1999 that figure dropped to just 13.9 percent. Those totals would have been even worse if many state and city governments had not given civil servants the right to join unions. In 1999, unions represented just 9.4 percent of the private-sector workforce but 37.3 percent of public-sector employees. There was some glimmer of hope as the 1990s came to a close, however. The Bureau of Labor Statistics said that total union membership in the United States climbed by 265,000 to 16.5 million members in 1999, with growth not just among government workers but from the private sector as well. The increase was the best growth for unions in two decades, as total union membership in the country had dropped by 25 percent since 1980.

The downward trend in numbers did not mean those in and around labor were devoid of optimism when it came to the future. However, there likely will be some drastic events that will follow a full, long-term cycle of labor-management relations. The first part of the cycle occurs with an economic downturn in which employers treat workers so badly that, when the economy improves to a certain point, workers then feel confident enough to join a union without fear of reprisal. That part of the cycle requires a strong economy in which unemployment is low. Economists who subscribe to this theory said workers have to want to unionize enough in a downturn that they actually take the leap to organized labor at the next upturn.

Mike Stanley, the last URW vice president, said he believed there will be a resurgence in labor. "But I think what we have to do is we've got to work on some strong labor law reform and we've got to change the personalities in Washington, D.C., and elect some officials who will make sure that labor is not run over and are doing some things to help the working people." Areas in need of labor reform are striker replacement and first-time contracts. "Labor has to push an agenda where we get some guarantees that there won't be any fear or intimidation placed on workers who want to organize," he said, including legislation that guarantees a first-time contract. "Winning the election is part of it. Then you have to go in and get a contract with that same company. There are no laws that say they have to give you a contract."

Gary Diceglio said some days he gets quite pessimistic about labor's future. He sees how union members vote in the political arena and it just amazes him, pointing out how the unionists were very astute about issues, but failed to tie the issues to the politician who brought the question up in the first place. For example, he saw unionists vote against a workers compensation measure that labor found undesirable—but they still voted for the politicians who had pushed it. Diceglio also is happy that organized labor was employing a lot more educated people with degrees. "In the URW, leaders generally had a high school education and had come up through the plant. I think those days are gone," Diceglio said. "In negotiating, you'd have lawyers and economists across the table from tire builders. The Steelworkers have attorneys available. They see that education as being very important."

Starting by educating young people in schools about the benefits of unions also is a must, said retired URW staff member Kenneth Finley. "Unfortunately, labor has done a very poor job of that. We should be at the school board meetings insisting that organized labor's history be incorporated into their curriculum, so students would know what organized labor has done for this country." Finley also fears the continued erosion of the middle class. While there are jobs available, many of them are not the type of positions that would allow a person to raise a family on one income. "It's taking two people to make a living for their families, and some of them two and a half jobs, with a part-time job. In my opinion, that leads to the decline of the family."

Stan Johnson said that labor entered the twenty-first century at a crossroads. "I think the generation that is currently involved will be the determining factor on the future of labor," he said. "The decision that we make will end up being final and binding on the movement as a whole. I think we have to recognize we can't do what we've always done. We maybe need to fall back to the roots of the 1930s and 1940s, where we build a member-to-member coalition and we build a communication network and connect to everyone. I believe certainly as Steelworkers today that we are working hard to keep our memberships informed, our memberships connected, our memberships vitalized, and our memberships willing to fight. But I think we all have to do that, and if we fail in the next few years than labor as a whole is at risk."

Canadian John Fuhrman believed the worst thing that could happen to the working man would be the downfall of unions. He knows some of the old-timers who had to run through backyards to attend union meetings because they would be blacklisted if their involvement came to light. "I don't know of any benevolent companies," Fuhrman said. "I think they'd be only too willing to get back to the old days of saying, 'Hey, don't bother coming in tomorrow. My nephew's going to take your job.'" Fuhrman has spoken to schoolchildren and told them that, despite what their parents may have told them, unions do want companies to make a profit. "If they don't make a profit, we don't get a raise," he said. "I was always proud to be a Rubber Worker. I was never ashamed of that. There are people who just see it as paying dues. They don't see what the benefits are."

Gates said while unions may not be organizing many new members, a lot of people actually are reaping the benefits of unionism without joining up, because companies often give equal pay and benefits to non-union workers to keep away the threat of an organizing campaign. But that can be a double-edged sword because those non-union workers are ignorant of the sacrifice it took to earn these benefits. "What's sad in some of those locations is the companies still can do what they want to do with the individuals, one at a time," Gates said. "Most of the people don't worry about an individual's problems if it's not at their doorstep. They say, 'That guy probably deserved to get fired.' Until it gets to be their turn; then they want everyone to help them."

Some of the old-timers about whom Fuhrman spoke had their own ideas on what labor unions need to survive and go forward. E. K. Bowers, who died in 2000, had a message to those who felt unions no longer are needed. "They just don't understand what has went on and what's going on," Bowers said. Otherwise, so many working young people would not support the Republican Party. "In order to support Republicans, they cannot be thinking about minimum wage, they cannot be thinking about child labor laws, and they cannot be thinking of Social Security and Medicare, because the Republicans opposed every one of those."

Bowers also said unions have to take some blame because they made it too easy on their members. When workers today get done at the plant, they go home or to the pool hall rather than going to the union hall to see what work needs to be done. He said even some of his sons are guilty of this. "Of my four boys, all belong to a union and pay dues. But when they have meetings, one boy you'll find working there. The others work and go home. They get in their fishing boats, or pick up their wives and go out and eat. They're not devoting their time and effort to the union and they could care less about politics." The former longtime Local 12 president also had a clear idea of what would turn things around. "Workers have got to hurt again," Bowers said. "I'd hate to see it go back like it used to be. I would not want my children to go through what I had to go through, but I'm glad I did go through it because I know what goes on."

Tom Jenkins said labor must make its mark in the first decade of the new century. "I think unions have maybe ten years to prove what they're going to do," he said. "Ten years is going to make or break these unions. If we don't get some organizing done, and show some proof of what we can do as a union for the working men, then they're going to be put out of business."

Walters of Local 351 was one who remained optimistic. He believed it will just take time. "I really believe this thing is coming back around to us slowly but surely. A lot of people haven't made a lot of sacrifices like our brothers and sisters at Bridgestone/Firestone," Walters said. "It's just going to take time for a lot of people who haven't been through a lot of these tough, hardship times to understand that this boss man isn't any different than he was in the damn '40s and '50s." When push comes to shove, only the bottom line matters, according to Walters. "He's here looking at that dollar bill, not what he can do for you."

As the leader of the group that once comprised the United Rubber

Workers union, Sellers said he remained hopeful, and that the Steelworkers had been a driving force in much of the positive change that had
occurred. "We have to keep pushing ourselves to make the changes that
we've got to make. We made a huge commitment to organizing," Sellers
said. "It's going to take some time before we fully realize the organizing
potential that we now have. Hopeful? Any of us who do this have to be
hopeful and have to be optimistic. You know you're going to get a bloody
nose occasionally. You get up and keep moving on."

PUTTING THE URW IN PERSPECTIVE

One of the most persistent arguments of merger opponents in 1995 was
that the URW members would lose their identity as Rubber Workers. They
feared that their sixty-year history would be forgotten as the larger Steelworkers union put its stamp on its new adopted child. To a certain degree,
that happened.

Dan Borelli said it was inevitable there would be some loss of identity
for URW members when they joined the USWA. "I think the concern was
there and I think it was justified," Borelli said. "Yeah, we have the Rub-
ber/Plastics Industry Conference of the Steelworkers, but we're still Steelworkers. I think that given all the other mergers with the Steelworkers, they
don't have a separate identity. I think as long as we have a separate identity
they're going to be treated different than the rest of the Steelworkers."

Borelli said it was difficult for some URW members to give up all the
history the union had. "It's almost like they were getting a divorce, and
believe me, a lot of them had a helluva time dealing with it," he said.
"Maybe we didn't prepare them enough for what would happen. Of
course some things happened we didn't think would happen. All in all, at
the end of the day, you have to ask, 'Was this best for our membership and
for this organization?' If you're honest you've got to say, 'Yes,'"

The Rubber Workers were, in fact, a good example of the unions that in
the 1950s and before were very powerful and militant. The union had risen
in an industry that had treated workers poorly and did all in its power to
keep organized labor out of its factories. But with a little help from the
government, the URW fought and slowly established itself as a force to be
reckoned with. The union often appeared larger than its numbers dictated
because URW-organized shops made the vast majority of tires in the U.S.
and Canada. "The URW's almost a classic example of that group of unions

that seemingly had grown to be quite strong and powerful through the sheer will of the existence of the members that they served," said Dan Nelson. "Then the wheels fell off."

Until the 1930s, in fact, it was these industrial plants, with thousands of workers, that were hardest to organize because the employer had so much power. Then there was the flip-flop in the 1940s when labor economists determined that the focus should be on these massive plants, because one successful organizing campaign at a huge facility with five thousand hourly workers could bring as many members as one hundred campaigns at small factories. "That is somewhat misleading, though, because during World War II there was a big emphasis on manufacturing," Nelson said. "The government created a situation where it was very easy to organize, so the labor movement was inflated by the mid-1940s." Then what really deceived people—and organized labor—was the absence of a postwar recession as there had been following World War I. Nelson said that created a certain complacency that things actually were like these boom years, when that period really was an atypical situation. Since the 1960s, it has been a reversion to the early pattern where it was easier for labor to organize smaller factories. Nelson said more aggressive management, coupled with a determined effort by employers to undermine the National Labor Relations Board, has made it tough on industrial unions.

By the 1990s the Rubber Workers union had become the symbol of just the opposite: the general decline of organized labor, except in the public sector. "By undermining the NLRB, or the system of labor laws from the 1930s and 1940s, and emasculating the government, then you go back to the situation of the earlier days where it becomes easier to get rid of the unions from the big plants than from the small plants—and easier to get rid of unions in manufacturing than in transportation or communications," Nelson said.

Frank Tully, Goodyear's chief negotiator from 1980 to 1993, believed that the URW was forced into a merger situation because as a group they refused to change. "They hung onto this pattern bargaining process, not recognizing early enough that in order to survive they had to do what their whole union was about—and that was to represent the individual working groups that they were elected and/or paid to represent," Tully said. "And they became structured. They became eventually like a lot of companies did. They lost touch and they tried to arrive at agreements through this target bargaining process that probably didn't exactly suit what any of the memberships wanted if the Goodyear chain was any indication. The ball game changed and the players changed, but the URW didn't change, in my opinion."

In the end, the URW was a union that still had the fighting spirit to take on the most tyrannical of employers, but not the might to back it up. While the companies the Rubber Workers faced had become bolstered by global acquisitions, the union was weakened by a membership base that had dropped by half, as old, URW-represented tire plants closed and were replaced by new, modern facilities that the union could not organize. The diminished URW found itself one battle it could not win away from being forced into drastic action. For the Rubber Workers, that battle was the War of '94 and the drastic action was the merger with the USWA.

Still, there are many good memories for the Rubber Workers. "I think it will be remembered as one of the most—if not the most—democratic union around," said Finley. "It will be remembered as an organization that provided quality service to its members. It was a very well-oiled international union."

Sellers said that the history of the Rubber Workers will include what has happened under the USWA. "This is part of our history right now," Sellers said. "Our history is still evolving. We exist as a conference within the Steelworkers. We have the largest employer within the Steelworkers— that's Goodyear. Those of our locals who have been in a fight can certainly recognize the difference in the resources we have today versus what we had before the merger."

John Cunningham—the former Local 677 president who told the merger convention delegates that history does not go away, "It's how you tell the story"—felt the Rubber Workers had done a good job of keeping the union's history alive. "The bottom line is if you don't have the bucks and you don't have the wherewithal, and things are going down that trail, it's semantics," he said. "Yeah, sure, everybody wants to keep your history, but one way to keep your history is to make sure you're alive to keep your history. If you're not alive, then your history is certainly going to die."

Stanley Johnson said the URW members have much to be proud of in their history, and even much more to be proud of in the future as Steelworkers. "I want people to remember that given the fact that we were small, we were a strong, dedicated union that took up the cross early in the fight for workers and carried that cross with a lot of vigor and fought some tremendous wars," he said. "We were fighters and we are still fighters. Rubber Workers, we believe, are a strong part of the mix of the Steelworkers today. The legacy has not died, has not gone, has not been forgotten. It's just become part of the history of another union. The Rubber Workers are still alive and vibrant. The Rubber Workers history is still alive and vibrant. We're just now very proud to be Steelworkers."

And that really was what the merger with the Steelworkers was all about: Living to fight another day—if not as the United Rubber Workers in name, then at least as the United Rubber Workers in spirit.

SOURCES BY CHAPTER

INTRODUCTION. "YEARNING FOR A UNION"

Books: An invaluable reference used here in researching the early efforts of organized labor's impact on the rubber industry was written by Daniel Nelson, a professor emeritus of history at the University of Akron. It is called *American Rubber Workers & Organized Labor, 1900–1941* (Princeton, New Jersey: Princeton University Press, 1988). Other books included Harold S. Roberts, *The Rubber Workers: Labor Organization and Collective Bargaining in the Rubber Industry* (New York: Harper & Brothers, 1944); Howard and Ralph Wolf, *Rubber: A Story of Glory and Greed* (New York: Covici-Friede Publishers, 1936); John D. House, *Birth of a Union,* unpublished book, courtesy of United Steelworkers of America; Steve Love and David Giffels, *Wheels of Fortune: The Story of Rubber in Akron* (Akron, Ohio: University of Akron Press, 1999); Maurice O'Reilly, *The Goodyear Story* (Elmsford, New York: Benjamin Co., 1983); Alfred Lief, *The Firestone Story* (New York: McGraw Hill, 1951); Patrick Renshaw, *The Wobblies: The Story of Syndicalism in the United States* (Garden City, New York: Doubleday & Co., 1967).

Interview: Dave Meyer, interview by author, tape recording, Akron, 5 February 1999.

Other Sources: *Rubber & Plastics News,* 22 August 1988 and 16 October 2000; Robert Cruden, *Five Years: The Story of the United Rubber Workers of America* (United Rubber Workers, 1941); John Newton Thurber, *Rubber Workers History: 1935–1955* (URW public relations department, 1955); William Abott and Joe Glazer, *25 Years of the URW: The Story of the Rubber Workers Union and the Men and Women Who Built It* (United Rubber Workers, 1960); *A Mighty Fine Union: A URW Golden Anniversary History* (United Rubber Workers, 1985); Labor Scrapbook, published by the United Rubber Workers, date unknown.

CHAPTER 1. THE BIRTH OF A UNION

Books: Nelson, *American Rubber Workers;* Roberts, *The Rubber Workers;* Wolf and Wolf, *Rubber: A Story of Glory and Greed;* House, *Birth of a Union;* Gary Fink, ed., *Biographical Dictionary of American Labor Leaders* (Westport, Conn.: Greenwood Press, 1974); O'Reilly, *The Goodyear Story.*

Interviews: Dan Borelli, interview by author, tape recording, Akron, Ohio, 8 December 1999; J. Curtis Brown, interview by author, tape recording, Akron, 6 December 1999; Glenn Ellison, interview by author, tape recording, Akron, 8 December 1999; George Freiberger, phone interview by author, tape recording, 7

February 2000; Tom Jenkins, interview by author, tape recording, Akron, 11 February 2000.

Other Sources: *Rubber & Plastics News,* 20 September 1999; Cruden, *Five Years;* Thurber, *Rubber Workers History;* Abott and Glazer, *25 Years of the URW; A Mighty Fine Union;* Gene Howard, *The History of the Rubber Workers in Gadsden, Alabama: 1933–1983* (URW Local 12, 1983); Charles Martin, "Southern Labor Relations in Transition: Gadsden, Alabama, 1930–1943," in *Journal of Southern History* (November 1981).

CHAPTER 2. THE PROSPERITY OF WAR:
THE URW MOVES FORWARD

Books: Nelson, *American Rubber Workers;* Roberts, *The Rubber Workers;* House, *Birth of a Union;* O'Reilly, *The Goodyear Story;* Kathleen L. Endres, *Rosie the Rubber Worker: Women Workers in Akron's Rubber Factories During World War II* (Kent, Ohio: Kent State University Press, 2000).

Interviews: J. W. Battles, interview by author, tape recording, Gadsden, Ala., 3 August 1999; E. K. Bowers, interview by author, tape recording, Gadsden, Ala., 4 August 1999; Leonard Bruder, interview by author, tape recording, Kitchener, Ontario, 18 March 1999; Jim Burdon, telephone interview by author, tape recording, 4 February 2000; Matt Contessa, interview by author, tape recording, Akron, 14 June 2000; John Cunningham, interview by author, tape recording, Kitchener, Ontario, 19 March 1999; John Cunningham, James Webber, Alan Turner, and Reginald Duguay, joint interview by author, tape recording, Kitchener, Ontario, 19 March 1999; Gary Diceglio, interview by author, tape recording, Cuyahoga Falls, Ohio, 23 January 2000; Ellison interview, 8 December 1999; Freiberger interview, 7 February 2000; John Fuhrman, interview by author, tape recording, Kitchener, Ontario, 19 March 1999; George Goebel, interview by author, tape recording, Kitchener, Ontario, 19 March 1999; Clark Lantz, interview by author, tape recording, Akron, April 2000; Gilbert Laws, telephone interview by author, tape recording, 10 February 2000; Doug Werstler, interview by author, tape recording, Akron, 9 December 1999.

Other Sources: *Akron Beacon Journal,* 6 January 1950 and 7 October 1978; United Rubber Workers official biography of Leland S. Buckmaster; Cruden, *Five Years;* Thurber, *Rubber Workers History;* Abott and Glazer, *25 Years of the URW; A Mighty Fine Union;* Memorandum from URW Research Director Keith Prouty to President George Burdon; George Burdon acceptance speech at 1964 URW convention; *Local 80 URW: 1937–1992,* published by Local 80, May 1992; Carlos Sousa, York University history major, *The United Rubber Workers of America and 1946: Prelude, Strike and Afterthoughts,* distributed at URW District 6 Annual Council Meeting, May 1986; Howard, *The History of the Rubber Workers in Gadsden.*

CHAPTER 3. THE BOMBER ALWAYS RISES TO THE TOP

Interviews: Borelli interview, Akron, 8 December 1999; Bowers interview, 5 August 1999; Brown interview, 6 December 1999; Burdon interview, 4 February 2000; Steve Clem, interview by author, tape recording, Akron, July 1998; Diceglio interview, 23 January 2000; Carl Dimengo, interview by author, tape recording, Akron, 8 December 1999; Ellison interview, 8 December 1999; Kenneth Finley, interview by author, tape recording, Akron, 19 April 1999; Jenkins interview, 11 February 2000; Mike Polovick, interview by author, tape recording, Cuyahoga Falls, Ohio, 22 April 2000; John Sellers, interview by author, tape recording, Akron, 8 February 2000.

Other Sources: The following issues of the *Akron Beacon Journal:* 12 September 1966; 13 September 1966; 14 September 1966; 15 September 1966; 16 September 1966; 18 September 1966; 2 July 1967; 30 July 1967; 18 June 1972; 4 October 1981; 6 July 1997.

United Rubber Workers official biography of Peter Bommarito; Letter from URW International officers to all URW locals not striking, 17 May 1967; United Rubber Workers report to International Executive Board members, 22 February 1974; *Wall Street Journal,* 5 September 1967; United Rubber Workers news release, 7 August 1967; Peter Bommarito, 1970 URW convention speech, September 1970.

CHAPTER 4. NEWS FLASH:
BOMMARITO WANTS TO CURE CANCER

Interviews: Louis S. Beliczky, interview by author, tape recording, Akron, 21 February 2000; Louis S. Beliczky and James Frederick, joint interview by author, tape recording, Akron, 21 February 2000; Annalee Benedict, telephone interview by author, tape recording, 21 January 2000; Bruder interview, 18 March 1999; Laws interview, 10 February 2000; Patrick Warlow, interview by author, tape recording, Kitchener, Ontario, 19 March 1999; Don Weber, telephone interview by author, tape recording, 17 December 1999.

Other Sources: *Akron Beacon Journal,* 4 June 1972, 14 December 1972, 16 September 1975, and 14 October 1975; Peter Bommarito and Louis S. Beliczky, "Seeds of Humble Origin Produce a Tree of Life," in *What's New in Labor Relations,* published by the Wharton School of Finance, Spring 1972; Peter Bommarito, 1970 URW convention speech; *Business Week,* 12 February 1972; United Rubber Workers Research Department report on the proposed Burke-Hartke legislation, June 1972; Peter Bommarito speech delivered at "Save Our Jobs" rally, 3 June 1972, Akron; Memorandum to Peter Bommarito from Steve Clem, assistant URW research director, 7 June 1971; URW research report, December 1972; Statement of the United Rubber Workers to the U.S. International Trade Commission, 25 April 1975; Letter from URW Research Director Steve Clem to Chad Hume, Summit County

Council, 4 November 1980; *Pictour Advocate,* 24 May 1972; Statement of Peter Bommarito before the U.S. International Trade Commission, 10 April 1975; James Nardello, testimony before the Trade Policy Staff Committee Office of the Special Representative for Trade Negotiations, 5 June 1975; James Nardello, letter to President-elect Jimmy Carter, 15 December 1976; *Wall Street Journal,* 19 April 1976; United Rubber Workers news release, 23 March 1973; Peter Bommarito, statement before the subcommittee on Manpower, Compensation, and Health and Safety, of the House Committee on Education and Labor, on the National Workers' Compensation Act of 1975—H.R. 9431, 16 March 1976.

CHAPTER 5. THE STRIKE OF 1976:
THE BOMBER HOLDS COURT

Interviews: Dan Baldwin, interview by author, tape recording, Gadsden, Ala., 2 August 1999; Bob Bianchi, interview by author, tape recording, Pittsburgh, 26 January 2000; Brown interview, 6 December 1999; Contessa interview, 14 June 2000; Kenneth Coss, interview by author, 1996; Kenneth Coss, telephone interview by author, tape recording, 7 December 1999; Ellison interview, 8 December 1999; Craig Hemsley, interview by author, tape recording, North Canton, Ohio, 30 December 1999; Jenkins interview, 11 February 2000; Jimmy Palmer, interview by author, tape recording, Gadsden, Ala., 2 August 1999; Ronnie Reed and Bill Willard, joint interview by author, tape recording, Gadsden, Ala., 2 August 1999; Tony Smith, interview by author, tape recording, Gadsden, Ala., 2 August 1999; J. Michael Stanley, telephone interview by author, tape recording, 21 December 1999; Doug Werstler, interview by author, tape recording, Akron, 3 February 1999; Mickey Williams, telephone interview by author, tape recording, 21 December 1999.

Other Sources: *Akron Beacon Journal* reporter Stu Feldstein's personal collection of 1976 strike stories was provided by Katie Byard. The following issues were used as sources: 14 January 1976; 22 January 1976; 24 January 1976; 10 April 1976; 18 April 1976; 20 April 1976; 21 April 1976; 25 April 1976; 27 April 1976; 5 May 1976, 9 May 1976; 10 May 1976; 12 May 1976; 13 May 1976; 16 May 1976; 17 May 1976; 21 May 1976; 27 May 1976; 29 May 1976; 8 June 1976; 16 June 1976; 18 June 1976; 21 June 1976; 23 June 1976; 13 July 1976; 14 July 1976; 17 July 1976; 23 July 1976; 30 July 1976; 2 August 1976; 12 August 1976; 15 August 1976; 17 August 1976; 23 August 1976; 24 August 1976; 25 August 1976; 27 August 1976.

Rubber & Plastics News, 7 October 1991; Peter Bommarito, 1973 New Year's Statement, issued 28 December 1972; United Rubber Workers news release, 24 March 1972.

CHAPTER 6. BOMMARITO'S SWAN SONG

Books: Charles Jeszeck, "Decline of Tire Manufacturing in Akron," in *Grand Designs: The Impact of Corporate Strategies on Workers, Unions and Communities*, edited by Charles Graypo and Bruce Nissen (Ithaca, New York: ILR Press, School of Industrial and Labor Relations, Cornell University, 1993); Nelson, *American Rubber Workers.*

Interviews: Benedict interview, 21 January 2000; Borelli interview, 8 December 1999; Brown interview, 6 December 1999; Clem interview, July 1998; Contessa interview, 14 June 2000; Coss interview, 7 December 1999; Kenneth Coss, telephone interview by author, tape recording, 15 December 1999; Cunningham interview, 19 March 1999; Cunningham, Webber, Turner, and Duguay joint interview, 19 March 1999; Diceglio interview, 23 January 2000; Finley interview, 19 April 1999; Fuhrman interview, 19 March 1999; Hemsley interview, 30 December 1999; Jenkins interview, 11 February 2000; Lantz interview, April 2000; Laws interview, 10 February 2000; Polovick interview, 22 April 2000; Sellers interview, 8 February 2000; Mike Stone, interview by author, tape recording, Akron, 24 July 1998; Larry Thrasher, interview by author, tape recording, Gadsden, Ala., 5 August 1999; Werstler interview, 3 February 1999; Williams interview, 21 December 1999.

Other Sources: The following issues of the *Akron Beacon Journal:* 30 August 1978; 11 September 1978; 17 September 1978; 1 October 1978; 5 October 1978; 8 October 1978; 10 October 1978; 11 October 1978; 12 October 1978; 13 October 1978; 14 October 1978; 3 March 1980; 19 March 1980; 29 March 1997.

The following issues of *Rubber & Plastics News:* 21 August 1978; 4 September 1978; 18 September 1978; 20 February 1979; 10 March 1980; 6 April 1998.

Letter from Local 831 President Charles R. Denny to URW President Peter Bommarito, 1973; Letter to the delegates of the 1978 URW convention from the presidents of the five Acme Boot Co. locals; Letter from the Bommarito for President Committee to URW members; *United Rubber Worker,* October/November 1978 and December 1978; Peter Bommarito, opening speech from the 30th URW Convention, 9–13 October 1978, Toronto, Ontario; Peter Bommarito, acceptance speech, 1978 convention; Report of the International President to the 31st URW Convention, 5 October 1981; *BFG Today,* 1978; Peter Bommarito, testimony before the U.S. House Committee on Education and Labor Subcommittee on Labor Standards, hearing on the National Employment Priorities Act, Akron, 9 May 1975; URW news release, 19 June 1980; Letter from SerVaas to Peter Bommarito; *Rubber World,* April 1980; Mario DiFederico and William Jones, testimony before the U.S. House Committee on Education and Labor Subcommittee on Labor Standards, hearing on the National Employment Priorities Act, Akron, 9 May 1975.

CHAPTER 7. THE URW IN TRANSITION:
THE MIKE STONE YEARS

Interviews: Brown interview, 6 December 1999; Clem interview, July 1998; Ellison interview, 8 December 1999; Polovick interview, 2 April 2000; Sellers interview, 8 February 2000; Stone interview, 24 July 1998.

Other Sources: *Akron Beacon Journal,* 4 October 1981, 6 October 1981, 8 October 1981, 9 October 1981, and 6 November 1985; *Rubber & Plastics News,* 26 April 1982, 20 March 1989, and 7 October 1991; URW Research Department report, December 1985; URW International Officers Report to 1990 Convention; Mike Stone, speech before the Economic Policy Task Force, Cleveland, Ohio, 7 December 1981; Bureau of National Affairs Inc.'s *Daily Labor Report,* 21 November 1985; Carl Dimengo, assistant URW research director, speech at AFL-CIO Conference, Chicago, 2–5 May 1982; *Newsweek,* 4 June 1984; URW 1985 Collective Bargaining Policy; U.S. Department of Labor, Bureau of Labor Statistics report, issued 30 November 1984; U.S. General Accounting Office Briefing Report to U.S. Senator Lloyd Bentsen, July 1986; *U.S. News & World Report,* 4 March 1985; *United Rubber Worker,* May–June 1990 issue; Bureau of National Affairs Inc., *Daily Labor Report,* 7 March 1984, Lynn Williams statement on plant closing bill (H.R. 2847) before the House Labor Subcommittee on Employment Opportunities; Steve Clem, testimony in hearing before the Trade Subcommittee of the House Ways & Means Committee on Trade Adjustment Assistance, Lorain, Ohio, 10 June 1985; URW Economic Background report for 1988 International Policy Committee, prepared by URW Research Department, Steve Clem, director; *Industry Week,* 28 April 1986; Mike Stone, speech at International Trade and Challenges to U.S. Labor Relations Labor/Management Conference, Nashville, Tenn., 2 April 1982, sponsored by Federal Mediation and Conciliation Services and Middle Tennessee State University.

CHAPTER 8. A FOUR-LETTER WORD: CONCESSIONS

Interviews: Bianchi interview, 26 January 2000; Brown interview, 6 December 1999; Clem interview, July 1998; Kenneth Coss, telephone interview by author, tape recording, 22 December 1999; Cunningham, Webber, Turner, Duguay joint interview, 19 March 1999; Diceglio interview, 23 January 2000; Roger Gates, interview by author, tape recording, Pittsburgh, 25 January 2000; C. V. Glassco, J. W. Battles, J. R. Countryman, joint interview by author, tape recording, Gadsden, 3 August 1999; Hemsley interview, 30 December 1999; H. W. Hudson, interview by author, tape recording, Gadsden, 2 August 1999; Jenkins interview, 11 February 2000; Nelson Lichtenstein, telephone interview by author, 28 August 1998; James A. Matthews III, telephone interview by author, 31 August 1998; Dave Meyer, interview by author, tape recording, Akron, 29 January 1999; Harry Millis, interview by author, 1996; Sonny Milton, telephone interview by author, tape recording, 10 February 2000; Daniel Nelson, interview by author, tape recording, Akron, 4 August

1998; Polovick interview, 22 April 2000; Sellers interview, 8 February 2000; Stone interview, 24 July 1998; Mike Stone, interview by author, 1996; Morry Taylor, telephone interview by author, 28 August 1998; David Thorley, interview by author, tape recording, Stow, Ohio, 11 February 2000; Frank Tully, interview by author, tape recording, Akron, 15 February 2000; Warlow interview, 19 March 1999; Jim Warren, interview by author, tape recording, Akron, 14 February 2000; Weber interview, 17 December 1999; Williams interview, 21 December 1999.

Other Sources: The following issues of *Rubber & Plastics News:* 7 December 1981; 26 July 1982; 11 March 1985; 1 February 1988; 8 February 1988; 22 February 1988; 25 April 1988; 9 May 1988; 23 May 1988; 4 October 1993; 12 August 1996; 20 September 1999.

Akron Beacon Journal, 29 March 1987, 14 May 1988, and 17 May 1988; Charles Jeszeck, "Structural Change in Collective Bargaining: The U.S. Tire Industry," in *Industrial Relations* 25, no. 3 (Fall 1986); URW 1985 Collective Bargaining Policy; *United Rubber Worker,* January-February 1985 and November-December 1989; Firestone company news release, 3 February 1988; [Cleveland] *Plain Dealer,* 16 May 1988.

CHAPTER 9. THE PERFECT CAMPAIGN:
KEN COSS TAKES OVER

Interviews: Bianchi interview, 26 January 2000; Borelli interview, 8 December 1999; Brown interview, 6 December 1999; Kenneth Coss, interview by author, 2 July 1995, Pittsburgh; Coss interviews, 7 December 1999, 15 December 1999, and 22 December 1999; Cunningham interview, 19 March 1999; Diceglio interview, 23 January 2000; Finley interview, 19 April 1999; Hemsley interview, 30 December 1999; Sellers interview, 8 February 2000; Stanley interview, 21 December 1999; Mike Stone, interview by author, Akron, 1990; Stone interview, 24 July 1998; Sam Torrence, interview by author, Akron, 1991; Kenneth Walters, telephone interview with author, tape recording, 2 February 2000; Williams interview, 21 December 1999.

Other sources: The following issues of *Rubber & Plastics News:* 20 August 1990; 1 October 1990; 8 October 1990; 21 January 1991; 11 February 1991; 18 March 1991; 29 April 1991; 13 May 1991; 20 May 1991; 7 October 1991; 15 February 1993; 26 July 1993; 12 April 1993; 13 September 1993; 27 September 1993; 4 October 1993; 11 October 1993; 15 November 1993; 27 December 1993; 21 February 1994; 28 February 1994.

Akron Beacon Journal: 20 August 1990 and 3 May 1993; *United Rubber Worker,* March-April 1987, May-June 1993, and September-October 1993; Letter signed by seven of the eleven URW International Executive Board members: Mary Boley, Larry Bridges, Dennis Brommer, Danny Bruce, Barbara Carter, David Jones, and J. Michael Stanley, 12 March 1990; Letter from Coss For URW International President Committee, 12 July 1990; Report of URW International officers to 35th URW Convention, 1993; United Rubber Workers Directory, January 1994.

CHAPTER 10. THE WAR OF '94:
THE UNWINNABLE BATTLE

Interviews: Borelli interview, 8 December 1999; Brown interview, 6 December 1999; Coss interview, 22 December 1999; Kenneth Coss, telephone interview by author, tape recording, 27 December 1999; Diceglio interview, 23 January 2000; Gates interview, 25 January 2000; Stanley Johnson, telephone interview with author, tape recording, 22 January 2000; Meyer interview, 5 February 1999; Milton interview, 10 February 2000; Polovick interview, 22 April 2000; Charles Ramsey, interview with author, Nashville, Tenn., November 1994; Peter Schofield, interview by author, tape recording, Cleveland Heights, Ohio, 16 June 2000; Sellers interview, 8 February 2000; J. Michael Stanley, telephone interview by author, tape recording, 23 December 1999; Stone interview, 24 July 1998; Thorley interview, 11 February 2000; Warren interview, 14 February 2000.

Other Sources: The following issues of *Rubber & Plastics News:* 7 October 1991; 22 June 1992; 6 July 1992; 27 July 1992; 7 December 1992; 2 May 1994; 27 June 1994; 12 September 1994; 21 November 1994; 5 December 1994.

Akron Beacon Journal, 26 April 1994 and 16 July 1994; *United Rubber Worker,* July-August 1985; *Des Moines* [Iowa] *Register,* 10 May 1995; Yokohama Tire Corp. news releases, 24 July and 5 October 1994; Dunlop Tire Corp. news release, 28 September 1994; Kovach Tire Report, August 1994; Associated Press report, 12 October 1994; *Nashville Banner,* 1 and 9 November 1994.

CHAPTER 11. "OFFICIALLY, WE ARE
NOW STEELWORKERS"

Interviews: Borelli interview, 8 December 1999; Kenneth Coss, interview by author, Pittsburgh, 2 July 1995; Coss interviews, 1996 and 27 December 1999; John Cunningham, interview by author, Pittsburgh, 2 July 1995; Cunningham interview, 19 March 1999; Diceglio interview, 23 January 2000; Kevin Fencil, interview by author, Pittsburgh, 1 July 1995; Finley interview, 19 April 1999; Fuhrman interview, 19 March 1999; Gates interview, 25 January 2000; Hemsley interview, 30 December 1999; Johnson interview, 22 January 2000; Milton interview, 10 February 2000; Sellers interview, 8 February 2000; J. Michael Stanley interview by author, Pittsburgh, 2 July 1995; Stanley interview, 23 December 1999; Thrasher interview, 5 August 1999; Walters interview, 2 February 2000; James Webber, interview by author, tape recording, Kitchener, Ontario, 19 March 1999; Werstler interview, 9 December 1999; Williams interview, 21 December 1999.

Other Sources: *Akron Beacon Journal,* 11 June 1995 and 30 June 1995; *Rubber & Plastics News,* 26 June 1995, 10 July 1995, 17 July 1995, and 25 August 1996; *United Rubber Worker,* March-April 1995.

EPILOGUE. THE USWA TAKES OVER—QUICKLY

Interviews: Benedict interview, 21 January 2000; Bianchi interview, 26 January 2000; Borelli interview, 8 December 1999; Bowers interview, 4 August 1999; Coss interview, 27 December 1999; Cunningham interview, 19 March 1999; Diceglio interview, 23 January 2000; Ellison interview, 8 December 1999; Finley interview, 19 April 1999; Fuhrman interview, 19 March 1999; Gates interview, 25 January 2000; Hemsley interview, 30 December 1999; Jenkins interview, 11 February 2000; Johnson interview, 22 January 2000; Meyer interview, 5 February 1999; Nelson interview, 4 August 1998; Polovick interview, 22 April 2000; Sellers interview, 8 February 2000; Stanley interview, 23 December 1999; Thrasher interview, 5 August 1999; Tully interview, 15 February 2000; Walters interview, 2 February 2000; Warlow interview, 19 March 1999; Warren interview, 14 February 2000; Webber interview, 19 March 1999; Werstler interview, 9 December 1999; Williams interview, 21 December 1999.

Other Sources: *Rubber & Plastics News*, 18 November 1996 and 11 August 1997; *Dayton Daily News*, 29 August 1995; USWA summary of proposed agreement between the union and Continental General Tire Inc.; *New York Times*, 20 January 2000.

BIBLIOGRAPHY

ARCHIVE COLLECTIONS

University of Akron Archival Services, Special Collections, Akron, Ohio
    United Rubber Workers International Research Department Collection
    United Rubber Workers International General Collection
    United Rubber Workers Local 5 Collection
    Goodyear Collection
United Steelworkers of America Local 12 files, Gadsden, Ala.
Reporter Stu Feldstein's personal collection of 1976 strike coverage

URW PUBLISHED HISTORIES

A Mighty Fine Union: A URW Golden Anniversary History. United Rubber Workers, 1985.

Abott, William, and Joe Glazer. *25 Years of the URW: The Story of the Rubber Workers Union and the Men and Women Who Built It.* United Rubber Workers, 1960.

Cruden, Robert. *Five Years: The Story of the United Rubber Workers of America.* United Rubber Workers, 1941.

Howard, Gene. *The History of Rubber Workers in Gadsden, Alabama: 1933–1983.* United Rubber Workers Local 12, 1983.

Labor Scrapbook. United Rubber Workers Education Department. Date unknown.

Local 80 URW: 1937–1992. United Rubber Workers Local 80, May 1992.

Thurber, John Newton. *Rubber Workers History: 1935–1955.* United Rubber Workers Public Relations Department, 1955.

NEWSPAPERS AND PERIODICALS

Akron Beacon Journal
BFG Today
Business Week
[Cleveland] *Plain Dealer*
Dayton Daily News
Des Moines [Iowa] *Register*
Industry Week
Nashville Banner

Newsweek
New York Times
Rubber & Plastics News
United Rubber Worker
U.S. News & World Report
Wall Street Journal
Wingfoot Clan

PERSONAL INTERVIEWS BY AUTHOR

Baldwin, Dan, tape recording, Gadsden, Alabama, 2 August 1999.

Battles, J. W., Countryman, J. R., and Glassco, C. V., joint interview, tape recording, Gadsden, 3 August 1999.

Beliczky, Lou, tape recording, Akron, 21 February 2000.

Benedict, Annalee, telephone interview, tape recording, 21 January 2000.

Bianchi, Bob, tape recording, Pittsburgh, Pennsylvania, 26 January 2000.

Borelli, Dan, tape recording, Akron, 8 December 1999.

Bowers, E. K., tape recording, Gadsden, 4 August 1999.

Bradley, Ray, tape recording, Gadsden, 2 August 1999.

Brown, J. Curtis, tape recording, Akron, 6 December 1999.

Bruder, Leonard, tape recording, Kitchener, Ontario, 18 March 1999.

Burdon, James, telephone interview, tape recording, 4 February 2000.

Clem, Steve, tape recording, Akron, July 1998.

Contessa, Matt, tape recording, Akron, 14 June 2000.

Coss, Kenneth, Pittsburgh, 2 July 1995; Akron, unknown date, 1996; telephone interviews, tape recording, 7, 15, 22, and 27 December 1999.

Cunningham, John, Pittsburgh, 2 July 1995; tape recording, Kitchener, 19 March 1999.

Cunningham, John; Reginald Duguay; Alan Turner; and Jim Webber, joint interview, tape recording, Kitchener, 19 March 1999.

Diceglio, Gary, tape recording, Cuyahoga Falls, Ohio, 23 January 2000.

Dimengo, Carl, tape recording, Akron, 8 December 1999.

Ellison, Glenn, tape recording, Akron, 8 December 1999.

Fencil, Kevin, Pittsburgh, 1 July 1995.

Finley, Kenneth, tape recording, Akron, 19 April 1999.

Frederick, James, tape recording, Akron, 21 February 2000.

Freiberger, George, telephone interview, tape recording, 7 February 2000.

Fuhrman, John, tape recording, Kitchener, 19 March 1999.

Gates, Roger, tape recording, Pittsburgh, 25 January 2000.

Godinho, Doug, telephone interview, 20 January 2000.

Goebel, George, tape recording, Kitchener, 19 March 1999.

Hemsley, Craig, tape recording, North Canton, Ohio, 30 December 1999.

Hudson, H. W., tape recording, Gadsden, 2 August 1999.

Jenkins, Tom, tape recording, Akron, 11 February 2000.

Johnson, Stanley, telephone interview, tape recording, 22 January 2000.

Lantz, Clark, Akron, April 2000.

Laws, Gilbert, telephone interview, tape recording, 10 February 2000.

Lichtenstein, Nelson, telephone interview, 28 August 1998.

Matthews, James A. III, , telephone interview, 31 August 1998.

Matthews, Lloyd, tape recording, Gadsden, 5 August 1999.

Meyer, Dave, tape recording, Akron, 29 January and 5 February 1999.

Millis, Harry, telephone interview, unknown date, 1996.

Milton, Lewis "Sonny," telephone interview, tape recording, 10 February 2000.

Nelson, Dan, tape recording, Akron, 4 August 1998.

Palmer, Jimmy, tape recording, Gadsden, 2 August 1999.

Polovick, Mike, tape recording, Cuyahoga Falls, Ohio, 22 April 2000.

Ramsey, Charles, Nashville, Tennessee, November 1994.

Reed, Ronnie, and Bill Willard, joint interview, tape recording, Gadsden, 2 August 1999.

Schofield, Peter, tape recording, Cleveland Heights, Ohio, 16 June 2000.

Sellers, John, tape recording, Akron, 8 February 2000.

Smith, Tony, tape recording, Gadsden, 2 August 1999.

Stanley, J. Michael, Pittsburgh, 2 July 1995; telephone interviews, tape recording, 21 and 23 December 1999.

Stone, Mike, Akron, unknown date, 1990; Akron, unknown date, 1996; tape recording, Akron, 24 July 1998.

Taylor, Morry, telephone interview, 28 August 1998.

Thorley, David, tape recording, Stow, Ohio, 11 February 2000.

Thrasher, Larry, tape recording, Gadsden, 5 August 1999.

Torrence, Sam, Akron, unknown date, 1991.

Tully, Frank, tape recording, Akron, 15 February 2000.

Walters, Kenneth, telephone interview, tape recording, 2 February 2000.

Warlow, Patrick, tape recording, Kitchener, 19 March 1999.

Warren, Jim, tape recording, Akron, 14 February 2000.

Weber, Don, telephone interview, tape recording, 17 December 1999.

Werstler, Doug, tape recording, 3 February and 9 December 1999.

Williams, Mickey, telephone interview, tape recording, 21 December 1999.

Williamson, Pat, tape recording, Gadsden, 3 August 1999.

Word, Troy, tape recording, Gadsden, 3 August 1999.

BOOKS

Boryczka, Raymond, and Lee Cary Lorin. *No Strength without Union: An Illustrated History of Ohio Workers, 1803–1980.* Columbus, Ohio: The Ohio Historical Society, 1982.

Brody, David. *In Labor's Cause: Main Themes on the History of the American Worker.* New York: Oxford University Press, 1993.

Craver, Charles B. *Can Unions Survive? The Rejuvenation of the American Labor Movement.* New York: New York University Press, 1993.

Dark, Taylor E. *The Unions and the Democrats: An Enduring Alliance.* Ithaca, N.Y.: Cornell University Press, 1999.

Endres, Kathleen L. *Rosie the Rubber Worker: Women Workers in Akron's Rubber Factories During World War II.* Kent, Ohio: Kent State University Press, 2000.

Fink, Gary M., ed. *Biographical Dictionary of American Labor Leaders.* Westport, Conn.: Greenwood Press, 1974.

Green, Max. *Epitaph for American Labor: How Union Leaders Lost Touch with America.* Washington, D.C.: AEI Press, 1996.

Jeszeck, Charles. "Decline of Tire Manufacturing in Akron." In *Grand Designs: The Impact of Corporate Strategies on Workers, Unions and Communities.* Edited by Charles Graypo and Bruce Nissen. Ithaca, N.Y.: ILR Press, School of Industrial and Labor Relations, Cornell University, 1993.

Kochan, Thomas A., Harry C. Katz, and Robert B. McKersie. *The Transformation of American Industrial Relations.* New York: Basic Books, 1986.

Lichtenstein, Nelson. *The Most Dangerous Man in Detroit: Walter Reuther and the Fate of American Labor.* New York: Basic Books, 1995.

Lief, Alfred, *The Firestone Story.* New York: McGraw-Hill, 1951.

Love, Steve, and David Giffels. *Wheels of Fortune: The Story of Rubber in Akron.* Akron, Ohio: University of Akron Press, 1999.

Nelson, Daniel. *American Rubber Workers & Organized Labor, 1900–1941.* Princeton, N.J.: Princeton University Press, 1988.

———. *Shifting Fortunes: The Rise and Decline of American Labor, from the 1920s to the Present.* Chicago: Ivan R. Dee, 1997.

O'Neill, Dennis J. *A Whale of a Territory: The Story of Bill O'Neil.* New York: McGraw-Hill Book Co., 1966.

O'Reilly, Maurice. *The Goodyear Story.* Elmsford, N.Y.: Benjamin Co., Inc., 1983.

Pappas, Gregory. *The Magic City: Unemployment in a Working-Class Community.* Ithaca, N.Y.: Cornell University Press, 1989.

Renshaw, Patrick. *The Wobblies: The Story of Syndicalism in the United States.* Garden City, N.Y.: Doubleday & Co., 1967.

Roberts, Harold S. *The Rubber Workers: Labor Organization and Collective Bargaining in the Rubber Industry.* New York: Harper & Brothers, 1944.

Taft, Philip. *The A. F. of L.: From the Death of Gompers to the Merger.* New York: Harper & Brothers, 1959.

Wolf, Howard, and Ralph Wolf. *Rubber: A Story of Glory and Greed.* New York: Covici-Friede Publishers, 1936.

OTHER SOURCES

"A Short History of American Labor." Adapted from *AFL-CIO American Federationist,* March 1981. Prepared for the 1981 Centennial of American Labor.

Bommarito, Peter, and Louis S. Beliczky. "Seeds of Humble Origin Produce a Tree of Life." In *What's New in Labor Relations.* Wharton School of Finance, Spring 1972.

Bommarito, Peter. 1970 URW convention speech.

——. Speech delivered at "Save Our Jobs" rally, 3 June 1972.

——. Statement before the U.S. International Trade Commission, 19 April 1975.

——. Statement before the subcommittee on Manpower, Compensation, and Health and Safety, of the House Committee on Education and Labor, on the National Workers' Compensation Act of 1975—H.R. 9431, 16 March 1976.

——. Opening speech at 1978 URW convention.

——. Acceptance speech at 1978 URW convention.

——. Testimony before the U.S. House Committee on Education and Labor Subcommittee on Labor Standards, hearing on the National Employment Priorities Act, Akron, 9 May 1975.

Burdon, George. Acceptance speech at 1964 URW convention.

Bureau of National Affairs Inc., *Daily Labor Report*, 21 November 1985.

Bureau of National Affairs Inc., *Daily Labor Report*, 7 March 1984, Lynn Williams statement on plant closing bill (H.R. 2847) before the House Labor Subcommittee on Employment Opportunities.

Clem, Steve. Testimony in hearing before the Trade Subcommittee of the House Ways & Means Committee on Trade Adjustment Assistance, Lorain, Ohio, 10 June 1985.

DiFederico, Mario, and William Jones. Testimony before the U.S. House Committee on Education and Labor Subcommittee on Labor Standards, hearing on the National Employment Priorities Act, Akron, 9 May 1975.

Dimengo, Carl. Speech at AFL-CIO Conference, Chicago, 2–5 May 1982.

House, John D. "Birth of a Union." Unpublished manuscript. Provided courtesy of United Steelworkers of America.

Jeszeck, Charles. "Structural Change in Collective Bargaining: The U.S. Tire Industry." In *Industrial Relations*, 25, no. 3 (Fall 1986).

Martin, Charles. "Southern Labor Relations in Transition: Gadsden, Alabama, 1930–1943." In *Journal of Southern History* (November 1981).

Nardello, James. Testimony before the Trade Policy Staff Committee Office of the Special Representative for Trade Negotiations, 5 June 1975.

——. Letter to President-elect Jimmy Carter, 15 December 1976.

Nelson, Daniel. "A CIO Organizer in Alabama, 1941." Reprinted from *Labor History* 18, no. 4 (Fall 1977).

Sousa, Carlos. "The United Rubber Workers of America and 1946: Prelude, Strike and Afterthoughts." Written by York University history major and distributed in May 1986 at United Rubber Workers District 6 Golden Anniversary Council Meeting.

Stone, Mike. Speech before the Economic Policy Task Force, Cleveland, Ohio, 7 December 1981.

——. Speech at International Trade and Challenges to U.S. Labor Relations

Labor/Management Conference, Nashville, Tenn., 2 April 1982, sponsored by Federal Mediation and Conciliation Services and Middle Tennessee State University.

United Rubber Workers statement to U.S. International Trade Commission, 25 April 1972.

United Rubber Workers report of the International President to the 31st URW Convention, 5 October 1981.

United Rubber Workers 1985 Collective Bargaining Policy.

United Rubber Workers Economic Background report for 1988 International Policy Committee, prepared by URW Research Department.

United Rubber Workers International Officers Report to 1990 convention.

United Rubber Workers International Officers Report to 1993 convention.

U.S. General Accounting Office Briefing Report to U.S. Senator Lloyd Bentsen, July 1986.

United Steelworkers of America summary of proposed agreement between the union and Continental General Tire, September 1999.

INDEX

Note: Page numbers in italics indicate an illustration.